Lebanon's Quest

In memory of my mother
Violette Sheena-Zamir
1925–1986

and my uncle
Yehezkel Sheena
1932–1986

LEBANON'S QUEST

The Road to Statehood 1926–1939

Meir Zamir

I.B.Tauris *Publishers*
LONDON · NEW YORK

Paperback edition published in 2000 by
I.B.Tauris & Co Ltd
Victoria House
Bloomsbury Square
London WC1 4DZ
175 Fifth Avenue
New York NY 10010
Website: http://www.ibtauris.com

In the United States of America
and in Canada distributed by
St Martin's Press
175 Fifth Avenue
New York NY 10010

First published in 1997 by I.B.Tauris & Co Ltd

A full CIP record for this book is available from the British Library
A full CIP record for this book is available from the Library of Congress

ISBN 1 86064 553 4

Printed and bound by SRM Production Services Sdn Bhd, Malaysia.

Contents

L'Invitation A La Paix

O Syrie, ô soeur,
Songe à la douceur
De vivre ainsi côte à côte;
De vivre, distinct,
Chacun son destin,
Le coeur serein, l'âme haute.
Je suis le Liban
Dont le soir tombant
Ceint le front d'ambre et de mauve;
Sois de ton côté,
Terre de beauté,
Sultane du désert fauve

Sois Syrienne – et me connais
Le droit d'être Libanais.

Te tournant vers l'est,
Laisse-moi l'Ouest
Et sa Méditerranée
Qui de mes aïeux,
Aux jours les plus vieux,
Vit fleurir la destinée.
A ses flots baigné,
Mon coeur a saigné
A ton épreuve aubie:
Il veut te laisser,
Pour le mieux penser,
Tous les baumes d'Arabie.

Sois Syrienne – et me connais
Le droit d'être Libanais.

J'ai toujours vécu,
Farouche, invaincu;
A ton tour te voici libre.
Toi, tendre, moi, fort,
Joignons notre effort
Pour nous mieux faire équilibre.
O vibrant matin
Où ton neuf destin
A mon vieux sort se fiance!
La main dans la main,
Partons vers demain,
Soulevés de confiance …

Sois Syrienne – et me connais
Le droit d'être Libanais.

Hector Klat, *Dans Le Vent Venu*, Beirut, 1937

Acknowledgements

This study, the result of extensive research in archives in France, Britain and Israel, could not have been completed without the help of a number of colleagues and institutions, and I am happy to thank them all. I am indebted to the Harry Frank Guggenheim Foundation in the United States and the Israel Academy of Sciences and Humanities, for providing funding. I am also grateful to the Moshe Dayan Center for Middle Eastern and African Studies at Tel Aviv University, and to its director at the time, Prof. Itamar Rabinovich. Much appreciation is due to the staff of the Archives diplomatiques du Ministère des Affaires Etrangères in Nantes and in Paris, the Service Historique de l'Armée in Vincennes, the Centre de Hautes Etudes sur l'Afrique et l'Asie Modernes in Paris, the Archives Départementales de la Corrèze in Tulle, the Public Record Office in London, the Ben-Gurion Archives in Sede Boker, and the Department of Middle Eastern Studies of the Faculty of Humanities and Social Sciences, Ben-Gurion University of the Negev.

Most of this work was written in the tranquil ambiance of Oxford University, while I was on sabbatical at St. Antony's College, and during repeated summer visits there. I am grateful to Roger and Margaret Owen; Nadim Shehadi, Director of the Centre for Lebanese Studies, with whom I had lively and fruitful discussions; and Fida Nasrallah. I wish to extend special thanks to the Oxford Center for Hebrew and Jewish Studies, its former and current presidents, Philip Alexander and Bernard Wasserstein, and to the staff there, especially Joan Sinclair, for their tireless assistance.

This project could not have been accomplished without the constant support of my wife Angela, who read the manuscript thoroughly and gave invaluable advice, and to my children Sharon, Tal and Yaniv, who patiently awaited its completion.

The book is dedicated to the memory of my mother and uncle, who were close throughout their lives and who passed away within months of each other while the work was in its initial stages.

Preface

The historian of Lebanon in the inter-war years faces a special challenge: the meta-narrative of Lebanese nationalism that dominated the country's historiography until the outbreak of the civil war in 1975. This version of history was compiled by the 'Khuri school'—a group of politicians, intellectuals, journalists and historians led by Beshara al-Khuri, independent Lebanon's first president, who fashioned a reconstruction of Lebanon's political history in the 1920s and 1930s. Glorifying the role of Khuri and his Constitutional Bloc in Lebanon's struggle for independence from France, the Khuri school systematically downplayed the role of their opponents, in particular Emile Eddé. They also created the myth of the 'Lebanese miracle' of peaceful Christian-Muslim coexistence within a Western parliamentary democracy and capitalist economy. Khuri's autobiography *Haqa'iq lubnaniyya*, which after publication in the early 1960s became a major source for Lebanese historians writing on the period, and is probably the most quoted book on the subject, may be the best example of such an interpretation.

Writing in 1988 on the state of Lebanese historiography, Kamal Salibi, a leading Lebanese historian, noted that a heterogeneous and divided society such as that of Lebanon cannot afford the luxury of a self-deceptive, fictionalized history. Salibi called upon the Lebanese to reappraise their past in an effort to understand their present predicament.

Such reappraisal was made possible by the declassification of French archives in the 1970s and 1980s, giving the historian access to a wealth of primary sources. This book is the second volume of a trilogy, based primarily on these sources, which seeks to reassess the political history of Lebanon under the French mandate (1918–1946). The mandate years were formative for the Lebanese state, determining its independence as a distinct entity, defining its borders, shaping its unique political system and capitalist laissez-faire economy.

The first volume, *The Formation of Modern Lebanon, 1918–1926*, studied the internal, regional and international developments leading to the establishment of the state of Grand Liban in 1920, when France and Britain redrew the political map of the Middle East following the Ottoman Empire's collapse. The book examined the Maronites' dominant role in the formation of the new state within its extended borders, as well as the political, social and

ix

economic repercussions of annexation of the coastal region, the Beqa valley and southern Lebanon—with their large Sunni and Shiite populations—to the predominantly Maronite and Druze Mount Lebanon.

The present work, encompassing the period between the declaration of the Lebanese Republic in May 1926 and the outbreak of the Second World War in September 1939, is devoted to the state-building process. It describes the attempt to form a nation-state based on the Western concept of parliamentary democracy, within a society divided along national, religious and sectarian lines. This effort is examined against the background of the political, social and economic changes sweeping Lebanon under the French mandate, and the conflicting pressures from Paris and Damascus. While the original premise of most historians has been that sectarianism, especially Maronite-Sunni rivalry, was the major factor in Lebanese politics, the picture that emerges is far more complex. Power struggles among political, religious and economic elites—some well-established and others newly-formed, frequently cutting across sectarian lines—were no less significant in moulding Lebanese society. Indeed, sectarianism was exploited by those elites to assure access to the new political institutions and wealth of the state. Factionalism and intra-sectarian rivalries often overrode inter-sectarian division: a marked example was the prolonged feud between the Maronites—Emile Eddé and Beshara al-Khuri—which dominated Lebanon's political scene from the 1930s into the 1940s.

Studying the politics of the Lebanese elites called for detailed research on the personalities involved: the sources of their power, their methods of gaining access to the political and administrative institutions, their internal power struggles, and their relations both with their followers and the French authorities. This was made possible only after the declassification in 1987 of the archives of the French High Commission in Syria and Lebanon. The archives, situated in Nantes—comprising over 3000 cartons, with hundreds of thousands of documents on all aspects of life in Syria and Lebanon under the French mandate, and containing detailed intelligence reports of the Sûreté Générale and the Service de Renseignements—enable the reconstruction of a fairly accurate picture of the Lebanese elites. To provide a more balanced viewpoint, Lebanese sources and archives in Britain and Israel were also extensively researched.

The French archives reveal a reality somewhat distinct from the one presented by Khuri and his circle. For example, the 1943 National Pact can be seen, not as a unique agreement between the far-sighted Beshara al-Khuri and Riad al-Sulh, but as the culmination of processes begun in the 1920s and 1930s, and in which Edde and the various French High Commissioners played a not insignificant role.

The numerous internal, regional and international forces involved, and the wealth of detailed primary sources, posed the question of how best to convey the complexity of this period of Lebanon's political and social history. Many subdivisions might have resulted in a fractured picture. I have therefore divided the work into four chapters, each presented without interruption, in an attempt to maintain the flow of the narrative. The study thus unfolds in overlapping, converging circles depicting the forces that shaped the Lebanese state: French policy in its mandated territories and French unease with Arab nationalism; Syria's political and territorial claims in Lebanon and their effect on the Lebanese domestic scene; the formation of the new political institutions and their adaptation to the Lebanese sectarian reality; inter- and intra-sectarian rivalry; the power struggle of the elites and the emergence of political clientelism within the state system; Beirut's political and economic development and its impact on Mount Lebanon and the peripheral regions; and the political involvement of Beirut's rapidly expanding Christian mercantile-financial bourgeoisie.

Chapter one addresses the question of Syrian unity following France's division of the country into six separate entities—the 'states' of Damascus and Aleppo, Jabal Druze, the Alawite region and Alexandretta, in addition to Greater Lebanon. It describes the Syrian Arab nationalist struggle for independence and unity, and argues that after the Syrian-Druze revolt, securing unification of all the territories under the French mandate became the nationalists' most pressing goal, superseding their demand for Syrian independence. The chapter analyzes the position of the Syrian nationalists on Lebanon's separate existence, as well as their territorial claims, in particular to Tripoli and the Beqa valley. Finally, it outlines French policy in the mandated territories under de Jouvenel and Ponsot following the 1925–1927 uprising.

The second chapter examines the development of Lebanon's political institutions—the presidency, the government and parliament—as their powers were defined and the interplay between them evolved during the Republic's first five years. Many negative aspects of Lebanese politics—political patronage and corruption, sectarianism and clientelism—emerged at that time and were integrated into the political system. The chapter explores attempts to change that system through two revisions of the 1926 constitution, and analyzes the consequences for the balance between the executive and legislative powers. The last section is devoted to the Eddé government crisis—a turning point in Maronite-Sunni relations that also marked the start of a bitter power struggle among the Maronite political elites.

Chapter three surveys inter- and intra-sectarian relations in the early 1930s against the background of the recession in the mandated territories and the unsuccessful Franco-Syrian treaty negotiations. It explores French policy toward Syria and Lebanon in the light of regional and international developments, including Iraqi independence, Italy's challenge to the French position in the Levant and the growing threat of war in Europe. Lebanese politics were dominated at that time by the struggle for the presidency between Emile Eddé and Beshara al-Khuri, and the chapter examines the impact of that struggle on Maronite-Sunni relations. The causes of the May 1932 crisis and the subsequent suspension of the constitution, the emergence of Khuri's Constitutional Bloc and the imbroglio within the Maronite church are discussed in detail. The chapter continues with a reassessment of the origins of the 1935 tobacco monopoly crisis, including the role of Beshara al-Khuri, Riad al-Sulh and the Syrian National Bloc in the confrontation between Patriarch Arida and the High Commissioner, de Martel. It concludes with Eddé's election as president in January 1936.

The final chapter opens with a review of the changes in French policy in the mandated territories following the collapse of the international order and the looming prospect of war in Europe. It reappraises Franco–Syrian relations and describes the motives behind the French decision, in March 1936, to resume negotiations on a treaty with the National Bloc; follows the negotiations until the conclusion of a treaty in September 1936 and examines the reasons for France's reluctance to ratify it. It then proceeds to look at Syria's political and economic claims over Lebanon during the Franco-Syrian negotiations and their effect on Christian–Muslim relations in Lebanon. The changes in the Maronite and Sunni stands on Lebanon's national identity are analysed, along with Lebanon's relations with Paris and Damascus following its own treaty with France, concluded in November 1936. The chapter describes the state of Lebanese politics under Edde's presidency and the renewed Eddé-Khuri power struggle, ending in September 1939 with the outbreak of the Second World War.

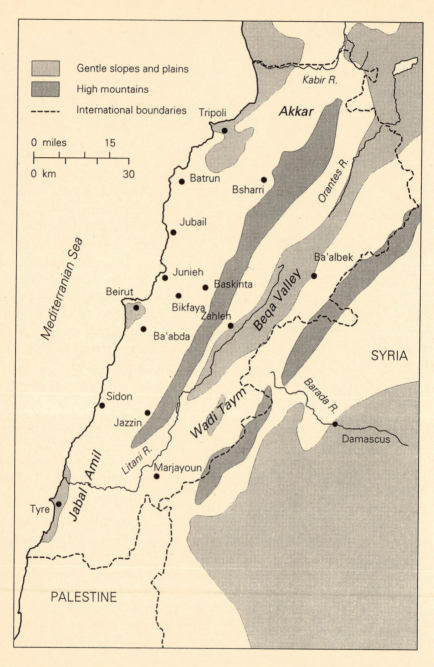

Lebanon after 1920

Topography based on Kamal Salibi, *The Modern History of Lebanon*, 1965

CHAPTER ONE

Syrian Unity and Lebanese Particularism

The history of modern Lebanon has always been closely linked with that of Syria. After the Syrian Arab and Lebanese national movements emerged at the beginning of the twentieth century, confrontation was inevitable. The Lebanese Christians, particularly the Maronites, strove for an independent Lebanese state—Grand Liban—within its historical and natural borders, extending from the Mediterranean in the west to the Anti-Lebanon mountains in the east, and from the Kabir river in the north to Ras Naqura in the south. With its capital in Beirut and its historic links with ancient Phoenicia, this state was to be a refuge for Christians in a Muslim-dominated Middle East. The Syrian Arab nationalists, however, had their own vision: that of a united, independent Arab nation, stretching from the Mediterranean in the west to the Syrian desert in the east, from Cilicia in the north to the Sinai desert in the south. This 'Greater Syria', with Damascus as its capital, was to restore to Syria the Golden Age it had enjoyed under the Umayyads in the seventh and eighth centuries.

An early attempt by the Arab national movement to define Greater Syria in political and geographical terms was made in 1915, when Husain, the Sharif of Mecca—who was secretly negotiating with the British authorities in Egypt to revolt against the Young Turks—sent his third son, Faisal, to Damascus to meet members of the underground, anti-Turkish, Arab nationalist groups. They presented Faisal with a plan for an independent Arab nation, including a Greater Syria. The Hashemites' adoption of this goal was a breakthrough for the nascent Arab nationalist movement; for the first time, a prominent Arab family, tracing its origins to the Prophet Muhammad, was willing to transform the nationalist idea into a concrete policy. Furthermore, the nationalists secured in the Husain–MacMahon correspondence, British backing—albeit perhaps somewhat ambivalent—for a Syrian Arab state. Arab nationalist aspirations thus gained a certain legal standing and international recognition at a time when the future of the Middle East was being decided by the European Powers. The Hashemites, who had emerged as a dominant political power in the Muslim Arab world, continued to aspire for a Greater Syria under their hegemony until well after the Second World War.[1]

Faisal, more than any other member of his family, espoused the Arab nationalist cause. It was under his leadership that Syria formed its first Arab government after four centuries of Turkish rule. Following his triumphal entry into Damascus on 1 October 1918, he began to lay the foundations for an independent Syria, working with former members of the Arab nationalist groups who had participated in the Arab Revolt. A government, administration and army were established and a Syrian congress elected. In July 1919, the congress, which included representatives from Lebanon and Palestine, voted for an independent Syrian Arab state within its geographical borders. The declaration of independence and the election of Faisal as king by the Syrian congress eight months later was a desperate attempt by the Arab nationalists to prevent France and Britain from implementing their secret war agreements for the partition of the Middle East. Their efforts, however, were in vain. At the San Remo Conference in April 1920, a mandate over Syria and Lebanon was granted to France, and a British mandate established over Palestine and Iraq. Three months later, the French army, under the command of General Gouraud, defeated the Arabs at Maisalun, occupied Damascus and expelled Faisal and his government from Syria, thus bringing their dreams for independence and unity to an abrupt and tragic end. For the next quarter-century, France would control Syria under the terms of the mandate laid down by the League of Nations.[2]

The battle of Maisalun, was engraved on Syria's collective memory as a symbol of the nation's heroic defence of its independence. It was the first devastating blow to the Arab Muslim nationalists during the long and bitter years of the French mandate. The nationalists regarded France not as a friendly nation—which was, as defined by the mandate, to help and guide them toward independence and statehood—but as a colonial, Christian, Western, anti-Muslim power, which had denied their national aspirations and was threatening their religion, culture and language. After being stripped of their independence, they received no less severe a blow when France shattered their dreams of unity by dismembering their country. They helplessly witnessed the partition of their lands and the imposition of artificial borders by two European powers, and watched as France surrendered the oil-rich Mosul region and Palestine to Britain, Cilicia and later Alexandretta to Turkey. France then carved up what was left of Greater Syria, exploiting its religious, ethnic, sectarian and geographic diversity, into what the nationalists regarded as artificial entities: Greater Lebanon, the Alawite region, Jabal Druze and the autonomous province of Alexandretta. The interior was further divided into the 'states' of Damascus and Aleppo. By pursuing its

'minorities' policy—relying on the more friendly minority communities—
France created what was to become the intractable problem of Syrian unity,
the issue that was to undermine its efforts to reach an agreement with Syria.
The question of unity would also be a constant source of tension between
the Arab Sunni majority and the minorities, and between Syria and Lebanon as well.[3]

Throughout the mandate period, the Syrian Arab nationalists struggled
to regain their independence and unity—inseparable goals, since only independence could ensure a united Syria. Despite their continued efforts, which
culminated in the Syrian–Druze revolt, France was determined to retain its
mandate. The nationalists thus feared that independence might be achieved
too late to secure their country's unity. Although they maintained that the
new 'states' had been artificially created against the people's wishes, they understood that they reflected the religious, sectarian and ethnic reality. They
knew that not only the Christians in Lebanon and Syria, but also the Druze,
Alawites and Turks in Alexandretta resented being minorities in an Arab
Muslim state dominated by Sunnis. Some of these communities even sought
the continuation of the French mandate to protect their rights and interests.
The Syrian nationalists feared that French backing could make these separate entities more viable. No longer content with local autonomy, they could
aspire to independence. The nationalists suspected that France might withdraw from the interior, but retain control over the coast and Jabal Druze.
These concerns gave rise to desperate attempts to force France to revise its
partition policy, and the refusal to sign any treaty that did not guarantee Syria's political unity.[4]

Although the Arab Muslim nationalists in Syria resented any minority community that collaborated with France and supported partition, it was the
Maronites they most abhorred. The belief that the Maronites, together with
France, were responsible for the Arab Muslim plight, was to determine the
nationalist stand toward Lebanon even after both countries gained independence. The Muslims were convinced that Maronite insistence on French
protection had given France a pretext to occupy Syria, and that its partition
into six artificial 'states' was the direct outcome of the Maronites' desire for a
state of their own. The formation of Greater Lebanon, they claimed, had
been a precedent for France's pursuit of its minorities policy in the whole of
Syria and for its decision to establish the separate Alawite and Druze entities. They believed that by maintaining the division of their country, France
had sought not merely to weaken Arab Muslim opposition and accommo-
date the population's ethnic, religious and sectarian composition, but to
strengthen a Christian Lebanon vis-à-vis a united Syria that threatened

Lebanon's existence as a separate entity. Continued Maronite hostility toward Syrian independence and unity reinforced this belief. In sum, the nationalists accused the Maronites of preventing the majority from realizing its aspirations for an independent, united Syria within its natural borders.[5]

Syrian Arab nationalist politicians and intellectuals often portrayed Lebanese nationalism both as an artificial idea supported by a small minority that refused to recognize the aspirations of the Arab nation, and as an isolationist movement inspired by religion and sect, led by the clergy and backed by a colonial power. While the Maronites, like the Zionist Jews in Palestine, were undermining Arab independence and unity, Arab nationalism, they declared, upheld equality for all, regardless of religion or sect. Yet despite these claims, their determined opposition to the Lebanese state attested to their recognition that, in contrast to the other entities created by the French, Lebanon was a unique phenomenon with its own distinct national and historical roots.[6]

The Syrian Arab Muslims were careful to couch their opposition to Lebanon in secular-nationalist terms, in order to forestall accusations of xenophobia or of discrimination against the Christian minorities. They pointed to the role played by Christians, including Maronites, in inspiring the revival of the Arabic language and its literature, as well as in the emergence of Arab nationalism. Indeed, many Syrian nationalists were secularists who genuinely believed that religion and sectarianism should be disassociated from Arab nationalism. They sought to enlist the support of the Christians in Syria and Lebanon by arguing that they were under no threat from their Arab Muslim brethren, and that France's alleged historic role of protecting the Christians in the Levant was merely a pretext to justify its colonial ambitions. But Arab nationalism could not be separated from Sunni Islam. After the collapse of the Ottoman Empire, the Sunni Muslim masses in Syria and Lebanon had wholeheartedly espoused Arab nationalism which, for them, had become synonymous with Islam. They hoped their nationalist beliefs would help them safeguard their religion and culture, their dominance in an Arab Syrian state and their independence and union with the rest of the Arab Muslim world, as well as dissuade the minorities from collaborating with the French mandate.[7]

The establishment of Greater Lebanon had profound national, political and economic consequences for Syria, particularly for Damascus, which emerged as the main focus of opposition to the French mandate and a separate Lebanese state. A conservative Muslim city, the fourth most important in Islam, proud of its long history as the seat of the Umayyad dynasty, Damascus had been an important regional, administrative and economic centre under Ottoman rule. Situated at the crossroads between Anatolia and

Aleppo in the north and Palestine, Egypt and the Arabian peninsula in the south, and on the historical trade route between Beirut and Palmyra, Mesopotamia and the Persian Gulf, it had long been a major trading centre. With the completion of the railroad to Beirut at the end of the 19th century, and the inauguration of the Hijaz railway in 1907—linking Damascus to Homs, Hama, Aleppo and Anatolia in the north and to Medina in the south—the city's status was further enhanced. It thus naturally became the capital of Faisal's newly-created Syrian Arab state.[8]

The division of Greater Syria into British and French mandates and the further partition of Syria by France isolated Damascus from the surrounding regions. To the south, it was separated by Lebanon and Jabal Druze from Palestine, Transjordan and the Hijaz. In the north, Aleppo, with its large Christian community and French backing, was reinforcing its position as a political and economic rival. To the east lay the new border with Iraq, while to the west, it was cut off from the sea by Lebanon, which now controlled the ports of Beirut, Tripoli and Sidon. Damascus subsequently lost much of its standing to Beirut, which became the main political, administrative, economic and cultural centre of the French mandated territories, enjoying its status as seat of the High Commission. The Damascenes envied Beirut's prosperity and believed it had been achieved largely at their expense. Indeed, there was a sharp contrast between prosperous, 'Christian–French' Beirut with its elegant quarters, wide avenues, modern universities and large European communities, and grim, conservative Muslim Damascus, parts of which had been destroyed during the Syrian–Druze revolt.[9]

The loss of the Beqa valley and Tripoli to Lebanon was particularly painful for Damascus, and was to become a major source of Syro–French and Syro–Lebanese tension throughout the mandate. Syrian leaders, both moderate and nationalist, were determined to restore control over these strategically and economically important regions. The Beqa valley, or the 'four qadas', as the Syrians referred to it, had been part of the vilayet of Damascus, and from 1918 to 1920 was under the administration of Faisal's Arab government. In August 1920, General Gouraud annexed the region to Lebanon to satisfy the Maronites, secure French domination over the area and isolate Damascus. The city was now less than 15 miles from the Lebanese border, and the vital road and railway systems in the Beqa valley linking it to Homs, Hama and Aleppo, and to Tripoli, Beirut and northern Palestine, were under French and Lebanese command. With the Beqa valley, Beirut and Tripoli within its territory, Lebanon now completely controlled access to Damascus from the sea. Syria's claim that Beirut's prosperity was based on its exploitation of Damascus and the Syrian interior was valid indeed.[10]

The Syrians maintained that Lebanon, Jabal Druze, the Alawite region and the sanjak of Alexandretta were an integral part of Syria. When faced with Lebanese Christian opposition, they were prepared to recognize Lebanon's separate existence, but only within its pre-war borders—namely the mutasarrifiyya. They insisted that the areas annexed to Mount Lebanon in 1920 be returned to Syria, or that a plebiscite be held to decide their future. However, they considered Beirut and south Lebanon as less critical than Tripoli and the Beqa valley, with which Syria shared a border. They were determined to regain the Beqa valley, which they insisted belonged to Syria, and regarded Tripoli, whose Sunni inhabitants were constantly demanding union with Syria, as the country's natural port. By detaching Tripoli from Lebanon, they also hoped to separate Lebanon from the Alawite region and undermine French designs to create a coastal base from which to retain control of the interior. In summer 1936, after realizing that France would not relinquish its hold on Tripoli, they requested that Sidon serve as Syria's port. This move was also aimed at separating the Christians in Lebanon from the Jews in Palestine.[11]

The French failed throughout the mandate to define a consistent policy to safeguard their strategic and economic interests in the Levant, fulfil their moral obligation to protect the Christians, and at the same time satisfy Arab Muslim aspirations for independence and unity. They could have maintained Syrian unity and granted it independence based on a treaty—as Britain had in Iraq—thereby countering accusations of an anti-Muslim bias and a policy of 'divide and rule'. But they chose to partition and control Syria, thus placing themselves in direct confrontation with the Arab nationalists and the Muslim majority.

It could be argued that France's policy of partition in the early years of the mandate was a natural reaction to its conflict with Faisal's Arab government. But by the mid-1920s, the High Commission was well aware that the issue of Syrian unity had become a major obstacle to any agreement with the Muslim majority. Moreover, the establishment of autonomous entities had created a large and inefficient administrative system, which hampered efforts to implement a coherent economic policy throughout the mandated territories. Politicians on the left, as well as officials, warned that by forming separate entities, France had weakened Syria's ability to withstand external pressure, whether from Turkey in Alexandretta and Aleppo, Iraq in the Jazira and Aleppo, or Transjordan in Jabal Druze.[12]

The origins of France's partition policy lay in its perception of the Arab nationalist movement, which had been largely shaped by its conflicts with Faisal's Arab government and with Britain during and after the First World

War. Indeed, like the Syrian Arab Muslims, the French were unable to extract themselves from the legacy of Maisalun. French officials and army officers in Beirut and Paris continued to view Arab nationalism as a militant, xenophobic and anti-French movement with which their country could not reach agreement. They realized that no distinction could be drawn between Syrian unity and independence: by granting unity, France would create a powerful state in the interior, which it would be unable to control. The question of unity was thus constantly deferred, either because the French government could not define a coherent policy on Syrian independence, or because the Quai d'Orsay and the High Commission tried to use the issue to impose a treaty on Syria's nationalists—on French terms. Another argument in defence of partition was that Syria comprised a mosaic of ethnic and religious groups and had never been a united political entity. Indeed, it was claimed that France was merely complying with the demands of minority groups for autonomy or independence. The partition policy was also exploited to justify creation of an organization under the High Commission's control, to administer the Common Interests. Since its own budget had been drastically cut and was closely scrutinized every year in the National Assembly, the High Commission became increasingly dependent on income from the Common Interests—which derived almost exclusively from customs duties—to finance its activities.[13]

Syria's partition was criticized in the National Assembly for its high cost, and because it was enlarging the bureaucracy and hindering the economic unity of the mandated territories. The left opposed it on the additional grounds that it antagonized the Muslims and precluded agreement with them. This criticism—together with the drastic cuts imposed on French forces stationed in the mandated territories, following recurrent financial crises—led subsequent French governments to twice revise the 1920 decision. In 1922, Gouraud created a Syrian Federation comprising the 'states' of Damascus and Aleppo, plus the Alawite region. His move, however, sprang from economic, rather than political, considerations. He even tried to convince the Maronite leaders that there could be economic advantages for Lebanon in joining the federation. But the Maronites refused, insisting on a separate budget and demanding that any economic ties between Lebanon and Syria be regarded as those between two independent states.[14]

The formation of the Syrian Federation did not satisfy the Arab nationalists either; they continued to insist on a united Syria including Jabal Druze, Alexandretta and Lebanon. After Gouraud's replacement by Weygand in the summer of 1923, they again demanded Syrian unity. In July 1924, Weygand decreed the creation of a Syrian state by uniting the 'states' of Damascus and Aleppo. The Alawite region, which had been part of the Syrian Federation, was not included. The decree was implemented in December 1925 by Henri de Jouvenel, the new high commissioner, but with the Druze revolt then at its peak, it had little effect.[15]

The minorities policy and the partition of Syria into entities based on religious, sectarian and geographical considerations, had been influenced, to a large extent, by France's decision to create Greater Lebanon as a separate state for the Christians. Unlike Jabal Druze, the Alawite region and the sanjak of Alexandretta, also formed at France's initiative, Lebanon had a well-established nationalist movement, with the Maronite community at its core. Even before the war, the Maronites had aspired to a Lebanese state within extended borders, separate and distinct from Arab Syria and closely linked to France. Indeed, there had been general support in France, both on right and left, for Lebanese Christian national aspirations. The French Catholic church and its missionary orders—particularly the powerful Jesuits, who had for centuries been involved in religious, educational and charitable activities in Beirut and Mount Lebanon—also promoted the establishment of a Christian Lebanon. Military circles in Beirut and Paris, which regarded Lebanon as a strategic stronghold of French influence over the hostile interior and the Mediterranean, endorsed independence and strongly opposed linking Lebanon with Syria. French officials in the Quai d'Orsay and the High Commission, as well as army officers and religious orders, used support for an independent Lebanese state to justify Syria's continued partition. They pointed out that a united Syrian state, with Damascus as its capital, would exert economic and political pressure on Lebanon and undermine its very existence. Similar arguments were voiced by the Lebanese Christians.[16]

Although the various French governments of the inter-war period agreed that France should retain Lebanon as a distinct and independent state, protecting it against threats from Syria, there was considerable disagreement over its borders, especially in the early years of the mandate. Some officials, led by Robert de Caix, Gouraud's secretary-general, advocated reducing Lebanon's territory by annexing Tripoli and the district of Ba'albeck, with their large Muslim populations, to Syria. Such a move, de Caix argued, would not only increase the Christian majority and thus create a more viable Lebanese state, but also weaken Syrian nationalist hostility toward France and Lebanon. He failed, however, to win the support of his superiors for such a policy. Henri de Jouvenel, the fifth high commissioner, sought to implement de Caix's recommendations; but he, too, met with strong opposition from officials and military circles in Paris and Beirut, as well as from the Maronites, whose church led the campaign against any revision of the borders.[17]

For five years after France was entrusted with mandates in Syria and Lebanon, three high commissioners—Gouraud, Weygand and Sarrail, all military men—strove to secure French control over these territories. In the summer of 1925, it seemed that their goal had been achieved and that the French policy of 'divide and rule' had succeeded in limiting opposition to the mandate. Yet within weeks, France was faced with an uprising of Druze and Syrian Arab nationalists. The revolt had profound repercussions on Syrian and Lebanese politics, as well as on France's Syrian policy throughout the next decade. As in 1920, the nationalists attempted to force France out of their country, and failed. But the rebellion evoked strong feelings of patriotism and transformed Arab nationalism into a major ideology in Syria and the Arab world. It also helped the Arab nationalists to gain prominence in Syria, and shaped the militant, volatile character of Syrian politics.[18]

The revolt came as a bitter surprise to the French, who had assumed that their control over the mandated territories had been finally secured. Instead, their Syrian policy was again thrown into disarray, and their pacification of the country was to cost them dear. The government was strongly criticized in the National Assembly and the French press, and the question of whether France should renounce its mandates over Syria and Lebanon became the focus of intense debate. The entire issue of France's Syrian policy—including the question of Syrian independence and unity and its relations and borders with Lebanon—was reopened. Moreover, the revolt led French politicians and officials, particularly Henri de Jouvenel, to acknowledge the influence of the Arab nationalist leaders on the Syrian public, and thus to advocate revision of the French stance on their demands.[19]

The revolt caused widespread havoc and exacted a heavy toll in human life as well as on the economy. More than 6000 Syrians and 2000 French troops were killed and thousands more injured. The civilian populations of Syria and Lebanon bore the brunt of the conflict from both sides. Parts of Damascus were destroyed, hundreds of villages sacked and crops burned, and the economies of Syria and Lebanon came to a near standstill. From the military point of view, the uprising may be divided into three distinct stages. The first, from Michaud's defeat in August 1925 to the Druze failure in November to capture Rashaya, was marked by a strong offensive led by Sultan al-Atrash and his brother Zayd. They aimed to disrupt French lines of communication in the Beqa valley and link up with the Druze in the Shuf region on southern Mount Lebanon. The Druze defeat at Rashaya forced the rebels to revise their tactics. During the second stage, from November 1925 until the French occupation of Suwayda and the Ghota in July 1926, the Druze and the Syrian nationalists resorted to guerrilla warfare to draw the French into negotiations on their terms. The third stage, which lasted until the end of the year, consisted of a 'mopping up' operation by the French army.[20]

As in the summer of 1920, Lebanon became an arena for military and political confrontation between the Syrian Arab nationalists and France. In October and November 1925, Druze forces advanced from Jabal Druze through Mount Hermon into Wadi al-Taym in the southern Beqa valley, while skirmishes took place between the Druze and the Maronites in the Shuf mountains. In the Anti-Lebanon Mountains, the central and northern Beqa valley and Jabal Akroun, northeast of Tripoli, two rebel bands of over 1000 men each, one headed by Tawfik Haidar and the other by Zein Muhi al-Din Ja'far, attacked French positions and convoys and cut off railways, roads and telephone and telegraph lines. Scores of Christian villages were sacked and cultivated fields burned, and trade in Beirut virtually halted. Hundreds of Lebanese Christians were killed or wounded; thousands fled from Syria and the Beqa valley and found refuge in Beirut.[21]

Lebanon played an important part in France's success in quashing the Syrian revolt: it was used as a base for rearming and reorganizing prior to operations, while Beirut served as a major port for reinforcements, as well as the main military and political headquarters. From their base at Rayak in the Beqa valley, French airplanes made reconnaissance flights and bombed rebel positions. Lebanese Christians and Armenians volunteered for the auxiliary forces, and weapons were distributed to the Christians to enable them to defend their villages.[22]

Lebanon's role in the revolt intensified the hostility of the Syrian Arab nationalists and the Muslim masses toward the Christians, particularly the Maronites. Indeed, many Syrians believed that, as in 1919–20, the Maronites had jeopardized their efforts to secure independence and unity and that its control over Lebanon had enabled the French army to avoid defeat. This perception was strengthened by the French right wing, which used the idea of France's moral obligation to protect Lebanese Christians to mobilize public backing for partition and direct administration. The Syrians resented in particular the Maronites' active participation in French military efforts. Declarations of support for the French mandate by Maronite leaders, including their patriarch, Hawayik, and the fears they voiced of an Arab Muslim victory, reinforced the nationalists' animosity. They took pains, however, to prevent the revolt from escalating into a religious and sectarian conflict by reassuring the Maronites that this was a national, secular struggle, and that their fears were groundless. Yet it was difficult to overcome the deeply-rooted religious and sectarian suspicions. After the Syrian defeat, anger at the Lebanese Christians mounted. It became customary for Syrian politicians, both moderate and militant, to adopt an anti-Lebanese stand in order to enhance their popularity among their own constituents. In meetings with the French, Syrian leaders strongly criticized Lebanon and its government. Khadour Bin Ghabrit, a pro-French Muslim Algerian, who had been sent by the Quai d'Orsay on a fact-finding mission to Syria, warned that French support for the Maronites was the main source of Syrian animosity toward France.[23]

The revolt and the strong criticism it generated at home, in the international community and in the League of Nations, convinced Prime Minister Briand of the need to revise his government's policy in the mandated territories. In November 1925, he recalled General Maurice Sarrail, who was being strongly attacked by the left, and replaced him with Henri de Jouvenel, the first civilian high commissioner in Syria and Lebanon. He entrusted de Jouvenel with the task of ending the revolt, restoring stability, and defining a long-term Syrian policy that would save France the embarrassment of having to face such uprisings every few years. A senator, journalist and diplomat who had represented his country at the League of Nations, Henri de Jouvenel was to make the first serious attempt to implement a more liberal policy in the mandated territories.[24]

De Jouvenel's policy was highly controversial and drew criticism from all sides. The French right wing opposed his plans for rapid emancipation of the mandated territories and negotiations on a pact with the Syrian Arab nationalists and rebel leaders. For their part, the nationalists suspected he was merely intending to suppress the revolt and restore French control over Syria. The Lebanese Christians accused him of pursuing a pro-Syrian, pro-Muslim policy that would jeopardize Lebanon's independence and territorial integrity. British diplomats in Beirut, Damascus and Paris described him as naive and opportunistic, claiming that few of his accomplishments had been of lasting value. He has also been harshly judged by historians, who maintain that he never really understood Syria's political problems. Yet a close examination of de Jouvenel's correspondence with Briand and the Quai d'Orsay reveals a man who was ahead of his time in grasping the faults in France's approach to Syria, and in defining a comprehensive and liberal solution for the mandated territories. Ten years later, when Blum's government sought to implement a similar policy, it was too late. With the threat of a new war in Europe, France would be reluctant to relinquish its control over Syria and Lebanon.[25]

De Jouvenel was critical of his predecessor's direct administration; he advocated following the true spirit of the mandate—to guide the inhabitants of Syria and Lebanon move toward independence and statehood. In contrast to the traditional view of the Syrian Arab nationalists as militant, xenophobic, anti-French and representative of only a small sector of the population, de Jouvenel saw them as influential patriotic leaders with whom France should negotiate an agreement. He opposed the minorities policy, which he believed was exacerbating religious and inter-sectarian tension in the mandated territories and creating weak, autonomous, sectarian 'statelets' unable to withstand outside pressure. He proposed instead to seek rapprochement with the Muslim majority and the Arab nationalist leaders by accepting their demands for Syria's independence and unity. Fully aware of the nationalists' deep suspicion and fear of France, he considered gaining their confidence crucial to the success of his policy. He therefore held an ongoing dialogue with their leaders in Paris, Cairo, Beirut and Damascus, outlining his policies and goals and asking for their full cooperation.[26]

A month after arriving in Beirut, de Jouvenel sent Briand a detailed plan for the mandated territories. He proposed granting independence to Syria and Lebanon through 30-year treaties, similar to the one Britain had signed with Iraq. Jabal Druze, the Alawite region and Alexandretta would be incorporated into Syria; the minority interests would be safeguarded through a decentralized administrative system. Organic laws would be elaborated with the participation of the elected representatives of Syria and Lebanon. After the Permanent Mandates Commission had approved the treaties and organic laws, the two countries would begin negotiations to solve their territorial dispute. France would retain its power of arbitration, but would try to persuade the Lebanese Christians to cede Tripoli and the Ba'albeck district to Syria. In January 1926, Briand approved de Jouvenel's proposals and instructed him to proceed with their implementation.[27]

De Jouvenel soon discovered, however, that he would be unable to execute his plan until the uprising had ended. The National Assembly and the French public would otherwise regard his liberal policy and the concessions he was ready to make as a surrender, an affront to French prestige. The Syrian nationalist leaders, moreover, rejected his appeals to end their armed struggle against France. Some regarded his policy as a sign of French weakness and advocated continuing the revolt to force France into relinquishing its mandate altogether, while others saw it as a means of obtaining further concessions. De Jouvenel consequently authorized the French army to step up the offensive against the rebels. Yet in his reports to Paris, he emphasized that he could see no long-term military solution and that army operations were intended merely to prepare the ground for a political settlement. He skillfully exploited the rivalries within the Syrian nationalist leadership, and met frequently with the moderates to weaken and isolate the militants. And he used the local press to convey directly to the Syrian public the need to end the revolt and begin negotiations. De Jouvenel did not share his predecessors' suspicions of Britain's Middle East policy, and coordinated his efforts with the British high commissioner in Palestine, in order to end the revolt. He constantly pressured British officials in London and the Middle East to curtail the political and financial support for the rebel bands coming from their national committees in Egypt, Palestine, Transjordan and Iraq. He used similar tactics with the Turkish Republic to prevent it from intervening in northern Syria.[28]

By the spring of 1926, de Jouvenel had succeeded in laying the groundwork for his plan. In Lebanon, a constitution was elaborated, a republic declared, a president and government elected. The former Representative Council, together with a senate whose members were appointed by the high commissioner and the Lebanese president, became a bicameral parliament. In Syria, the combination of military and political pressure had considerably reduced the rebels' activities and weakened Syrian public support for them. Nationalist leaders were now willing to end the revolt and begin negotiations on a compromise agreement with France. In April, Ahmad Nami was appointed to head a provisional government that included three nationalist ministers. During discussions on forming the government, de Jouvenel and his aides assured the nationalists of their support for a treaty, as well as for Syria unity and annexation of Tripoli and the Ba'albeck district to Syria. They pointed out, however, that tactically, Syria's unity and the revision of its borders with Lebanon would be more readily achieved if the Syrian government would negotiate directly with representatives of the minority groups and with Lebanon. Thus, Nami's governmental platform, which was approved by de Jouvenel, contained the well-established nationalist demands: Syria's right to formulate its own constitution and a 30-year treaty, with access to a port and Syrian unity to be secured through negotiations.[29]

De Jouvenel, however, no longer enjoyed his government's backing. Paradoxically it was precisely his success in suppressing the revolt that reduced French willingness to support conclusion of an agreement with the nationalists. Officials in the Quai d'Orsay, especially Philip Berthelot, the influential secretary-general, criticized de Jouvenel's attempts to emancipate the mandated territories and negotiate with the nationalists. He was accused of undermining Lebanon's very existence and of weakening the Lebanese Christians, France's most loyal allies in the Levant. Opposition was also raised by the military establishment, both in Paris and Beirut, which backed General Gamelin's insistence that France should first crush the rebellion and restore its forces' tarnished image, and only later impose a political solution. The uprising in the Rif in Morocco further undermined de Jouvenel's efforts to win his government's support. In the Ministries of War and Colonies, and among the deputies and senators on the right, concern was voiced that his liberal policy might be seen as a sign of weakness in North Africa. The success of France's military campaigns against the rebels in the Rif strengthened the position of those who advocated similar tactics in Syria.[30]

Briand, under attack in the National Assembly over his handling of the franc crisis, was anxious to avoid giving the opposition further cause to criticize the government over its Syrian policy. Although he shared many of de Jouvenel's liberal views, when faced with domestic political constraints, Briand favored revising and slowing down the implementation of his high commissioner's policy. De Jouvenel, however, insisted that his plan be executed without delay. At the end of May, he returned hastily to Paris to counter his critics and ensure government backing for his policy. He met with Briand and other ministers, officials in the Quai d'Orsay, and senators and deputies in the National Assembly, and granted numerous interviews to the Parisian press. In all his meetings and interviews, he emphasized the achievements of his policy and reiterated his belief that there was no military solution to the Syrian problem. Only an agreement with the Syrian Muslims and their nationalist leaders, he argued, would enable France to maintain its influence in the Levant in the long run. In contrast to its previous harsh criticism of France's Syrian policy, the Permanent Mandates Commission endorsed de Jouvenel's plan in June.[31]

While de Jouvenel was attempting to gain support in Paris, however, his policy was being undermined in the mandated territories by General Gamelin, commander of the French forces in the Levant; Colonel Catroux, the head of the intelligence services; de Reffye, secretary-general and acting high commissioner; and Solomiac, the delegate to Lebanon. Together, they sought to demonstrate that his conciliatory policy had failed, and persuade the government to send reinforcements for a large-scale offensive against the two main centres of the uprising—Damascus and Jabal Druze. Exploiting the rebel attacks on French positions and on the Christians in Lebanon, they warned Paris that France's prestige and influence in the Levant were in danger. They purposely exaggerated their descriptions of rebel operations in Lebanon, well aware of the effect of such reports on the government, the National Assembly and the French public. They accused Syrian nationalist leaders of encouraging the rebel attacks in order to force France to bow to their demands, while simultaneously negotiating an agreement with de Jouvenel. They also blamed the Syrian government, particularly the nationalist ministers, for promoting anti-French and anti-Lebanese activities. And they exploited the heated exchanges between Dabbas and Ahmad Nami over Syrian territorial demands in Lebanon to reinforce their claim that the Syrian government was seeking to undermine Lebanese independence. In June, de Reffye instigated a governmental crisis in Syria which culminated in the resignation of the nationalist ministers. Officers in the Service de

Renseignements discreetly urged Alawite and Druze notables to oppose the incorporation of their regions into Syria. Maronite leaders who had deferred to de Jouvenel and agreed to cede territories to Syria were encouraged by the High Commission to change their stance and publicly denounce him for pursuing a pro-Syrian policy at Lebanon's expense.[32]

Reports from the High Commission criticizing de Jouvenel were leaked to the French press, intensifying opposition to his policy in the government and the National Assembly. A growing number of ministers now supported the Ministry of War's position that France had first to end the revolt by force before seeking a long-term political solution. Suppression of the revolt in the Rif gave the Ministry of War the opportunity to concur with General Gamelin's request for additional troops. On 20 July, the first French reinforcements arrived in Beirut from Morocco; shortly thereafter, the army began its offensives in the Ghota and Jabal Druze, which effectively quashed the revolt.[33]

Briand's resignation following the franc crisis, and the formation of a right-wing government by Poincaré, marked the end of de Jouvenel's tenure as high commissioner. Although Briand continued as foreign minister in the new government, his influence was limited and he was no longer able to uphold de Jouvenel's programme. In a last-minute attempt to salvage his policy, de Jouvenel met Poincaré at the end of July, but failed to win his support. The conservative Poincaré had been advocating, since the war, that France retain control over the Levant and fulfil its obligations to protect the Christians. He was reluctant to endorse what he regarded as unnecessary appeasement of the Syrian nationalists, now that they had been defeated.[34]

On 3 August 1926, de Jouvenel sent Briand a letter urging the government to take advantage of its military success to define and implement a coherent policy without delay. He noted that France had two options: continue using military force or seek a political solution through diplomacy. The first option might appear tempting in the wake of the military victories; but in the long run, he warned, it would lead to further uprisings and undermine French prestige. Moreover, it would necessitate stationing a large army in the mandated territories for an indefinite period of time. He thus proposed that France seek an agreement with the Arab Muslims in Syria, but cautioned that French support of Lebanon's Christian minority was a major obstacle: the Muslims regarded the French mandate as a 'Maronite' mandate. The establishment of Grand Liban had been a mistake. It had created a state in which the Christians enjoyed only a slim majority, which they would be unable to maintain for long, and had inflamed the animosity of two million Syrian Muslims toward France. De Jouvenel agreed that Lebanon be maintained as a separate state, provided its territory was reduced. Such a move, he argued, was endorsed by the Lebanese government as well as Maronite leaders. France, he noted, should not attempt to be 'more Lebanese than the Lebanese themselves'. With regard to the Syrian constitution, he reiterated that it should take the form of a treaty, similar to the pact between Britain and Iraq. Indeed, he believed that France should pursue a policy in Syria and Lebanon which would be seen by the population as more liberal than that of Britain in its own mandated territories. A few days later, after Poincaré turned down his proposal, de Jouvenel resigned.[35]

De Jouvenel's resignation was greeted with much satisfaction in the Quai d'Orsay, the High Commission and the military establishment, as well as by the Maronites. Although the Muslims and the Syrian nationalist leaders had been critical and suspicious of his motives, they were now disappointed. The resignation ended France's most serious attempt to revise its minorities policy and reach an agreement with the Syrian Arab nationalists. In the years that followed, various French governments and high commissioners would give lip service to de Jouvenel's liberal ideas, while in fact reverting to their previous policies. Lebanon, with its Christian population, along with the minority communities in Syria, were again perceived as France's main allies in its attempts to safeguard its interests in the mandated territories.[36]

Following the controversies surrounding Sarrail and de Jouvenel, the French government now sought a neutral candidate for the position of high commissioner, acceptable to both right and left. The Quai d'Orsay, as a consequence of its stormy relations with the outsider de Jouvenel, preferred an experienced diplomat who could be trusted to follow its policies closely. Henri Ponsot, who succeeded de Jouvenel in September 1926, was the antithesis of his predecessor. A professional diplomat, he had joined the Quai d'Orsay in 1904 at the age of 27 and had held various posts in Paris and abroad, including that of consul in Bangkok and consul-general in Montreal. He also had experience in Muslim affairs, having served as director of the interior in Tunis and later as assistant chief of the African and Levant section in the Quai d'Orsay, where he helped define French policy in North Africa and Syria. In contrast to the flamboyant de Jouvenel, who had ignored officials in the Quai d'Orsay, Ponsot closely coordinated policy with his superiors. He shared de Jouvenel's liberal views, but was reluctant to enter into confrontations with the Quai d'Orsay or the military establishment. Well aware of the obstacles facing him, Ponsot adopted a cautious approach, leading Syrian and Lebanese politicians and foreign diplomats to regard him as overly hesitant. He rarely took the trouble to explain his stand to the local public or press, adopting a distant and reserved attitude, with the result that he was considered enigmatic and aloof.[37]

Having turned down de Jouvenel's proposals, the Quai d'Orsay had to re-formulate its policy in the aftermath of the Syrian–Druze revolt. Anxious to meet the September deadline set by the Permanent Mandates Commission for granting Syria a constitution, officials in Paris prepared draft organic laws for Syria, Jabal Druze and the Alawite region. Ponsot's task was to secure the approval of the local governments and representative councils, with a minimum of modification. Before Ponsot's departure, however, Briand sent a copy of the proposed laws to de Jouvenel. The former high commissioner criticized them, arguing that in contrast to his organic laws, which had taken the form of a treaty approved by the representatives of the Syrian people, the Quai d'Orsay was seeking to impose its own legislation on the mandated territories. In such circumstances, he observed, problems were bound to resurface. In light of the Syrian constitutional crisis two years later, it is worth noting his warning that an article in the constitution granting veto power to the high commissioner would inevitably provoke a confrontation with the Syrians. He reiterated the importance of taking immediate action while France's military victory was still fresh, before the nationalists could restore their influence. There was an urgent need to solve Lebanon's problems by revising its borders, he stressed: 'To rely on a Christian majority in Lebanon and reduce it to 52 per cent by annexing its opponents ... while there are four times as many Syrians as Lebanese, is to play a losing game.' This time, despite opposition in the Quai d'Orsay, Briand heeded de Jouvenel's warnings. Ponsot was first sent to Beirut on a mission of inquiry. Only after he returned to Paris with his findings did the government finalize its policy in the mandated territories.[38]

While politicians and officials in Paris were defining French policy in Syria and Lebanon, army officers in Beirut, backed by the Ministry of War and the majority of the staff of the High Commission, attempted to restore direct administration. A memorandum from General Gamelin to the minister of war presented the views that were circulating in Beirut at the time. Gamelin's arguments and recommendations derived largely from the army's experience in the revolt. He strongly opposed annexation of the Alawite region or Jabal Druze to Syria and advised against granting Syria control over the Beqa valley and Tripoli. He described Damascus as the 'centre of Pan-Arab intrigue and xenophobia', and the Syrian nationalists as 'agitators' who represented a small minority of the population. The masses, in his view, desired only a 'firm administration, which will enable them to benefit peacefully from the fruits of their labour'. Gamelin warned that the establishment of a Greater Syria would be the first step toward creation of an Arab empire backed by Britain. From the military point of view, the revolt had demonstrated the need for French control over the coast. France therefore had to maintain the Alawite region as an autonomous entity. Syrian claims in Tripoli had also to be rejected, as they would separate Lebanon from the Alawite region. Pointing out the pivotal role played by Lebanon, with its ports, roads and railways, in France's success in suppressing the revolt, he recommended that Lebanon be maintained as a loyal base within its present borders. With regard to Jabal Druze, Gamelin advocated reconciliation with its 'warlike inhabitants' and preservation of its autonomy under close French supervision in order to isolate Damascus from the south.[39]

For almost a year after de Jouvenel's departure, Syria and Lebanon were without a high commissioner, and de Reffye, the acting high commissioner, together with General Gamelin and Colonel Catroux, enjoyed considerable freedom of action. They aimed to strengthen France's control over its mandated territories and forestall any further attempts at an uprising. Harsh measures were taken against those who supported the rebels, and the army began a large-scale operation to disarm the local population. Under Catroux, the Service de Renseignements was expanded and reorganized, and French intelligence officers were stationed throughout the territories. Officers in the Alawite region continued to encourage local leaders to oppose annexation to Syria and demand the retention of autonomy under French control. The administration in Jabal Druze was reorganized under the close supervision of the army. Anxious to regain the cooperation of the Druze and distance them from the Syrian nationalists, the High Commission adopted a conciliatory policy toward them, thereby provoking a strong reaction from the Lebanese Christians. Hundreds of young Alawites and Druze were drafted into the local auxiliary forces, whose ranks were thus considerably expanded.[40]

One of the lessons learned from the revolt was the urgent need for good rail and road networks to enable the rapid movement of troops from one region to another. An ambitious plan to improve the road system in order to facilitate access to outlying areas was implemented in 1926–27. New roads were built from Beirut to Suwayda, detouring through south Lebanon and Kuneitra in order to avoid Damascus. Similarly, Beirut was linked to Tripoli, Latakia, Aleppo and the Euphrates, allowing trade with Mesopotamia to bypass Damascus. Plans were drawn up for a rail link between Tripoli, Beirut and Haifa, and work began on improvements to the port of Beirut. These projects further enhanced Beirut's economic standing. Additional police and gendarmerie stations were built and the telephone and telegraph systems upgraded. Thus, while there was pressure in Paris to limit France's direct administration in the mandated territories, the High Commission, through the Service de Renseignements, effectively strengthened its control. De Reffye also initiated a modest plan to repair some of the damage caused by the war and revive the economy. He granted the Lebanese government FF 5 million for compensation in south Lebanon, particularly in Rashaya, most of which had been destroyed. The Syrian government, on the other hand, received a mere FF 2 million to pay for damage to Damascus. In addition, funds were allocated to the agricultural sector, which had been badly affected by the revolt, in the form of loans to peasants for the purchase of seed and cattle.[41]

On the eve of Ponsot's arrival in Beirut in mid-October 1926, tension was running high in the mandated territories. The politicians and the public had been waiting since de Jouvenel's departure in the spring for the French government to decide on its policy, and were now expecting to learn of the new high commissioner's plans for solving their pressing political and economic problems. Yet the uncertainty remained. Ponsot met first with officials in the High Commission and assured them he had no intention of making any staff changes. He then met the Lebanese president and the Syrian prime minister and informed them that he had come merely to conduct an inquiry; the French government would decide on the future of the region after reviewing his findings. The news of Ponsot's mission and his refusal to make any public commitment further exacerbated public anxiety. Accompanied by Colonel Catroux, Ponsot left on a tour of Damascus, Jabal Druze, Dir al-Zor and Latakia. In the months that followed he met with a stream of delegations, conversed with notables and officials and received numerous petitions and letters. The requests and complaints conformed to a familiar pattern. In Syria, they included demands for unity, a 30-year treaty, a constituent assembly to promulgate a constitution, a general amnesty, a national army, admission to the League of Nations, diplomatic representation abroad, compensation for losses incurred in the revolt, the return of the districts annexed to Lebanon in 1920 and access to a port in Tripoli. The Syro–Palestine Congress sent Ponsot a letter stressing its desire for peace and requesting an agreement with France that would safeguard both Syrian national aspirations and French interests. It also proposed continuing the negotiations begun with de Jouvenel in Paris in July. However, in Jabal Druze and the Alawite region, Ponsot encountered opposition to Syrian unity. In Lebanon, Hawayik, the Maronite Patriarch, criticized de Jouvenel's pro-Syrian policy and objected to modification of Lebanon's borders. He also renewed his proposal that the High Commission take advantage of the Druze flight from the southern Beqa valley to settle the Christians there. Yet the Sunnis of Tripoli and Beirut, as well as some Shiite and Druze notables from other regions, supported Syrian unity. At the end of January 1927, accompanied by Catroux, Ponsot returned to Paris. Satow, the British consul-general in Beirut, who met him on the eve of his departure, observed that if the French did not fully support their new high commissioner, they 'would probably lose their last chance of making a success of the Syrian mandate'.[42]

The results of his inquiry deepened Ponsot's apprehension of the difficult task lying ahead. He was sceptical of the importance de Jouvenel had attached to the nationalists, particularly the Syro–Palestine Congress in Cairo. He did not share de Jouvenel's style of public diplomacy and opposed the haste with which he had attempted to implement his policy. But he did accept his main recommendations—that the mandate be replaced with a treaty, that Syrian unity be implemented on the basis of administrative decentralization, and that France arbitrate in the Syro–Lebanese border dispute.[43]

From February to May 1927, Ponsot held discussions in the Quai d'Orsay with officials of the Ministries of War and Finance, but failed to reach an agreement. Both the army and the Quai d'Orsay opposed negotiations with the Syrian nationalists, advocating direct administration of the mandated territories and retention of the minorities policy. Some, taken aback by the scope of the revolt and the destruction it had wrought, warned that unless France adopted a conciliatory policy toward the Muslims and the nationalists, as de Jouvenel had recommended, it might face another costly and embarrassing uprising. Ponsot argued that the government could not retract de Jouvenel's public pledges, and proposed continuing his predecessor's policy, but with certain modifications.[44]

Deliberations in the Quai d'Orsay on the future of the mandated territories were increasingly overshadowed by a severe financial crisis which forced Poincaré's government to reduce expenditure drastically. Members of the Committees for Finance and Foreign Affairs in the National Assembly and representatives of the Ministry of Finance made it clear that the government had to cut the budget for Syria. The Ministry of Finance proposed that the mandated territories pay for maintaining the French army and the local auxiliary forces there. This was rejected after Ponsot warned of possible political repercussions and the fact that the local economy would be unable to bear the financial burden. In mid-April, at a joint meeting of representatives of the Quai d'Orsay and the Ministries of War and Finance, it was decided that the number of troops in the mandated territories be reduced by the end of the year to 26,000, of whom 16,000 would be French, and 10,000 local.[45]

This decision had immediate repercussions on France's Syrian policy. The government reluctantly concluded that it would be impossible to maintain the minorities policy, which necessitated a large military presence. Some officials even suggested adopting a 'littoral' policy—retaining direct control over Lebanon, the Alawite region, Alexandretta and Jabal Druze, while withdrawing the French army from the interior. But this proposal was rejected as unviable, one which could lead to civil war as well as confrontation between Syria and Lebanon. Alienated and politically isolated, and with no access to the sea, Syria, it was claimed, would turn to the areas under the British mandate—Palestine and Transjordan—or would seek an alliance or even unity with Amir Abdallah, or a confederation with Iraq. It was therefore recommended that France pursue a more liberal policy in order to weaken Arab Muslim hostility. The government recognized that Syria's partition had become a major source of this hostility; in order to solve the security problem, France had to revise its stand toward nationalist demands for unity.[46]

In May, after four months of lengthy discussion, details of the policy Ponsot was to implement in the mandated territories were finally worked out. It was recognized that Jabal Druze and the Alawite region should be united with Syria, while continuing to enjoy a large degree of administrative and financial autonomy. Union with Syria would be attained through negotiations between their elected representatives and the Syrian government, under the arbitration of the high commissioner, while Syria's territorial claims in Lebanon should be settled. Seeking to forestall a reduction of Lebanon's territory, some officials proposed that it be reorganized on a decentralized basis similar to that of Syria, by granting a certain measure of autonomy to the annexed regions. This idea was rejected, however, on the grounds that Lebanon was too small: decentralization would enable Syria to undermine its territorial integrity and political stability. It was subsequently recommended that the border dispute between Syria and Lebanon be resolved in negotiations between the two governments. If these failed, the high commissioner would impose his own solution. Ponsot advocated that de Jouvenel's proposals be adopted, and Tripoli and Ba'albeck annexed to Syria. Once the border dispute was settled, the two governments would negotiate an agreement on the nature of economic ties. He suggested that economic unity between the two states be maintained through the organization of the Common Interests. As for the Syrian nationalists' demands for a treaty, France should follow Britain's example in Iraq. Only after Syria had an elected government and parliament and a constitution, and the issues of Syrian unity and Syro–Lebanese relations were settled, would the High Commission begin negotiations on a treaty.[47]

During deliberations in the Quai d'Orsay, it was decided that the Lebanese constitution should be revised before Syria was granted its own organic law. The power of the president should be strengthened, it was proposed, and that of parliament weakened by abolishing the senate. This decision evolved partly from the incessant confrontations between the Lebanese president and his government on the one hand, and the bicameral legislature on the other, as well as between the chamber of deputies and the senate. The major reason, however, was fear that Syrian politicians would use the Lebanese constitution as a precedent for their own demands. The High Commission would thus have to face a powerful and uncontrollable Syrian senate and chamber. It was also assumed that the High Commission would have better control of the two states if each had a president willing to cooperate closely with France.[48]

Shortly before his departure for Beirut, Ponsot outlined his plans and timetable for implementing the policy determined in Paris. He proposed issuing a statement presenting its main principles to the inhabitants of the mandated territories. This statement should be vague and uncommited, to prevent unnecessary tension. Ponsot would then initiate revision of the Lebanese constitution. In Syria, a new prime minister would be appointed, willing to work closely with the High Commission and able to help ensure election of a friendly constituent assembly. This assembly would be allowed to freely elaborate a constitution; the authority of the Mandatory Power would be guaranteed through articles similar to those added to the Lebanese constitution of May 1926. The Syrian government would then open deliberations with Druze and Alawite representatives on the terms of their annexation to Syria. Syria and Lebanon would hold talks to define their borders and economic ties, and In the final stage, France would negotiate with the Syrian government on the replacement of the mandate with a treaty. The question of ending the mandate in Lebanon was left open, although Ponsot suggested that France grant Lebanon a treaty as well.[49]

Despite claims to the contrary by Briand and Ponsot, the policy defined in the spring of 1927 differed considerably from de Jouvenel's programme. Aware of the Syrian nationalists' influence on the general public, and their ability to incite opposition to France, de Jouvenel had been willing to compromise on their demands for independence and unity, and integrate them into the Syrian government. Ponsot, however, was not permitted to negotiate with the Syrian nationalist leaders or include them in the government. Instead, he was given the task of choosing a Syrian prime minister who could isolate the nationalists and gain Syrian support for an agreement on French terms. Over the next decade, both Ponsot and de Martel, who succeeded him, failed to accomplish these goals. The Syrian politicians they appointed, Taj al-Din al-Hasani for example, willingly cooperated with France, but were unable to mobilize public support for an agreement. With the High Commission rejecting their requests for independence and unity, undermining their influence and preventing their access to the government, the nationalists were determined to oppose the French mandate. Ponsot's decision to refrain from publicizing his plans only served to reinforce their suspicions of French intentions. Thus, after France had lost the opportunity to exploit the nationalist defeat and secure agreement to safeguard French interests, Ponsot was given the difficult task of implementing a far less liberal policy, at a time when the nationalists were already restoring their prestige.[50]

Ponsot returned to Beirut in June 1927 and immediately faced a severe political crisis. Tension had arisen following rumours that the High Commission planned to revise the constitution in order to facilitate a reduction in Lebanon's terrority. International press reports of France's intentions to relinquish its mandate in Syria and Lebanon only served to worsen matters. Anxious not to commit himself to any specific obligation, Ponsot instructed Catroux to deliver a statement outlining French policy. On 26 July, Catroux convened a group of journalists in Beirut and read out a vague declaration that was open to various interpretations. He strongly denied the rumours of a pending withdrawal and restated France's determination to uphold its mandate and carry out its obligations in accordance with the League of Nations charter. France favoured Syrian unity, he claimed, but would safeguard the rights of minorities. Disagreements between the states or communities would be settled through negotiations, with France retaining the power of arbitration. France would encourage elaboration of a constitution and promote the political and economic development of the states, but would not tolerate any activity that threatened its mandate, law and order, or the Common Interests. For the inhabitants of the mandated territories, who had been waiting a whole year for France to define its policy, the future still remained uncertain.[51]

Lebanese Christians, especially the Maronite church, welcomed Catroux's statement, seeing it as the end of de Jouvenel's pro-Syrian policy. But the Muslims in Syria and Lebanon were deeply disappointed: the statement reinforced their belief that, following its military victory, France was unwilling to allow them to realize their national aspirations. The fact that Catroux himself had made the declaration increased nationalist suspicion, since he was known for his uncompromising stand on their demands. France did not intend to grant them political unity, a treaty, access to the sea, an end to martial law or a general amnesty. The idea of negotiations to resolve the issue of Syria's political unity, along with reference to the need to respect minority rights, strengthened the impression that France would not alter the status quo. Noting that France had created Jabal Druze, the Alawite region, the sanjak of Alexandretta and Greater Lebanon, they argued that it should return the first three regions to Syria. The revision of the Lebanese constitution in October 1927 convinced the nationalists that Ponsot had departed from de Jouvenel's declared goals, and that the High Commission had reverted to its former policy. They rightly suspected that this move, together with the weakening of the Lebanese parliament's authority, was intended to prevent their elaborating a constitution that provided for a strong legislature. They also resented the fact that the constitution reaffirmed Lebanon's separate existence within its 1920 borders, while Syria's territorial claims had not been settled.[52]

Catroux's declaration afforded the nationalists an opportunity to regain the public support they had been losing since the previous summer. Their reaction was delayed, however, by the division and rivalry within their ranks. The revision of the Lebanese constitution prompted them to hold a meeting in Beirut in October, attended by representatives from cities in Syria and Lebanon, at which they defined their response. Significantly, it was in Beirut that a new movement, the National Bloc (al-Kutla al-Wataniyya) was established; it would lead the struggle against France for Syrian independence and unity over the next two decades. The decision to convene in Beirut rather than Damascus was intended to convey the nationalists' message directly to the high commissioner and confirm their position on Lebanon's independent existence. But the statement they issued on 25 October was of a conciliatory nature: although it denounced Catroux's declaration and reiterated their by now familiar demands, it also reflected willingness to 'cooperate honorably' with France.[53]

Ponsot criticized the Syrian nationalists for their inability to grasp the nuances of his statement. Their negative reaction, however, prompted him to meet with the Syrian leaders, present his plans in more detail and request their cooperation. He convinced some, but even they doubted his ability to implement his policy in the face of the strong opposition in conservative, colonial, military, and pro-Lebanese-Christian circles in Beirut and Paris. Indeed, members of his own staff and officers in the Service de Renseignements constantly undermined Ponsot's programme. His authority was challenged particularly by Colonel Catroux, who opposed any attempt by the high commissioner to pursue what he considered a policy of appeasement toward the rebel leaders. In November, their disagreement burst into the open following publication by the right-wing *Action français* of a confidential letter from Ponsot to the Quai d'Orsay, recommending that amnesty be granted to Sultan al-Atrash. There was little doubt that Catroux had leaked this information as well as other reports in the French press attacking Ponsot's handling of affairs in Syria. The embarrassed Quai d'Orsay had no choice but to ask the Ministry of War to recall Catroux.[54]

Increasing criticism of his slow progress in Paris and the mandated territories, and the prospect of the Permanent Mandates Commission meeting scheduled for June 1928—at which France was required to present an organic law for Syria—prompted Ponsot to take action. In December 1927, he convened his top officials and instructed them to ensure that a Syrian constitution be ready by June. During the following months, however, he was placed in a quandary: he believed that nationalist cooperation was essential to successful implementation of his policy, but his attempts to negotiate with them or include one of their leaders in the government were vetoed by the Quai d'Orsay. Despite opposition from his own staff, in mid-March 1928 he granted partial amnesty to the nationalist leaders who had participated in the revolt. This move drew further criticism from rightist deputies in the National Assembly and the French press, which accused him of allowing France's enemies to return to the mandated territories and resume their subversive activities.[55]

In April 1928, elections for a 70-member constituent assembly were held in Syria. The success of Ponsot's Syrian policy now depended on the ability of the officers of the Service de Renseignements and the newly-appointed prime minister, Taj al-din al-Hasani, to ensure election of a controllable parliament. The vote was rigged by the High Commission and the Syrian prime minister, and only 22 deputies allied with the National Bloc were elected. Yet the nationalists emerged as an influential force in Syrian politics and would successfully resist France's attempts to impose its own solution on Syria.[56]

Although they comprised less than a third of the constituent assembly, the nationalist deputies exercised considerable influence in the committee formed to elaborate the constitution. Through it, they hoped to compel France to acquiesce in their demands for unity and a treaty. Article 2 thererfore declared that Syria, including Lebanon, Transjordan and Palestine, was one indivisible country. The French government clearly could not accept such a provision, which not only negated their plans for Lebanese independence, but pertained to regions under the British mandate. When confronted by the French and the Lebanese Christians, the nationalists responded that when the Lebanese constitution was being formulated, de Jouvenel had undertaken to allow Syria, like Lebanon, to specify its territorial aspirations in its own constitution. Other articles gave the Syrian government the right to organize a national army and empowered the president to conclude treaties, receive ambassadors, grant amnesty and declare martial law. These were unacceptable to Paris. For the next three months, Ponsot desperately strove to narrow the gap between the Quai d'Orsay and the nationalists in order to ensure ratification of the constitution, but to no avail. In August, he adjourned the constituent assembly after the nationalist deputies attempted to win approval for the constitution, including the controversial articles. He was summoned to Paris, and upon his return to Beirut again failed to reach a compromise with the nationalist deputies. In February 1929, Ponsot finally dissolved parliament and Franco–Syrian relations reverted to the familiar pattern of confrontation, hostility and suspicion.[57]

Ponsot never recovered from his failure in the Syrian constitutional crisis and, for the next three years, his policies became increasingly indecisive. His position and prestige in Paris severely undermined, he was criticized in the Quai d'Orsay for mishandling the whole affair. The Syrian problem once again became a source of embarrassment for the French government in the National Assembly and the press. The right wing saw the constitutional crisis as further evidence that a liberal policy could not succeed in Syria, while the left argued that an understanding with the nationalists was the only option. Rumours resurfaced that France would abandon its mandate in the Levant. Ponsot's image in the mandated territories fared no better. He was regarded as weak, and local politicians continually attempted to bypass him and deal directly with Paris.[58]

A decade after receiving the mandate, France had failed to define a Syrian policy acceptable to the Arab Muslim majority that would also secure French interests. The issues of unity, a treaty, and an organic law, along with the disputes over Syria's borders and its relations with Lebanon, remained unresolved. French delegates and officers of the Service de Renseignements stationed in Jabal Druze, the Alawite region, the sanjak of Alexandretta and the Jazira, continued to promote the separatist tendencies of the minority communities there. French officials once again regarded Christian Lebanon as essential to safeguard their country's interests in the Levant. They gave Lebanon priority in allocation of the Common Interests budget, and substantial funds were invested in development projects, particularly the port of Beirut. The Syrian constitutional crisis also increased calls in the High Commission and the Quai d'Orsay to restore close supervision over Lebanon's political institutions. To justify their stand, the French exploited the instability of the Lebanese political system and often exaggerated the Lebanese politicians' incompetence in running the country.

The Lebanese Christians, particularly the Maronites, were pleased with the Syrian constitutional crisis and with Ponsot's failure to reach an agreement with the Syrian nationalists. Maronite politicians and clergy claimed the situation proved once again that only Lebanon, with its Christian population, could serve as a loyal base for France in the Levant. But Maronite satisfaction with the strained relations between France and Syria was shortsighted, as the issue of Lebanon's independence and borders became more deeply entangled in the Franco–Syrian imbroglio. As tension between Syria and France grew, so did the hostility of the Syrian public toward Christian Lebanon. Furthermore, the struggle against France radicalized the Arab nationalists, who in any case regarded Lebanon as an artificial entity created by France. They now linked the question of Syria's unity and independence directly to their ability to undermine the Lebanese state, and would soon incite Muslims on the coast to oppose Lebanon's separate existence.

Also shortsighted was Maronite contentment with the failure of de Jouvenel and Ponsot to settle the Syro–Lebanese border dispute by returning Tripoli and Ba'albeck to Syria. Such a step would have removed one of the major causes of Syrian hostility to Lebanon—the lack of a port. Moreover, with the detachment of Tripoli and Ba'albeck, Lebanon would have been rid of two militant, Muslim, anti-Lebanese centres, whose continued demands for union with Syria were radicalizing the entire Muslim community. Whatever Beirut might have lost economically if Tripoli had become a Syrian port, Lebanon would have gained politically.

CHAPTER TWO

In Search of a Viable Political System

With the promulgation of the constitution on 23 May 1926, the Lebanese Republic began a long and arduous journey toward independence and national unity. Transformation of the diverse communities into a civil society would prove to be far more difficult than the establishment of Greater Lebanon. For the next six years, the country was to undergo a unique process in which a society divided along religious, sectarian and national lines sought to adopt a Western, democratic parliamentary system. Although restricted by the French mandate, Lebanese politicians were to play a significant role throughout. By 1932, however, the experiment had failed: the constitution was suspended and France resumed direct administration.

Lebanon could hardly have begun its quest for a national consensus and a Western political system in less favourable circumstances. The Syrian–Druze revolt was far from over, and clashes between armed rebel bands and the French army were still taking place throughout the country. There was widespread destruction in south Lebanon and the Beqa valley; thousands of refugees were fleeing to Beirut; and the economy was at a standstill. The revolt and the confrontation over the constitution had left the population deeply divided, with national, religious and sectarian tension resurfacing. Six years after the establishment of Greater Lebanon, the Arab Muslims in Syria and in the regions annexed to Mount Lebanon continued to oppose a separate, enlarged, Christian-dominated Lebanon. The Lebanese Christians, for their part, feared the repercussions the Syrian revolt might have on the independence and territorial integrity of their newly-established state. The open support for Syrian unity of the Muslims of the annexed regions reinforced the Christians' belief that they were alien to Lebanon.[1]

The elaboration of the constitution and the proclamation of the Republic was a turning-point in Lebanon's political history. These events, together with the establishment of Greater Lebanon in 1920 and the National Pact in 1943, were crucial stages in the Christian effort to transform Lebanon, within its extended borders, into a viable, modern state. With its own constitution and elected representatives, Lebanon was no longer a 'mandated territory', the Christians claimed. They thus embarked on transforming the symbols of their new statehood—the constitution, the presidency, the government and the parliament—into reality.[2]

Of all the peoples in the Middle East of 1926, the Lebanese, particularly the Christians, seemed most prepared to adjust to a parliamentary democracy. With their comprehensive educational system, they were the most literate in the region. Exposed for generations to Western culture, they aspired to modernize their society. Many of the young generation, educated in Beirut's two universities or in France, despised the former Muslim–Ottoman administration and were confident of their ability to introduce Western political institutions into the new Lebanon.

The constitution provided Lebanon with a political framework within which the elements of a polarized, sectarian society could coexist and pursue a national consensus. However, the various groups and communities differed in their perception of the constitution. Some viewed it as the manifestation of their country's independence, sovereignty and its affinity with the West, while others regarded it as an expression of Christian and French colonialist domination. Some considered it almost a miraculous solution to Lebanon's religious and sectarian divisions, while others saw it as guaranteeing their share in the political system or their dominance of the state. The constitution thus embodied two conflicting concepts: a genuine desire to implement a Western political system based on equality and universal suffrage, regardless of religion or sect; and sectarianism, which was deeply entrenched in Lebanon's political and social culture.

The constitution defined Lebanon as a 'Republic' with legislative power vested in two houses—a senate and a chamber of deputies. The senate comprised 16 members, seven appointed by the president and nine elected, for a period of six years. The chamber was composed of 30 deputies, elected for four-year terms. Senators and deputies were elected by two-stage universal (male) suffrage in accordance with the 1922 electoral law. As in the constitution of the Third Republic, both houses initially enjoyed considerable power, including election of the president, voting confidence in the government and approval of the annual budget. The executive power was exercised by a president and a government. The president was elected for a three-year term by both houses at a joint session, with the right to re-election for an additional term. He had the authority to designate the prime minister, appoint and dismiss ministers, dissolve the chamber with the approval of a three-quarters majority in the senate, and initiate revision of the constitution with the approval of the two houses. He was assisted by a government, whose ministers were individually responsible to the chamber. Each new prime minister was required to present a statement of policy to the chamber and request a vote of confidence. Every October, at the beginning of the winter session, he was to submit to the chamber a budget estimating revenue and expenditure for the coming year, to be discussed and approved, article by article.[3]

Article 95, guaranteeing sectarian representation, albeit provisionally, was appended to the constitution by the Lebanese drafting committee, headed by Shibl Dammus. Although it appeared under the heading of 'concluding and temporary provisions', it was to become an integral part of the constitution. The article read as follows: 'As a provisional measure and according to Article 1 of the Charter of the Mandate and for the sake of justice and amity, the sects shall be equitably represented in public employment and in the composition of the Ministry, provided such measures will not harm the general welfare of the state.' Two additional articles stated that 'personal status and religious interests of the population, to whatever religious sect (*millet*) they belong, shall be respected' (Article 9), and that there should be 'no violation of the right of the religious communities (*tawaif*) to have their own schools.' These articles contradicted, to a certain extent, others in the constitution, which stipulated that 'every Lebanese shall have the right to hold public office, no preference being made except on the basis of merit and competence' (Article 12) or that 'a member of the Parliament shall represent the whole nation' (Article 27).[4]

The constitution laid down the framework of the political system, but it was the politicians, religious leaders, businessmen, journalists and others in the liberal professions who gave that system its distinct Lebanese character. Some of its traits were new, while others, deeply rooted in the society, became even more pronounced. This was a formative period, during which the characteristics of the new political institutions—the presidency, government and parliament—were moulded, and the interplay between them determined. Their shortcomings soon became apparent, as conflicts arose between the executive and legislative powers, and between the senate and chamber. Relations between the newly-formed institutions and the mandatory authorities also had to be redefined. Some of the problems were solved after a period of trial and error, by revising the constitution. Lebanon's relationship with France was eventually settled at the end of the Second World War, when the country gained independence. But many of the negative political trends which emerged during these years were inherited by independent Lebanon. Particularly damaging were the infiltration of political sectarianism into the new, Western, parliamentary system and administration; the emergence of political patronage and clientelism; and the strong influence of the Christian mercantile-financial bourgeoisie elites of Beirut on political life.

The negative effects of sectarianism in Lebanon have been examined in numerous studies. It has never been merely a question of Christians against Muslims or Maronites against Sunnis; the situation has always been far more complex—often influenced by personal, familial, factional, regional and ideological considerations rather than confessional allegiance. Thus, to refer to viewpoints as 'Maronite', 'Sunni', 'Shiite', 'Druze', 'Greek Orthodox' or 'Greek Catholic', is to oversimplify Lebanese politics. For example, the rivalry between the two Maronite leaders, Emile Eddé and Beshara al-Khuri, split their community and dominated Lebanese politics well into the 1940s. The Sunnis were geographically and ideologically divided, while regional differences and family–clan rivalries were to plague the Shiite community throughout the mandate years. The age-old conflict between the Jumblatts and the Yazbaks in the Druze community continued unabated, while the other two major sects—the Greek Orthodox and the Greek Catholics— were also far from united.[5]

The interests of the Lebanese people and its various communities were not necessarily better served by the new parliamentary system or the adoption of political sectarianism in the 1926 constitution. These new institutions considerably enhanced the power of a small group of prominent Christian families on the Mountain and in Beirut; Shiite and Sunni land-owning feudal families on the peripheries; and later, Sunni notables in the coastal towns. Thus, despite religious, sectarian, regional and national differences, members of this dominant class cooperated with each other because they shared a similar interest—exploitation of the institutions of the new state to strengthen their positions and increase their wealth. Indeed, they used sectariansim more as a tool to exact privileges for themselves, their relatives and their clients than to protect the interests of the communities to which they belonged. Hence the cynical view held by the ordinary Lebanese citizen, who associated politics with the pursuit of position, intrigue, nepotism, patronage, opportunism and corruption. Only politicians predisposed to these methods were able to succeed in the Lebanese political arena. Those who genuinely strove to transform Lebanon into a democratic, pluralistic and equitable society either had no influence or were forced out of the system altogether. Politics as practiced under the auspices of the Republic became a ruthless game. There were no real political parties or sustained positions, but rather a continuous grouping and regrouping, resulting in the extremely volatile character of Lebanese politics: during the first six years of the constitution there were eight governments. Only a just and democratic political system would have enabled a deeply divided Lebanon to evolve into a truly civil society. Such a system never had a chance.[6]

Nevertheless, the new institutions, especially parliament, helped channel the sectarian, religious, regional and national conflicts into a defined political discourse and prevented the tension from escalating into open violence. The often stormy parliamentary debates not only reflected rivalry between the politicians, but testified to deep dissension over fundamental issues within Lebanese society. It was in parliament and the government that the old Ottoman political traditions of the vilayet and the Mutasarrifiyya were integrated into new Western institutions, thus creating a political culture unique to Lebanon.[7]

The deputies differed radically among themselves, not only in sectarian origin, but in background, education, profession, social status and age. There was little in common, for example, between Habib al-Sa'ad and Omar Da'uq, whose political and adminstrative experience had been gained under the Mutasarrifiyya and the vilayet of Beirut, and Emile Eddé and Beshara al-Khuri, young Western-educated lawyers, whom the High Commission had introduced into the Lebanese administration in the early years of the mandate; or between members of feudal families like Yusuf al-Zein and Abud Abd al-Razak, or Ayub Tabet and Auguste Adib, who had spent many years abroad. Yet they all became part of Lebanon's new political elite. Although they had initially boycotted the Lebanese state, the prominent Sunni notables of Beirut, Tripoli and Sidon would also integrate into this small, privileged class. Moreover, parliament was seldom divided on a clear-cut religious or sectarian basis—regionalism also played a significant role. The electoral law of 1922, which encouraged candidates from the same electoral district to form one multi-sectarian list, had reinforced this division. Thus, deputies from the same region, regardless of religion or sect, would frequently unite to protect their common interests. And paradoxically, the continued political intrigues and shifting alliances helped establish working relationships which, in turn, led to the emergence of the concept of compromise as a major tenet of Lebanese politics.[8]

The success of the mainly Maronite political elite in strengthening its authority through the new political and administrative systems was accompanied by the growing intervention in politics of Beirut's Christian mercantile-financial bourgeoisie. These two processes were to shape Lebanon's political and economic character, both under the mandate and during independence, and would to a large extent lead to the eventual collapse of the Lebanese Republic. A class of affluent Christian merchants and financiers had already emerged in Beirut in the second half of the nineteenth and the beginning of the twentieth century. They had amassed their wealth as intermediaries between foreign, mainly French, capital and commercial interests on Mount Lebanon, especially in the silk trade. The inhabitants of the

Mountain had endured hardship and famine during the war, while the merchants, financiers and a small number of prominent Sunni families in Beirut and Tripoli who controlled the grain trade, were exploiting the lack of commodities and the black market to make huge profits. They used their vast fortunes to acquire large tracts of land in Beirut, the Mountain and the Beqa valley. The swift growth of trade with Europe and America during the mandate enabled them to enhance their positions as major intermediaries. After 1920, and especially after 1926, they used their considerable wealth to gain favours from officials in the High Commission, as well as from ministers, deputies and high ranking bureaucrats in the Lebanese administration. Merchants, bankers and entrepreneurs entered into joint ventures with politicians or their relatives. There was also a rise in intermarriage between prominent Maronite families from the Mountain and rich Christian families in Beirut. Under the Republic, affluent bankers and traders not only supported politicians financially, but often became directly involved in politics. Indeed, this close alliance between the politicians and the wealthy became a dominant feature of Lebanese politics. Such an association is never desirable; in Lebanon it had dire consequences, corrupting and undermining the political and administrative fabric of the state.[9]

The tight relationship between Maronite politicians from the Mountain and non-Maronite Christian businessmen in Beirut can best be observed in the unique ties between Beshara al-Khuri and his brother-in-law, the banker Michel Chiha. For more than a quarter of a century, these two men largely shaped the political and economic character of the Lebanese Republic. From 1926 until 1952, when he was forced to resign in disgrace following accusations of corruption and nepotism, Khuri played a central role in Lebanon's political life—initially as a minister and later as prime minister in three governments, in his relentless pursuit of the presidency in 1932 and 1936, and as leader of the opposition to Eddé after 1936. His political career culminated in his election as independent Lebanon's first president in 1943 when, together with Riad al-Sulh and others, he laid the foundations for the National Pact. In contrast, Chiha, apart from a short period in which he was involved directly in politics, for the most part remained in the background, whether financing Khuri's political career or serving as his chief ideologist. Khuri rarely made any serious decision without prior consultation with Chiha.

Khuri was a controversial figure, and uncovering his political intrigues and tactics poses a challenge to the historian. A shrewd, accomplished, manipulative and patient politician, he tended to act behind the scenes. After independence, he and his close circle of friends and followers effectively rewrote the history of Lebanon in the inter-war years. The best example is Khuri's autobiography, *Haqa'iq lubnaniyya*, published in the early 1960s. Khuri emerges from his memoirs as a committed national leader who dedicated his life to serving his people and country, ceaselessly defending its independence and sovereignty in the face of the colonial power. He portrays himself as the pillar of Lebanon's constitution and parliamentary system, who, from the start, advocated Christian–Muslim coexistence and cooperation with Syria and the rest of the Arab world.[10]

His critics, on the other hand, see him as a weak and uncharismatic leader: an opportunist motivated by an insatiable thirst for power, allowing his relatives, friends and a small group of affluent Christian financiers and merchants in Beirut to exploit him and his position to promote their own political and economic interests. Khuri's detractors reject his democratic posture and hold him, more than any other politician, responsible for making nepotism and corruption acceptable norms in Lebanese politics. They discard his claim to have been a steadfast opponent of the French mandate, and point out that he loyally served France, changing his stance only after the High Commission backed his sworn enemy, Emile Eddé, in his bid for the presidency.[11]

Khuri's biography resembles that of many other sons of affluent Maronite families from Mount Lebanon, who grew up in the last decades of the Ottoman Empire, and whose political careers were launched under the French mandate. He was born in 1890 in the village of Rishmaya near Ba'abda, to a family with a tradition of public service in the Mutasarrifiyya. At the Jesuit College in Beirut, he relates in his memoirs, Khuri acquired his early political education, love for his country, and exceptional mastery of the Arabic language. Studying with the Jesuits also provided him with the skills he was to employ effectively in the political arena. The Jesuits were impressed by his diligence, religious fervour and academic achievements, and played a significant role in promoting his political career. It was at the Jesuit College that he became acquainted with Michel Chiha and Riad al-Sulh, who would accompany him throughout his political life, the former as a close friend and ally, the latter as a bitter rival. In 1909 he went to France, where he earned his law degree from the University of Paris. After returning to Beirut in 1912, he began his training in Eddé's law office. With the outbreak of the war, like many other young Christians, he and two friends, Michel Chiha and Hector Klat,[12] fled to Egypt, where he practiced as a lawyer in Cairo and Alexandria. In 1919 he went back to Beirut and rejoined Eddé's office. With the help of his influential cousin, Bishop Abdallah al-Khuri, and Father Catan, director of the Jesuit College and head of the Medical School at St Joseph University, he was appointed to the Department of Justice, and in

February 1920 became secretary to the government of Mount Lebanon. In 1922 he was nominated as head of the Court of Appeal, a position which brought him into close contact with Charles Dabbas, director of the Justice Department. In 1926, the French, who valued his loyalty, chose him to serve as a judge in a special court set up to deal with the violence that had erupted between Druze and Maronites in the Shuf region. His appointment at the age of 36 as minister of interior in Auguste Adib's government was a natural outcome of his background and qualifications.[13]

Khuri's marriage in 1922 to Michel Chiha's sister, and that of his elder brother, Fuad, to Renée Darwish-Hadad, linked the Khuris with some of the most affluent Christian families in Beirut. These ties provided him with the means to promote his political career and considerably influenced his political and economic viewpoints. They also exposed him to accusations of nepotism and corruption. An intimate circle of relatives and friends comprising his brothers, Chiha, Pharaon and Taqla would rally together and, in coordination with Bishop Abdallah al-Khuri, strive relentlessly to bring about his election as president while undermining all other contenders. Members of this close-knit circle, joined later by Michel Zakur, Farid al-Khazin, Hamid Faranjieh, Charles Amoun and Camille Chamoun, would form the core of the Constitutional Bloc established in the 1930s, which brought together Maronite politicians from the Mountain and Beirut's Christian bourgeoisie. The Bloc's ideology, which reflected its members' particular interests, profoundly influenced the political and economic character of the Lebanese state.[14]

Despite Khuri's attempts, after independence, to emphasize both his role in the struggle against France throughout the mandate period, and the contrast between his stand and that of Eddé on Lebanon's Muslims, his political outlook differed little from that of other Maronite leaders. In 1912 he joined the 'Lebanese Society of Beirut', which advocated an independent Lebanon within extended borders, dominated by the Maronites and closely linked to France. The group, whose members included Eddé and Yusuf Gemayel, appealed to Georges-Picot, the French consul, for France's protection. While in Egypt, he became involved in the activities of the 'Alliance libanaise', and established close contacts with Yusuf al-Sawda, the head of its Alexandria branch.[15] After returning to Lebanon, in May 1919 and March 1920, he took an active part in the opposition to Faisal's claims over Beirut and Mount Lebanon. In 1921 he joined the Progressive Party, which advocated the independence of a Greater Lebanon under a French mandate and fiercely opposed any political ties with Syria. Among its members were the Marquis de Freige, Emile Eddé, Na'um Bakhus, Alfred Naqash, Michel Chiha and Yusuf Gemayel. Khuri was also affiliated with circles that called for the revival of Lebanon's Phoenician heritage. Despite a later claim that he had always pursued Christian–Muslim coexistence, his cooperation with Muslim politicians evolved more from political expediency—namely to win their backing for his bid against Eddé for the presidency—than from a genuine belief in the need to grant the Muslims an equal share in the Lebanese state. In fact it was Eddé who, from the start, had supported the nomination of Sunnis to the positions of president of the parliament and prime minister. It was no surprise, therefore, that Muslim politicians were suspicious of Khuri, whom they regarded as a 'Maronite from the Mountain' and, for the most part, preferred to back Eddé.[16]

Neither Khuri's successful career nor his political and economic outlook can be understood without taking into consideration the influence of Michel Chiha. The latter not only provided the financial means to sustain Khuri's political career, but developed the ideology that guided him and the Constitutional Bloc as a whole, and eventually determined Lebanon's political and economic orientation. Chiha may be seen as the principal architect of what has been defined as the 'Lebanese system'—a delicate balance between the sects, clans and regions, along with a capitalist laissez-faire economy based on trade and services. Chiha's influence peaked after 1943, during Khuri's term as president. Even after his death in 1954, it continued to be felt through his many disciples and admirers, who held key positions in Lebanon's political, economic and educational institutions. A myth grew up around him and he was credited, often unjustifiably, with many of Lebanon's political and economic achievements.[17]

Chiha was born in Beirut in 1891 to an affluent Chaldean-Catholic family originating in Iraq. The Chihas, together with the Greek-Catholic Pharaon family from Beirut, established the Pharaon–Chiha Bank, which accumulated most of its wealth from the silk trade. As was customary, the two families consolidated their business links through intermarriage: Chiha's mother was from the Pharaon family, and he himself married his cousin, the sister of Henri Pharaon.[18] As with Khuri, his education at the Jesuit College in Beirut left its mark on his Catholic beliefs, discernible in his way of thinking and in his writings. Unlike Khuri, however, Chiha made no effort to master the Arabic language and preferred to speak and write in French, in which he was well-versed. His Jesuit education also influenced his political outlook, which was similar to that of many other young Catholics in Mount Lebanon and Beirut at that time. His stay in Egypt during the war and time spent in England exposed him to the liberal British legal and administrative traditions, which he later attempted to emulate. Chiha returned to Beirut in 1919 and shortly thereafter, upon his father's death, left his studies and joined his uncle, Philippe Pharaon, in managing the family bank. He soon became director, a position he held throughout his life. As a banker, he established close ties with representatives of French concessionary companies in Beirut, as well as with officials in the High Commission. His appointment as a director in the Banque Syrie–Liban enabled him not only to promote the financial and commercial interests of the family bank, but also provided him with considerable political clout.[19]

Yet Chiha was not satisfied with merely being a businessman. Since his youth he had been attracted to politics. He was one of the founders of the Progressive Party and a member of the 'Young Phoenicians', a group of Lebanese Christians influenced by the ideas of Charles Corm, as expounded in the *Revue Phénicienne*.[20] In 1925 he was elected to the Representative Council in Beirut's minority seat. As a member of the Shibl Dammus Committee, and through his close ties with Paul Suchier, who had been appointed by de Jouvenel to advise the committee, he played an important part in drafting the 1926 constitution. Chiha served in Lebanon's first parliament as president of the finance committee, where he devoted most of his time to matters concerning the budget and taxation. His experiences in those years led him subsequently to advocate limited governmental and parliamentary intervention in the economy. After 1929 he ceased to be directly involved in politics, and chose to act behind the scenes to ensure Khuri's election as president. Together with his brother-in-law and business partner, Henri Pharaon, he provided the financial means to bribe deputies and journalists to support Khuri. In August 1934, he established *Le Jour*, with the aim of promoting Khuri, as well as of undermining Eddé, who was being backed at that time by the High Commission. In *Le Jour*, which became the mouthpiece of the Constitutional Bloc, Chiha expounded his views on numerous political, social, cultural and economic issues.[21]

Chiha was a highly sophisticated and versatile figure, with a wide variety of interests, and a keen observer of Lebanese politics and society. He was a man of many talents: a banker, a politician, a poet and prolific writer, as well as a philosopher. An autodidact and a devout francophile, he was immersed in French history, culture and literature. His political and economic views were formed during the 1920s and 30s. His editorials in *Le Jour* in the second half of the 1930s and his book *Le Liban d'aujourd'hui*, published in 1942, reveal a well-established philosophy. Chiha's main accomplishment was his ability to take existing ideas and mould them into a comprehensive ideology reflecting Lebanon's geography and history, as well as the political and economic reality of the time. Thus, in his thinking we can observe Lammens' idea of Lebanon as a refuge for persecuted Christian minorities, Corm's 'Phoenician' and 'Mediterranean' response to Arab nationalism, Nujaim's interpretation of the Mutasarrifiyya and Sawda's fervent Lebanese–Maronite nationalism. He was also influenced by French thinkers, in particular Renan and Barrès, as well as by Britain's liberal political economy and constitutionalism. Chiha offered the young, educated, secular Christians, troubled by the question of Lebanon's national identity, and facing the challenge of Arab nationalism, a complete ideology—one that not only justified Lebanon's separate existence within its 1920 borders, but imbued them with a feeling of great pride in their country's uniqueness and its contribution to Western civilization. He strove to combine the populistic and conservative traits of Maronite nationalism—which was the driving force behind the establishment of Greater Lebanon—with the liberal, cosmopolitan outlook of the non-Maronite Christian communities of Beirut. In his personality and views, Chiha, the Beiruti financier, complemented Khuri, the Maronite politician from the Mountain. His main contribution, however, was in transforming the capitalist laissez-faire economy advocated by Beirut's mercantile-financial Christian bourgeoisie into the mainstay of Lebanon's economic policy, thus laying the foundations for what later became the 'merchant republic'.[22]

Chiha's philosophy evolved from his belief in 'geographical determinism', the concept that geography determines, to a large extent, the history, culture and economy of nations. Situated at the crossroads of three continents, Lebanon, with its mountains and sea coast, is both a maritime nation and a bridge between East and West. It is also a union of Mount Lebanon, traditional refuge for oppressed minorities, and Beirut, a trading port on the Mediterranean, with its open, cosmopolitan atmosphere. The Lebanese, Chiha maintained, are not an Arab, but a Mediterranean people, a pluralistic society comprising a mix of minority communities, Christians and Muslims, and reflecting this unique fusion. Playing the role of intermediaries between the Christian West and the Arab Muslim East, the Lebanese are the true descendants of the Phoenicians. Greater Lebanon was the result of its geography and history; within its frontiers, the unique Lebanese genius would be able to express itself, as in the past, both in the economic and cultural spheres.[23]

Despite Chiha's apparent sophistication and his articulate, rational arguments, his ideology was inconsistent and fraught with contradictions, frequently masked in metaphysical or religious terms. This inconsistency resulted from the fundamental gap between the Lebanese Christians' vision of their state, which Chiha shared, and the reality of Greater Lebanon. While the Christians continued to strive for a modern, Western state under Maronite control, half of Lebanon's population were in fact Muslims, who rejected its national identity and challenged its very existence. While the Christians considered Lebanon to be part of Europe and Western civilization, their country was situated in the Arab, Muslim Middle East, a part of

Asia, which had for centuries been in religious, cultural and political conflict with the West. Finally, while Lebanon rejected any political ties with Syria, its economy relied heavily on trade with, and the provision of services to, the Arab Muslim population in the interior. Thus, when Chiha refers to equal sectarian representation, he in fact means Christian hegemony; when he speaks of a 'Mediterranean identity', he is rejecting Arab nationalism; and when advocating a capitalist laissez-faire economy, he envisages the transformation of Syria, Iraq, Iran, Transjordan and the Arabian Peninsula, in addition to the peripheral regions annexed to Lebanon, into an economic hinterland for Beirut and Mount Lebanon. Precisely for those reasons, Chiha firmly rejected Eddé's proposal to sever parts of the areas with predominantly Muslim populations that had been annexed to Lebanon in 1920. He feared that this would make Lebanon merely a bastion of Western Christianity, isolated from the surrounding region and thus unable to retain its economic, and subsequently its political viability. Chiha especially opposed the annexation of Tripoli to Syria, lest it undermine Beirut's position as the main port and trading centre for the interior.[24]

Politically, Chiha's thinking expressed more the *'dhimmi'* attitude of Christian Beirut than the fervent 'Maronitism' of the Mountain. Chiha was acutely aware of the potential for inter-sectarian violence between Maronites and Druzes on Mount Lebanon, as well as the religious and national conflict between Muslims and Christians. He thus aspired to a formula that would contain the violence and help preserve peace in Lebanon. He saw the solution in political sectarianism. He was one of its main proponents, for, he believed, it was deeply embedded in Lebanon's political, social and cultural traditions; through it, harmony and stability between the various communities, vital for the country's survival, would be ensured. Convinced that in the long run, sectarianism would facilitate true integration of the Muslims and the newly annexed regions into Lebanon, Chiha envisioned a country resembling Switzerland, but comprising a federation of communities rather than cantons.[25]

Chiha's support of political sectarianism was undoubtedly influenced by his business background. He believed in a system of give and take that would benefit all sides; hence his view of parliament not as an institution representing the sovereignty of the Lebanese people, but a marketplace where the political and economic elites of the various communities could meet, exchange views, bargain and reach agreements based on compromise, rationalism, tolerance and conciliation. He thus did not object to the High Commission's initiative to modify the constitution in order to weaken the power of the deputies, particularly in financial and budgetary matters. But he did oppose dissolution of parliament and suspension of the constitution; he regarded them as essential for preserving order and stability.[26]

Notwithstanding its intellectual, geographical and historical elements, Chiha's philosophy was, above all, determined by the economic, political and cultural reality of Beirut after the establishment of Greater Lebanon. Beirut had already become an important commercial and financial centre in the Levant before 1914. During the war, the city was severely affected by the blockade imposed on Ottoman ports by the British and French navies. Under the mandate, Beirut, with its numerous banks, commercial houses, wholesalers and traders, took advantage of the rapidly expanding demand in the Middle East for consumer goods from Europe. Its financiers and merchants played a significant role in the import trade, not only for Syria, but for Iraq, Transjordan and Iran and to a lesser extent the Arabian Peninsula. Between 60 and 80 per cent of all imports to the mandated territories passed through Beirut.[27]

France's decision to locate its High Commission in Beirut transformed the city into the main political and administrative centre of the mandated territories. In accordance with the 1926 constitution, it became the official capital of the Lebanese Republic and the seat of its government and parliament. As the new political institutions and the administrative system established themselves in the city, Beirut gradually extended its influence throughout the country. With the construction of a modern road network, improved education and the spread of newspapers and later of radio, the residents of the periphery became better informed and more aware of the political scene unfolding in Beirut.[28]

The High Commission and the Lebanese government attached much importance to modernizing the city, which had been partially destroyed in the war. The French saw it as a showcase for their accomplishments in the Levant; for the Lebanese, it was an expression of their modern, prosperous and vibrant state. In the 1920s and 1930s substantial investments were made. Old neighbourhoods were pulled down and elegant new quarters erected, with wide avenues leading to the centre of the city, where the parliament was built. A national museum, public buildings, squares and gardens were constructed, streets were widened and paved, and a comprehensive sewage network was laid. The port was enlarged and a free-trade zone established. Radio Orient, a new and powerful communications station, linked Beirut to Europe and America. Students from throughout the region sought an education in the city's two universities, where they were exposed to its unique cultural mix of East and West. In the cafés around the universities, students, faculty, politicians and journalists mingled, forming many of the new ideologies and political movements that emerged in the next two decades. By the

1930s, Beirut had become a major economic and cultural centre for the whole Middle East.[29]

Beirut's population grew at an unprecedented pace, more than doubling from 77,820 in 1921 to 161,382 in 1932. Although members of all communities moved to Beirut, the majority were Christians, thereby reinforcing the city's Christian character. Thousands of foreigners, attracted by Beirut's European ambience and expanding business opportunities, also came to settle there. The focus of Lebanese politics thus shifted from the Mountain, with its conservative Maronite and Druze communities, to Beirut, with its pluralistic and cosmopolitan society. Ministers, deputies and a rapidly growing number of state bureaucrats moved to the city or rented houses there. Beirut's expansion, accompanied by a rapid rise in the value of land and real estate, enabled landowners and contractors to accumulate considerable wealth, giving rise to widespread corruption. French officials, Lebanese politicians, civil servants, journalists, intellectuals, bankers, traders, contractors and industrialists mingled politically and socially. Financiers and entrepreneurs sought the support of politicians and bureaucrats to promote their new ventures, and the latter rarely hesitated to take advantage of the opportunities offered to them.[30]

Political life in Lebanon was not confined to the government or parliament, but became a public spectacle, with all its drama and comedy. Signs of religious, sectarian and national conflict, as well as political intrigue and corruption, could be seen daily on the pages of Lebanese newspapers, whose numbers rapidly increased during the 1920s and 1930s. Published in Beirut in Arabic and French, they were read avidly by politicians, officials in the High Commission and a growing young, educated and politically aware sector of the population, which comprised what could be termed 'public opinion'. The press became an arena where all major issues were openly debated. It enabled the Lebanese to follow closely as their elected representatives exercised power in the newly-created political institutions. The newspapers, which backed various communal, national and political causes, reflected the pluralism of the society and contributed to the liberal character of its political culture, while journalists not only provided information, comment and criticism, but participated directly in politics. Access to the press was thus essential for politicians, some of whom even established their own publications. The ownership of newspapers became a profitable enterprise, with politicians paying handsomely to expound their views or criticize their opponents. A major source of income for many newspapers and journalists was the 'financial support' they received for their services, both from politicians and the High Commission.[31]

Lebanese politicians faced pressure not only from the financial-commercial sector, but also from the Christian clergy, both Lebanese and foreign. Religious leaders actively intervened in politics, either at their own initiative, or at the request of the politicians themselves. This was particularly true with regard to the Maronite church. Following the central role of its patriarch in the establishment of Greater Lebanon in 1920, the church believed it had a special duty to defend the country's independence and territorial integrity. Its involvement in politics, however, exacerbated religious and sectarian differences, as well as the rivalry and factionalism within the Maronite community. It also reinforced Muslim and Arab nationalist resentment of the Lebanese state and strengthened their long-held belief that Lebanon was a creation of French colonialism and the 'separatist' Maronite clergy, and thus unworthy of allegiance. Moreover, Church activism served as a precedent for religious leaders from other communities, especially the Sunnis, to seek a similar role. Thus, the Mufti of the Republic and the Qadi of Beirut began not only to voice their concern for the rights and interests of their community, but to become directly involved in national issues.[32]

Intense rivalry among the Maronite bishops deeply affected their community. Although the elderly, ailing Patriarch Hawayik continued to enjoy the admiration and love of his people, he was steadily becoming less able to fulfil his duties. Unity in the church and community, in which he had invested so much, was lost as his bishops became engaged in a bitter power struggle to succeed him. The two main contenders were the patriarchal vicar, Bishop Abdallah al-Khuri, and the outspoken Bishop of Beirut, Ignatius Mubarak. Since the early 1920s, Bishop Khuri had exploited the power vacuum to emerge as a dominant force in the church, as well as in Lebanese politics. The rapid rise of his young cousin, Beshara al-Khuri, owed much to his support. Other bishops backed their own favourites, often intervening on their behalf in the High Commission. Arida's election as patriarch after Hawayik's death in December 1931 did little to improve the situation; the Maronite community and Lebanese politics continued to suffer the consequences of the deep divisions among the clergy throughout the following decade.[33]

The intervention of the Jesuits and that of Frediano Gianini, the apostolic delegate, in Maronite politics weakened the church and sharpened the conflict among its bishops. The Jesuits had long exercised considerable influence in Christian Lebanon through their control of its leading educational institutions, especially St Joseph University. After 1920 many of their graduates attained prominent positions in Lebanon's political and economic institutions. The Jesuits also promoted their views through the newspaper *al-Bashir*, which they controlled. Following Sarrail's failure to check their influence, they further strengthened their power under Ponsot. They backed Bishop

Khuri's efforts to succeed Patriarch Hawayik, as well as Beshara al-Khuri's bid for the presidency. Gianini used the power vacuum created by Hawayik's weakening status in the Maronite church as an opportunity to intensify his intervention in its affairs. This conformed with Vatican policy at the time: to extend its authority over the Eastern Catholic churches in the Levant. Like the Jesuits, Gianini, who had close ties with Bishop Khuri, supported the latter's efforts to take over Hawayik's position.[34]

To criticize Lebanon's political institutions is by no means to suggest that there was a better alternative; only a democratic parliamentary system would have enabled its multi-sectarian society, with neither a clear-cut Christian or Muslim majority, to evolve into a genuine civil society. Mistakes were bound to occur, especially in the early stages, when a Western political system was adopted by a society that had lived for centuries under Muslim and Ottoman rule. Indeed, the *raison d'être* of the mandate was for a European power to educate and guide the countries under its control, including Lebanon, through the difficult transitional phase. Yet the question remains: why did the negative aspects of those early years become rooted in Lebanon's political culture?

To what extent were the new political institutions able to exercise their power? Article 90 stipulated that 'the constitution shall be in force in addition to the preservation of the rights and duties of the Mandatory Power in accordance with Article 22 of the Charter of the League of Nations and the Act of Mandate.' The high commissioner, his delegate in Lebanon and the French advisers in the various ministries and departments continued to exert considerable influence on the Lebanese political and administrative systems even after promulgation of the constitution. Yet, until he suspended the constitution in May 1932, Ponsot, who was reluctant to intervene in what he regarded as local intrigues, allowed Lebanese politicians more freedom than any other high commissioner before or after him. His stand, frequently criticized not only by French officials, but by some Lebanese, resulted both from his cautious character and the circumstances under which he had assumed office. In the aftermath of the Druze–Syrian revolt, and in light of the precedent established by de Jouvenel in Lebanon, Ponsot was wary of imposing a direct administration. His interpretation of the mandate was far more liberal than that of most French officials in the High Commission. Moreover, aware of the influence wielded in Paris by the Maronite church and the Lebanese Christian politicians, he was especially careful to preclude accusations of undue interference. He feared that close control of the new political institutions, as advocated by many of his staff, would antagonize the Christians and drive them to cooperate with the Arab Muslim nationalists. Moreover, he sought to demonstrate to the Syrians the benefits of cooperating with France in promulgating their own constitution and electing a parliament and government. Ponsot argued that as long as Lebanese politicians did not interfere with French interests in the mandated territories, it was preferable to leave them to their own devices. This policy, however, not only proved to be unrealistic but, in the long run, discredited both the high commissioner and the new Lebanese political institutions. Satow, the British Consul General in Beirut, who was constantly criticizing Ponsot's attitude, described its shortcomings in detail: 'The present policy seems to be to leave more and more to the Lebanese Government. In theory this is no doubt excellent, but as regards practical results it is less so. Most branches of the public service are inefficiently conducted, and in several of them, notably the police, public works and health departments, serious scandals came to light during the years.'[35]

The first president of the Lebanese Republic was Charles Dabbas, a Greek Orthodox lawyer and former director of the Department of Justice. He had spent the pre-war years in Paris and was married to a French woman. By choosing a Greek Orthodox, de Jouvenel sought to silence Patriarch Hawayik's demands for a Maronite president and end the intense rivalry among the Maronite candidates—which had been delaying promulgation of the constitution—while at the same time allaying Muslim fears of Maronite domination of the new state. Thus, on 26 May 1926, at a joint session of the senate and chamber, Dabbas was elected president by a majority of 44 votes. His election, celebrated at a grandiose ceremony in the best of French traditions, barely concealed the fact that he neither enjoyed public support nor had any political base of his own. The Maronite church, particularly Bishop Mubarak, opposed his appointment, arguing that a Maronite should have been elected president, while the Muslims regarded him as merely a French puppet. Even his own community had its reservations, and the prominent Greek Orthodox families in Beirut, led by the Sursuks, constantly sought to undermine his influence.[36]

Dabbas faced the unenviable task of transforming the presidency into a symbol of national consensus. He had to maintain a middle course between serving the French, who had installed him in his position and were the driving force behind his presidency, and his duty to pursue his country's interests. But his weak and indecisive character made it more difficult for him to attain these goals. Not content with ceremonial duties or the role of an honest broker between the various communities and ambitious politicians, Dabbas immediately involved himself in political intrigue in an attempt to strengthen his own position. He tried to enhance his popularity in the Maronite church and community by demonstrating his loyalty to Greater Lebanon. A mere two weeks after his election, he announced his commitment to the integrity of Lebanon's borders to an audience of enthusiastic Christian students at St Joseph University in Beirut. His declaration, made during an intense border dispute with Syria, antagonized many Muslims in Lebanon and drew a strong reaction from the Syrian prime minister, Ahmad Nami. During a visit to the main mosque in Beirut a few days later, Dabbas was insulted and his speech interrupted.[37]

Since a Greek Orthodox had been elected to the presidency, a Maronite had to be nominated to the premiership. De Jouvenel chose Auguste Adib Pasha, a pro-French financial expert who had spent most of his professional life in the Egyptian administration. It was hoped that with his experience, he would be able to rejuvenate Lebanon's economy, which had been devastated by the war. Like Dabbas, the new prime minister had no political base of his own. After receiving a vote of confidence from the two houses, the first Lebanese government put forward an ambitious and detailed platform emphasizing the need to restore law and order, repair the damage caused by the revolt, reduce administrative costs and revitalize the economy. Satow justifiably observed that the Lebanese would be satisfied even if only part of the programme were implemented.[38]

The formation of the new government raised the question of the distribution of portfolios among the various communities. For the next six years, the issue of whether there would be three or seven ministers, and the competition for these positions, were major sources of Lebanon's political instability. There was a strong argument for a small, efficient government. Yet many politicians favoured a larger one, pointing to the need for representation of each of the six major communities. Moreover, an expanded government provided more ministerial positions, and thereby access to power, prestige and material reward. The principle of sectarian representation was subsequently adopted, and the first government comprised seven ministers: two Maronites and one representative of each of the other large communities: Greek Orthodox, Greek Catholic, Sunni, Shiite and Druze. The most influential member of the government was the minister of the interior, Beshara al-Khuri. Both President Dabbas and Prime Minister Adib considered him a useful link to his influential cousin, Bishop Abdallah al-Khuri, and to the Maronite church.[39]

A serious problem faced by the Lebanese Republic in its early years was the imbalance between the executive and legislative branches. Although the constitution granted the presidency considerable power, in reality both Dabbas and Adib, lacking a political base of their own, were unable to effectively exercise their authority in the face of ambitious senators and deputies. Confronted with strong opposition in the senate, particularly from Eddé,

who considered himself better suited to the presidency, Dabbas strove to secure the backing of the deputies. Adib, whose government depended on the
support of both houses, was in an even more vulnerable position. The Lebanese Republic, whose constitution was modelled after that of the Third
Republic, had inherited all the weaknesses of the latter's political institutions.
But when the High Commission concluded that the bicameral system was
too complicated and costly, and attempted to abolish the senate and reduce
the number of deputies in order to strengthen the authority of the president
and government, it faced strong opposition from both houses.

Political life in the first year of the Lebanese Republic was dominated by
power struggles and personal rivalry between senators and deputies. The two
houses disagreed on nearly every issue, ranging from the size of the government and the budget, to reform of the costly administration. Without the
need to stand for re-election every four years, the senators adopted a firmer
stand on these questions than did the deputies. The latter, who had considerably enhanced their influence and prestige by participating in the
elaboration of the constitution, were hostile to the senators' attempts to increase their own power. Most of the senators were former deputies who had
been defeated in the 1925 elections for the Representative Council, which
had been rigged by Leon Cayla, the former governor of Lebanon, together
with Habib al-Sa'ad and Musa Namur. These senators, led by Emile Eddé
and Ayub Tabet, were determined to undermine the standing of Namur, now
president of the chamber.[40]

The positions of president of the senate and of the chamber entailed considerable political power, and their election before each March and October
session invariably involved political intrigue and inter-sectarian rivalry. As the
two top executive posts were held by Christians and the head of the chamber was a Maronite, in May 1926 de Jouvenel endorsed the election of a
Sunni—Muhammad al-Jisr from Tripoli—as president of the senate, while
Omar Da'uq retained his position as vice-president of the chamber. The task
of re-electing the presidents of both houses loomed again before the October session. Namur was the winner of an intense contest that left the
deputies deeply divided, but not, however, along sectarian lines: Namur was
supported by many Muslim deputies, including Omar Da'uq and Omar
Bayhum, while his Sunni opponent, Khalid Chihab, was favoured by a
number of Christians. In the senate, Eddé and Ayub Tabet backed Jisr
against Habib al-Sa'ad. To prevent Maronites presiding over both houses, the
High Commission again intervened to secure Jisr's election.[41]

Although Adib's government had undertaken to improve the economy
and streamline the administration, it accomplished very little. Some ministers were simply unqualified, having been appointed for sectarian or political

reasons. Once in office, these ministers often selected inefficient and super-
fluous officials from among their supporters and communities. These
officials, in turn, felt obliged to provide positions for their own relatives and
friends. Thus political patronage and the clientele system became integrated
into Lebanon's new institutions. Hundreds of unnecessary positions were
added to the administration, which had been rapidly expanding since 1920.
Consequently, over 75 per cent of the budget was spent on sustaining an
overextended and costly bureaucracy (compared with only 40 per cent in
Syria), leaving little for improving the economy. After raising salaries in the
public sector yet again, the government was obliged to ask the High Commission for loans from its future share of the Common Interests. Scandal
and corruption in the administration were continually exposed by the press,
which strongly criticized the president, the ministers and the conduct of the
senators and deputies. Their criticism was no doubt politically motivated in
part, but it also reflected public disappointment with the way the new political institutions were being run. Instead of trying to solve the problems,
however, President Dabbas and his ministers responded by temporarily suspending publication of the newspapers—a measure they would frequently
adopt in the future.[42]

Faced with growing public discontent and pressure from the High Commission to balance the budget, Dabbas and the government sought to use the
1927 budget to reduce expenditure and stimulate the economy. At the beginning of the winter session in October 1926, the senate and chamber began
debating the proposed budget, but a conflict soon arose between the two
houses. With his budget still not approved and his government under attack
from senators and deputies, Adib lacked the resolve for a political struggle.
He left in December for Paris, where he spent the next few months representing Lebanon in discussions on the Ottoman Public Debt. In the absence
of Ponsot, who was also in Paris, de Reffye, the acting high commissioner,
and Solomiac, the French delegate to the Lebanese Republic, were unwilling
to intervene, and left Lebanese politicians to find their own way out of the
crisis. For the next four months President Dabbas and Beshara al-Khuri, the
acting prime minister, shuttled between the senate and the chamber in a desperate attempt to persuade the two houses to come to an agreement, but to
no avail. The budget was finally approved in April 1927 but by then, damage had been done both to the Lebanese economy and the standing of its
political institutions.[43]

Deputies and senators alike claimed that their refusal to approve the
budget had been motivated by their concern for the public welfare. In fact,
the disagreement between the two houses had grown out of a struggle for
power and prestige, reinforced by personal ambitions and rivalries. Some

senators had been eager to demonstrate their authority vis-à-vis the deputies, or to prolong the crisis in order to expose Dabbas' weakness. Both senators and deputies had sought to topple the government, hoping to secure ministerial positions. In the absence of Auguste Adib Pasha, Beshara al-Khuri had conspired to secure the premiership for himself. On the eve of the March parliamentary session, with the help of Salim Taqla, the director of the interior, Khuri had encouraged a group of deputies, led by Georges Tabet, to bring down the government. But his plans had been foiled; the deputies were unable to agree over the distribution of portfolios, while de Reffye and Solomiac opposed any change in government.[44]

The government had hardly survived the assault by Khuri and the deputies, when it again came under attack—this time by a group of senators led by Eddé, Ayub Tabet, Qashu'a and Jisr. Their aim was to replace Auguste Adib with Jisr, and thereby improve their position vis-à-vis the president and the chamber. Well aware of this plan, de Reffye and Solomiac informed Ponsot, but advised against intervention: this was 'an internal matter which does not interest the Mandatory Power'.[45] Ponsot heeded their recommendations, and suggested that if the senators did succeed, the opportunity should be taken to reduce to five the number of ministers in the new government. In April 1927, the senate presented an ultimatum to the government demanding the reduction of its ministers to three, along with reform of the administration and the judicial system. The senators' demands, however, were opposed by the deputies. When informed by Khuri of the ultimatum, Adib, who was still in Paris, resigned, and Dabbas had no choice but to ask Jisr to form a new government.[46]

The senators' scheme had gone smoothly thus far. But it ultimately failed, as Jisr was under pressure from his own community, which feared his election would be tantamount to Muslim recognition of the Lebanese state. Once again, personal rivalry was involved. Omar Da'uq, Omar Bayhum, and Abd al-Hamid Karameh, who were leading the campaign against Jisr, sought to prevent him from strengthening his position. Thus sectarian division played a secondary role: Jisr's bid for the premiership was supported by many Christian politicians but opposed by members of his own community.[47]

Their failure to obtain the premiership for Jisr was a setback for the senators, but a victory for Dabbas and the deputies. Some of them insisted that all senators stand for election, while others stepped up their campaign for complete abolition of the senate. Dabbas—who since his election a year before had been harassed and maligned by deputies and senators (albeit more so by the latter), criticized and ridiculed by the press, and treated with little respect by French officials—considerably enhanced his position. With the senators and deputies continually at loggerheads, he seized the opportunity to play an important role in forming the new government. After obtaining de Reffye's and Solomiac's agreement, he asked Beshara al-Khuri, his close ally, to head it. Despite their ultimatum on limiting the number of ministers to three, the senators eventually voted in favour of a new government, again comprising seven ministers. The vote reflected their weakness, as well as the fact that their move had actually been designed to topple the government. For its part, the High Commission had failed to ensure formation of a smaller government. In a telegram to Ponsot, de Reffye explained that it would have been impossible to reduce the number of ministers to five without provoking another crisis.[48]

The new government, which enjoyed the support of the majority of the deputies, was expected to be more stable than its predecessor. Two of its ministers, Georges Tabet and Khalid Chihab, were prominent figures in the chamber's two main factions. In order to promote stability and improve the government's relations with the senate, Ponsot nominated Beshara al-Khuri as a senator. Khuri's appointment testified to his success in becoming, within one year, a force to be reckoned with in Lebanese politics. But despite initial hopes, the government was again short-lived, and failed to solve the pressing problems of the budget, the economy and the inefficient administration. Discord among the ministers was rife, each striving to promote his own policies and interests, while deputies and senators resumed their intrigues. A year after proclamation of the Republic, it was clear to the High Commission, as well as to the Lebanese people, that the political system was in urgent need of reform. From July to October 1927, therefore, attention focused on amending the constitution.[49]

The reckless behaviour of the senators and deputies during the first year of the Lebanese Republic undermined the prestige of both houses and paralysed the political system. The High Commission was determined to weaken the legislative and strengthen the executive power. This was deemed all the more necessary in light of the Quai d'Orsay's decision to renew efforts to elaborate a constitution for Syria. Ponsot feared that the Syrians would use the Lebanese constitution as a precedent for demanding a strong senate and chamber. Having had to contend with the problems of a bicameral system in Lebanon, he was anxious to prevent a similar and potentially even more dangerous situation from developing in Syria. Yet contrary to the claims of Lebanese politicians and the press, modifications had not been imposed by the French merely to serve their own interests. Changes had been requested by many Lebanese, and President Dabbas and Prime Minister Khuri had willingly cooperated with the High Commission to implement them. In Paris in December 1926, Prime Minister Auguste Adib Pasha had already stressed the need to strengthen the government in relation to the senate and chamber. Dabbas, for his part, had repeatedly asked the High Commission to extend the president's authority, especially after the senators' campaign against him in February 1927. The budget crisis finally convinced Ponsot and the Quai d'Orsay that action had to be taken. But no move was made until Ponsot returned to Beirut.[50]

In June, after consulting Dabbas and Khuri and his aides in the High Commission, Ponsot informed the Quai d'Orsay of his plans to proceed with revision of the constitution. He argued that the constitution granted to Lebanon the previous year was too close to the French model—it was too costly and complex for a state the size of Lebanon, with a population of only 600,000. Moreover, it had failed to provide Lebanon with a stable and efficient government. Ponsot did not expect much opposition; there had been strong public criticism of the constitution from the president, as well as the prime minister, who were demanding that their power be increased vis-à-vis the senate and chamber.[51]

Ever cautious, Ponsot initially refrained from using his authority as high commissioner to impose the revisions, preferring that they be implemented by Lebanon's elected representatives, in accordance with the constitution. He hoped thereby to avoid accusations in the Mandates Commission and in Lebanon, as well as in Syria, that France was seeking to restore direct control now that the Syrian revolt was over. He thus entrusted Dabbas and Khuri with the task of introducing the necessary modifications. During the summer, together with Solomiac, they prepared a detailed draft for a revised constitution that weakened the legislature and considerably strengthened the presidency. The High Commission's aim was to gain a better hold on the Lebanese administration through a strong and trusted president. Dabbas, for his part, had long been striving to extend presidential power, and thus his own. While he had misgivings, Khuri, then prime minister, was keen to co-operate with Ponsot, Solomiac and Dabbas—to whom he owed his position—and thus wary of voicing his doubts. He already harboured ambitions to succeed Dabbas in 1929 and deemed it beneficial to take such a step. Although he later attempted in his memoirs, to minimize his role, Khuri fully participated in revising the constitution. In a letter to the high commissioner introducing the proposed amendments, he set out in detail the difficulties of the government in exercising its authority in the face of a strong senate. Apart from giving the government more 'cohesion and stability' by replacing individual with collective ministerial responsibility, all his proposals were concerned with enhancing the power of the president. Consequently, he failed to raise the issue of extending the authority of the government, which was essentially the multi-confessional governing body.[52]

On 24 August 1927, Ponsot sent Briand a detailed proposal for revising the constitution which, he explained, was intended to improve the efficiency and stability of Lebanon's political system. The new provisions included abolition of the senate and the fusion of the two houses into one parliament comprising 45 deputies, of whom two-thirds would be elected and one-third nominated by the president. To justify his proposal that both elected and appointed deputies serve in the same parliament, Ponsot argued that this would enable the High Commission 'to choose men favourable to our action' and 'to correct the results of the elections, in which the majority of the participants are illiterate and whose votes are not always guided by reasons of general interest'. The deputies were, in fact, to be nominated mainly for political convenience or their willingness to cooperate with the High Commission. Ponsot also proposed promoting government stability by introducing collective ministerial responsibility and increasing to two-thirds the number of deputies necessary for a no-confidence vote. The focus of the plan, however, was on strengthening the power of the president against that of parliament by granting him the right not only to nominate one-third of the deputies, but to legislate laws and initiate revision of the constitution. The president was also given more freedom in financial matters. The proposals were examined by officials in the Quai d'Orsay and approved by Briand in the middle of September. Although Briand agreed on the need to ensure a sound administration for Lebanon, he stressed that the High Commission should 'intervene as infrequently and as indirectly as possible in the governing of the country'.[53]

Despite Briand's instructions and Ponsot's reluctance to exercise authority, the High Commission had no alternative but to impose the revised constitution on a defiant, resentful senate and chamber. Both houses had learned of Ponsot's intention to amend the constitution at the beginning of July, when Solomiac had informed their presidents and requested their cooperation. Jisr and Namur had been placed in a difficult situation. While they opposed the French initiative, they were anxious not to antagonize the High Commission. Nevertheless, for the next three months, senators and deputies buried their differences and united against it. They were proud of the role they had played in elaborating the constitution, believing it truly reflected the will of the Lebanese people. It had became a symbol of Lebanon's sovereignty and independence, for which they assumed responsibility. Some feared that the French intended to restore their direct administration of Lebanon, and accused the High Commission of being motivated more by its policy needs in Syria than by a genuine desire to solve Lebanon's problems. Senators and deputies, who for the previous two years had been accustomed to exerting a strong influence on the president and the government, were unwilling to relinquish their power. They especially opposed their fusion into one house or a reduction in their numbers, insisting that such a step would undermine the principle of confessional representation and the division of the electoral districts. Instead of the radical revisions sought by the High Commission, they offered to approve urgent measures that would facilitate the government's ability to exercise its authority, particularly in financial matters.[54]

Solomiac, Dabbas, Khuri, Jisr and Namur discussed the revisions until the middle of September, but produced no results. The presidents of the chamber and senate employed delaying tactics, hoping that with the winter session due to begin on 15 October, in which the 1928 budget was to be approved, the High Commission, Dabbas and Khuri would drop their initiative. For precisely that reason, Khuri, in his letter to Ponsot on 10 August, stressed the need to finalize the revisions before parliament convened. Unable to persuade the deputies and senators to agree to the modifications, Ponsot and Dabbas decided to force the issue. Exercising his power in accordance with Article 76 of the constitution, Dabbas officially presented both houses with a draft revision on 23 September. The legislators, who had no choice but to debate the draft, formed two commissions: the deputies restored the Dammus Committee, which had originally written the constitution, while the senators moved to establish a committee comprising all members of the senate. Neither convened until the end of the month. Ponsot and Dabbas attempted to mobilize public support by publishing the proposed draft in the press, but the senators and deputies succeeded in instigating campaigns against the revisions, which they described as a setback to Lebanon's national goals. Solomiac wryly remarked that while the press had criticized the political system in the past, it now unanimously opposed any change. By the end of September, emotions were running so high that Colonel Catroux summoned several editors whose newspapers had been especially outspoken, cautioning them to cease their attacks.[55]

Impelled by the High Commission, the chamber and senate formed a joint committee, which made a counter-proposal rejecting fusion of the chamber and senate; it offered to consider the option at a later stage and if necessary initiate a revision of the constitution. The committee suggested that both houses meet in the meantime to discuss specific issues, including approval of the budget, and vote on bills considered urgent by the government. The senators and deputies were clearly willing to make concessions as long as they could delay union of the two chambers.[56]

Ponsot, however, was reluctant to wait any longer. He threatened to exercise his authority in accordance with Article 1 of the mandate, while Colonel Catroux undertook to 'persuade' the reluctant parliamentarians to accept the High Commission's proposals. The senate was the first to yield;

on 6 October, 12 of its members voted in favour of the draft revision. The chamber passed a similar resolution the following day, with a majority of 21 deputies out of the 29 present voting in favour. After his proposals had been adopted, Ponsot was ready to make minor adjustments to appease the two houses and restore their prestige. A new committee of eight deputies and four senators was formed to study the draft in detail. Its main concern was that all serving legislators be included in the combined parliament, and that both nominated and elected deputies enjoy equal status. At a joint session on 12 October, the two houses approved the draft by a majority of 31 votes. Omar Da'uq and Omar Bayhum, the two Sunni deputies from Beirut, did not participate in the debate; they made a different proposal: to abolish the May 1926 constitution altogether and return to the 1861 regime of the Mutasarrifiyya.[57]

The modifications of October 1927 were indeed extensive, with 52 of the original 102 articles amended. Most of the revisions advocated by Dabbas, Khuri and the High Commission were adopted. The senate was abolished; but faced with strong opposition from both senators and deputies, Ponsot did not reduce the number of deputies, as originally intended, or hold new elections. Consequently, the former senators and deputies continued to serve together in the joint parliament. Article 24 of the revised constitution stipulated that parliament comprise both elected and appointed deputies, and that 'the number of appointed deputies be equal to half the number of those elected', that is, 30 elected and 15 appointed. This arrangement had its obvious advantages for the High Commission and President Dabbas, as well as for the senators themselves, who were able to remain in office without having to stand for re-election. Some deputies, led by Shibl Dammus, objected to this article, but they were ignored. The 'new' parliament thus lost its cohesion, power and prestige, while rivalry between elected and appointed deputies remained a source of political instability. Yet the deputies' prerogative to elect the new president enabled them to retain considerable influence over the presidency. This was to become apparent after the 1929 parliamentary elections, when a contest for the presidency developed between Eddé and Khuri.[58]

One of the declared goals of amending the constitution had been to provide Lebanon with a stable, efficient government. The previous system of individual ministerial responsibility to parliament was replaced with collective responsibility. A no-confidence vote now required the presence of at least two-thirds of the deputies, and this was increased in May 1929 to three-quarters (Article 69). Yet subsequent governments continued to be voted out of office, and their efficiency hardly improved. On the other hand, parliament succeeded in raising from three to four the number of deputies allowed to serve as ministers, in a seven-member government.[59]

The May 1926 constitution, modelled after that of the Third Republic, had entrusted executive power to the prime minister rather than the president. In the revised constitution, however, presidential power was enhanced vis-à-vis that of both the parliament and the prime minister, who was obliged to rely on the president's support. The High Commission had clearly favoured extending the authority of the president, assuming that since he would be less exposed to parliamentary influence, it would be better able to control his actions. The president could now manipulate parliament through his ability to nominate one-third of the deputies, a prerogative that had previously been entrusted to the prime minister (Article 24). He had also gained authority to dissolve the legislature (Article 55). He could temporarily postpone laws passed by parliament (Article 57) and promulgate urgent legislation himself, albeit with government approval (Article 58). In addition, he was given the right to enforce the budget if parliament failed to approve it during the ordinary or extraordinary sessions (Articles 85 and 86). Moreover, his power to initiate amendments to the constitution was also extended (Article 76).[60]

The constitution in its new form lost much of its credibility and respect, as well as its ability to become, as the Dammus committee had envisioned, a symbol of Lebanon's independence and sovereignty. And a dangerous precedent had been established: the constitution could be modified to serve immediate political needs. Thus instead of shaping the structure of Lebanese politics, the constitution increasingly reflected their negative characteristics. One could perhaps blame the elected representatives, whose pursuit of their own interests had precipitated the constitutional crisis. But such a claim ignores the fact that according to the mandate, France was ultimately responsible for helping Lebanon adjust to a modern political system. Mistakes were bound to be made, and despite their belief to the contrary, Lebanese politicians lacked the experience to implement a Western parliamentary system successfully. Indeed, Briand had instructed Ponsot to act in the spirit of the mandate. Undoubtedly some modifications were necessary in order to create a more stable and efficient Lebanese administration. But Ponsot allowed the old guard in the High Commission, led by de Reffye, Solomiac and Catroux, along with a self-centred president and a hesitant prime minister, to introduce changes enabling continued French control of Lebanese politics—albeit indirectly. He may have solved an immediate crisis, but he had created far worse problems for the future. The outcome of a strengthened presidency would become apparent in the presidential elections of 1932 and 1936. With so much at stake, the Maronites and their church were deter-

mined, more than ever before, to attain the presidency, and Maronite politicians were to struggle relentlessly for the post.[61]

The High Commission's decision to unite the two houses raised the question of whether Namur or Jisr would head the combined parliament. Indeed,
Solomiac and Dabbas used this issue to weaken opposition to the revised
constitution. The senators initially sided with Jisr, and the deputies with
Namur, but they soon began to shift from one candidate to another according to their own immediate interests. Since the two highest positions, president and prime minister, were already held by Christians, Namur offered to
endorse Omar Da'uq's candidacy for the premiership in return for the latter's support for his own election as speaker. Da'uq and Omar Bayhum also
sought to prevent Jisr's election, and as the latter's chances improved, they
offered their backing to Ayub Tabet. Emile Eddé, who argued that the position should go to a Sunni, played an important part in mobilizing support
for Jisr. He had his own motives: to ensure the election of a close ally and
the defeat of Namur, an old rival. Eddé held intensive discussions with Bishops Khuri, Mubarak and Bustani to gain their backing for Jisr. Bishop Khuri
willingly cooperated, seeking to ensure that his cousin retain the premiership.
He even undertook to visit Habib al-Sa'ad, with whom his relations were
strained, in order to persuade him to endorse Jisr. The latter was also favoured by the High Commission, which recommended that a member of the
Sunni community hold one of the three high political posts. Consequently,
Jisr was elected as speaker of parliament, with Habib al-Sa'ad as his deputy.
Thus began Jisr's rapid rise to prominence in Lebanese politics. Once again,
sectarian considerations had played a secondary role, with deputies voting
according to their own interests: Jisr was supported by the Maronite Church
and by Christian as well as Muslim deputies, Namur by many Muslim deputies. After his election Jisr praised France and undertook to cooperate with
all members of parliament. His declaration of allegiance to the Lebanese
state, in which he vowed to 'defend it until death', might have scored some
points with the Christians, but it raised more than a few eyebrows among
members of his own community.[62]

The fusion of senate and chamber, together with Namur's defeat, led to
a shift in the balance of power in parliament. The 'Namurists', who had
dominated the former Representative Council and later the chamber, lost
much of their cohesion, and some of their members sought to join the new
coalition led by Eddé, Jisr and Sa'ad. It also sparked a new government crisis, as Khuri was attacked from both sides for his role in revising the
constitution. In return for his support of Jisr, Sa'ad pressured Eddé to back
his own bid for the premiership. Eddé also intended to force Minister of the

Interior Georges Tabet, Namur's ally, out of the government. And there were always politicians who would not balk at initiating a government crisis in order to secure ministerial positions for themselves. The deputies, however, had learned from the mistakes of the previous year, and refrained from using the issue of the budget to topple the government; the 1928 budget was approved in record time. In order to enhance his popularity, Georges Tabet raised salaries in the public sector, providing Eddé and Sa'ad with further ammunition to bring down the government. The deputies were already engaged in intrigues over division of the ministerial positions in the next administration. Anxious to hold on to his post, Khuri offered to exclude Tabet from the government he intended to form. The Eddé–Jisr–Sa'ad alliance, however, endorsed Sa'ad's bid for the premiership, with Khuri as minister of interior. Namur, who also wanted to settle his score with Khuri, attempted to gain the support of deputies for his own government, in which Tabet would retain his position. Khuri succeeded twice in thwarting his opponents' attempts to force him from office by blocking the quorum now required in parliament under the revised constitution. After coming to an agreement with Dabbas, however, he tendered his resignation.[63]

With his newly-acquired power, President Dabbas considerably enhanced his standing in Lebanese politics. No longer was he willing to tolerate deputies who ignored his authority or attempted to undermine the government. In his discussions with Ponsot and Solomiac, it was agreed that the opportunity to form a narrow government headed by Khuri, had to be seized. Ponsot insisted that Ayub Tabet serve as minister of the interior; having opposed Tabet's bid for the position of speaker, this was compensation for his continued loyalty. Moreover, Ponsot hoped that Tabet would implement some of his long-desired proposals to cut costs and reform the administration. But the nervous and short-tempered Tabet proved to be a burden to his prime minister, who did not share his determination to reduce expenses drastically by dismissing government employees. Left to choose the third minister, Khuri offered the position to Husain al-Ahdab, the Sunni administrator of Beirut. Ahdab declined at first; only after Khuri threatened to dismiss him from his post in Beirut did he agree to serve as minister of finance, public works and agriculture. With Ahdab out of the way, Khuri installed his trusted ally, Salim Taqla, former director of the interior, in Ahdab's previous position. Commenting on the new government, Satow wrote:

> The life of the new ministry will presumably be a short one but how long it will remain in office cannot be foreseen and does not perhaps much matter. The doings of the ministers and the politicians in general have but little connection with the general interests of the country. They are all interwoven with personal intrigues

and jealousies. They add considerably to the expense of administration but yield practically nothing in return. Politics as played here is a rather futile and expensive game, and it is unfortunate that the de Jouvenel Constitution has given such encouragement to it.[64]

Caught by surprise by Dabbas and Khuri, Eddé and Namur, after clashing for three years, decided to cooperate. Referring to his new alliance with Eddé, Namur remarked:

> As long as we are divided, the parliament cannot get any work done and will neglect important matters. The president and Beshara al-Khuri will exploit this to do whatever they want. We had proof of this in the composition of the government. We are now going to try to present a united front against the government.[65]

Beshara al-Khuri's close cooperation with Dabbas and his willingness to head a three-member government angered not only his opponents, but many of his allies. Maronite politicians accused him of serving Dabbas' interests, but their attempts to win their church's support to force his resignation were thwarted by Bishop Khuri. Deputies voiced their opposition to Dabbas and Khuri at a session in which the latter requested the parliament's vote of confidence. To prevent lengthy debate, Khuri briefly outlined his government's intentions to cut the budget and reform the administration. He was strongly criticized, especially by the Shiite deputies, who complained that their community, which was already under-represented in the administration, now had no minister in the cabinet. Yet Khuri still managed to secure a majority for his government. His success, however, was due less to the support he enjoyed among the deputies, than to the expanded power of the president, who was able to manipulate and exert influence on parliament. Some deputies feared that Dabbas, seeking re-election, would make use of a prolonged government crisis to dissolve parliament and hold new elections, and would thus be able to nominate one-third of the deputies, in accordance with the revised constitution. Others were tempted by promises of political and personal favours to cooperate with the government. Eddé and some former senators, who had long argued for a small, efficient administration, could not openly oppose Khuri's cabinet without losing their credibility. Namur and his supporters, however, boycotted the parliamentary session, while Dammus gave the government his 'temporary vote of confidence'.[66]

Khuri's government initially had more success than its predecessors. Public expenditure was reduced, hundreds of officials dismissed, changes introduced into the judicial and health systems, attempts made to reorganize the police force and gendarmerie, and additional resources allocated to public works, mainly road construction. Many of these measures, especially the dismissal of government employees, were extremely unpopular. Deputies who were no longer able to grant favours to their relatives and clients, or whose protégés in the administration had been dismissed, raised an outcry. The government discredited its own policy by politicizing the administration: most of those dismissed had been allied with the opposition or were Muslims—leading Sunni and Shiite deputies to accuse the government of failing to maintain sectarian and regional balance. Tabet repeatedly clashed with politicians and officials, forcing Khuri to contend with one crisis after another. Newspapers, especially *L'Orient* and *al-Ahrar*, accused the ministers of corruption and embezzlement of public funds, and of using their power to grant lucrative public work contracts to relatives and friends. Khuri's attempts to silence criticism by suspending publication of newspapers evoked strong protests from their editors and journalists to the High Commission and the Quai d'Orsay.[67]

In July 1928, the opposition, led by Namur and Subhi Haidar, collected enough signatures to force President Dabbas to convene an extraordinary meeting of parliament. At a particularly tumultuous session on 9 August, Khuri exchanged bitter recriminations with his opponents. After the opposition succeeded in passing a resolution demanding an increase in the number of ministers from three to five, in order to ensure that all the major communities were represented in the government, Khuri resigned.[68]

Some deputies undoubtedly had their own motives for raising the issue of sectarian representation. Nevertheless, the government was obliged to implement this basic tenet, which had been integrated into the constitution. Yusuf al-Zein, a Shiite deputy from the south, remarked that deputies were elected to parliament not to receive salaries and further their own positions, but to represent and defend the interests of their communities. He questioned whether a government should use the need for a more efficient administration to justify its reluctance to comply with Article 95. The Shiite and Sunni deputies regarded government policy as a pretext for the Christians to avoid granting their communities equality. Dr. Salim Talhuk, a former Druze minister, warned that:

> Lebanon is currently composed of communities which replace the political parties of other countries. Any community which does not have a share in the power considers itself wronged. We must take all possible steps to attain unity between the communities, none of which should be sacrificed. It was with this intention that Article 95 was included. To calm things down, each citizen should participate in public affairs. Laws are made to create harmony among all citizens of the nation that we aspire to form. Everyone is expected to obey the law. I repeat, we want to attain unity gradually, not by force; a method which has clearly succeeded in nations comprising heterogeneous communities which thereby became homogeneous and indivisible.[69]

Such a statement by a member of parliament was rare, and barely made an impression on most Lebanese politicians. The president, the prime minister, ministers and deputies were all engaged in endless games of political manoeuvreing and intrigue. This was clearly illustrated in the efforts to form the new government in August 1928. Dabbas was keen to improve his relations with the opposition in order to ensure his re-election. Maronite candidates, most noticeably Habib al-Sa'ad, had already announced their intention to run for election, and Sa'ad and other Maronite deputies met with Bishop Mubarak in May to obtain his backing for a Maronite president. Dabbas therefore sought to remove Sa'ad from the race and gain the support of the Maronite church, as well as of Namur and Subhi Haidar. For his part, Jisr, who faced re-election in October, was eager to prevent Namur from participating. And all the politicians were in a state of agitation as the parliamentary elections of June 1929 drew closer. These considerations were to determine the composition of the new government, which was headed by Habib al-Sa'ad and comprised five ministers, as requested by parliament. Namur was appointed minister of the interior, and Subhi Haidar minister of finance. The downfall of his government must have been a disappointment for Beshara al-Khuri. To add insult to injury, he was replaced by his relative and rival, who had also, as Khuri tells us in his memoirs, deposed his father from his position during the Mutasarrifiyya. But Khuri was an accomplished and patient politician and did not openly take offense at Dabbas' volte-face.[70]

Presenting his government's platform to parliament, Sa'ad undertook to strengthen the economy and invest additional resources in agriculture and road construction, using the funds saved from the previous year's budget. The money was indeed rapidly put to use, but for less worthy causes. Sa'ad also told the deputies that his government would guarantee freedom of the press, alluding to the record of the former prime minister. In early October, Namur and Haidar staged presidential visits for Dabbas to their respective home towns of Zahle and Ba'albeck. A somewhat nervous Dabbas, who still remembered the stormy reception accorded him by the Muslims of Beirut after his election, was welcomed by Ba'albeck's Shiite notables and religious leaders, who proclaimed their allegiance to the Lebanese state. The event was particularly remarkable because Subhi Haidar had represented Ba'albeck at a congress for Syrian unity held in Damascus in June. Dabbas hoped his visit would prove to the Maronite church and community his determination to uphold Lebanon's territorial integrity. He demonstrated his new-found concern for the Beqa valley by rejecting complaints by Shiite deputies from the south that Haidar was giving preferential treatment to that region. With Namur out of the race, Jisr faced little opposition, and was re-elected as speaker of parliament. All efforts to reduce the budget and reform the administrative system came to an abrupt halt, however, as Lebanese politicians turned their attention to the upcoming presidential and parliamentary elections, and disregarded the deteriorating economic and social situation.[71]

While Dabbas laboured diligently to preclude any threat from a Maronite contender to his re-election, he was challenged by an outside candidate, George Lutfallah. The latter's bid for the Lebanese presidency transformed an otherwise predictable campaign into a colourful event, and at the same time enhanced the financial standing of many politicians and journalists. George Lutfallah was one of three brothers whose Greek Orthodox Lebanese father had emigrated in the nineteenth century to Egypt, where he amassed a considerable fortune. The eldest brother, Michel, had been involved since the war in financing the Syrian Arab nationalist struggle against the French mandate. After the failure of the Syrian–Druze revolt, however, the family sought to improve its relations with France. Together with his rich and influential father-in-law, Najib Sursuk, George Lutfallah attempted to win the High Commission's support for his presidential bid. Ponsot had no intention of allowing Lebanon to be governed by a member of a family known for its hostility to France. Nevertheless, he discreetly encouraged Lutfallah's ambitions in order to sow discord in the ranks of the Syrian Committee in Cairo. Ponsot and Lutfallah used plans to construct a railway linking Tripoli and Beirut with Naqura in northern Palestine as a cover to conceal the true nature of their contacts. In September 1927, George Lutfallah and Najib Sursuk accompanied a French senator, Etienne Lamercy, who had come on a fact-finding mission to the mandated territories. Sursuk took the opportunity to meet Ponsot and hold long discussions with de Reffye, in which he offered the Lutfallah family's cooperation with France in return for the High Commission's support of George Lutfallah as the next Lebanese president. If Ponsot was reluctant to take this step, Sursuk stated, he was willing to stand for election himself. Dabbas was alarmed by the French officials' meetings with Lutfallah and Sursuk, and Ponsot's explanations did little to reassure him. He feared that Lutfallah's connections in Paris and his father-in-law's influence in Beirut might help him obtain French endorsement of his candidacy. Lutfallah's visit to Beirut, on his way to Paris in the summer of 1928, and the intensive campaign on his behalf in the Lebanese press, added to Dabbas' apprehensions. His rival's return to Beirut from Paris in December 1928, on the same boat as Ponsot, left him in total panic.[72]

For the next three months, George Lutfallah invested large sums of money in rallying support for his candidacy among Lebanese politicians and the public. He visited towns and villages, met with delegations and dignitaries, and undertook to use his personal fortune to bolster the Lebanese economy. Numerous articles were published in the newspapers backing him and criticizing Dabbas. In order to participate officially in the elections, however, he required Lebanese citizenship, which the government was reluctant to grant him. Lutfallah's followers campaigned in the press and petitioned the Lebanese government and the High Commission, arguing that being of Lebanese descent, he was no less qualified for citizenship than the Armenians who had only recently settled in Lebanon. Meanwhile, his representative in Paris, Georges Enkiri, attempted to persuade the French government to urge the high commissioner to back him. Concerned that he might have overplayed his hand, Ponsot brought forward the elections, originally scheduled for April, to the first day allowed by the constitution. On 26 March, Dabbas was re-elected with a majority of 42 votes for another three-year term. Since parliamentary elections were due to take place in June, few deputies had been willing to defy Ponsot or Dabbas.[73]

With the parliament paralysed, Ponsot and Dabbas initiated yet another revision of the constitution in April 1929, further extending presidential power vis-à-vis parliament. The president's term of office was extended to six years; he could now dissolve parliament almost at will (Article 55), and choose ministers from outside it (Article 28). Although the High Commission claimed that the revisions were necessary in view of the deputies' irresponsible conduct, its initiative had no doubt been motivated by the constitutional crisis in Syria. The National Bloc's success in gaining control of the Syrian parliament, along with Ponsot's failure to convince the nationalist deputies to omit certain articles of their proposed constitution, further underlined the need to weaken the power of both parliaments. Unlike the deputies' reaction in October 1927, this time there was barely any opposition from the Lebanese parliament. The government, including Namur, who had previously campaigned against modifying the constitution, now cooperated willingly.[74]

While the president, ministers and deputies were preoccupied with the presidential and parliamentary elections, Lebanon's economic and social problems deteriorated further. It was true that Beirut was enjoying economic prosperity and the real estate market flourishing, but it was the affluent and well-established families who benefited most from the situation. For average citizens, however, who were moving in ever-growing numbers to the city, the cost of living was rising sharply. In the south, the Beqa valley, Tripoli and north Lebanon, economic conditions improved little. Despite the promises of the various governments, few resources were invested in those regions. The agricultural sector was neglected. Complaints were voiced against the high taxes and the diversion of most of the budget to maintain the overextended, inefficient and corrupt political and administrative systems. Since many families relied on remittances from relatives in North America, Lebanon was also soon to feel the repercussions of the global economic crisis. Newspapers reflected the disillusionment of a growing number of young and educated Lebanese, many of whom were unemployed. The political intrigues, corruption and nepotism exposed in the press further antagonized the public. Ministers and deputies undermined their standing by trading insults and recriminations. A comment in one of the newspapers expressed the mood at the time:

> We have seen men come to power whose patriotism and talent are undisputed. Men well aware of the hopes and needs of the country, and who came with a plan and a goal. All their efforts were in vain. Each time they tried to rectify the situation in the national interest, they encountered considerable opposition, a coalition of interests, ambitions, hate, greed and ignorance, which are the very essence of this parliamentary system. This is the environment in which they were called upon to serve. To do exceptionally useful work and assure a majority, they had to conclude the strangest alliances; to surrender to degrading bargaining, at the cost of the most burdensome concessions; to obtain approval for projects whose use for the general public is most questionable.[75]

As the parliamentary elections drew near, Sa'ad and his ministers, Namur and Haidar, openly exploited their positions to mobilize public support, leading the press to accuse them of pillaging national resources to further their political goals. Dissension in the government grew as Namur plotted to topple Sa'ad, in an attempt to replace him in the premiership. Namur also clashed with Haidar over the distribution of deputies among the various sects and electoral districts. Many opposition deputies feared that Sa'ad and Namur would rig the elections, as they had in 1925. Indeed, Dabbas was anxious to replace Sa'ad before June to prevent him from supervising the vote. With the presidential elections over and the constitution revised, this goal could now be realized. Publication in the press of a list of the candidates whom, it was alleged, Sa'ad intended to support, raised an outcry from his opponents and gave them the opportunity to oust him. On 8 May, after 23 deputies signed a motion of non-confidence in the government, Sa'ad handed in his resignation to President Dabbas.[76]

With the new parliament to elect the next president in 1932, Ponsot, Solomiac and Dabbas chose Khuri to head the government that would supervise the parliamentary elections. Although two of its three ministers were not even members of parliament, few deputies were willing to oppose Dabbas and Khuri openly. In a statement to parliament, the latter pledged to hold free elections and prevent any unlawful interference in them. However, neither the High Commission, Dabbas, Jisr and the deputies, nor Khuri himself had any intention of keeping such promises: there was too much at stake to rely on the free will of the voters.[77]

On the eve of the elections, Omar Bayhum gave an ominous warning to his colleagues in parliament. The fact that it came from a declared opponent of the Lebanese state did not detract from its weight:

> We have been, my dear friends, the principal scourge of the country. Your only concern was to look after your own interests. You have filled the administration with your people. The public good —the general interest—never concerned you. I hope that most of you will not return in the next parliament and that it will be less evil, less harmful and less shameful than the present one. The country needs people other than demagogues, who will bring to its service something other than words, and who can understand that the public funds at their disposal are not for them to waste on the interests of their clients.[78]

The ministers and deputies, however, paid little heed to the public criticism or to warnings of the repercussions of their conduct on the country's future. Expectations that the 1929 elections, the first to be held under the Lebanese Republic, would reflect the genuine wishes of the people any more than had those of 1925, were soon dashed. Instead, they revealed all the negative aspects of a parliamentary system as practiced by Lebanese politicians. They generated intense rivalry, but it was not of a sectarian nature: the most violent conflicts took place between candidates from the same community, often from the same clan and family.

The elections were held in accordance with the electoral law of March 1922, in which the various communities were proportionally represented in parliament according to their size and geographical distribution. They were indirect and based on universal male suffrage. In the first round, the voters chose an 'electoral college' in each of the six electoral districts. In the second round, each electoral college voted for a certain number of deputies assigned to the district from a list of candidates who had received a majority in the first round.[79]

Disagreement over distribution of the 30 elected and 15 nominated deputies among the different sects and electoral districts had surfaced more than six months before the elections. Subhi Haider, then minister of finance in Sa'ad's government, argued that both elected and appointed deputies should be calculated together, while Musa Namur, minister of the interior, advocated a separate calculation. The two proposals were identical with regard to sectarian representation, but the High Commission preferred Haidar's proposal, because it enabled the French authorities to 'restore a little balance with the people of our choice'. The deputies were consequently distributed as follows: Maronites - 15 (ten elected and five nominated); Sunnis - nine (six elected and three nominated); Shiites - eight (five elected and three nominated); Greek Orthodox - six (four elected and two nominated); Druze - three (two elected and one nominated); Greek Catholic - three (two elected and one nominated); Minorities - one (elected).[80]

Although the seats were distributed along sectarian lines, the system encouraged candidates from the different communities to organize themselves on a joint list in each electoral district. A successful list was one whose members had secured large numbers of voters from all sects. Yet Shiite feudal families in the south and the Beqa valley, or Sunni feudal leaders in Akkar, who controlled large numbers of followers, had a clear advantage. Moreover, the system of electoral colleges enabled candidates to exert pressure and bribe delegates in the second round.[81]

In the first round of the elections on 2 June, 148,701 eligible voters were to elect 706 delegates. In the second round on 16 June, the delegates were to elect deputies from a list of the 182 candidates remaining from the original 360. Many dropped out of the race, either because they realized they had little chance, or were discreetly 'encouraged' to do so by the High Commission or the government. The distribution of the candidates between the various communities was significant. While nine Shiite candidates competed for five seats and 23 Sunnis for six, in other communities the race was much more intense: 83 Maronite candidates competed for ten seats; 19 Druze for two; 27 Greek Orthodox for four; 14 Greek Catholics for two; and seven minorities for one. The Shiite and the Druze communities were both dominated by feudal families, but whereas in the former the notables reached an agreement, in the latter a deep division emerged, not only between the leading families, but also within them.[82]

Preparations had begun almost a year before the elections, with the candidates concluding deals when compiling the lists in each electoral district. In the south, which had to elect six deputies, the two prominent feudal families, the As'ads and the Zeins, reached an agreement at an early stage, whereby Yusuf al-Zein headed a list that included a member of the As'ad family, as well as Najib Usayran, another leading Shiite from Tyre. The Sunni candidate on the list was Khalid Chihab, a former minister from Hasbaya. Zein chose relatively lesser-known Maronite and Greek Catholic candidates to join his list, in order to be able to influence their stand in parliament. Gabriel Khabaz, editor and owner of *L'Orient*, who was also running for the Greek Catholic ticket, was thus forced to withdraw from the race.[83]

In the Beqa the three prominent Shiite clans—the Haidars, Hamadehs and Husainis—reached an understanding to maintain the balance of power between them. The Husainis obtained a seat in parliament through nomination. Ibrahim and Subhi Haidar initially tried to secure the two remaining

Shiite seats, but faced with strong opposition from the Hamadehs, Subhi Haidar withdrew, allowing Ibrahim Haidar to head the list. This list also included Sabri Hamadeh, Musa Namur representing the Maronites, Shibl Dammus the Greek Orthodox, Elias Sakaf the Greek Catholics, and Husain Kazoun the Sunnis.[84]

In the north however, a bitter struggle for the Maronite seat took place between Wadia' Torbay, who was on the list of Abud Abd al-Razak, a prominent Sunni feudal notable from Akkar, and Kablan Faranjieh, who represented the Maronite stronghold of Zgharta. Muhammad al-Jisr of Tripoli ensured his position through nomination. The candidate for the elected seat was Rashid Adib, who declared that his only task in parliament was to defend Tripoli's economic interests. Although Abd al-Hamid Karameh and other Arab nationalists boycotted the elections, they tacitly supported Adib.[85]

The Sunni community of Beirut ostensibly boycotted the elections as a demonstration of defiance to the Lebanese state. But many of its prominent leaders, including radical Arab nationalists, either participated or tried to influence the results. The two former deputies, Omar Da'uq and Omar Bayhum, were challenged by new candidates, Muhammad Fakhuri and Dr Salim Kaddura. Bayhum soon withdrew his candidacy. Da'uq, after failing to persuade Fakhuri to join him on the same list, attempted to win the High Commission's support for his nomination—but again to no avail. Riad al-Sulh initially supported Aref Na'amani, a rich merchant with an anti-French record, but after the latter withdrew his candidacy, Sulh joined a group of young Muslim Arab nationalists, headed by Salah al-Din Bayhum, in supporting Fakhuri. Kaddura was backed by Muhammad al-Katsi, the Qadi of Beirut, and Salim Tiara. The fact that Georges Tabet, the leading candidate for the Maronite seat, ran on the same list as Fakhuri and Kaddura, reflected the growing pragmatism of the Sunni leadership in Beirut, and the significance of the mutual political interests of the Maronite and Sunni elites. Georges Tabet, however, refused to allow Ayub Tabet, who was running for the minority seat, to join the list, although they shared a similar stand on Lebanon and the French mandate. Again the overriding factor was personal rivalry. Tabet was supported by Bishop Mubarak and Beshara al-Khuri, and received financial backing from Henri Pharaon. His rival was Abdallah Ishaq, an Armenian Catholic. The Greek Orthodox seat was virtually secure for the veteran Petro Trad, who was on the Tabet–Fakhuri–Kaddura list. Consequently, Gebran Tuaini, owner and editor of *al-Ahrar*, who was supported by many Sunnis and Arab nationalists, withdrew from the race.[86]

The election campaign was especially tense on Mount Lebanon, where it left villages and families in the Maronite and Druze communities deeply divided. Maronite bishops intervened directly in an attempt to enhance their influence and prestige in their community. The main struggle took place between Habib al-Sa'ad and Beshara al-Khuri. Although he could have secured his seat through nomination, Sa'ad decided to run for election, hoping to use his position as prime minister to ensure the election of deputies from among his own followers. In February he organized a list of lesser-known candidates, thus antagonizing many of the Maronite deputies and renewing his rivalry with Yusuf al-Khazin. The latter, together with Michel Zakur, Ibrahim Munzir, Rukhus Abu-Nader and Emile Tabet, were backed by Bishop Abdallah al-Khuri and Beshara al-Khuri, who was guaranteed a seat through nomination. Bishops Aql, Mubarak and Bustani, on the other hand, supported Habib al-Sa'ad. The intense rivalry among the Maronite candidates exacerbated divisions in the Druze community. Sa'ad's inclusion of Tawfik Arslan and Jamil Talhuk on his list antagonized Fuad Arslan and the Jumblatts, who consequently cooperated with Bishop Khuri and Yusuf al-Khazin. After losing his position as prime minister in early May, Sa'ad's ability to influence the elections greatly diminished and his list disintegrated.[87]

Despite the intensive campaigning, only 55,843 voters, or 37 per cent, participated in the first round of the elections. There were, however, considerable differences in the turnout of the six electoral districts: in Tripoli a mere 13 per cent voted; in Beirut, 19 per cent; in the north, 34 per cent; in the Beqa, 37 per cent; in the south, 48 per cent; and on Mount Lebanon, 52 per cent. The low turnout in Tripoli and Beirut underlined the fact that, nine years after their annexation, many Sunnis were continuing to boycott the Lebanese state. The broader participation of voters in the Beqa and the south attested to the success of the Shiite feudal lords in mobilizing large numbers of their followers. Significantly, many of the well-educated urban population in Beirut and other cities also refrained from voting, indicating their disillusionment with the entire political process.[88]

During the two weeks before the second round, delegates in the electoral colleges came under strong pressure from the candidates. As expected, the list headed by Yusuf al-Zein in the south and the Haidar–Hamadeh–Namur–Dammus list in the Beqa won by an overwhelming majority. Rashid Adib in Tripoli and the Georges Tabet–Fakhuri–Trad list in Beirut were also elected. Ayub Tabet, however, was defeated by Abdallah Ishaq. In the north, the elections deteriorated into an open confrontation between Kablan Franjieh and Wadia' Torbay. Although he had been prevented from campaigning in Zgharta, Torbay secured a majority for his election. Unwilling to concede defeat, Franjieh and his followers descended upon Tripoli, where the electoral college was due to vote. Fearing that tension between the supporters of the two candidates might escalate into violent clashes between the inhabitants of Tripoli and Zgharta, the French authorities reinforced the gendarmerie and police in the city. Despite the outcome of the first round, Prime Minister Khuri pressured Torbay to withdraw his candidacy. On the day of the elections, skirmishes broke out between Franjieh's supporters and the gendarmerie, and in two separate incidents, three people were killed and over 20 injured. Surrounded by hundreds of Franjieh's followers, who threatened to kill him if he won, Torbay withdrew and was replaced on the winning list by Franjieh, who was subsequently elected. On Mount Lebanon, Sa'ad was defeated and the candidates backed by Bishop Khuri and Beshara al-Khuri were elected. A bitter conflict developed between Tawfik and Fuad Arslan over the remaining Druze seat. Tawfik Arslan was elected only after the High Commission exerted strong pressure on the delegates to vote against Fuad Arslan.[89]

The 1929 elections left the politicians—particularly the Maronites, Druze and Sunnis—deeply divided. Bishop Khuri, Beshara al-Khuri and Yusuf al-Khazin had scored a clear victory over Sa'ad and Bishops Aql and Mubarak. Jisr's success deepened the rift between supporters and opponents of the Lebanese state among the Sunnis. The Druze community lost much of its coherence, and during the next decade was to lack any real leadership. Bribery was rampant; political patronage more deeply entrenched; and the successful candidates were those who controlled large numbers of followers, either due to their feudal status or the services they could provide to their clients through access to the government. Despite his declaration prior to the vote, Khuri intervened to ensure the election of his own allies. He also cooperated closely with Solomiac, whose main concern was to prevent the election of candidates hostile to France. Religion and inter-sectarian division played a secondary role.[90]

On 17 June, President Dabbas announced the list of the 15 nominated deputies, which he had prepared together with Solomiac and Khuri. Khuri and Eddé retained their seats, as did Sa'ad, despite his defeat in the elections. Khuri secured the nomination of two of his close friends, Yusuf al-Sawda, a Lebanese nationalist and outspoken critic of the mandate, and his brother-in-law, Henri Pharaon. Commenting on the results of the election, a newspaper noted: 'Begun as a comedy, the Lebanese electoral farce ends in tragedy. The new chamber is born under the sign of violence, fraud and corruption. Two months ago we complained that Sa'ad's government was a government of patronage. Those were the good times.'[91]

The way in which the elections had been conducted reinforced the High Commission's doubts on the ability of the Lebanese politicians to exercise power. While some French officials were genuinely concerned for the future of Lebanon's political system, others merely sought a pretext to tighten their control over the administration. Throughout the summer, the High Commission received numerous complaints of government intervention in the elections.Khuri was sharply criticized by the defeated candidates, and the press, led by *L'Orient* and *al-Ahrar*, accused him of unlawfully interfering in the elections and condemned his handling of the Torbay affair. Khuri responded, as before, by suspending publication of certain newspapers.[92]

Khuri also came under attack in the newly-elected parliament, which had yet to grant his government its vote of confidence. The deputies strove to regain some of the power they had conceded to the president and the prime minister before the elections. New alliances were formed and old ones renewed. Some, including Georges Tabet, Namur, Haidar and Zein renewed their efforts to form a larger government of five ministers, seeking thereby to secure positions for themselves. Muslim deputies sought the cooperation of their Christian colleagues in organizing a 'Reform Party' aimed at defending the 'rights and interests of the country and attaining political union with Syria'. After criticizing Jisr for his part in the elections, a group of Sunni deputies, headed by Khalid Chihab and Muhammad Fakhuri, attempted to prevent his election as speaker of parliament. In a stormy session on 13 July, Khuri secured a majority for his government and Jisr was re-elected as speaker, with Henri Pharaon as his deputy. Thus, despite strong opposition, Khuri and Jisr were still able to command a majority, a lesson which Eddé was to learn painfully eight months later.[93]

On 18 September 1929, Khuri tendered his resignation to President Dabbas. His decision was motivated partly by the continual public criticism of his government, as well as by Dabbas' diminishing support after its lack of popularity had become apparent. He was offered the post of legal adviser to the newly-formed Lebanese branch of Bank Misr, and he hoped, as he told Tetreau, the acting French high commissioner, that this would improve his financial situation. But the main reason for his resignation was his desire to run for the presidency in 1932 without facing daily attacks in the press and continual challenges from the parliament.[94]

Even before the parliamentary elections, an increasing number of Lebanese had begun to realize that their country was in urgent need of radical political, administrative and economic reform. Various ideas were aired in the press and some were presented to the High Commission. Two plans, one by Habib Trad, a banker and a nominated senator from Beirut, and the other by Emile Eddé, attracted the attention of the High Commission, which judged them 'objectively better predisposed to remedy Lebanon's continued malaise'. Trad's proposals included cutting the number of deputies to 27 (18 elected and nine nominated); selecting the nominated deputies from the business sector; replacing the government with one minister of state chosen from outside parliament and responsible to it only on financial matters; changing the electoral law; reorganizing the administration into six decentralized districts instead of the existing 11; reforming the judicial system; cutting the budget by reducing the number of state employees; investing the money saved in large public projects; and revising customs duties. Eddé's plans placed more emphasis on administrative, judicial and financial reform than on political change. They also included administrative decentralization, but based on five districts (divided into 17 *qadas* instead of 36 *mudiriyyas*, with *mukhtars* being nominated instead of elected); reorganization of the judicial system; preparation of a personal law for the Christian community; cutting the budget by drastically reducing the number of state employees; and reforming the fiscal system. He also proposed granting the government extraordinary power—the right to issue decrees—for a limited period, to enable it to implement its programme.[95]

By 1929 many Lebanese, especially the young educated Christians in Beirut, had come to believe in the need for a strong leader to cleanse the corrupt and inefficient political and administrative systems and remove the old generation of politicians who had inflicted their backward 'Ottoman' habits upon the nation. Some even yearned for a dictator like Mussolini, who would help build Lebanon as a modern, efficient and prosperous state. These views were reflected by the newspapers, which daily voiced harsh criticism and called for reform. One name continually raised as Lebanon's last hope was that of Emile Eddé. He was the one leader, argued his supporters—particularly in *L'Orient*—capable of saving the country. The Quai d'Orsay and the High Commission also reached the conclusion that drastic measures had to be taken. Some French officials in Paris and Beirut believed that only Eddé could shoulder the difficult task of cutting the administration and reducing the budget deficit. A French report described the mood in Lebanon at the time:

> Beshara al-Khuri's failure and resignation poses a serious question for the future. To whom should one turn to head the government? Since May 1926, when the Lebanese constitution came into effect, all the people able to play an important role in public life have been called to power but none could remain there. For many Lebanese Eddé is the main hope, and certain newspapers have even gone so far as to declare that his downfall would have grave consequences for the country's political regime. If all these honest, intelligent and educated people have failed, it must be a sign that it is impossible for the government to work as long as the parliament, by virtue of the constitution, is able to oppose it. This is the current situation; despite their pride, the Lebanese would not hesitate to turn to the

mandatory power and ask it to readapt the constitutional and administrative organization of Lebanon to its general needs and economic capacity.[96]

Satow, the British consul general, described a similar mood in his despatches, but was skeptical of Eddé's ability to introduce the necessary reforms. He too predicted that if Eddé failed, France would have to resume direct administration. But in contrast to the French officials, he warned that such a move would face strong opposition:

> There seems to be a tendency in the press to regard M. Eddé, who is reported to enjoy the confidence and to be able to count on the support of the French authorities, as the last hope of the Lebanon. It is suggested that if he fails to bring about an improvement in the general situation and in the administration of the country, there will have to be drastic constitutional changes. This may be so, but it seems more likely that when he fails someone else will gladly take on the task. There is undoubtedly much latent discontent, but the time is probably far off when a drastic revision of the cumbersome and costly constitution devised by M. de Jouvenel will be demanded by Lebanese public opinion such as it is. The French certainly cannot initiate a change. Complaints are made that they, having invented the Constitution, are responsible for what goes wrong, but these complaints would be as nothing compared to the complaints which would arise if they of their own initiative introduced changes. Things will therefore probably muddle along as they do now, and nothing much more will be achieved by M. Eddé than by his predecessors. The administration is undoubtedly inefficient, its cost is excessive and is growing, and the number of officials is absurdly high. On the other hand, the politicians are enjoying themselves, and with so many useless posts there seems to be a place in the administration for almost any idler who wants one.[97]

Eddé played a prominent role in Lebanese politics during the inter-war years. His rivalry with Beshara al-Khuri took on almost mythical proportions and was, to a large degree, to shape Lebanon's future political development. Like Khuri, Dabbas and Adib, he was part of a new Christian, mainly Maronite, political elite, whom the French had enlisted after 1918. His family background, loyalty to France, French education, profession and experience had made him well-suited to France's political and administrative needs in the early years of the mandate. Both Eddé and Khuri had risen through the political system to become part of this elite, which dominated Lebanese politics after 1926. Eddé was a controversial politician, whose contribution to the creation of the Lebanese state has often been underestimated or misrepresented. Following his defeat in the 1943 presidential elections, Lebanon's inter-war history was reinterpreted by the victorious Khuri and his group. This one-sided view of the history of that period can best be seen in Khuri's autobiography *Haqa'iq lubnaniyya*. His critical and negative portrayal of Eddé influenced the way many Lebanese, including historians, perceived him. According to Khuri, Eddé was arrogant and authoritarian and disregarded the constitution. He was a manipulative, anti-Muslim fanatic, alien to Arabic culture and language, who opposed Arab nationalism and aimed for a Christian Lebanon isolated from the Muslim Arab world, and permanently linked to and protected by France. In contrast to himself, who was loved and admired by the Lebanese people, Eddé owed his career to French support, and connived with the High Commission to prevent Khuri from being democratically elected as president both in 1932 and 1936. He had collaborated with the Vichy regime during the Second World War and later with Free France against the Lebanese nationalists, led by Khuri, in their struggle for independence and sovereignty.[98]

In reality, neither image is accurate: not that of Eddé as a dictator, nor Khuri's portrayal of himself as defender of the constitution, champion of independent Lebanon and its sovereignty, and founding father who laid the ground for Christian–Muslim cooperation. To argue this would be to accept the notion that the National Pact was a unique agreement between two far-sighted Maronite and Sunni leaders, rather than the culmination of processes begun in the 1930s, in which Eddé played a not insignificant role. All such questions should be examined in the context of the 1920s and 1930s, as well as the radically altered international and regional situation produced by the war, France's defeat by Germany, and the occupation of Lebanon and Syria by Britain in 1941.[99]

Eddé was born in 1883 in Damascus, where his father was a dragoman in the French Consulate. He studied at the Jesuit College in Beirut, but unlike Khuri, he was not a devout Christian, and did not maintain close ties with the Jesuits in later years. In 1900 he went to France, where he studied law at the University of Aix-en-Provence. He returned to Beirut in 1912 and began his career as legal adviser to the French Consulate. His marriage to Lodi Sursuk the same year gave him direct access to prominent and affluent Greek Orthodox families in the city. Before the war, like other young, educated Maronites, Eddé had advocated an independent, Christian–Lebanese state under French protection. At the start of the war he fled Lebanon for Egypt, as did many Christians known for their pro-French stand, fearing reprisals or conscription into the Turkish army. Eddé spent the war years in Alexandria, where he participated in the activities of the Syro–Lebanese immigrant groups and helped the French form the Légion d'Orient. In January 1919, he returned to Beirut, where he was appointed political adviser to Georges-Picot. Together with Beshara al-Khuri, Michel Chiha and Charles Corm, he joined the Phoenician Society, and later helped establish—at the initiative of the Marquis de Freige—the Progressive Party, which aimed to secure Greater Lebanon's political independence under the French mandate.

He was a member of the third Lebanese delegation, headed by Bishop Abdallah al-Khuri, that went to Paris in February 1920 to obtain the French government's support for an independent Greater Lebanon. In the same year, Gouraud appointed Eddé to the Administrative Council, and in 1922 he was elected to the Representative Council.[100]

Eddé was immersed in French history, and admired its culture and language. With his French education and his family's long service to France, he regarded it as his second homeland. In contrast to other Maronites who saw the role of the French as merely to protect and help them attain their national aspirations, he believed that Lebanon should maintain close ties with France. Yet his relations with some high commissioners and French officials in Beirut were often strained, and he did not hesitate to criticize their policy. He was self-confident and could be overbearing and tactless. With his education and wealth, he felt superior to those officials and was not prepared to let them treat him as a 'Levantine native'. He often turned down their advice, considering himself to be more knowledgeable about local affairs and thus better qualified to judge Lebanon's needs. Members of the High Commission resented his direct access to the Quai d'Orsay and to French politicians in Paris. In 1922, de Caix foiled his attempt to be elected president of the Representative Council, and in 1925, Sarrail thwarted his election as governor, a move that sparked an open confrontation between Eddé and the High Commission. In the same year, Cayla prevented his election to the Representative Council, but in 1926, de Jouvenel appointed him as a senator in the newly-created Lebanese Republic. Ponsot disliked him, preferring to work with Beshara al-Khuri. Antoine Privat-Aubouard was one of the few close friends he made in the High Commission, and Eddé often used this to his advantage.[101]

Although he advocated an independent, Christian Lebanon linked politically, culturally and economically to France and the West, Eddé was one of the few who, early on, understood the inherent danger for Lebanon in retaining the 1920 borders. Throughout the 1920s and early 1930s, he therefore advocated severing parts of the annexed areas with large Muslim populations in order to ensure a Christian majority. Yet he was not the fanatic anti-Muslim portrayed by his opponents. As long as the Christians were protected by France, Eddé was willing to grant the Muslims of Lebanon a fair share in running the state. He continually turned down offers from Lebanese Muslim leaders to cooperate with him or back him politically if he gave up his call for French protection. Despite their reservations, the Syrian Arab nationalists, who were well aware of his support for the return of Tripoli and the Beqa valley to Syria, attempted to reach an agreement with him on several occasions. In the 1930s, however, as the Muslims became more willing to accept the Lebanese state within its existing borders—provided it was linked closely to Syria and the Arab world—Eddé came to symbolize the concept of a Christian Lebanon which they deeply resented.[102]

Unlike other Maronite politicians, Eddé lacked a real power base on the Mountain, where he was always considered an outsider, and never felt at home, as did Khuri, with its politics. He was a Beirut man, well placed in the political life of the city, maintaining close social and economic ties with its wealthy, influential Greek Orthodox and Sunni families. Throughout his political career, he devoted much effort to developing and modernizing Beirut. He rarely allowed the church to dictate his position, and his association with the Maronite bishops was based on mutual interest. His relations with Bishop Khuri became strained, however, as the latter strove to secure the presidency for his young cousin. Eddé was an affluent landowner with properties in Beirut, the Beqa, Egypt and Palestine. He also ran a prosperous law office, in which two of his future rivals, Khuri and Chamoun, received their training. He had close ties with Gabriel Khabbaz, the owner of the influential *l'Orient*, through which he expressed his views or criticized his opponents. Unlike Khuri, Eddé was not a team player; he lacked the patience and sometimes the tact to maintain the support of, and working relations with, politicians whom he despised. These traits proved to be a handicap on more than one occasion.[103]

Relations between Eddé and Dabbas had never been particularly friendly, and Eddé did not conceal his contempt for the latter. He had opposed de Jouvenel's decision to appoint Dabbas as president, considering himself better suited to the post, and often rejected Dabbas' attempts to improve relations and cooperate with him. For his part, Dabbas regarded Eddé as a threat to his position and prestige. He envied his direct access to French politicians in Paris and his influence over the Maronite church and community. Indeed, Dabbas' support for Beshara al-Khuri after 1926 was partly intended to counter Eddé's authority. Eddé's relations with Khuri were cordial at first, but as Khuri allied himself closely with Dabbas, began to build his own political base and emerged as a strong contender for the presidency, the two began to drift apart. Nevertheless, Eddé voted for Khuri's first and second governments, though he abstained from voting for the third. He would later hold Khuri responsible for corrupting the political and administrative systems in order to promote his personal interests, as well as those of his relatives and friends.[104]

Throughout 1927 and 1928, Eddé was content with building his political power and his reputation as a presidential candidate. He often exercised his influence behind the scenes, first in the senate and later in parliament. He was reluctant to become directly involved in running the administration and turned down offers to serve as prime minister. His law firm and business activities, along with his efforts to prepare a personal law for the Christian community, took up most of his time. In September 1929, however, he changed his mind and agreed to form a government—a decision he was later to regret. Eddé had come under mounting pressure from his friends and supporters to shoulder the task of solving the country's pressing economic and political problems, and believed he could succeed where his predecessors had failed. The main consideration in his decision, however, was his concern that Khuri, having increased the number of deputies allied to him, would jeopardize Eddé's own bid for the presidency. He hoped that by serving as prime minister, he would strengthen his popularity and political power and enhance his chances of being elected president in April 1932. For precisely that reason, Khuri was determined to see him fail.[105]

Eddé, however, had learned from the experience of previous prime ministers, and was willing to accept the position provided he received the prior commitment of the Quai d'Orsay and Ponsot to back his comprehensive reform programme. While visiting Paris in September, he secured the support of Briand and officials in the Quai d'Orsay. Shortly before leaving for Beirut, he presented his plans to Ponsot, who endorsed them. Dabbas thus had no choice but to ask Eddé to form a new government.[106]

Immediately after returning to Beirut, Eddé held extensive discussions with members of parliament and on 12 October announced his government. It comprised five ministers: two 'technical' ministers from Khuri's government (Husain al-Ahdab and Najib Abu Suan); two deputies (Musa Namur and Ahmad Husaini); and a new position—that of under-secretary for economic affairs—to which he appointed a Greek Orthodox, Gabriel Menasa, in order to placate his community. This was Eddé's first real test in the complex task of forming a government. He had deferred to the deputies and departed from his long-held stance favouring a narrow government. Already at this stage, his limitations in negotiating a coalition of conflicting factions and deputies were becoming apparent. The new parliament was deeply divided: by giving ministerial positions to some, he antagonized others. The Shiite deputies in the south complained that their region was not represented in the government. The nomination of Husaini angered his rivals, the Haidars, while Namur's appointment was resented by many Maronites, particularly in the church, who expressed doubt as to whether he could be trusted to defend the community's interests. The strongest opposition was voiced by Maronite and Druze deputies from the Mountain, who claimed that the government was dominated by ministers from the new 'annexed' areas of Beirut and the Beqa. It took 40 days for Eddé to overcome the difficulties, secure a majority in parliament and prepare his reform plan. On 22 November, he finally presented his government's platform to parliament, but by then he had lost his initial drive and was exposed to criticism and manipulation.[107]

Unlike Khuri, who would present parliament with a brief outline of government policy, thereby limiting discussion to a minimum, Eddé submitted a detailed plan. He was determined to resist any attempt to modify his reforms, and insisted that the government be granted exceptional power for a three-month period to enforce them. These reforms were based on the proposals he had submitted to Ponsot in July. They entailed: cutting the budget and investing the savings in public works, decentralization and revision of the administration by restoring the original five larger districts; reorganization of the judicial system; adoption of a personal law for the Christian communities; and the implementation of ambitious development projects in Beirut, using loans from France.[108]

The deputies, who had already been forced to relinquish some of their authority to the president in the two previous constitutional revisions, objected to granting Eddé what they considered dictatorial power. Empowering the prime minister to promulgate his own laws, even for a limited period, they argued, would diminish parliament's role as a legislative body. Publication of the planned reforms in the press generated strong resentment among those affected. Deputies came under pressure from relatives, friends, clients and communities to safeguard their vested interests, but were initially reluctant to confront Eddé, who enjoyed the support of the public, the High Commission and the Quai d'Orsay. During the parliamentary debate, the strongest opposition was voiced by Sawda and Khuri, who was subsequently elected to head a parliamentary committee to examine the government's reforms. Nevertheless, on 17 December, the deputies voted 30 to six to grant Eddé emergency power for three months to enable him to implement his programme. The veiled threat to dissolve parliament was sufficient to convince the opposition to approve his programme. In light of the events that followed, it is worth noting that all the Christian, mainly Maronite, deputies, including Khuri, Sa'ad and Tabet, who were competing with Eddé for the presidency, opposed the government, while all the Muslim deputies supported it.[109]

Upon obtaining parliamentary approval, Eddé immediately began to put his reforms into effect. During the second half of December and in January 1930, scores of decrees were issued and steps taken to cut costs by drastically reducing the number of government employees. The High Commission's decision to decrease Lebanon's share in the revenue from the Common Interests forced the government to take even harsher measures than it had originally intended. Its plan to make large investments in Beirut provoked criticism from other regions, especially Mount Lebanon. The Shiites in the south protested against the government's failure to allocate resources to agriculture in their region. The dismissal of government employees raised an outcry, not only from the officials themselves, but also from politicians who had given jobs to their relatives and friends and depended on the clientele system for their power.[110]

The government's decision to return to the former five-district administrative system roused fears among the Maronites that the division between Mount Lebanon and the 'annexed regions' would be restored—a first step toward revision of Lebanon's borders. In November 1929, rumours circulated that Eddé had reached a secret agreement with Muslim leaders to sever Tripoli and part of the Beqa valley from Lebanon and annex them to Syria. It is not clear whether such an understanding had in fact been reached, or whether the talk originated with Eddé's opponents in the Maronite community. Eddé's support for the detachment of Tripoli and part of the Beqa valley was well known, and the rumours no doubt reflected the anxieties of those who stood for a Greater Lebanon, including Khuri, Zakur and Sawda. Indeed, Sawda had expressed such fears during the parliamentary debate on the reforms. True or false, the reports stiffened their determination to prevent Eddé from implementing his policy.[111]

One of the reforms in particular—the closure of 100 state schools—proved to be most controversial, and provoked a crisis that would lead to the eventual downfall of Eddé's government. The question of their children's education had always been extremely sensitive for the Muslims of Lebanon, especially the Sunnis in the coastal towns of Beirut, Tripoli and Sidon. They felt vulnerable to the activities of the various Christian missionary orders that dominated Lebanon's educational system, and were concerned that their schools, and those established by the local Christian communities, were undermining not only their Arabic culture and language, but also their religion. The Muslims were well aware of the consequences of France's 'mission civilisatoire' on their coreligionists in North Africa, and feared that they would be exposed to a similar cultural colonization. Yet many upper and middle class Muslim families, recognizing that a Western education would enable their children to compete with their Christian counterparts, had long been sending them to Christian schools. The overwhelming majority of Muslim pupils, however, attended state schools, whose standards were generally low. Many of their teachers were unqualified and the physical facilities inadequate, because of the limited resources allocated to them by the High Commission and the Lebanese government. The closure of these schools was therefore seen as yet another example of discrimination against the Muslims. Some even claimed that the move was a ploy to force Muslim children into the missionary schools. Their apprehensions were reinforced by rumours that the French and some Lebanese Christians intended to replace Arabic script with Latin letters, as Mustafa Kemal had in Turkey. Eddé's decision was therefore regarded with much suspicion and provoked deep resentment among the Muslim public.[112]

The schools crisis was far from just a spontaneous reaction of Lebanese Muslims to what they regarded as unjust and insensitive measures taken by an anti-Muslim prime minister. It was in fact a well-organized campaign, in which old rivals—whether Muslim or Christian politicians, supporters or opponents of the Lebanese state and the French mandate—rallied together. All had their own motives, whether personal, sectarian or national—but they shared a common goal: to bring about Eddé's downfall.

The schools closure had initially been raised by Khuri and Sawda during a parliamentary debate on the government's programme. On 22 November Khuri, a former minister of education, had criticized the proposal, arguing that it would undermine education in the Muslim sector. The Muslim deputies, however, had chosen to ignore the issue altogether. In reply to Khuri's criticism, Eddé had stressed that the matter at stake was the standard of the schools and not their number. The need for reform in the government's educational system had indeed been raised on numerous occasions. It had been argued that some schools were half empty and often staffed by unqualified teachers, resulting in low standards and unnecessarily high expenses. In November and December, Muslim leaders and politicians pleaded with Eddé to rescind his decision to close the schools, but he refused, reiterating that Muslim pupils would benefit from the reforms. He was determined not to bow to the usual demands from sectors anxious to safeguard their own interests, but to proceed with his policy of cost-cutting. In January 1930, teachers and other employees dismissed from the educational system raised an outcry and called upon the Muslim politicians to intervene. But the government, assuming it was in full control of the situation, went ahead with the reforms.[113]

Toward the end of the month, however, an organized campaign to topple the government began in Tripoli with strikes and demonstrations. Petitions and telegrams flooded the Quai d'Orsay, Ponsot, Dabbas, Eddé and the Permanent Mandates Commission, demanding that the government rescind its decision. The Sunnis in Beirut and Sidon immediately followed suit, while Shiites and Druze were urged to join in the struggle. The Muslim Council of Beirut, headed by Sheikh Mustafa al-Ghailani, seized the opportunity to call for convening a congress of Lebanese Muslims to discuss their interests, including the return of the waqfs to the community's control.[114]

Faced with growing criticism in the Sunni community and the Muslim newspapers, Eddé sought to appease them. Explaining that the closed schools had been half empty, and staffed by unqualified or incompetent teachers, he declared that their closure would enable the government to raise the standards of the remaining schools, whose numbers would answer the needs of the Muslim population. He also declared his willingness to reconsider some of his reforms. Eddé's assurances and his decision to bestow the title of 'qadi of the qadis' upon the Qadi of Beirut, failed, however, to impress the Muslim and Arab nationalist leaders, who were already sending urgent messages to the kings of Saudi Arabia, Egypt and Iraq, the Amir of Jordan, and Hajj Amin al-Husaini, the Mufti of Jerusalem, requesting their support. By then, demonstrations were taking place and press campaigns being waged against France and the Lebanese government throughout the neighbouring Arab countries, in which Eddé's decision was presented as a Christian offensive against the Muslims. The protests were especially vociferous in Palestine. In February, *al-Ahd al-Jadid* published a letter sent to Ghailani by the Mufti of Jerusalem declaring his willingness 'to provide him with any help he needed at the first signal'. Eddé responded by closing the newspaper *sine die*. [115]

The strongest support for the Muslims of Lebanon came from Syria, where numerous petitions were signed and demonstrations and strikes were held. Provocative articles were published daily in the Syrian press, describing Eddé as a Christian fanatic, while the closure of the schools was presented as a ploy to force Muslim children to give up not only their Arab culture and language, but also their religious beliefs. The offensive took on an increasingly strident tone, as Christian and Muslim newspapers traded insults and recriminations. The month of Ramadan, which coincided with the conflict, reinforced its religious character, and Muslims were urged to turn the Bairam (the last day of Ramadan) into a national day of mourning. It was also alleged that Eddé had told Abd al-Hamid Karameh that the Muslims could emigrate to the Hijaz if they objected to his decision. In an article in the Syrian newspaper *al-Sha'b* entitled 'Emigrate or become Christians', Ahmad Zaki Afiuni, a journalist, wrote:

> The Muslims on the Syrian coast and in Lebanon cannot tolerate the crime committed against them by the Lebanese government, nor approve the criminal reorganization it is carrying out, especially the reorganization of public education in which 101 schools were closed in a country whose inhabitants number fewer than 800,000 and in which only the Muslims are discriminated against, depriving thousands of Muslim children of the right to learn, to be enlightened and to live, seeking to throw them into the bosom of missionary establishments ranging from those of the Frères to the Jesuits, Americans, Italians and Syriacs and even the devil. It is as if Eddé, the dictator, had said to the Muslims in their country: emigrate or become Christians. [116]

The campaign against Eddé was spearheaded by Karameh and the inhabitants of Tripoli. Indeed, there was a certain truth in Karameh's claim that it was he who had brought down Eddé. Throughout the crisis, he maintained close contact with Muslim and Arab nationalist leaders in Beirut and Damascus and persistently opposed any compromise with Eddé. He even met with his sworn rival, Muhammad al-Jisr, as well as with Dabbas, the president of a state he refused to recognize, in order to rally their support against Eddé. In Beirut, the opposition to Eddé was led by Riad al-Sulh, who put special emphasis on enlisting the cooperation of Christian politicians. Karameh, Sulh and other Muslim Arab nationalists on the coast exploited the schools crisis to mobilize the Muslim community against the Lebanese state and the French mandate. Their campaign was encouraged and coordinated by the leaders of the National Bloc in Syria, especially Fakhri al-Barudi. In the aftermath of the constitutional crisis, the Syrian nationalists, whose relations with the High Commission were already strained, used the problems in Lebanon to step up their pressure on the High Commission. Neither the Arab-Muslim unionists in Lebanon nor the National Bloc in Syria had any wish to see Eddé succeed in solving Lebanon's political and economic problems. Their stand was clearly expressed by Karameh at a meeting in Dabbas' office, when he told Eddé that he bore no personal grudge against him, but would do his utmost to overthrow him, since he did not wish to see him using his talent to help Lebanon prosper. He went so far as to declare that he hoped to see the Lebanese, like the Syrians, plunged into misery, disgusted and disheartened by the governments established by France, so much so that they would prefer to emigrate to the Hijaz, where they would be free of the tutelage of any foreign power.[117]

The support they received for their campaign against Eddé from Muslims in Lebanon, Syria and neighbouring Arab countries, united the Sunni leaders. Some, like Omar Da'uq and Omar Bayhum, who had failed in the elections, seized the opportunity to regain their positions and influence, while others had no choice but to join the public condemnation of Eddé and his policies. Muslim deputies were pressured to withdraw their support of his government. Muhammad al-Jisr's decision to join the opposition was particularly damaging to Eddé, strengthening his opponents within parliament. Jisr's standing in Lebanon's Muslim community was based on an extensive network of clients—whom he placed in the administration—and on his ability, like that of other prominent Muslim politicians, to protect the interests of his coreligionists. The closure of the government schools, the dismissal of his supporters from the administration and the subsequent outcry from the Muslims were serious blows to his prestige. Moreover, his attempts to persuade Eddé to abolish the decrees were abruptly rejected.

Eddé's remark that Jisr enjoyed too great a political influence, and Jisr's harsh criticism, voiced in *L'Orient*, exacerbated the already strained relations between the two. As Karameh's prestige rose among the Sunnis, Jisr had no choice but to take a firmer stand in defence of their interests. Indeed, by joining the opposition, Jisr considerably enhanced his standing in his community and, for the first time, his opponents, including Karameh, were ready to cooperate with him to protect the interests of the Muslims of Lebanon.[118]

Although the Maronite leaders were facing the most extensive Muslim and Arab–Syrian nationalist opposition since the crisis over the constitution in the spring of 1926, they failed to close ranks. Even the church, which in the past had played a unifying role in defending community interests, was divided, with its bishops engaged in a struggle to succeed Patriarch Hawayik. Prominent politicians—Beshara al-Khuri, Georges Tabet and Habib al-Sa'ad—competing with Eddé for the presidency, plotted to remove their rival from the race. They ignored their country's need for reform, overlooking the fact that the Muslim offensive was directed not only against Eddé, but against the very existence of the Lebanese state. Most active behind the scenes was Khuri: determined to humiliate Eddé completely, he cooperated with the Muslim opposition, rejecting any compromise that would enable Eddé to retain the premiership. Henri Pharaon, his brother-in-law, and Michel Zakur, together with Jisr, coordinated the campaign against Eddé in parliament. Pharaon's sumptuous home became the centre of the campaign, where opposition leaders frequently met to plan their moves to topple the government.[119] At the same time, newspapers were encouraged to attack Eddé and portray him as a dictator whose policies were undermining Christian–Muslim coexistence. The press attacks were led by Zakur's *al-Ma'arad* and Tuaini's *al-Ahrar*, which had previously criticized Khuri for his failure to reform the administration. For its part, *L'Orient* reacted by accusing Khuri and other Christian politicians of betraying the Lebanese cause in order to further their own interests. The stand taken by Khuri and his colleagues against Eddé sowed the seeds of a bitter and vengeful rivalry between the two Maronite leaders in later years.[120]

As Muslim opposition to Eddé intensified, Dabbas distanced himself from his prime minister, fearing that the crisis might escalate into inter-sectarian violence. Although he attempted to mediate between Eddé and the Sunni leaders, he privately told his Muslim interlocutors that he disagreed with government policy, a stand that did little to encourage compromise. Indeed, after a meeting with Dabbas, Karameh was left with the impression that Eddé was isolated and that the president supported the Muslims' demands. Dabbas' reserved attitude also weakened Eddé's position in parliament, and Ponsot used this to justify to the Quai d'Orsay his reluctance to back Eddé.[121]

Ponsot had initially underestimated the severity of the crisis, treating it as just another case of intrigue among Lebanese politicians who opposed reforms that threatened their positions, and Muslim leaders' hostility to the French mandate. He ignored French officials who had warned against the closure of the schools, assuming that the campaign would weaken after the month of Ramadan. As the crisis escalated, however, Ponsot was faced with a difficult choice. He deemed the reforms necessary and was certain that the schools crisis was being used to influence Muslim public opinion. Moreover, he was well aware of the backing Eddé enjoyed in Paris, and felt obliged to convey to the Quai d'Orsay his own support for him. Yet he was anxious to prevent the situation from deteriorating into violent anti-France demonstrations. He therefore urged Eddé to modify some of his original plans and met with some of the Sunni leaders in an attempt to appease them. But Ponsot's moves sent the wrong message: the Arab Muslim nationalists and the deputies interpreted his hesitant stand as a sign that Eddé no longer enjoyed the full support of the High Commission. In March 1930, as the campaign against Eddé intensified and urgent reports arrived from French diplomats on violent anti-French demonstrations in neighbouring Arab states, Ponsot—who had never liked the independent-minded Eddé—left him to his own devices. In a letter to the Quai d'Orsay after Eddé's resignation, he wrote:

> Eddé's personal qualities are beyond discussion and are no doubt, in Lebanon, beyond comparison. But the most eminent statesmen must adapt to the rules of the system that they serve and from which they draw their authority ... Eddé had his first taste of power; it was good for his country and revealed him capable of meeting the expectations and trust laid in him. Today he just has to break away from his former philosophy, draw conclusions and prepare himself for a future, all of whose roads are open to him if he approaches them with wisdom and moderation.[122]

The schools crisis revealed Eddé's shortcomings as a politician. He was stubborn, overconfident and presumptuous, traits which had won him many adversaries. He was insensitive to the complaints of the Muslim leadership and ignored the strong reaction his decision had provoked in their community. He underestimated Muslim resentment as well as the ability of his Maronite rivals to mobilize opposition. When he did realize the severity of the situation, it was already too late: Karameh and other Arab Muslim nationalists had transformed the crisis into a power struggle between the Muslims in Lebanon and the government. Eddé could not yield to them without losing prestige. His dispute with Jisr proved to be a serious political error, which drove the Muslim opposition and his rivals in parliament to join forces against him. His failure to come out in support of Husain al-Ahdab, the Sunni minister for public affairs (whom *L'Orient* had accused of corruption and misconduct), also played into the hands of his opponents, who claimed that the campaign was yet another example of his anti-Muslim stand. Indeed, the intense campaign conducted by *L'Orient* against Eddé's opponents often backfired. Its inflammatory criticisms of the Muslim opposition and its reaction to articles in Muslim newspapers contributed to escalation of the crisis into a religious, sectarian and cultural confrontation, and reinforced Eddé's image as an anti-Muslim, Christian fanatic. His reluctance to consult with Ponsot during the crisis, and his failure to seek the Maronite church's backing for his reforms, further weakened his position. Yet the question of whether he actually was justified in believing that only radical reform could cure Lebanon's ills still remained.[123]

Eddé's failure to gauge the severity of the situation enabled his opponents in parliament, led by Khuri and Jisr, to outmanoeuvre him. Up until the last minute, he believed he could overcome the crisis. He rightly suspected that some of his ministers, particularly Namur, were secretly collaborating with his rivals, and therefore worked out a plan to upstage them by forming a new government. On 18 March, on the eve of the parliamentary session, 18 deputies met at Pharaon's house and undertook to vote against him. Two days later, when a motion of no confidence was tabled, some deputies from Eddé's camp joined his opponents. There was no debate, and the government resigned en masse after the motion had been passed by a majority of 27 with no opposition. Pressed by Eddé and his supporters, Dabbas asked him to form a new government. For the next five days, a power struggle raged, unparalleled in Lebanese politics. Sunni leaders, headed by Karameh, inundated Dabbas and Ponsot with protests against Eddé's reappointment. At the same time, they pressured the Muslim deputies to refrain from supporting or participating in any new government formed by Eddé. In parliament, Jisr, Khuri, Tabet, Sa'ad and Pharaon, together with Salim Taqla, the administrator of Beirut, stepped up their efforts to prevent Eddé from obtaining a majority. Jisr told undecided deputies that Ponsot was taking a neutral stand, a claim the high commissioner did not deny. For his part, Dabbas made it clear to the deputies that he had had no choice but to appoint Eddé, but that he opposed him and would not help him form a new government. In an attempt to secure a majority, Eddé offered ministerial positions to 12 candidates, but they all turned him down, an unprecedented event in Lebanese politics. On 25 March, Eddé conceded defeat and informed Dabbas of his failure.[124]

Eddé's defeat had far-reaching repercussions on political life, as well as on intra- and inter-sectarian relations in Lebanon. This had been the first serious attempt to introduce radical reforms into an inefficient and corrupt system dominated by political patronage, clientelism and sectarian interests. Lebanon was to pay a heavy price for its failure. No Lebanese politician, not even Eddé himself, would be willing to repeat this endeavour. In the years to come, Lebanese politicians would exploit the system for their own interests, and the limited attempts of the High Commission to remedy the situation would not have any lasting impact. After six governments and two constitutional revisions, it was clear that the parliamentary system as practiced in Lebanon was a complete failure. The situation also strengthened the conviction of many French and Lebanese that de Jouvenel's initiative of May 1926 had been premature.

The stage was thus set for the bitter feud between Eddé and Khuri, which was to dominate Lebanese politics for the next 13 years. Eddé, convinced that Khuri and his supporters had been responsible for his downfall, never forgave them for his humiliating defeat; two years later, he would take revenge. The rivalry between its two most prominent leaders left the Maronite community weakened and deeply divided. A precedent had been established: Maronite politicians had cooperated closely with Sunni leaders known for their opposition to a Christian Lebanese state, to overcome a Maronite rival. The only prominent Maronite who openly advocated relinquishing areas with large Muslim populations had been defeated. From now on he would be reluctant to raise the issue publicly for fear that his opponents would use it against him. Furthermore, a rift had opened between Eddé and the Muslims which, despite his attempts, he was never able to heal. On the other hand, Khuri began to lay the basis for his future political cooperation with the Sunni leadership. For the first time since their annexation to Lebanon, the Sunnis had scored a clear victory. The outcome of the crisis strengthened their self-confidence and spurred some of their leaders to demand their fair share in the Lebanese state, while others sought union with Syria. Jisr's bid for the presidency in 1932 was the direct result of his new-found confidence and that of his community.

Humiliated and bitter as he witnessed his opponents celebrating his defeat, Eddé angrily remarked to Auguste Adib Pasha, the new prime minister, 'Je ne suis pas encore mort'.[125]

CHAPTER THREE

The Struggle for the Presidency

A decade after undertaking—in accordance with Article 22 of the League of Nations Charter—to guide the mandated territories toward independence, France had made little progress. Syria had neither an organic law nor an elected parliament or government, while Lebanon's constitution, even after two revisions, had failed to provide a stable political system. France had been unable to define a coherent policy that would at once safeguard its strategic and economic interests in the Levant, fulfil its moral obligations to protect the Lebanese Christians and satisfy Arab Muslim aspirations for independence and unity. Its failures were highlighted by Britain's success in concluding a treaty with Iraq in June 1930. With no solution of its own, France turned to Britain's Iraqi policy for inspiration and, in the early 1930s, attempted to develop a similar policy in Syria. For three years, the High Commission negotiated unsuccessfully with the Syrian government and the National Bloc on replacing the mandate with a treaty. Once again, the question of Syrian unity proved to be the major obstacle.

As the second decade of the mandate progressed, France's policy in its mandated territories was dominated by global and regional developments: the Great Depression and its repercussions on Syria and Lebanon; the collapse of the international order and the mounting threat of war in Europe; chronic political instability in France; the Italian challenge in the Levant; Britain's Middle East policy; and the emergence of independent Arab regimes, particularly in Iraq. France's Syrian policy must therefore be examined in the context of these events.

In the first half of the 1930s, political issues in the mandated territories were overshadowed by a severe economic crisis that forced the High Commission and the Lebanese and Syrian governments to cut their budgets drastically and curtail public spending. The rapid increase in unemployment and decrease in the standard of living led to widespread social unrest. As a result, France came under harsh criticism both for its political policy and its failure to manage the economy of the mandated territories. The National Bloc initiated a campaign to free the Syrian economy from the control of

French and other foreign concessionary companies, and exploited the worsening economic situation to mobilize public support for its demands for independence and unity. Increasingly disillusioned, the Christians in Lebanon now began to question the wisdom of relying on French protection.[1]

Although the economic crisis in Syria and Lebanon was a direct result of the Depression, it was aggravated by local conditions. Changes in the Lebanese economy since the beginning of the mandate—the expansion of the financial sector and the emphasis on the transit trade and export of agricultural products—made it especially vulnerable to the decline in the international and regional markets. As world commerce disintegrated into protectionist trade blocs, including the Middle East, with each power safeguarding its own economic interests, Beirut—which relied heavily on trade and financial services—was seriously affected. The import-export trade of the mandated territories decreased from just over FF 1 billion in the first nine months of 1931 to FF 744 million in the same period of 1932, a reduction of 26.5 per cent. Total imports for Syria and Lebanon, most of which passed through Beirut, dropped by 50 per cent during the recession: from FF 729 million in 1929 to FF 339 million in 1936. At the same time, exports decreased from FF 255 million in 1929 to FF156 million in 1934, and rose only to FF 219 million in 1935. Merchants in Beirut were left with large stocks of goods, and hundreds of companies went bankrupt. The financial sector was also badly hit as traders were unable to repay loans. The recession was further exacerbated by the crisis of the French franc in 1932, and its consequent devaluation, as well as by the instability of other currencies, including the US dollar and the Turkish pound, which was still in widespread use. The devaluation of sterling also affected trade with Palestine and Iraq.[2]

The Great Depression in North and South America and subsequent restrictions on the transfer of funds considerably reduced the flow of remittances from Lebanese emigrants, upon which many Christian families, particularly those living on Mount Lebanon, depended. Real estate markets, in which many of these emigrants and their families had tended to invest, also depreciated.[3]

Economic difficulties in Lebanon were compounded by a stagnation in tourism which had become an important sector by the end of the 1920s. Encouraged by the French, Lebanese entrepreneurs had built hotels in Beirut and guest houses in villages on the Mountain. Thousands of tourists had been flowing in from neighbouring countries, particularly Egypt, but a recession there, coupled with foreign currency restrictions, considerably reduced their numbers. In 1935, the situation improved to some extent, mainly as the result of a rise in Jewish tourism from Palestine, but the revolt there the following year disrupted this source of income.[4]

Britain's decision to build a modern port in Haifa added to the problems of the commercial and financial sectors in Beirut. Fears that Haifa would compete with Beirut as a major trading centre with the Arab countries under British influence were subsequently justified when, after the inauguration of its modern port in October 1933, Haifa took over a growing part of the transit trade, especially with Iraq and Transjordan.[5]

The decline in Lebanese agriculture, which had begun before the First World War, continued during the mandate. The French had little interest in this sector, and their investment in it was minimal. Nevertheless, in the 1930s over half of the population was still engaged in farming. The world recession led to a drop in the demand for Lebanese agricultural products, particularly silk. Traditionally a major source of income for the inhabitants of Mount Lebanon, the silk industry had been in decline since the end of the nineteenth century, but in 1914 it still provided 50 per cent of their earnings. French efforts to revive the industry, which had been decimated by the war, did have some success; at the end of the 1920s, silk production reached two-thirds that of the pre-war years. But the slump in prices following the recession, the import of artificial silk, and the collapse of the silk industry in France, Lebanon's main market, almost annihilated this branch. The High Commission encouraged the peasants of Mount Lebanon to replace silk cultivation with terraced fruit and vegetable farming, but the results of these efforts would not be felt until the Second World War. The fall in the price of tobacco, which provided a livelihood for many of the inhabitants of the south, the Beqa valley and Mount Lebanon, aggravated the situation. Furthermore, a severe drought in 1932 affected the entire agricultural sector, particularly the cultivation of olives for oil.[6]

By the end of the 1920s, local industry had already felt the impact of large-scale importation of western manufactured goods, the mandated territories having become a market for French and other foreign products. The low customs duties applied as a result of the 'open door' policy, a French obligation under the mandate, had offered little protection. As a result, thousands of workers in traditional industries—mainly textiles and food—had been made redundant. It was not until the High Commission raised customs duties in June 1932, in order to increase revenues, that local industry was afforded further protection. The recession, however, had opposite effects on Lebanese industry: on the negative side, it was difficult to export local products to neighbouring countries at a time when the High Commission was being pressed by French industrialists to increase their exports to the mandated territories. On the other hand, low prices encouraged Lebanese entrepreneurs and well-to-do returning emigrés to invest in selected sectors, including construction, textiles and food.[7]

The recession had profound social and political repercussions in Lebanon. A rapid rise in unemployment was aggravated by the cancellation of development programmes in the public sector and the dismissal of government employees. The standard of living dropped further as the Syrian pound was devalued and wages cut. Mounting social unrest was manifested in demonstrations, strikes and violent confrontations between employers and workers, while anger at foreign—mainly French—concessionary companies was expressed in boycotts, affecting trains and tramways especially. The High Commission frequently blamed Arab nationalist and communist agitators, particularly Armenians, but the unrest was clearly the result of economic hardship suffered by the working classes. As the agricultural sector contracted, thousands of people from Mount Lebanon, the Beqa valley and the south moved to Beirut seeking employment. The mood in Beirut darkened as the prosperity of the preceding years was replaced by severe recession, felt primarily by the middle and lower classes. The recession also worsened communal and regional tensions. The Christians of Mount Lebanon claimed they were far worse off than the inhabitants of Beirut; the Shiites protested the lack of government investment in their regions; and the Sunnis complained that although the main tax burden fell on the inhabitants of the annexed areas, most of the budget was invested in Mount Lebanon.[8]

Lebanese politics were no less affected. The public and the press protested corruption, the squandering of public funds and the inflated administrative system, urging the government and parliament to reduce expenses and improve the economic situation. Tension grew between Lebanon and Syria over economic policy and division of the revenue from the Common Interests. At the same time, politicians, financiers and merchants of Beirut were growing more conscious of Lebanon's economic dependence on Syria and other neighbouring Arab countries.

Both Syrians and Lebanese blamed the High Commission's economic policy for exacerbating the crisis. They accused the French of using a large portion of the revenue from the Common Interests to finance an inefficient and corrupt administration, in which French officials received high salaries, while those of local officials had been drastically reduced. French concessionary companies were denounced for exploiting the local economy. The Lebanese compared the rapid economic growth in Palestine and Iraq, which they saw as the outcome of a successful British policy, with the failure of French policy in Syria and Lebanon. Criticism came not only from Muslims and Arab nationalists, but from many Christians, including Maronites—

leading in 1935 to a direct confrontation between the Maronite Patriarch and the High Commission over the tobacco monopoly.[9]

During the first months of 1930, the High Commission, together with the local government, prepared comprehensive development plans. In a letter to the foreign minister, Ponsot presented France's economic achievements in the mandated territories, laying special emphasis on Lebanon, and outlining an ambitious programme proposed by the High Commission and Eddé's government. It entailed an investment of FF 392 million, or three and a half times the Lebanese budget for 1929, in several large projects including construction of a railway linking Tripoli to Beirut (FF 140 million); enlargement of the port of Beirut (FF 80 million); building of a seaplane port in Tripoli (FF 20 million); and improvement of the telephone network (FF 20 million). A year later, however, the mandated territories plunged into a severe economic recession, and the High Commission had to struggle to remain within its budget. The recession, which was to last for five years, placed Ponsot and de Martel, who succeeded him in October 1933, in an unenviable position. Faced with administering the mandated territories at a time when the political situation was deteriorating under worsening economic conditions, they were often required to give priority to improving the economy instead of solving political problems.[10]

From the beginning of the 1920s, successive high commissioners had been under constant pressure from France to ensure that the mandated territories bore the financial burden of their administration, including the budget of the High Commission. By the early 1930s, this had been accomplished—apart from the upkeep of the military forces, which was still financed by France. But now, the High Commission was required to ensure that the territories also contributed to military expenses. The recession had led to a sharp drop in revenue from customs duties, which furnished a large share of the Common Interests budget. This budget financed the High Commission's activities, as well as a substantial portion of the expenses of each local government. In an attempt to augment its income, the High Commission raised customs duties and imposed new direct taxes, measures which generated deep resentment throughout the mandated territories, particularly among the Lebanese. The direct taxes were not progressive; they affected mainly the lower and middle classes, leading to strikes and demonstrations. Meanwhile, the commercial sectors strongly opposed the rise in customs duties, complaining that transit trade was being undermined at a time when Beirut was facing more competition from Haifa. Moreover, higher duties resulted in the smuggling of goods from Palestine, where tariffs remained low. The industrialists, however, welcomed the move, which protected local industry.[11]

Despite the political and social problems, the High Commission was determined to balance its budget, which had been cut by nearly one quarter, from FF 623,491 million in 1928, to FF 503 million in 1932. It attempted to reduce expenses, but the main burden fell on the local governments, which were obliged to cut costs sharply. In 1934 the High Commission embarked upon reviving the economy. Plans were made to enlarge the port of Beirut and establish a free trade zone to enable it to compete with Haifa. At the same time, to encourage the transit trade, work began on improving roads and rail links to northern Syria and Iraq. Efforts were also made to promote local industry and agriculture, but the Lebanese economy did not emerge from the recession until 1937.[12]

From the Treaty of Versailles onwards, France had been obsessed by its search for security, its main concern being to contain Germany. At first it tried, without success, to obtain the agreement of Britain and the United States to come to its aid in the event of German aggression. Then, under Poincaré, France resorted to seeking military alliances with other European countries that shared its fears of Germany. France insisted on application of the Treaty of Versailles on disarmament, reparations and control over the left bank of the Rhine. The Lucarno Agreement, the financial settlements with Germany, and the latter's admission to the League of Nations, obliged France to acknowledge that its attempts to isolate Germany had failed; integration of Germany into the European and international order was now the aim. This policy, inspired largely by Briand, saw the League of Nations as a guarantor of international order and the balance of power in Europe, and as a major factor in maintaining French security. The League of Nations thus became a cornerstone of French foreign policy and France's prestige and international standing was considerably enhanced by the influence it exercised in Geneva. Briand's efforts had culminated in the 'Paris Agreement' of August 1928, in which representatives of the United States, Britain, France, Germany, Italy and Japan agreed to strengthen the League of Nations and refrain from employing force in international disputes. France enjoyed rapid economic growth following Poincaré's success in stabilizing the franc, and by the early 1930s had amassed one of the largest gold reserves in the world. Its army and air force were the second largest in Europe, after those of the Soviet Union. Within a few years, however, the European order for which Briand had striven, collapsed. Divided politically and socially, France again faced a growing threat from Germany.[13]

During the 1930s, France's policy in its mandated territories was influenced by Italy's growing military and economic presence in the Mediterranean. Italian involvement in the Middle East would have significant political and ideological repercussions on the countries of the region, including Syria and Lebanon. In a mere decade Mussolini had transformed Italy from an agricultural country with a marginal role in European diplomacy into an industrial power with one of the largest and most modern armies on the continent. He was to exploit its military might and pursue an aggressive policy of territorial expansion, with the aim of establishing a second Roman empire and turning the Mediterranean into *mare nostrum*. To achieve this, he built up a strong navy and air force, the most advanced in Europe. Italy's occupation of Corfu, the Dodecanese Islands and Libya and its intervention in the Spanish Civil War were assertions of his ambition.[14]

Mussolini sought to secure a foothold in the Levant by undermining France's position and bringing an end to its mandate there. He employed propaganda and subversion extensively, while his representatives on the Permanent Mandates Commission criticized France's Syrian policy. In the early 1930s, Italy stepped up its economic, educational and religious activities in Syria and Lebanon. Its banks and maritime companies competed with those of France, while schools were established and aid given to educational institutions which taught the Italian language. Plans were also made to build an Italian university and hospital in Beirut. The Italian Consul General, who enjoyed direct access to Mussolini, placed special emphasis on fostering relations with Christian leaders and politicians, especially from the Maronite community. In meetings with them, he repeatedly stressed that Italy was a rising Catholic power, able to offer the Christians better protection than France, which was on the decline. Commanders of Italian warships anchored in Beirut paid their respects to the Maronite patriarch and bishops, and Maronite clergy were invited to Rome. These efforts were also intended to strengthen Italy's influence in the Holy See and replace France in its traditional role of protecting the Christians of the Levant. Visits to the Vatican by religious leaders from the Maronite and other Christian communities were exploited to gain their support for Italy, while Italian clergy, including those serving in the Vatican, were encouraged to promote their country's interests in the region. Indeed, the French suspected that Frediano Gianini, the apostolic delegate in Beirut, was tacitly supporting Italian ambitions in the mandated territories. At the same time, Italian representatives sought to cultivate ties with the Muslims of Syria and Lebanon, openly supporting the Arab nationalist struggle against France. These tactics did in fact undermine French attempts to conclude a treaty with Syria in 1933.[15]

Propaganda played a major role in Italians efforts to improve their position in Syria and Lebanon. Italian diplomats presented their country's military, industrial and scientific achievements, while substantial sums of money were offered to local newspapers and journalists to promote Italy's stand. Articles published in the Italian press and statements made by Italian delegates at the League of Nations criticizing France's Syrian policy were frequently reproduced in Syrian and Lebanese newspapers. Radio Bari, which began to broadcast in Arabic in 1934, continually aired attacks on French and British policy in the Arab world, while praising Italy's support of Islam and Arab nationalism. Although this propaganda failed to persuade the Syrians or Lebanese to support Italy, it did have some impact on local public opinion and further undermined France's position in its mandated territories.[16]

Fascism, with its emphasis on patriotism, a strong leader, modernization and science, and on the role of youth in building the state, appealed to many young and educated Christians and Muslims in the mandated territories, who had either witnessed the failure of the democratic parliamentary system in France or rejected communist ideals. The Italians encouraged young people to form their own fascist organizations throughout the region. At the end of December 1933, Mussolini addressed the opening session of a congress of Asiatic youth organizations in Rome, attended by many delegates from the Arab world, including Syria and Lebanon. The congress was convened again a year later.[17]

Although Germany's activities in the mandated territories were limited, they generated much suspicion and resentment among the French, particularly after the rise of Nazism. German representatives in Syria and Lebanon promoted their country's economic interests, and encouraged the local press to publish articles praising Germany's opposition to Jews and Zionism, its support for Arab independence and unity and its backing for the Syrian Arab nationalist struggle against France. Ruppel, the German delegate to the Permanent Mandates Commission, often joined his Italian colleague in criticizing France's Syrian policy. His visit to Syria and Lebanon in April 1933 and his meetings with Syrian nationalist leaders only added to French apprehensions.[18]

This Italian and German activity reinforced doubt among the populations of Syria and Lebanon regarding France's intention or ability to retain its mandate, and fuelled rumours of an impending withdrawal. Information sent from Geneva by Shakib Arslan and Ihsan al-Jabiri, concerning Italian and German support for their cause, encouraged the Syrian Arab nationalist leaders to take an uncompromising stand in negotiations with France. Ponsot accused the Italian and German representatives on the Permanent Mandates Commission of jeopardizing his negotiations with the Syrian government. French diplomats in Rome tried to foil Mussolini's attempts to use Italian clergy in the Vatican to promote Italy's standing among the Christian communities in the Levant. In Beirut the High Commission, which was closely

following Gianini's activities, constantly pressed the Quai d'Orsay to intervene in the Vatican for his replacement with a Frenchman. Although France
was obliged by the League of Nations to implement an 'open door' policy in
its mandated territories, it employed various means to undermine Italian and
German activities there. Italian and German companies encountered numerous difficulties in operating in Syria and Lebanon, while local newspapers
were encouraged to publish articles criticizing Italy's treatment of the Muslims in Libya.[19]

France came close to civil war on several occasions in the 1930s, when the
country was sharply divided on ideological, political, social and economic issues. The bitter conflict between left and right, added to the frequent
political and economic crises, undermined national morale. The political system reflected the deep divisions: between 1930 and 1940 there were 24
changes of government. France's political instability seriously undermined its
position in its mandated territories. Although the Third Republic had frequently undergone such crises in the 1920s, repercussions on France's Syrian
policy had been limited. During most of that decade, Briand had served either as prime minister or foreign minister. The experienced Philippe
Berthelot, who had followed the Syrian question since the first World War,
served as Director-General of the Quai d'Orsay, while Robert de Caix,
France's representative to the Permanent Mandates Commission, continued
to be involved in defining its Syrian policy. After the rise of Edouard
Herriot's leftist government in 1932, both Briand and Berthelot retired, and
although de Caix continued to hold his position in Geneva, he lost much of
his influence. The position of foreign minister was then held by politicians
who either had little knowledge of Syrian affairs, or did not remain in office
long enough to formulate a policy. Thus French policy in Syria and Lebanon
lacked inspiration and was, for the most part, content with solving pressing
problems. Ponsot and de Martel had to face repeated crises, but were unable
to initiate or implement long-term policies.[20]

During the annual debates on the Syrian budget in the National Assembly, communist and socialist deputies continually criticized government
policy and called for withdrawal from the mandated territories, thereby reinforcing doubts in Syria and Lebanon of France's intent to maintain its
mandate. Overestimating the left's criticism, and believing that a change in
French policy was imminent, the National Bloc was reluctant to moderate
its stand in negotiations with the High Commission. French weakness and
rumours of its impending withdrawal increased the fears of the Christians
of Lebanon and Syria that they would be left with no protection against the
Muslim majority.[21]

In early 1930, Henri Ponsot could hardly have been content with the situation in the mandated territories. After more than three years in office he had attained few of the goals he had set out to achieve. France's Syrian policy was again in disarray, unable to free itself from the conflict between advocates of the status quo and supporters of a liberal policy. France had yet to fulfil its international obligation to the League of Nations to grant organic laws to its mandated territories. With no constitution or elected parliament and government, Syria was administered by an appointed prime minister who was responsible more to the French than to his own people. Jabal Druze and the Alawite region were under military control, with army officers, mainly from the Service de Renseignements, supervising the key positions. The Lebanese constitution, even after two revisions, had yet to provide the country with a stable political system. The National Bloc, enjoying considerable public support, continued to demand independence and unity, exploiting the deteriorating economic situation and the growing resentment of France's economic policy to encourage strikes and demonstrations. After failing to persuade the Syrian parliament to approve the constitution, Ponsot lost his self-confidence, and his position and prestige in both Paris and Beirut were severely weakened. His indecisiveness in handling the crisis of Eddé's government aroused further criticism. His standing in the High Commission was undermined by his staff and army officers who opposed his liberal policy. Often he was unable to control the personal rivalry among his own delegates. Increasingly isolated, he became reluctant to make any new moves and paradoxically, this was interpreted by the Syrian nationalists as a sign of aloofness.[22]

The conclusion of the Anglo–Iraqi treaty in June 1930 convinced Ponsot and officials in the Quai d'Orsay that France had to take the initiative in order to break the deadlock in its mandated territories. Britain, which at first had sought to limit confrontation with the Muslim population and the Arab nationalist movement, had reached an agreement with the Iraqi government that safeguarded British imperial interests while allowing Iraq to run its own affairs. Having failed to define their own policy, the French were continually seeking inspiration from Britain's success in Iraq: in 1926, de Jouvenel had proposed following the example of Britain's Iraqi policy of 1922; and in 1930, Ponsot attempted to emulate the Anglo–Iraqi treaty in Syria and Lebanon. But right-wing French politicians, officials and army generals opposed these attempts, arguing that unlike Britain, France had a moral obligation to protect the Christian minorities in the Levant. Moreover, unlike Iraq, Syria lacked a stable central government with which a long-term agreement could be negotiated. This argument was, to a large extent, groundless: the French themselves had expelled Faisal from Damascus and had divided Syria, precluding the emergence of a strong, elected central government.[23]

News of the impending conclusion of the Anglo–Iraqi treaty fuelled opposition to the French mandate in Syria. France's colonial policy was compared unfavourably with Britain's more liberal attitude in Iraq. It was alleged that although Syria was more advanced, Iraq was soon to achieve its independence. With tension in Syria building, and the Permanent Mandates Commission scheduled to meet in June, the Quai d'Orsay and Ponsot came under pressure to demonstrate that progress had been made. Thus, on 14 May 1930, Ponsot published six decrees comprising organic laws for the mandated territories (Syria, Lebanon, the government of Latakia, Jabal Druze and the Alexandretta region) and for the Common Interests. In June he presented them to the Permanent Mandates Commission in Geneva, declaring that France intended to emulate Britain's example by replacing the mandate with treaties to be negotiated with elected local governments. These assurances were repeated during the following months by Briand, Paul-Boncour and de Caix. De Jouvenel's treaties policy was thus finally to be put to the test. For the next four years, negotiations were held between France and Syria on ending the mandate. This was to be the last opportunity to reach an agreement before the disintegration of the international order and the growing threat of war in Europe made it impossible to pursue this strategy.[24]

During the second half of 1930, Ponsot held intensive discussions in the High Commission to explore the various aspects of implementing a treaties policy. In November, he sent a memorandum to Briand analysing French policy in the mandated territories and presenting his arguments for the conclusion of treaties with Syria and Lebanon.[25] It was one of the few occasions that Ponsot departed from his cautious diplomatic style and openly criticized those in Paris and Beirut who opposed his more liberal stand. He denounced what he defined as the 'colonialist approach' that had dominated French Syrian policy since 1920. Those who advocated such a strategy, he claimed, considered the mandate a facade behind which they sought to control the Levant, as they had North Africa. This colonial state of mind had lasted for too long and had manifested itself each time liberal solutions were proposed. Ponsot accused the colonialists of seeking to maintain tight control over the mandated territories, although this would have entailed maintaining the status quo for an undetermined period of time. He charged that the colonialists had not considered the Allied pledges to the Arabs during the war, nor the transitory character of the mandate, whose goal had been to prepare Syria and Lebanon for independence. As in 1925, they failed to recognize the influence of Arab nationalism, which would necessitate a more liberal policy.

He pointed out that between 1920 and 1930 the number of French troops in the Levant had fallen from 80,000 to 14,000, while the budget of the High Commission had been reduced from FF 185 million to FF 11 million. The entire staff of the High Commission now numbered no more than 356. France had therefore to adapt its policy to its limited means. Moreover, the question of the mandated territories did not exist in a vacuum; the Syrians were closely following Britain's liberal policy in Iraq and were demanding similar treatment from France. Under the circumstances, a colonialist policy could be sustained only by allocating sufficient military forces to the territories, which France was unwilling to do.[26]

In 1926, Ponsot noted, the French government had agreed to the principle of replacing the mandate with treaties, as recommended by de Jouvenel, but no action had been taken for four years. Since French economic and financial interests in the mandated territories were limited and could be protected without a mandate, he proposed negotiating treaties with Syria and Lebanon based on the Anglo–Iraqi agreement of 1930. In any such pact, France would have to maintain its traditional role as protector of the Christian minorities, as well as of its cultural and educational institutions. With regard to its military interests, he recommended that France follow the precedent established by Britain in its treaty with Iraq. He advised that the Ministries of War, Navy and Air coordinate their efforts and allocate the necessary resources to construct military facilities. He pointed out the importance of protecting French oil interests, proposing establishment of air and military bases along the oil pipeline, and development of Tripoli, its terminal, into a major military, air and naval base for French operations in the eastern Mediterranean. Ponsot stressed that Lebanon was no less interested in a treaty than Syria, and suggested that it be granted one and admitted to the League of Nations simultaneously with Syria. He noted that while Syria regarded a treaty as a means of limiting French control, Lebanon saw it as a safeguard against its abandonment by France. He was therefore confident that Lebanon, wary of its Syrian neighbour, would welcome the continuation of a French military presence on its soil. Despite his mistrust of the Syrian nationalists, he believed it was possible to negotiate an agreement with them, since they had been insisting on a treaty and admission to the League of Nations since 1926. He suggested that a treaty with Syria be concluded within two years, before Iraq joined the League of Nations, and that this period be used to resolve standing issues, including the question of Syrian unity (the status of the governments of the Alawite region and Jabal Druze); Syrian territorial claims in Lebanon, especially over Tripoli; and an agreement between the two states on dividing the revenue from the Common Interests. He admitted that his recommendations might arouse some controversy, but stressed that they were not entirely new, being based on principles acknowledged years before, which could now be applied. He warned that the High Commission would face difficulties in implementing the constitution in Syria and emphasized the need for the French government to provide its representatives with comprehensive instructions regarding French policy in the mandated territories, to enable them to solve the problems that would inevitably arise.[27]

In order to implement a treaties policy, it was essential that elections be held for a Syrian government with which to negotiate. But the election period did not begin until December 1931, ending in the following April. It was not until June 1932, two years after promulgation of the organic law, that Syria had its own elected parliament, president and government. This delay was partially caused by the inability of the French government and the bureaucrats in Paris and Beirut to define a new policy, as well as by the decision to prepare the ground carefully in Syria before proceeding with elections. After Ponsot's failure in 1928, the Quai d'Orsay sought to ensure that a more manageable parliament would be elected this time. Moreover, Ponsot and his staff had to devote much of their time to solving urgent financial problems. A major reason for the long delay was the opposition of conservative politicians in the National Assembly, officials in the Quai d'Orsay and, in particular, of the French military establishment.[28]

Throughout the discussions held in Beirut and Paris in 1931, officers in the army, navy and air force insisted that in any treaty, France's military interests in the mandated territories should be taken into account in the event of local uprisings, regional threats (especially from Turkey) or a general war in Europe. They pressed for control over lines of communication and military and air bases, as well as close supervision of the Syrian army. Adamantly opposed to application of the treaties policy in Lebanon, the Alawite region, Alexandretta or Jabal Druze, they argued that control over the coastal regions, with the ports of Beirut, Tripoli and Alexandretta, was essential to French strategic interests in the eastern Mediterranean. The importance of retaining these areas would increase after completion of the pipeline to Tripoli, they pointed out. The mounting threat from the Italian navy, particularly after Italy's occupation of the Dodecanese Islands and Libya, was another concern. Finally, they cautioned that French assent to Syrian nationalist demands for integration of the Alawite region and Jabal Druze could lead to a general uprising, especially among the Druze. And a united Syria, they warned, would be better positioned to undermine Lebanon's separate existence and Christian character.[29]

Like de Jouvenel, Ponsot was well aware that the National Bloc and the overwhelming majority of Muslims in Syria and Lebanon regarded Syrian unity as a national goal as important as independence. Along with other civilian officials, he argued that the army was ignoring political considerations, and noted that Great Britain was content with looser military control over Iraq. He pointed out that the Lebanese, including the Christians, were also demanding a treaty and independence, and that France would be better able to secure its military interests in Lebanon through a bilateral agreement. As in 1920 and 1926, the French government was again facing the difficult choice of whether to continue its 'minority policy', which would entail maintaining direct control over Lebanon, the Alawite region and Jabal Druze, or to reach an agreement with the National Bloc and the Arab Muslim majority, thus necessitating a revision of its stand over Syrian unity. Without such a revision, there was little chance of reaching an agreement.[30]

On 16 November 1931, shortly after returning from Paris, Ponsot was instructed by Briand to hold elections in Syria and form a government. He was given a draft treaty, with military and financial protocols to be negotiated and approved by the elected government and parliament. The treaties policy, however, was not to be applied to Lebanon, the Alawite region or Jabal Druze; the mandate was to be maintained in those areas. The government clearly preferred to postpone a decision on Syrian unity and the issue of a treaty for Lebanon.[31]

Briand's instructions, however, hampered Ponsot's efforts to reach agreement with Syria. Ponsot had to persuade the National Bloc and the Syrian public to shelve their demands for unity for the time being and be content with a treaty. His most pressing task was to ensure election of a moderate parliament and a government with which a treaty could be negotiated. Ponsot had learned the lesson of the 1928 constitutional crisis and was well aware of the National Bloc's ability to undermine his policy. He therefore pursued a strategy of sowing discord in the ranks of the National Bloc by courting its moderate wing—centred in Damascus and headed by Jamil Mardam—while simultaneously weakening the radical faction in Aleppo, led by Ibrahim Hananu. For that reason he rejected demands to publish the proposed treaty before the elections, knowing that such a step would play into the hands of the militants. The elections were held in December 1931 and January 1932, accompanied by much tension and violence, and the High Commission was forced to hold another round in Hama and Damascus at the end of March and beginning of April. French officials openly intervened to prevent election of candidates hostile to France, such as Hananu. The National Bloc was left deeply divided, and the resentment harboured by Hananu and his supporters would severely undermine Mardam's efforts to negotiate a treaty with Ponsot.[32]

In June 1932—two years after his declaration in Geneva of France's intention to adopt a treaties policy in its mandated territories—Ponsot was
finally able to begin negotiations with an elected Syrian president and government. Two moderate nationalists, Ali Abid and Haqqi al-Azam, had been
elected president and prime minister respectively. Two of the government's
four ministers, Mazhar Raslan and Jamil Mardam, were members of the National Bloc; the latter would play a key role in negotiations with the French
the following year. The preliminary discussions were soon cut short by the
May elections in France, which returned the left to power after an eight-year
absence. In light of the left's past record on the Syrian question, the National
Bloc hoped that the new government, headed by Edouard Herriot, would be
more receptive to their demands. Their hopes were shared by Ponsot, who
expected to be given a freer hand in concluding a treaty with Syria.[33]

Ponsot remained in Paris from July to October, helping to re-evaluate
French policy in the mandated territories. It soon became clear, however, that
Herriot, who also served as foreign minister, could not depart from Briand's
policy, particularly on the issue of Syrian unity. The military establishment
insisted on retaining direct French control, through the mandate, over Lebanon, the Alawite region and Jabal Druze. Officials in Paris and Beirut warned
that the Syrian nationalists would not be content with integration of the
Alawite region and Jabal Druze with Syria, but would continue to demand
the Beqa valley, south Lebanon and Tripoli as well, thus undermining Lebanon, France's main base of influence in the Levant. Others argued that France
should not abandon the minorities who had placed their fate in its hands.
Indeed, Christian leaders in Syria, especially the influential Syrian-Catholic
Patriarch Tapuni, expressed fear for their future and appealed to France to
ensure that the treaty would safeguard their interests. A similar concern was
voiced by Pope Pius XI, who urged Ponsot, at a meeting in November 1932,
to protect the Christian communities in Syria and Lebanon. In view of Italian attempts to undermine France's traditional role as protector of the
Catholic communities in the Levant the Pope's appeal carried considerable
weight.[34]

Iraq's admission to the League of Nations on 3 October 1932 and the convening of the Permanent Mandates Commission the following month
pressed Herriot into reaching a decision on France's Syrian policy. The feeling of urgency was expressed in a memorandum to the prime minister which
stressed: 'The time of promises is over—we have to take action.' On 12 October, the French government reaffirmed its intention to conclude a treaty
with Syria based on the Anglo–Iraqi agreement, and approved the new draft
prepared by Ponsot: Syria would be granted independence and admitted to
the League of Nations after a transitional period of three to four years. No

major changes were made on the question of Syrian unity, and a decision on the Alawite region and Jabal Druze was postponed until the end of the transitional period. Their future would then be decided in negotiations between the Syrian government and their elected representatives—provided the two regions continued to enjoy administrative and financial autonomy. The issue of a treaty with Lebanon was also deferred. Ponsot was instructed to return to Beirut and reach an agreement in principle with the Syrian government, based on the proposed draft, within a month. He was then to leave for Geneva to present the Mandates Commission with the results of the negotiations, and return to Paris, where any unsolved problems could be reexamined.[35]

Ponsot returned to Beirut on 21 October and proceeded immediately to Damascus, where he announced that France would grant Syria a treaty more liberal than Britain's pact with Iraq. Tension in Syria had been mounting since June, in anticipation of the French government's decision; it was manifested in the widening rift in the National Bloc between supporters and opponents of the treaty. On the eve of Ponsot's arrival, Bloc leaders had met in Sofar in Lebanon, but had failed to reach an agreement. At a second meeting in Homs at the beginning of November, however, Mardam and his allies obtained approval for their participation in the negotiations. Ponsot subsequently held talks with President Abid, Prime Minister Azam and Mardam on the proposed treaty, urging them to conclude an agreement with France. In response to their demands for Syrian unity and revision of Lebanon's borders, he declared that the time was not yet ripe for a decision on these issues; they should be deferred until the end of the transitional period.[36]

On 22 November, Ponsot left for Geneva, confident that he would be able to reach an agreement after his return. But during the following month, France's policy in Syria and Lebanon was again thrown into disarray and any hopes he may have had of immediately concluding a treaty were shattered. French efforts were undermined by the Italian and German members of the Permanent Mandates Commission. On 1 December, Ponsot, accompanied by de Caix, appeared before the Commission. He described events in the mandated territories since his previous report of June 1930, and informed its members of the current negotiations on a treaty with Syria. The Italian chairman, the Marquise Theodoli, immediately asked Ponsot whether the Alawite region and Jabal Druze would be incorporated into Syria. Instead of answering in general terms, Ponsot made the mistake of giving a detailed review of France's stand on Syrian unity. He compounded the blunder by referring to Syria as a 'treaty zone', and to Lebanon, the Alawite region and Jabal Druze as a 'mandate zone'. For the next few hours, the Italian and German representatives interrogated him on numerous sensitive issues: French intervention in the elections, specifically in Aleppo; Syria's territorial claims in Lebanon and its access to the sea; and the suspension of Lebanon's constitution. Italian and German attempts to undermine French Syrian policy continued for several months, as they effectively exploited the unity issue to thwart attempts to conclude a treaty with the Syrian government. Representatives of the two countries called for details of the proposed treaty to be submitted to the Commission before being approved by the French and Syrian governments. Italian diplomats encouraged the Syrians to adhere to their national goals, while the Italian press began criticizing French policy in the Levant. German delegates joined the Italian initiative; Ruppel visited Damascus in April and met with Syrian leaders, including Jamil Mardam. In view of Britain's success in securing its military and economic interests in Iraq through a bilateral treaty, Italy and Germany were clearly anxious to prevent France from concluding a similar treaty with Syria.[37]

Throughout his negotiations with the Syrian leaders, Ponsot had maintained a vague stand on the question of Syrian unity. But the tactics of the Italians and Germans in Geneva frustrated his efforts. News of his distinction between a 'treaty' and a 'mandate' zone, and criticism of French Syrian policy by members of the Permanent Mandates Commission were widely publicized in the Syrian and Lebanese press, arousing a strong public reaction. Encouraged by international support of their stand, opponents of the treaty in the National Bloc stepped up efforts to prevent the Syrian government from compromising Syrian unity. Nationalist leaders abroad, including Shakib Arslan and Ihsan al-Jabiri in Geneva, and Abd al-Rahman al-Shahabandar in Cairo, joined the campaign against the proposed treaty, as did the Iraqi government through its representatives in Geneva, Damascus and Beirut. At a meeting in Aleppo on 16 February, Hananu and Atasi succeeded in reversing the National Bloc's previous decision, winning support for their stand that unity should be secured before any treaty was concluded.[38]

Ponsot hastened back to Beirut on 6 January 1933 to counter the growing Syrian opposition to the treaty. But at this critical stage in the negotiations he had to remain in Beirut for three weeks to resolve a political crisis in Lebanon, and deal with pressing financial problems. He issued the statement he had made in Geneva to the local press, accompanied by comments on France's policy. The High Commission also encouraged newspapers to publish articles criticizing the Italian and German intervention. At the beginning of February, Ponsot summoned Abid and Mardam to Beirut, and warned them that Italy and Germany were seeking to undermine French efforts to grant independence to Syria, since their own economic and cultural interests would be better protected under a mandate system. He urged them to mobilize public support for the treaty.[39]

Negotiations continued throughout February and March, but little progress was made. Ponsot assured the Syrians that France indeed intended to address the unity issue by the end of the transitional period; in the meantime, Syria would attain economic unity and the inhabitants of Jabal Druze and the Alawite region would be defined in their passports as 'Syrian' citizens. His efforts, however, were unsuccessful; the Syrian government was under pressure by the radicals, who had succeeded in transforming the question of Syrian unity into a matter of general concern. In April, the Quai d'Orsay sent de Caix to Damascus but he too failed to persuade the Syrian leaders to endorse the proposed treaty. His visit was also intended to counter that of Ruppel, the German representative on the Permanent Mandates Commission. In an attempt to salvage the treaty, Ponsot suggested negotiating an agreement on the technical protocols, but it soon became evident that even on these issues, the Syrian government was unable to make any progress. He repeatedly asked the Quai d'Orsay to transfer the talks to Paris, where the Syrian representatives would not be under public pressure and the French negotiators would have direct access to their government. The Quai d'Orsay refused, however, arguing that such a move would weaken Ponsot's position in the mandated territories. The French government was clearly reluctant to hold the talks in Paris for fear they would attract the attention of the French public, opening the way for the opposition and the press to criticize its Syrian policy. On 20 April, pushed by the radicals in the National Bloc, Mardam and Raslan resigned. Although negotiations continued under the new government, the resignations marked the end of Ponsot's three-year effort to conclude a treaty with Syria.[40]

The Permanent Mandates Commission was scheduled to meet in June and hear Ponsot's report on his progress. As the date drew closer, the Quai d'Orsay re-evaluated its stand on Syrian unity. Ponsot, however, opposed making any concessions, arguing that they would fail to satisfy the National Bloc while weakening France's position in Syria and Lebanon and encouraging the minorities to cooperate with the nationalists. Druze and Alawite opposition to their annexation to Syria reinforced the stance of those French officials who claimed that the nationalists were using France to impose Syrian unity on the minorities.[41]

The French government was anxious not to afford the Italian and German representatives on the Permanent Mandates Commission another opportunity to attack its Syrian policy. But Ponsot's proposal that the Quai d'Orsay ask for the June meeting to be postponed was turned down, for fear it would attract further criticism. Instead, the Quai d'Orsay adopted de

Caix's suggestion that Ponsot inform the Mandates Commission, shortly before he was to leave for Geneva, that he was unable to participate for reasons of ill health. Toward the end of the month, rumours spread that Ponsot had fallen ill. At the meeting in June, de Caix presented the Commission with a general report, stating that a detailed account would be submitted by the high commissioner at the next meeting in November. On 2 July, it was announced that Ponsot had ended his term as high commissioner, and shortly thereafter he returned to Paris.[42]

Ponsot had served almost seven years in Syria and Lebanon, by far the longest term held by any high commissioner. During that time he had acquired an intimate knowledge of the political, social and economic conditions in the mandated territories. His arrival in October 1926 had raised hopes that he would continue the liberal policy to which his predecessor had aspired. But when he left in 1933, few of the problems that had been troubling the mandated territories since 1920 had been resolved. His critics in the Quai d'Orsay and in the High Commission, as well as the Syrian nationalists and Lebanese Christians, accused him of being slow and indecisive. He had failed to win the respect of his superiors in the Quai d'Orsay, who had distrusted his judgment since the Syrian constitutional crisis. While this criticism may have been valid, it did not consider the obstacles Ponsot had faced. The various foreign ministers had expected him simultaneously to remove the Syrian question from the public and political agenda in France, safeguard French interests in the Levant, and maintain France's traditional role of protecting the minorities, while solving the problem of its relations with the Arab Muslim majority. He had been expected to cut costs and ensure that the mandated territories cover the expenses of French administration, while promoting the economy and implementing development plans at a time of severe financial crisis, both in France and the mandated territories. His attempts to adopt a more liberal policy had met with strong opposition from the army, conservative officials in the Quai d'Orsay and the High Commission, as well as from groups with religious-cultural or economic-financial interests in the Levant. Ponsot had understood that a solution to the question of Syrian unity, acceptable to the National Bloc, had to be found if a Franco–Syrian agreement was to be achieved. But his efforts had been frustrated by those who advocated retaining the status quo and the traditional 'minoritaire' policy. In retrospect, France had lost a unique opportunity to implement a consistent policy in its mandated territories, a policy that could have led Syria and Lebanon to independence, while safeguarding its own interests there. At the time, France still enjoyed considerable freedom of action in its dealings with the Syrian Arab nationalists, particularly after their defeat in the revolt of 1925–27. By the mid-1930s, however, it would face tight local, regional and international constraints, that would make these goals almost unattainable—as the Blum government was to learn after 1936.[43]

The seventh high commissioner in Syria and Lebanon, Comte Damien de Martel, was also a professional diplomat; but he lacked any administrative experience. This was one of the few characteristics he shared with his predecessor, as the inhabitants of the mandated territories soon discovered. He came from an aristocratic family and had joined the Quai d'Orsay in 1901 at the age of 22. He had served in various diplomatic positions in the Far East and, during the war, in the Caucasus; later he represented his government in the Baltic states. In 1924 he was appointed to the embassy in Peking and four years later was transferred to Tokyo, where he reached the rank of ambassador. After the hesitant Ponsot, the Quai d'Orsay was seeking an authoritative figure who could take decisions: the cynical, business-like and pragmatic de Martel, who enjoyed direct access to the Quai d'Orsay, was a man of action. Unlike Ponsot, he did not become involved in the local political scene, keeping his distance from politicians, whom he despised for the most part. He also did not share his predecessor's commitment to carry out France's educational mission in accordance with the mandate. His first year in office marked an attempt to return to the tight control exercised by the high commissioners who had preceded de Jouvenel, a policy that was to draw him into sharp confrontation with both the Syrians and the Lebanese.[44]

Before assuming his post in Beirut, de Martel participated in the re-evaluation made by the Quai d'Orsay of French policy in the mandated territories. It soon became apparent that the French government was reluctant to revise its stand on the question of Syrian unity. Their attitude was reinforced by two events in Iraq in the fall: the massacre of the Assyrians by the Iraqi army and the death of King Faisal. The massacre vindicated France's position regarding the protection of minorities. Members of the Permanent Mandates Commission now denounced Britain for its haste in granting Iraq independence and for its failure to include in the treaty provisions for safeguarding the minorities. Italy, which had spearheaded the campaign against France, was now criticized both by Christians in the Levant and officials in the Vatican for undermining French efforts to protect Christian minorities. The massacre also reinforced doubts in the government and National Assembly as to whether the Arab Muslims would be able, as they had hitherto pledged, to establish a democratic, secular state in Syria in which all citizens would enjoy equal rights, regardless of religion or sect. In September 1933, the death of Faisal, who had enjoyed the support of certain factions in the National Bloc, further weakened the pressure on France to revise its Syrian policy. The

French had always viewed Faisal's efforts to secure Iraqi–Syrian unity as a Hashemite, pan-Arabist threat to their control in the mandated territories. They believed that, with his death, Iraqi intervention in Syria and Lebanon would diminish, and that rivalries within the National Bloc would increase.[45]

Officials in the Quai d'Orsay questioned whether France could reach agreement with a Syrian government continually pressed by the National Bloc, especially with the question of Syrian unity still in dispute. Nevertheless, Prime Minister Paul-Boncour, who served also as foreign minister, de Martel and others in the Quai d'Orsay sought to exploit the support France now enjoyed in the Permanent Mandates Commission to conclude a treaty with the Syrian government without delay. It was also argued that France would be better able to ratify the treaty with the existing Syrian parliament, which was considered friendly. De Martel was therefore instructed to resume negotiations with the Syrian government immediately, based on Ponsot's draft proposal.[46]

De Martel arrived in Beirut on 12 October 1933. After the customary meetings with local dignitaries, heads of religious communities and delegations and tours of the mandated territories, he devoted much of his time to negotiating with President Abid and Premier Azam. He described the repercussions of events in Iraq in Paris and Geneva, and urged them to accept the proposed treaty. The two Syrian leaders were aware that the National Bloc had succeeded in swaying public opinion in favour of unity before the conclusion of a treaty. Azam, however, believed that under the circumstances it was preferable for Syria to accept the treaty, and signed it on 16 November. For the next five days, both the High Commission and the National Bloc tried to influence parliament, which had to approve the treaty. As in 1928, the National Bloc succeeded in mustering the support of the majority of the deputies, who rejected it. Among those who voiced opposition to the treaty was a large group of deputies representing the Christian minorities in Aleppo, who believed that their interests and security would be better protected under a French mandate.[47]

Rejection of the pact by the Syrian parliament marked the suspension for the next two years of France's efforts to conclude a treaty. In March 1934 de Martel dismissed Azam's government and appointed al-Hasani to head a narrow cabinet. After twice suspending sessions of the parliament, he dissolved it in November 1934. The National Bloc initially regarded the French failure to have the treaty approved as a major victory that strengthened the radicals, headed by Hananu and Atasi. But moderate leaders, especially Mardam, soon realized they had given France a pretext not only to maintain direct control over Syria, but to suspend its elected parliament and government. Mardam's attempts to resume negotiations and restore the constitution were rejected by de Martel and opposed by the radicals. Throughout 1934 and 1935, the National Bloc was beset by personal and ideological rivalries; it lost much of its popularity and ability to mobilize the Syrian masses against the French. For his part, de Martel turned his attention to reviving the economy and solving Lebanon's political problems.[48]

Negotiations on the Syrian treaty had serious repercussions in Lebanon, which became a major arena for Franco–Syrian confrontation. They affected French policy in Lebanon, led to further Syrian intervention there, and exacerbated tensions between Christians and Muslims. The Lebanese again found themselves torn between two conflicting forces and were compelled to reassess their stand on fundamental issues: separatism or unity; mandate or treaty; territorial reduction or a Greater Lebanon. The political history of Lebanon of those years should therefore be examined in the light of Franco–Syrian relations.

With the prospect of Syria soon to achieve independence, France needed to re-evaluate Lebanon's role in its Middle East strategy. It was essential for France to maintain its influence on the coast, in the face of a hostile, independent, Arab Muslim Syria in the east and a growing threat from Italy in the west. But disagreement arose on whether Lebanon should also be granted a treaty. During the discussions in 1931 and 1932, the military establishment had insisted on retaining direct control over Lebanon through the mandate. Ponsot and officials in the Quai d'Orsay, however, had argued that a long-term bilateral agreement would more effectively secure French interests there. Moreover, a treaty and membership in the League of Nations would reinforce Lebanon's international status as an independent state separate from Syria. In the past, some French officials, including Ponsot, had been willing to consider revising Lebanon's borders, particularly in the Beqa valley. Now there was strong opposition to conceding any territory to Syria, especially Tripoli, whose strategic and economic importance had been considerably enhanced by its designation as the terminal for the oil pipeline from Iraq. Syria's territorial claims in Lebanon were therefore rejected, as were new proposals by some Lebanese Christian leaders, including Eddé, to detach Tripoli and the Beqa valley.[49]

The Franco–Syrian negotiations also influenced Ponsot's stand toward Lebanon. With his attention focused on concluding a treaty with Syria, he devoted less time to Lebanon's pressing political problems, allowing them to escalate into a major crisis. He overestimated the ability of the National Bloc and its supporters on the coast to undermine French interests in Lebanon, and sometimes confused Muslim demands for a greater share in the Lebanese state with the Syrian Arab nationalist struggle against France. He was therefore careful not to antagonize the Maronites, for fear that they might be lured into cooperating with the Muslims, now that France intended to withdraw from Syria.

The French criticized what they saw as the National Bloc's uncompromising stand in the negotiations, accusing its leaders of being xenophobic, shortsighted and driven by personal ambition. In fact, the National Bloc had ample reason to be wary of France's motives in seeking a treaty. Well aware that French military and civilian officials were insisting that the mandate in Lebanon and the Alawite and Jabal Druze regions be retained, they suspected that France was seeking to rid itself of what it considered a hostile Arab Muslim interior, while maintaining direct control in those three minority regions. With France retaining military bases in Syria, their independence would be merely a facade. Syria, they feared, would become a continental 'island' with no access to the sea—isolated from Palestine and Transjordan by Lebanon and Jabal Druze, and bordered on the north by a powerful Turkish Republic that still harboured territorial designs on Alexandretta, Aleppo and the Jazira. No longer able to rely on an international guarantee by the Permanent Mandates Commission, Syria would have to face a France armed with a 25-year bilateral treaty. Moderate Syrian leaders, including Mardam, were reluctantly prepared to allow the Alawites and the Druze to maintain a certain administrative and financial autonomy, but only if France agreed that they be part of Syria. As for economic unity, which French officials were presenting as a first step toward Syria's political unity, they suspected that this was a ploy to retain economic control through the Common Interests, as well as to continue favouring Lebanon's economy.[50]

During the Franco–Syrian negotiations, resentment of the Lebanese Christians intensified in Syria. The Arab Syrian nationalists accused the Maronites of once again undermining Syria's unity and independence, as they had in 1920 and 1926. Adding to this resentment was Ponsot's declaration to the Permanent Mandates Commission, on 1 December 1932, that France resolved to maintain its mandate on the coast. As its opposition to the French-imposed treaty became more vocal, the National Bloc stepped up its intervention in Lebanon. Muslims on the coast were asked to send petitions to the High Commission, the Quai d'Orsay and the Permanent Mandates Commission in support of Syrian unity. These activities culminated in the 'Conference of the Coast' convened in Beirut in November 1933 as part of the National Bloc's campaign against the treaty.[51]

At the same time, Syrian leaders sought to reinforce Lebanese Christian doubts over France's ability to protect them, and attempted to persuade them to reach an understanding with Syria now that it was about to gain independence. They exploited the deteriorating economic situation and the resentment it generated among both Muslims and Christians to counter France's influence. They warned Lebanese Christians that if they continued to insist on separatism, Syria might direct its trade through Haifa instead of Beirut. They were also quick to take advantage of any tension between the Maronite church and the High Commission, as well as the rivalries among Christian leaders—notably between Eddé and Khuri—to promote Syrian goals.[52]

The Syrians regarded negotiations with France as the last opportunity to claim Tripoli and the Beqa valley before a treaty was signed. Despite Ponsot's insistence that Syria's territorial ambitions in Lebanon were not on the agenda, its leaders repeatedly raised their country's need for a port and de- manded annexation of Tripoli. They realized that apart from economic considerations, which had been amplified by construction of the oil pipeline terminal in Tripoli, their control over the city would drive a wedge between Lebanon and the Alawite region and thus weaken French control of the coast. They therefore urged the Sunnis in Tripoli to press for immediate un- ion of their city with Syria. The National Bloc was encouraged by the support for this idea expressed by Lebanese Christian leaders, particularly Eddé. The issue was raised again in April 1933 by Mardam, who insisted on territorial concessions from Lebanon as one of the preconditions for conclud- ing a treaty with France. In a letter to de Martel, he claimed that Syria's vital interests had not been taken into account when the borders of the Lebanese Republic were defined; they should now be modified through direct nego- tiations between Syria and Lebanon, in order to safeguard Syria's rights and guarantee its access to the sea. During a visit to Paris in August that year, Subhi Barakat also argued that the return of Tripoli and the Beqa valley to Syria would facilitate conclusion of a treaty, as well as restore homogeneity to Lebanon and ensure good future relations between the two states.[53]

Following the schools crisis and Eddé's resignation in March 1930, relations between Christians and Muslims in Lebanon were strained. Ponsot's decla- ration in Geneva of the French intention to grant treaties to the mandated territories, and the subsequent Franco–Syrian negotiations, exacerbated the tension. For the next three years, a unique debate would take place in Leba- non on the country's future in light of impending Syrian independence. The debate was not limited to political, religious, intellectual or economic circles, but was openly conducted in the press and followed closely by the public. Fundamental issues were addressed: Lebanon's political and economic ties with an independent Syria; whether Lebanon should also demand a treaty; and the implications for Christian–Muslim relations. The exchanges, often of a sectarian nature, contributed to a long and arduous process in which each community defined its own interests and learned of those of the others. While radical solutions like territorial reduction or political union with Syria were proposed, a compromise was also suggested, based on Christian–Muslim coexistence in an independent Lebanon within its 1920 borders. As in the past, Maronites and Sunnis took opposing stands. The two communities, however, were also divided from within, and different ideological and political trends would emerge on the question of Lebanon's independence and its relations with Syria and France.

The success of the Sunni and pan-Arab leaders of Lebanon in ousting Eddé considerably enhanced their prestige among the Muslim masses not only on the coast, but also in Syria and the neighbouring Arab states. Encouraged by the division among the Maronites and Ponsot's indecisive policy, they loudly demanded equality and political and economic ties with Syria. Their achievements reinforced the National Bloc's belief that they were important partners in the struggle against France and its Lebanese Christian allies. Leaders from Iraq, Transjordan and Palestine now frequently visited Beirut and Tripoli to coordinate tactics.[54]

The Franco–Syrian negotiations and the prospect of Syria shortly gaining independence caused unrest among the Sunnis. Their three most important political protests—the 'Conferences of the Coast' in November 1933 and March and October 1936—were closely linked to these negotiations. Despite their greater confidence, they still feared the Syrian leaders would give priority to their immediate interests and abandon them to French and Lebanese Christian domination. The demand by both military and civilian officials for direct French control over Lebanon, and the Lebanese Christians' request for continuation of the French mandate strengthened their fears. Throughout the Franco–Syrian negotiations, they stepped up their campaign for Syrian unity and urged the National Bloc to raise the question of their future. Yet while many Sunnis genuinely strove for union with Syria, others regarded it merely as a means to induce the High Commission and the Christians to grant them an equal share in the Lebanese state. Various solutions were proposed by politicians through the Muslim press: detachment of all or part of the areas annexed to Lebanon in 1920 and their incorporation into Syria; formation of a Syro–Lebanese confederation; granting of autonomous status to Beirut and Tripoli; or even a population exchange between Syria and Lebanon.[55]

During the 1930s, three schools of thought were to emerge among the Muslims. There were those who accepted integration into the Lebanese state provided they were granted full equality; those who demanded immediate union with Syria; and those for whom the most pressing issue was neither equality nor borders, but securing Lebanon's independence by severing

Maronite ties with France. These trends were manifested in the ideas and activities of, respectively, Muhammad al-Jisr, Abd al-Hamid Karameh and Riad al-Sulh.

Muhammad al-Jisr was often portrayed by his opponents as an ambitious politician who collaborated with France merely to promote his own interests. But these accusations should not detract from the role he played in legitimizing the Muslim participation in the Lebanese political system. Many Muslim politicians, including some of his severest critics, would try to follow in his footsteps, but few would attain the influential position he held in Lebanese politics between 1926 and 1932. Unlike other Sunni politicians, who either boycotted Lebanon's political institutions or held positions while publicly denouncing the Lebanese state, Jisr served in the Lebanese administration from the early stages. In 1926 de Jouvenel appointed him to the newly-created senate, of which he later became president. He used his post as speaker of the combined parliament to augment his political power, and cunningly exploited divisions among the Christian politicians, as well as the French desire to win the support of Sunni leaders, to strengthen his position. The role he played in bringing down Eddé's government considerably enhanced his prestige. His achievements should be judged in view of the opposition he faced, not only from Christians and the Maronite church, but from his own community. In Tripoli, he was continually challenged by Karameh, while in Beirut, the prominent Sunni families, who regarded him as an outsider and a threat to their influence, cooperated with the Christian leadership to undermine his authority.[56]

Unlike other Sunni politicians, Jisr was unwilling to pay lip service to Syrian unity in order to enhance his popularity among the Muslim masses. He genuinely believed that the interests of the Muslims on the coast would be better served by their integration into Lebanon, and that by fully participating in Lebanese politics they would eventually gain equality with the Christians. He saw no need to confront the French and sought their support in the Muslim struggle for a greater share in the Lebanese state. But he nevertheless exploited the Franco–Syrian negotiations and French and Christian fears of the Muslim reaction to promote his own interests as well as those of the Muslims of Lebanon.

Abd al-Hamid Karameh was remarkable for his unwavering struggle against the French mandate and the Lebanese state. Whereas in the 1920s he was considered an unsophisticated local leader, during the following decade he became a national figure, and Sunni politicians in Beirut, heads of the National Bloc, and leaders from neighbouring Arab states often visited him in Tripoli. He became deeply involved in numerous Muslim causes, including the Palestinian struggle against Britain and the Zionists, and protests against the Italian occupation of Libya. His role in toppling Eddé's government was a turning point in his career. The Anglo–French decision to designate Tripoli as the terminal for the oil pipeline from northern Iraq to the Mediterranean considerably enhanced the city's strategic and economic importance and consequently Karameh's own position. In the past, the High Commission had often detained or imprisoned him for his anti-French activities, but it was now careful not to antagonize him. During the Franco–Syrian negotiations, French officials frequently met with him to discuss France's plans to develop the city and its port. The National Bloc, on the other hand, sought his support for the annexation of Tripoli to Syria. Lebanese Christian leaders, including Beshara al-Khuri and even Emile Eddé, also attempted to improve their relations with him.[57]

Karameh had served as the Mufti of Tripoli before the war and as governor of the city under Faisal. He had little knowledge of the West and its culture, and saw the French mandate as a threat to the religious and national interests of Arab Muslims in Syria and on the coast. His hostility to the Lebanese state was no less pronounced than his opposition to France. He considered Lebanon to be a 'Christian republic', alien to Muslim beliefs and national aspirations. He often expressed to French officials his preference for direct French control over Tripoli, rather than that of a Lebanese administration in Beirut. He made no distinction between Islam and Arab nationalism, regarding the latter as a means to ensure the independence and unity of all Arab Muslims in Syria. He unceasingly tried to convince the French and the Maronites that Lebanon would be better off without Tripoli. He, and many of the city's inhabitants, assumed that union with Syria would enable it to become a major port and invigorate its economy. Tripoli's geographical location and Muslim character, added to Syrian insistence on its annexation, made his demands for immediate union with Syria seem an obvious solution.[58]

An ardent pan-Arabist, Riad al-Sulh was dedicated to the struggle for Arab independence and unity. He was a committed opponent of the mandate, and frequently outwitted the French authorities, who invested much effort in following and countering his activities. An American report described him as 'a finished politician, resourceful, subtle, persuasive, dynamic and shrewd. As a master he plays with first one side, then another, always gaining something, compromising only when necessary but always at the right moment.'[59] Sulh was born in Sidon in 1896 to a prominent Sunni family which had served in the Ottoman administration. His father, Rida, had represented the vilayet of Beirut in the Ottoman parliament. His education at the Jesuit College in Beirut equipped him with a good knowledge of French, and prepared him to deal with the Lebanese Christian politicians and French officials on an equal footing. He had been inspired at an early age by the ideals of Arab nationalism and in 1916, together with his father, was charged with conspiracy by the Turkish authorities and sentenced to death. The sentence was subsequently commuted to deportation to Izmir, but Sulh was allowed to study in Istanbul, where he received a law degree. After the collapse of the Ottoman Empire, he wholeheartedly supported Faisal's Arab government in Damascus, in which his father had been appointed minister of interior, and he himself served, for a short while, as governor of Sidon. His association with Faisal's administration to a large extent shaped his political outlook and laid the groundwork for his close ties with many prominent Arab leaders. At that early stage, Sulh proved to be a determined and sophisticated opponent of the French administration on the coast. In the summer of 1920 he played a major role in Faisal's attempt to lure members of the Administrative Council of Mount Lebanon into an agreement against France. For these activities he was sentenced to death, but escaped to Cairo and later proceeded to Geneva, where he joined Shakib Arslan and Ihsan al-Jabiri in the Syro–Palestinian Congress. For the next four years he gained firsthand experience of the League of Nations and the Permanent Mandates Commission, of which he would make good use in later years. In 1924 he was permitted to return to Beirut, and in the following year assisted in the Syrian–Druze revolt. In June 1926, he was sentenced to exile on the island of Arwad, but once more escaped to Cairo, continuing to Geneva, where he again joined up with Arslan and Jabiri. In April 1928, with the help of Emile Eddé, he was allowed to return to Beirut, after his father had undertaken not to become involved in politics. Nevertheless, shortly after his return, Sulh joined the National Bloc and resumed his struggle against the French mandate. During his years of exile in Europe, he had cultivated close ties with various organizations and politicians in France, particularly on the left. In the National Bloc he was considered an expert on French politics, and was frequently sent to Paris to mobilize the support of French politicians for the Syrian nationalist cause. In 1929, together with his cousin, Khazim al-Sulh, he established the Beirut newspaper *al-Nida*, in which he aired his views.[60]

During the next decade, Sulh was involved in Syrian and Lebanese politics and in the National Bloc's campaign against the French mandate, especially in Lebanon. His close association with the pan-Arab movement, his marriage into the prominent al-Jabiri family of Aleppo, and his familial ties with Afif al-Sulh, accorded him a unique position in the National Bloc. Because his family had originated on the coast, he was regarded by some Syrian leaders as an outsider; in fact, his role in the National Bloc has been largely unrecognized. Yet his involvement in Syrian politics also led many Lebanese to consider him an outsider. The leading Sunni families of Beirut—the Bayhums, Salams and Da'uqs—were wary of his and his family's attempts to acquire prominence in the city. Sulh nevertheless succeeded in building up his influence among the young and educated Arab Muslims there. He also exploited the longstanding ties between his family in Sidon and the Shiites in Jabal Amil, to mobilize them in the struggle against the French. His involvement in both the Syrian and Lebanese political systems gave him a unique position and enabled him to play the role of mediator.[61]

Sulh's attitude toward the Lebanese state evolved from his pan-Arabist belief that the borders imposed by Britain and France were artificial and would become irrelevant after the Arabs gained independence. He therefore considered the immediate goal to be independence for Syria and Lebanon. When that was achieved, he claimed, political, economic and cultural links would naturally develop between the two countries, and between them and other independent Arab states. He regarded the ties between France and the Maronites as a major obstacle to independence. As long as the Maronites insisted on French protection, he believed, no French government would be able to relinquish, morally or politically, the role its country had played for centuries. Sulh deemed it essential to allay Maronite fears of the Muslims. He repeatedly warned their leaders that they could not rely on the protection of France, an eclipsed power that would abandon them as it had the Armenians in Turkey. Their future, he argued, lay in cooperation with their Arab Muslim brethren in a common struggle for independence. He opposed Lebanese separatism and tried to convince the Christians that Arab nationalism, based on secularism, would bridge the religious and sectarian gap in Lebanon. He objected to the attempts made by Karameh and other Muslim leaders on the coast, as well as by the National Bloc, to detach Tripoli and the Beqa valley, arguing that such a step would antagonize the Maronites and drive them further into the French grasp. Moreover, with a Maronite majority in a smaller state, Lebanese separatism was bound to become more pronounced. On the other hand, he claimed, maintaining the present borders would ensure Lebanon's Arab character and its ties with Syria and other Arab states. He was less concerned with securing political or economic equality for the Muslims of Lebanon, believing these issues could be resolved after gaining independence. Instead, he sought to undermine Maronite confidence in France and exploited every opportunity to deepen their distrust and resentment of the mandate. His efforts culminated in the National Pact of 1943, which would become the basis for Christian–Muslim coexistence in an independent Lebanon.[62]

The united stand of the Sunni leaders in their campaign against Eddé's government sharply contrasted with the divisions within the Maronite community. These were reinforced by the bitter struggle for the presidency between Eddé and Khuri and by infighting among the bishops to succeed the old and ailing Patriarch Hawayik. France's hesitant policy, as manifested in Ponsot's failure to support Eddé against the Muslim opposition, added to their feeling of vulnerability. The deterioration of the economy led them to criticize the High Commission's economic policy and accuse the French concessionary companies of exploiting Lebanon. Christians on the Mountain even began to express the view that they had been better off politically and economically under the Mutassarifiyya.[63]

Britain's decision to grant independence to Iraq, and France's declaration in June 1930 of its intention to pursue a similar policy in its mandated territories fuelled the apprehension of many Christians. They feared that after the withdrawal of Britain and France, Lebanon would be overwhelmed by the Islamist, pan-Arabist tide that was already spreading throughout the region. They followed the Franco–Syrian negotiations closely, and became alarmed at any sign of French concessions, especially on Syrian unity. Syria's renewed territorial demands and the growing support of the Lebanese Muslims for Syrian unity underlined their country's precarious position. They accused the Sunnis of disloyalty to Lebanon, charging that they were exploiting every opportunity to undermine its political institutions and incorporate it into Syria. Yet they were acutely aware of Lebanon's economic dependence on Syria, which had been highlighted by the recession. With Syria soon to be granted independence and unity, the Christians were faced with the agonizing problems of their relations with Damascus and Paris. They had the choice of joining the Syrians in demanding a treaty and independence, and thereby severing their traditional ties with France, or advocating continuation of the mandate, and thus arousing the hostility of both an independent Syria and the Muslims of Lebanon. As France's internal and international weaknesses were revealed, a deal with the Lebanese Muslims and the Syrian leaders began to seem more tempting for some as a way of ensuring their country's independence and territorial integrity. Others were willing to consider a more radical solution: to acquiesce in Syria's territorial demands.

The Anglo–Iraqi pact and the National Bloc's campaign to force France to grant a treaty to Syria generated intense public debate in Lebanon. At a parliamentary session in April 1930, at which Auguste Adib Pasha presented his government's platform, Khalid Chihab requested that the mandate in Lebanon be replaced with a treaty similar to that granted by Britain to Iraq. In fact, Riad al-Sulh, hoping to raise the issue for public discussion, had been behind this initiative. An article published in *L'Orient*, known for its close links with Eddé, in support of a treaty, spurred public debate and added to the High Commission's concern. Encouraged by *L'Orient's* positive reaction, Sulh offered Eddé the backing of the Arab nationalists in Lebanon and Syria in return for his agreement to lead a campaign for ending the mandate in Lebanon. But Eddé turned down the offer, emphasizing that in contrast to Sulh, he sought to prolong the mandate, considering it a guarantee of Christian security.[64]

One of the most revealing public debates took place following a proposal made by *L'Orient* for the detachment of Tripoli, the Beqa valley and Jabal Amil from Lebanon and an exchange of populations between Lebanon and Syria. The newspaper argued that only such a step would ensure Lebanon's national homogeneity, Christian character and independence. The proposal generated much controversy among the politicians and the press, since it was believed to have been initiated by Eddé. In a series of four articles, Habib Bustani, a Maronite intellectual who opposed the prevailing political system, criticized the plan which, he claimed, was seeking to 'amputate an integral part of the Lebanese homeland', and rejected the idea of a population exchange as impractical. There was no real enmity between Christians and Muslims in Lebanon, he argued, and the differences between them were no more pronounced than the ethnic, religious or political differences in some European countries. The two communities had common social and economic interests, and he believed that with no external interference, a Christian–Muslim entente, based on secularist ideals, could be reached. A balance between Christians and Muslims could be maintained within Lebanon's present borders. Moreover, it would be possible in the long run to abolish sectarian representation altogether and achieve genuine national unity. On the other hand, territorial reduction would not create a 'foyer chrétien' but a 'foyer de discord', with the Maronites becoming the dominant community. He called for independence, arguing that French presence was only exacerbating religious and sectarian divisions in Lebanon. He did not regard Arab nationalism or Arab unity as a threat to Lebanon's independence or unique character. Such unity, he stressed, did not necessarily have to be expressed politically, but could be based on cultural and moral grounds, similar to the ties between the 'Latin European states' of France, Italy and Spain.[65]

L'Orient maintained that although the aspirations and ideals presented by Habib Bustani were noble, they were, unfortunately, utopian, lacked 'historical reality' and were merely a 'pipe-dream'. Pointing to the events of 1926, the newspaper claimed that the religious, sectarian and national conflicts in Lebanon were not over. The country, in its present borders, lacked national unity, and was exposed to internal and external threats. Muslims and pan-Arabists were not content with cultural or moral ties, but were striving for political union with Syria. Indeed, Arab nationalists, such as Sulh and Karameh, were seeking to hoist an Arab flag over Lebanon. Any attempt to ignore that truth revealed a basic lack of understanding of the situation. Without territorial reduction, all the Christians' sacrifices for a state of their own would have been in vain and Lebanon would become just another Arab state. The continued presence of France, which had played a historical role in protecting the Christians of Lebanon, was essential. Bustani and those who shared his views on maintaining Lebanon's territorial integrity appeared to take a more patriotic stand, but they were dangerous; those who supported them were merely burying their heads in the sand. The newspaper had a responsibility to present a solution to the public, even if it was unpopular and seemed unpatriotic. 'However small Lebanon might be in its revised borders, it will retain its Lebanese character and be more viable than a Greater Lebanon with half of its population still refusing to be Lebanese.'[66]

These and similar exchanges among the Christians did not reflect disagreement on whether Lebanon should retain its separate identity, but rather on the best way to ensure it. The differences were to be manifested later, in two schools of thought that took on increasingly ideological and political characteristics. These two approaches, if one is to follow *L'Orient*'s definition, could be described as 'revisionist' and 'integralist'. The former emphasized the differences between Christians and Muslims, and between Lebanese and Arab nationalism. It regarded close ties with France and the revision of Lebanon's borders as the only way to ensure the country's independence and Christian character. The integralists also aspired to ensure Lebanon's independence, but they were determined to retain the 1920 borders. They believed that both goals could be obtained through an agreement with Syria and the Lebanese Muslims.

There were fundamental weaknesses in both approaches, however. The revisionists were unable to provide a satisfactory answer to the question of whether the Christians could ultimately depend on French protection; France's defeat by Germany in 1940 would demonstrate that they could not. They also failed to explain how a smaller Lebanon, isolated from Syria and the rest of the Arab world, could remain economically viable. The integralists faced no less difficult dilemmas. Many Christians and Muslims doubted that religious, sectarian and national differences could be bridged and national unity achieved. They questioned whether it would be possible to reconcile the goals of the Maronites for a 'foyer chrétien' and those of the Sunnis for Syrian and Arab unity. How could the Christians, they asked, ensure that they would not become a minority in an Arab Muslim Lebanese state—the very reason for which they had established their state in the first place. Who would protect Lebanon from Syrian ambitions after they gave up French protection?

Paradoxically, many Christians denounced those who advocated a smaller Christian Lebanon for their willingness to relinquish part of its territory, while some Muslims supported such a solution. On the other hand, even those Christians who doubted the possibility of a Christian–Muslim entente sided with the integralists. The Muslims were similarly divided: some opposed and distrusted the integralists, while others were willing to cooperate with them in order to obtain Lebanon's independence from France.

The ideological debate over Lebanon's national identity, its borders and ties with the West and the Arab Muslim world became progressively entangled in the bitter 13-year struggle for the presidency between Emile Eddé and Beshara al-Khuri. It is impossible to analyse the political history of Lebanon in the 1930s and the course it followed after 1943 without examining this confrontation in detail. The rivalry between the two men was not limited to politics or ideology, but was reflected in intra- and inter-sectarian relations. It further factionalized Lebanese society and politics and weakened the Christian camp at the very time it was facing crucial internal and external challenges. It also enabled Muslim politicians to exercise considerable influence on, and facilitate their integration into, the Lebanese political system. The contest for the presidency became a political spectacle that the Lebanese followed voraciously on the front pages of the newspapers. It widened the gap between the public, which was feeling the effects of the recession, and the politicians, who were involved in their endless intrigues. The scandals and accusations of corruption published daily not only discredited the politicians but undermined the very foundations of the Lebanese state. The large sums of money that changed hands in the campaign enabled affluent bankers and financiers, as well as foreign concessionary companies, to intervene, further corrupting the political system. Lebanese politicians devoted more time and energy to their feuds than to solving their country's social and economic problems. Deeply divided, the Lebanese Christians were less and less able to withstand Syrian intervention and attempts by the High Commission to tighten its control.[67]

The conflict between Eddé and Khuri in the 1930s, as it was presented later from the point of view of Khuri and his followers, is shrouded in misconceptions. An examination of their rivalry in the context of the events of that period reveals a far more complex picture. French officials in Beirut at the time and historians, later, tended to emphasize the personal aspects of the contest. Personal ambition, hatred and vengeance were undoubtedly involved, but there were also clear ideological and political elements. Contrary to Khuri's claims that his opponent was motivated merely by a thirst for power, Eddé had in fact defined his views on issues such as Lebanon's borders, its relations with France, and integration of the Muslims, at a much earlier stage. Khuri, on the other hand, had initially been less committed on these issues; only after failing in his bid for the presidency in 1932 did he adopt a clearer ideological stand, criticizing French policy and calling for restoration of the constitution.[68]

The political history of Lebanon from 1930 to 1936 may be divided into three periods: the first, from the formation of Adib's government on 25 March 1930, following Eddé's resignation, until the decree of 9 May 1932, which dissolved the parliament and government and suspended the constitution; the second, from May 1932 until 30 January 1934, when the constitution was partly restored and a new parliament elected; and the third, from January 1934 until Eddé's election as president on 20 January 1936. In the first period, political life was centred around the presidential elections scheduled for April 1932. During the second period, Lebanon was again administered directly by the High Commission, with Dabbas serving as head of state with a small executive council. The third period was dominated by the escalating confrontation between the Maronite patriarch and the high commissioner over economic policy, as well as by resumption of the struggle in parliament between Eddé and Khuri over the presidency.

Although Khuri and his supporters had succeeded in discrediting Emile Eddé and forcing his resignation, they continued to regard him as their main rival. Throughout 1930 and 1931 Khuri, together with Chiha, Pharaon, Taqla and Zakur carefully planned their moves to ensure Khuri's election as president. They maintained a low profile, working behind the scenes to prevent their opponents, particularly Eddé, from drawing Khuri into a public confrontation. The large sums of money made available, especially by the Chiha–Pharaon Bank, were used to bribe deputies and journalists. Attempts were also made to sow discord between Emile Eddé, Habib al-Sa'ad and Georges Tabet, and to lure Musa Namur, Tabet's principal ally, into supporting Khuri.[69]

Such tactics were used in Auguste Adib's formation of a five-member government in March 1930. In contrast to the governments of the previous four years, short-lived and plagued by intrigue, the new government served for 26 months—one of the longest under the mandate (25 March 1930 to 22 July 1931 and 22 July 1931 to 9 May 1932). With Ponsot's approval, Dabbas, Khuri and Jisr chose Auguste Adib as prime minister; he was a weak politician without a powerbase of his own, whom they could control. The strong man in the government was Musa Namur, the minister of interior and health. His appointment was intended to reward him for his role in ousting Eddé and to weaken his support of Georges Tabet. Husain al-Ahdab, the target of criticism from Eddé's supporters, was retained in his former position as minister for public works, while Ahmad al-Husaini, a Shiite, served as minister of justice. The most controversial nomination was that of Jubran Tuaini, a Greek Orthodox and owner of *al-Ahrar*, as minister of education. His appointment was in recognition of the campaign he had conducted against Eddé, and was intended to ensure his future support. It was opposed, however, by the Maronite church, due to his association with the Freemasons. Adib undertook to continue his predecessor's reforms, but the new government did little apart from reopening 75 state schools that had been closed by Eddé, and reinstating some 700 government employees. Despite the worsening economic situation and rising demands on the budget following the reduction in revenue from customs duties, the government failed to cut administrative costs or improve the economy.[70]

In June 1931, Khuri officially announced his candidacy for the presidency. The elections were scheduled for March 1932 and, in accordance with the 1929 amendments to the constitution, the president was to be elected for a six-year term. Khuri had worked hard throughout the previous year to form a powerful coalition backed by politicians, including Dabbas and Jisr, and leading businessmen in Beirut. He may have failed to win the backing of the Patriarch Hawayik, but enjoyed the support of his cousin, Bishop Abdallah al-Khuri, who exercised considerable influence over seven deputies, as well as of the Jesuits in Beirut, headed by Père Chanteur and Père Bonneville. At the same time he attempted, through Salim Taqla, the administrator of Beirut, to win its prominent Sunni families over to his side. He also used Michel Zakur to liaise with the Arab nationalist leaders, including Riad al-Sulh. Zakur's *al-Ma'arad* and Tuaini's *al-Ahrar*, and other newspapers that had received handsome sums of money, promoted his candidacy and attacked Eddé.[71]

Khuri had already established close ties with Solomiac, the influential delegate to Lebanon, but he needed to secure Ponsot's support in order to ensure his election. Lacking Eddé's direct access to political circles in Paris, and facing opposition from Georges Samné and other Lebanese immigrants in France, only Ponsot could persuade the Quai d'Orsay to approve his candidacy. Officially maintaining neutrality, Ponsot hardly concealed his opposition to Eddé, resenting the latter's attempts to bypass his authority and deal directly with Paris. Following Eddé's resignation, relations between them were strained, particularly after Eddé had accused Ponsot of failing to back him. Preoccupied with preparations for negotiating a treaty with Syria, Ponsot sought to end the Lebanese presidential campaign as soon as possible. He feared that Eddé's election might antagonize the Syrian nationalists as well as the Lebanese Muslims. Ponsot regarded Khuri, on the other hand, as a less controversial candidate who could gain the support of both Christians and Muslims, and would not be resented by the Syrians. He had worked closely with Khuri, who had served as prime minister in three governments. Moreover, Khuri was willing to introduce reforms that Ponsot deemed necessary in the political, administrative and financial systems. Although in his dispatches to the Quai d'Orsay Ponsot was careful not to declare openly his preference for Khuri, he actively promoted his candidacy.[72]

After his defeat, Eddé frequently expressed his disillusionment with Lebanese politics and devoted most of his time to his law practice. But he was determined to take revenge on Khuri and his allies, whom he held responsible for his downfall. As the elections drew nearer, he dedicated his efforts to preventing Khuri's election. With his opponent enjoying a majority in parliament and the backing of the high commissioner, his task was by no means easy. He initiated a campaign in *L'Orient*, in which he accused Khuri of having undermined his attempts to cleanse and reform the administration in order to promote his own political ambitions. As the economic situation deteriorated, public criticism of Khuri, Dabbas and Jisr grew, holding them responsible for the corrupt, inefficient political and administrative systems of the previous five years. Eddé, on the other hand, began to be regarded increasingly as a man who stood for reform.[73]

With his popularity growing, Eddé stepped up efforts to undermine Khuri's candidacy and promote his own. He focused on winning over the Maronite church and the French government, and cultivated close ties with Bishop Khuri's main opponent, Bishop Mubarak. With the latter's mediation, Sa'ad, Tabet and Eddé coordinated their moves against Beshara al-Khuri. Bishop Mubarak also strove to win Hawayik's backing for Eddé, but his initiative was undermined by Bishop Khuri. In September 1931 Eddé travelled to Paris, seeking to persuade the Quai d'Orsay and prominent French politicians to endorse his candidacy. His attempts, however, were thwarted by Ponsot, who had already arrived there. Eddé's views in support of revising Lebanon's borders were immediately leaked to his opponents in Beirut, and were exploited by Khuri's camp. Some newspapers went so far as to accuse him of treason and questioned whether he should serve as president since, according to the constitution, the elected president had to swear to defend Lebanon's territorial integrity.[74]

Toward the end of 1931, opposition to Khuri intensified. Warnings were voiced of the danger of the 'Khuri clan' taking over the two prominent positions—the presidency and the head of the Maronite church. His opponents presented him to the Maronite community as a weak politician who would be unable to defend their interests against Jisr's expanding influence, and to the Muslims as a 'Maronite from the Mountain' who could not be trusted. He was accused of corruption and of exploiting his political position to further the financial interests of his relatives and friends. It was also alleged that, as prime minister, he had received bribes from Bank Misr to promote its interests in Lebanon. Some deputies who had previously backed him withdrew their support, while others now hoped to become last-minute compromise candidates themselves. The appointment of Solomiac as a delegate in Damascus further weakened Khuri's position. Nevertheless he and his friends continued to believe that with Ponsot's help and the majority he still enjoyed in parliament, he would be elected. In the first four months of 1932, however, their elaborate plans collapsed as Lebanon underwent one of the most severe crises of the mandate period. It began with a succession struggle in the Maronite church and ended with suspension of the constitution.[75]

On 25 December 1931, Elias Pierre Hawayik died at the age of 89. Since his election in 1899 he had acquired a unique moral authority among the Maronites, who remembered his defense of their autonomy against Jamal Pasha and his efforts to help the community through the famine during the war. Above all, he had become a symbol of 'Grand Liban' in whose formation he had played a crucial role. It was he who had travelled to Paris and secured Clemenceau's pledge to support Christian aspirations for a state of their own. His death marked the end of an era. The Western and secular Lebanon that was to emerge, centred around Beirut, half of whose population was Muslim, was far from the Christian refuge envisaged by the Maronite church.

Hawayik's death triggered an intense struggle for succession among the Maronite bishops. The conflict that had begun in the 1920s between the two most prominent candidates, Bishop Abdallah al-Khuri, the patriarchal vicar, and Ignatius Mubarak, the Bishop of Beirut, intensified in 1930. In June that year Bishop Khuri, with the help of Gianini, Père Chanteur and Père Bonneville, had secretly attempted to win papal support for his appointment as Hawayik's coadjutor, arguing that the latter was no longer capable of fulfilling his duties. His nomination would have greatly improved his chances of succeeding Hawayik. But Bishop Khuri's opponents, led by Bishops Mubarak and Awad, hastened to inform Hawayik of this ploy. They also began a campaign in the Lebanese press accusing him of seeking to undermine Hawayik's position and the Maronite church's autonomy, and of promoting Italian interests in the Levant. This incident generated much resentment on both sides, leading to a bitter confrontation after Hawayik's death.[76]

The process of electing a Maronite patriarch had been defined in 1736; it involved the convening of the synod comprising all the bishops, in seclusion, on the ninth day after the death of the patriarch. Election required the votes of two-thirds of the synod which, in 1932, consisted of 15 bishops. If no decision was reached, the patriarch would be appointed by the pope. From 2 January until 8 January, the bishops repeatedly cast their ballots, but neither Mubarak nor Khuri received the required majority. In an attempt to break the deadlock, Mubarak and Awad proposed that their ally, Bishop Antoine Pierre Arida of Tripoli, be a compromise candidate, but he was rejected by Bishop Khuri. On the advice of Gianini, Bishop Khuri also turned down the candidacy of his own ally, Bishop Feghali, who could have secured the necessary ten votes, since he was confident that if the deadlock continued, he himself would be appointed by the Pope. On the sixth night, however, Mubarak intercepted a letter from Gianini to the hesitant Feghali, pressing him to continue to vote for Khuri. This was considered undue interference in the electoral process and Mubarak threatened to publish it in the press. Bishop Khuri was consequently forced to withdraw his candidacy, and the following day Arida was elected unanimously as the patriarch of the Maronite church.[77]

Arida's election, however, did not end the rivalry within the church, which remained sharply divided throughout the 1930s and 1940s. The new patriarch failed to impose his authority on his bishops and his community. He was 70 years old at the time of his election and lacked any experience in politics or international affairs. He was impulsive, outspoken and arrogant, traits that often caused friction with his bishops, the Vatican and the High Commission. His election was also opposed by the influential Jesuits of Beirut, who supported Bishop Khuri and continued to undermine Arida's authority. His naivete was exploited by his opponents in the church as well as by politicians and his own relatives. The fact that he came from an affluent family with large investments in the north of Lebanon led to allegations that he was taking advantage of his position to further his family's interests. Arida's involvement in economic issues would bring him into direct confrontation with de Martel.[78]

Bishop Khuri, who had spent years preparing himself for the position of patriarch, was embittered by Arida's election, and became even more resentful when he was replaced as patriarchal vicar by his opponent, Bishop Paul Aql. He would subsequently strive to regain his position in the church and in Lebanese politics, and to take revenge on his opponents—Arida, Mubarak, Aql and Awad—often with much success. His relations with the High Commission were tense, for he suspected that French representatives in Beirut and in the Vatican had played a part in his defeat.[79]

The rivalry in the church had profound repercussions on Lebanese politics. With the Maronite clergy and politicians divided and engaged in endless intrigues, the community was left without leadership or a clear sense of direction. The situation also deeply influenced the presidential elections. Since 1926, the church had repeatedly asked the High Commission for a Maronite president, but it failed to agree on a candidate, the patriarch and his bishops having become directly involved in political intrigue. The defeat of his cousin, who had played an important role in rallying support for his election, considerably weakened Beshara al-Khuri's candidacy. Although Arida, Mubarak, Awad and Aql sought to enhance their influence by ensuring the election of a Maronite president, they also aimed to prevent Beshara al-Khuri from occupying the position. They backed the candidacy of Habib al-Sa'ad, who was related to both Arida and Awad. With the race open, various politicians tried to promote themselves as compromise candidates and win the support of the new patriarch and his bishops. For his part, Bishop Khuri was determined to prevent the election of Sa'ad, his major rival on Mount Lebanon. Indeed, when the latter's chances appeared to have improved, he met secretly with Jisr and expressed his willingness to support him against Sa'ad. Assisted by Gianini and Père Chanteur, he stepped up his efforts to promote his cousin. Yet, as Bishop Khuri's position weakened, Gianini and Chanteur began to promote candidates from other Catholic communities. Even the threat of a Muslim president could not convince the Maronite clergy and politicians to close ranks. After failing to come to an agreement with his bishops on a candidate, Patriarch Arida conceded in despair to a French official: 'We are to blame.'[80]

Jisr's decision to present his candidacy for the presidency transformed the struggle within the Maronite community into an open confrontation between Christians and Muslims and highlighted the question of Lebanon's national identity, already being publicly debated in anticipation of Syria's independence. The rift was to lead to a constitutional crisis with long-term repercussions on Lebanon's political structure. There is no need to present the numerous intrigues, secret deals, and political manoeuvres that accompanied the elections; it is sufficient to examine the key processes and the stands of Ponsot and the main candidates—Jisr, Khuri and Eddé.

The Lebanese constitution did not preclude a Muslim president and Jisr, an ambitious politician, had on various occasions expressed his desire to stand for election. He had realized, however, that such a move would force him into confrontation with Maronite religious and political figures, as well as with the High Commission. With Beshara al-Khuri poised to win— backed by a powerful coalition of Ponsot, Dabbas, and Bishop Khuri—Jisr, a sophisticated and cunning politician, had also declared his support for him. But as the elections drew near and rivalry between the Maronite contenders intensified, Khuri's election no longer seemed certain, and Jisr began to promote his own candidacy.[81]

Jisr's decision to participate in the elections was considerably influenced by the support he received from his former opponent, Emile Eddé. After the collapse of his government, Eddé had severed ties with Jisr, holding him responsible for his defeat. Returning from Paris, where Ponsot had foiled his efforts to undermine Khuri's candidacy and further his own, Eddé decided to 'play the Muslim card', as his opponent had in 1930. He thus began to encourage Jisr to run for the presidency and was soon joined by Sa'ad and Tabet. It was a clever move, for Eddé was confident that the Quai d'Orsay would not permit a Muslim to be president. Jisr was conscious of Eddé's motives, but still believed he stood a chance if rivalry between the Maronite contestants continued. He was determined to stand, assuming that even if he was not elected, he would thereby strengthen his position and prestige.[82]

The 1932 census was an important factor in Jisr's strategy: he expected it to demonstrate that the Muslims comprised a majority, and thus reinforce his bid for the presidency. The census issue had initially been raised by Jisr and other Muslim deputies. After boycotting it ten years before, they hoped a new census would strengthen their demands for equality both in the political and administrative systems and in allocation of resources. The High Commission had seen no reason to oppose this initiative and therefore, on 27 May 1931, the Lebanese parliament had adopted a resolution to carry out a census. Christian deputies, especially Maronites, who soon realized the possible implications for the presidential elections and the representation of their communities in public life, sought to delay the census or prevent it altogether. Nevertheless, when parliament convened for the winter session, Jisr and other Muslim deputies urged the government to make immediate preparations to conduct the census. On 24 November, despite opposition from Christian deputies, parliament passed a law authorizing the census to take place on Sunday, 31 January 1932.[83]

Jisr's candidacy practically transformed the census into a referendum on whether Lebanon was a mainly Christian state, or had become a Christian–Muslim state in which a Muslim could hold the highest position. Jisr and his supporters began a campaign to encourage the Muslims to participate, while Shiites and Druze were asked to count themselves as 'Muslim'. The census was fraught with irregularities as Muslims and Christians attempted to influence the results. Identity cards were issued to thousands of Syrian workers and Alawites who had settled in the Tripoli and Akkar regions, and rumours spread that the census would serve as a basis for taxation and enlistment into the army. For their part, the Christians, especially the Maronites, insisted on the inclusion of thousands of emigrants. The High Commission's decision to acquiesce in part of their requests, and the granting of Lebanese nationality to thousands of Armenian immigrants, aroused the Muslims' ire. Although the final results revealed that the Christians comprised only 52 per cent of the population, they were greeted with relief by the High Commission and the Christian communities.[84]

The census increased tension between Christians and Muslims, in particular between Maronites and Sunnis, as each community accused the other of fraud. The Maronite church demanded that the number of Muslims should be readjusted by subtracting thousands of Muslims it alleged were Syrian, while the Muslims claimed that the inclusion of emigrants and Armenians had distorted the results and denied them a majority. They also argued that since the Muslims now comprised half the population, Lebanon could no longer be considered a Christian state. Throughout February the recriminations continued. Arida's visit to Beirut to mark his election as patriarch turned into a political demonstration, with thousands of Maronites cheering his appearance in the streets. The high commissioner, President Dabbas and Premier Adib honoured him at elaborate ceremonies, in sharp contrast to the muted reaction to Tawfik Khalid's appointment as Mufti of the Lebanese Republic a few months earlier. In speeches and interviews, the outspoken Arida and Mubarak criticized Jisr for vying for the presidency: since their community was the largest, the position should be held by a Maronite. Muslim newspapers hurled insults at the two religious leaders and significantly, their attacks were secretly encouraged by Bishop Khuri.[85]

The controversy over the census galvanized the Muslim community and considerably enhanced Jisr's popularity; the masses now regarded him as the defender of their interests. They eagerly awaited his election as president, hoping thereby to counter the Maronite claim that Lebanon was a Christian state; Jisr and his followers encouraged them, calling for Muslims to unite and support his candidacy. Yet prominent Sunni politicians in Beirut and Tripoli, as well as pan-Arabist groups and the religious establishment, opposed Jisr. They regarded him as a collaborator with the French and a politician whose only ambition was to promote his own interests, and resented his increased popularity. Although they refrained from openly opposing his candidacy, for fear of being accused of dividing the community and jeopardizing the election of a Muslim president, they tacitly cooperated with Christian politicians against him. Karameh, who was competing with Jisr for influence in Tripoli, even asked Arida to press Ponsot to intervene in order to prevent Jisr's election. Sulh also opposed Jisr's bid for the presidency, fearing it would drive the Maronites to turn to France, while the Syrian government was concerned that his candidacy would undermine its territorial claims over Tripoli and the Beqa valley.[86]

As the pressure of public opinion rose, Sunni politicians were compelled to modify their stand and demonstrate support for Jisr. At a meeting held in Salam's home and attended by Jisr, it was decided to endorse the latter's candidacy and if he withdrew, to back Sa'ad. Despite his doubts, Sulh, who met secretly with Jisr, also declared support for him. In March and April the Muslim deputies came under strong public pressure to vote for Jisr. In Syria, hope was expressed that election of a Muslim president in Lebanon would help to achieve Syrian unity. The Syrian government, however, continued to be extremely cautious for fear of possible repercussions on its negotiations with France.[87]

Jisr's candidacy became the focus of the presidential campaign, with the four leading Maronite contestants—Khuri, Sa'ad, Eddé and Tabet—using it to block each other. His presence made any agreement on an outside compromise candidate impossible. Jisr believed that if divisions in the Maronite camp continued, he could win the election, with the backing of the Muslim deputies; he therefore manipulated his four Maronite rivals by playing one against the other. His main concern, however, was to convince the High Commission not to veto his candidacy. At meetings with Ponsot and other French officials, he reiterated his loyalty to France, pointed to his supporters among both Christian and Muslim deputies, and asked that parliament be allowed to exercise its power and elect the next president. According to the constitution, he stressed, every Lebanese citizen had the right to present his candidacy. To a French official he commented ironically, that it appeared France was seeking to establish a 'foyer chrétien' with a Muslim majority, and a parliamentary system that did not allow this majority to affirm itself.[88]

Well aware of Ponsot's criticism of the political and administrative systems, Jisr presented him with a detailed plan for revising the constitution and cutting the administration and budget; he pledged to resign if he failed to implement reform within two years. His promise to reduce administrative costs from 70 to 30 per cent of the budget was viewed with cynicism by Ponsot, however, following Jisr's role in enlarging the inefficient and costly administration in the first place. By the end of April, Jisr had to a large extent lost his freedom of action. He was imprisoned by his own success in winning the support of the Muslim public; he could not renounce his candidacy without losing his standing in the community. Nevertheless, he offered to withdraw his candidacy if Khuri, Eddé, Sa'ad and Tabet withdrew theirs; but neither Ponsot nor Khuri was willing to consider this option.[89]

Jisr's decision to run for the presidency undermined Khuri's majority in parliament. Muslim deputies transferred their support to Jisr; neither bribes offered by Pharaon and Chiha, nor discreet attempts by the High Commission, could persuade them to change their stand. They were willing to vote for Khuri only if Jisr gave up his candidacy. Moreover, Namur and Khazin, who had previously backed Khuri, now promoted themselves as compromise candidates and frequently met with Jisr in an attempt to win his endorsement. Although his position had been considerably weakened, Khuri refused to withdraw his candidacy and continued to try to force Jisr out of the race. Until the last minute he hoped that he could, with Ponsot's assistance, convince Jisr to change his mind, thus ensuring his own election.[90]

Eddé was pleased to see his tactics succeed and his opponent lose ground. Referring to Khuri and his own support for Jisr, he told a French official: 'This despicable person represents for me all the corruption of the regime. To make sure that he does not return to power, I have made an alliance with the person who caused my downfall and with whom, for that reason, I haven't spoken for the last two years.'[91] Although he declared himself reluctant to return to politics, he continued to promote his candidacy, assuming that his chances of election had improved. He offered the premiership to Jisr in return for his backing, but Jisr declined. He also attempted to bypass Ponsot's opposition to his candidacy by appealing directly to the French prime minister, Tardieu, with the help of his friends in Paris. His time was limited, however; the French government was in the midst of an election campaign in which it faced a strong challenge from the left. As the French elections drew nearer Eddé began to suspect that Ponsot and Khuri were intentionally prolonging the crisis in order to use a possible change in government to ensure the latter's election. He was therefore determined to force Ponsot's hand.[92]

Ponsot played a controversial role in the elections by becoming directly involved in the political intrigue. He had expected that Khuri, with the support of the majority of the deputies, would be elected, despite vociferous opposition outside parliament. He had assumed, like many Lebanese politicians, that Jisr's declaration of his intention to run was merely a tactical move intended to strengthen his position vis-à-vis Khuri and enhance his prestige in his own community. He therefore remained in Damascus to supervise the parliamentary elections there. On 9 April, however, after being informed that Jisr insisted on maintaining his candidacy, he hastened to Beirut. Although he was anxious to return to Damascus, where a new Syrian president was being elected and a government formed, Ponsot remained there for a month in an attempt to solve the crisis. The French government clearly could not allow a Muslim president in Lebanon. Jisr's election would antagonize the Maronites and increase the danger of an open Christian–Muslim confrontation. It might also undermine the French pursuit of a treaty with Syria. Indeed, Ponsot repeatedly warned the Quai d'Orsay that the Lebanese crisis was reinforcing the intransigence of radical elements in the National Bloc who opposed a treaty with France. Sulh's meetings with Jisr heightened Ponsot's suspicion of the Syrian nationalists' involvement. He was also concerned that election of a Muslim president would underscore the vulnerability of French interests in Lebanon and thus harden opposition by the French military establishment to a treaty. The French government was in the midst of elections and feared criticism in the National Assembly, the press and the French public. It thus urged Ponsot to prevent Jisr's election and bring an immediate end to the crisis. But Ponsot could not veto Jisr's candidacy merely because he was a Muslim: such a step might generate a strong reaction from the Muslims not only in Lebanon and Syria, but in North Africa. A possible solution, raised by Jisr and accepted by Eddé, would have been for him and the four prominent Maronites jointly to retract their candidacies. Yet Ponsot, who still believed that Jisr would back down and leave the way open for Khuri, rejected this proposal and continued to urge Jisr to withdraw from the race, a move that clearly prolonged the crisis. But as the deadlock persisted and the pressure from Eddé intensified, Ponsot began to consider another solution—postponing the elections and dissolving parliament.[93]

Ponsot and other officials in the High Commission had long been critical of Lebanon's political and administrative systems. They accused Lebanese politicians of promoting their own rather than national interests, with nepotism, clientelism and corruption rife in the administration. Aware of the need to cut expenses following the recession, Ponsot deplored the generous salaries that the president, ministers and deputies had allocated to themselves. He also objected to the pension law passed by parliament in 1931, which would have placed a heavy burden on the budget. The presidential crisis had strengthened his conviction that the 1926 constitution needed to be revised again. He had already begun to advocate reducing the power of parliament and increasing that of the president. Yet despite appeals by some Lebanese leaders and French officials, Ponsot had refused to restore direct French administration, fearing criticism from Paris, Geneva and Damascus. His experience in Lebanese politics had convinced him that any attempt to reimpose French control over Lebanon would be met with opposition, not only from the Muslims, but also from the Christians. Indeed, he had supported Khuri, in the hope that he would carry out the political, administrative and financial reforms he had promised. As opposition to Khuri grew, however, Ponsot decided to implement the necessary reforms himself.[94]

Whether Ponsot had prolonged the crisis to ensure Khuri's election, justify suspending the constitution, or merely because of his failure to make a decision, Eddé forced him to make a move. On 20 April, Eddé hastened to present Jisr with a telegram he had just received from his brother in Paris, informing him that the Quai d'Orsay would soon instruct the High Commission to support his own election. The news caused great concern among the other candidates, as well as in the High Commission. Jisr, who had already agreed to Ponsot's request to postpone the elections, was now anxious they be held before the Quai d'Orsay could veto his candidacy. He therefore urged his followers to petition the French government in support of his bid for the presidency. Ponsot, taken unawares by Eddé's move, sent angry dispatches to the Quai d'Orsay requesting clarification and repeating his warnings that Eddé's election would antagonize the Muslims of Lebanon and Syria. Tardieu's answer—that he trusted Ponsot's judgment on the matter, yet still recommended Eddé—did little to calm his fears. When he received a telegram from the Quai d'Orsay at the beginning of May, informing him that a French politician and journalist, known for his close ties with Eddé, planned to arrive in Lebanon to cover the elections, Ponsot was driven to action. He immediately sent messages to Paris pressing for postponement of the elections and dissolution of parliament, arguing that it was the only way to prevent election of a Muslim president. Moreover, he claimed, this would afford the High Commission time to reform Lebanon's political system and make the necessary budget cuts. On 9 May, with the approval of the French government, Ponsot suspended the constitution, dissolved the government and parliament and appointed Dabbas as head of state.[95]

The aborted presidential campaign and suspension of the constitution had a long-term effect on Lebanon's political structure and inter-sectarian relations, as well as on France's Lebanese policy. It was clear that the constitution granted by de Jouvenel six years earlier had failed to provide the country with a stable political system or efficient administration. The new political institutions, especially the parliament and the government, had indeed brought together members of the various communities and regions which now formed Greater Lebanon, but they had become, to a large extent, a marketplace where deals were made between politicians who sought to promote personal, familial and sectarian interests. The political climate which had emerged in these institutions was not conducive to promoting values of national interest. The presidential elections revealed this sad reality: for more than two years politicians had been turning the Lebanese state into a playground where they fought unrelentingly to indulge their ambitions. Could the high commissioner, who had allowed the situation to deteriorate to this point, accomplish the task of introducing the necessary reforms?

Suspension of the constitution left open the question of the presidency, with many scores yet to be settled. After the first two rounds had ended in stalemate, the struggle between Eddé and Khuri continued to dominate

Lebanon's political life. Khuri was bitterly disappointed with the suspension of the constitution. His political influence had been weakened by the dissolution of parliament, and his public image tarnished. Determined to restore his power, clear his name and take revenge, he collaborated closely with his cousin, Bishop Khuri, and his friends, Chiha, Pharaon and Taqla. He had learned a lesson from his defeat and would now continually seek to improve his relations with the Muslim community. Disillusioned with France's policy in Lebanon, he would attack the mandate, taking on the role of champion of the constitution and the parliamentary system.

Eddé greeted the dissolution of parliament, his rival's power base, with much satisfaction. He pressed for a thorough investigation of corruption and embezzlement of public funds under the previous regime, and demanded that those responsible be brought to justice. He continued to advocate radical reform of the political system and administration, and offered to cooperate with the High Commission to implement them. Eddé also realized the importance of gaining the support of Muslim political figures, and would strive to better his ties with them. The presidential crisis strengthened his belief in the need to sever regions with large Muslim populations from Lebanon. While in Paris in August 1932, he addressed a letter to the Quai d'Orsay pointing out the inherent danger in maintaining the 1920 borders. He again proposed detaching Tripoli, the Beqa valley and south Lebanon in order to ensure Lebanon's Christian character and its role as a stronghold for the French in the region.[96]

The presidential crisis also reinforced doubts about Christian–Muslim coexistence. It deepened Christian fears of an Arab Muslim take-over, and underscored their dependence on France, whose intervention had prevented the election of a Muslim president. Many Muslims regarded suspension of the constitution as proof that they could never achieve equality in a Lebanese Christian state, and they continued to seek their detachment from Lebanon. Yet there were others in both communities who reached different conclusions. Some Christians considered Jisr's candidacy as evidence that the Muslims could eventually be integrated into Lebanon. They held the French responsible for exacerbating tension between the two communities in order to promote their own interests. Such views were shared by a growing number of Muslims. Encouraged by their community's prominent role in the elections, they believed they could change Lebanon's national identity from within and subsequently achieve full equality.[97]

Ponsot intended to maintain the provisional government for six months, during which he would defuse tensions, balance the budget, reform the administration and prepare a plan for revising the constitution. This plan was to be discussed and approved during his forthcoming visit to Paris, so he could present it in Geneva in November and counter any criticism from the Permanent Mandates Commission. Following publication of the decrees, Ponsot began to mobilize public support for his move. He and his delegates met with religious and political leaders and members of the financial and commercial sectors, declaring that suspension of the constitution was only a temporary measure, until the political and economic crises were solved. They pointed out that dissolution of the costly political institutions and reduction of the large and inefficient administration would enable considerable savings to be made, easing the tax burden and diverting resources to rejuvenate the economy. The reformed political and administrative systems would be efficient and compatible with the size and needs of the population, they promised. The High Commission also initiated a press campaign to gain the support of the Lebanese public.[98]

The welcome that greeted the French decision attested to public resentment of the previous regime. The newspapers reflected these feelings, calling for a thorough investigation of abuses and the embezzlement of government funds. It was hoped that within a short time the tax burden would be eased and the economy revive. Many Lebanese politicians were deeply angered, however, regarding the suspension of the constitution as an affront to their country's independence and sovereignty. Some even suspected it had been a French ploy to ensure continued control over Lebanon after Syria gained independence. Ministers and deputies, having lost their positions as well as an important source of income, initiated a campaign to restore the constitution. They admitted that the political and administrative systems had been in need of revision, but argued that parliament should have been allowed to initiate the reforms, as it had in 1927 and 1929. Such an argument, however, ignored the fact, which Ponsot was quick to point out, that the deputies would have opposed any attempt to limit their power or reduce their numbers. Khuri and his circle questioned whether Ponsot would succeed in introducing reform, lower taxes or rejuvenate the economy. *al-Ahrar* gave voice to these doubts:

> The high commissioner's explanation for the decrees does not justify suspension of the constitution. That is why we hasten to protest against the harm done to parliamentary life. The reforms called for by the people could have been implemented within the framework of the constitution. There was no need to resort to such drastic measures which put the constitution at the mercy of the high commissioner. Lebanon has always asked for a republican parliamentary system and it won't give up now. We cannot claim that the country truly prospered under the constitutional system, and we criticized the governments which followed the proclamation of the Republic. But that does not imply that the parliamentary system is responsible for all the mistakes made. The ones to blame

are those who governed against the spirit of the constitution. Since 1926 we have been warning the deputies that sooner or later their abuses would provoke a reaction. The result was not slow in coming. The people will no doubt regret the suspension of the constitution. They will learn that these calamities are not the fault of the constitution itself, but of those who caused waste and who ruined it by raising direct and indirect taxes such as customs duties. The constitution has been suspended. But will the people benefit from a tax reduction? Won't they discover for themselves that the money they assume will be saved by the dismissal of the deputies and ministers, will be embezzled and won't lead to any reduction in taxes?[99]

While the dissolution of parliament and the government received widespread support, Ponsot's decision to retain Dabbas as head of the provisional administration provoked sharp criticism in Beirut and Paris. After six years as president, Dabbas was constitutionally ineligible to remain in office. His appointment as 'head of state' was considered further proof of France's disregard of the constitution. Critics questioned the wisdom of appointing him, when he had been responsible for many of the abuses of the previous governments. They doubted that he would be capable of helping reform the political system and cleansing the administration, or bringing those responsible to justice. His former colleagues, led by Khuri, accused him of betraying his oath to defend the constitution. His appointment was also opposed by the Maronite church, particularly by Bishop Mubarak. Only after Ponsot stressed that it was for a six-month period, did Arida and Mubarak acquiesce. Dabbas' conduct did not make Ponsot's task any easier. He had his own ambitions and objected to the period of his appointment being defined. In the months that followed, he came increasingly under attack from the opposition and would prove to be a weak point in the provisional administration.[100]

The suspension of the constitution and the appointment of Dabbas turned out to be one of the rare occasions when Ponsot succeeded in overriding the Quai d'Orsay. Exploited the fact that the government was in the midst of elections, he presented his recommendations at the last minute as the only solution to the crisis, thereby leaving the Quai d'Orsay no alternative but to approve them. But his move was not fully endorsed by his superiors, and soon came under fire from members of the National Assembly, who claimed it contradicted the treaties policy that France had undertaken to implement two years before. Fears were also voiced that Ponsot's move would undermine negotiations with Syria and expose France to attacks from the Permanent Mandates Commission. As criticism mounted, the Quai d'Orsay pressed Ponsot to justify his decision, and Prime

Minister Tardieu took the unusual step of reproaching him for retaining Dabbas.[101]

In his dispatches to Paris, Ponsot repeatedly described the possible effect of Jisr's election both on French policy and Christian–Muslim relations in Lebanon, stressing that he had had no choice but to take immediate action, since the 'house was already on fire'. As for Dabbas' appointment, he argued, it had been intended to convey the impression of continuity, in order to limit criticism in the Permanent Mandates Commission. He claimed that Dabbas had retained his neutrality in the elections, that he was acceptable to the Muslims, and that his past experience would facilitate implementation of the necessary reforms. Moreover, the appointment of another candidate might have been regarded as an indication of the High Commission's future preference and thus have generated further tension. Throughout May and June, Ponsot sent the Quai d'Orsay copies of letters and petitions from Lebanese leaders, as well as press cuttings, to demonstrate public support for his decision. But criticism in Paris mounted, particularly after the rise to power of Herriot's leftist government. Ponsot was thus forced to take hasty and more extreme measures to justify his decision, thereby jeopardizing his own plans and antagonizing a large sector of the Lebanese population.[102]

Following instructions from Ponsot, Dabbas and officials in the High Commission immediately embarked upon reforming the financial and administrative systems. The most urgent problem was the deficit in the 1932 budget following the decline in revenue from direct taxes and customs duties. Decrees were issued drastically cutting the salaries of former ministers, deputies and government employees. Hundreds of civil servants and gendarmes were laid off, government and municipal departments reorganized, and the pension law radically revised. Within a month, expenses dropped by 12 per cent. But efforts to lower taxes and divert resources to reviving the economy were largely unsuccessful. In fact, with the deepening recession, the High Commission had to seek new sources of revenue. Its decision in June to double customs duties undermined the transit trade and sparked an outcry from commercial and financial sectors in Beirut. The silk and olive oil industries continued to decline, while the price of tobacco slumped due to over-production. The living standards of thousands of peasants and laborers deteriorated. To the large number of unemployed were added thousands more, who had either been dismissed from the administration or laid off after public projects had been cancelled or cut back.[103]

In May, Ponsot asked Antoine Privat-Aubouard, the French delegate, to draw up a plan for reforming the political system. The latter prepared a plan for revision of the constitution, effectively transforming Lebanon into a presidential republic. According to this scheme, the government was to be abolished and the executive power to be held by the president, assisted by a minister of state and a council of directors. As long as the mandate was in force, the president would be nominated by the high commissioner for a three-year term, either according to his choice or from a list of three candidates submitted to him by parliament. The minister of state would be appointed by the president and would be responsible only to him. The power of parliament would be considerably reduced: it would comprise 32 deputies instead of 45, and the existing two-stage vote would be replaced by direct suffrage. Privat-Aubouard also recommended that the electoral district be based on the qada rather than the larger sanjak, and that the 'list' system be abolished.[104]

This plan was modified, however, following opposition from Dabbas, who played an important role in the following month in preparing the revised constitution. He too supported a presidential system, but insisted that the principle of proportional sectarian representation be retained and that the number of deputies be reduced to 17. The president would have the power to nominate an additional five deputies. Dabbas accepted direct suffrage, but suggested adopting a system from the former Belgian constitution, whereby certain sectors, based on education and income, would have more than one vote. He advocated maintaining the 'list' system, and proposed that the sanjak continue to serve as the electoral district, arguing that under the system of qadas, it would be difficult to attain equal representation of the various communities and regions. He recommended that the French government appoint the president for a three-year term, but proposed that this term of office be renewable indefinitely; he wished to benefit from this arrangement himself. Thus, instead of considering reforms to serve Lebanon's national interest, the High Commission and a self-centred president sought to use the situation to further their own goals. The idea of a parliament with greatly reduced power, and a president nominated by the high commissioner and responsible to him, rather than the Lebanese people, inevitably provoked strong opposition from politicians who continued to demand restoration of the 1926 constitution.[105]

Ponsot's controversial decision to conduct an inquiry into the corruption and embezzlement under the previous governments, and to bring those responsible to justice, caused an outcry from politicians and bureaucrats alike. It is doubtful that he had originally intended to carry out such an investigation. He knew it would generate opposition from former ministers and deputies and some of his own staff, along with criticism from Paris for having allowed the situation to deteriorate. But after a campaign by opponents of the previous regime, and demands from Paris to justify suspending the constitution, he had no choice but to proceed. He nevertheless preferred that the investigation be carried out by the Lebanese authorities themselves. During the following months, under pressure from Eddé, the press and the public, Dabbas went ahead with cleansing the political and administrative systems. Special judges appointed to conduct the inquiries soon discovered instances of widespread corruption, nepotism and embezzlement of public funds. With the newspapers exposing new scandals daily, Dabbas was forced to continue the investigation despite mounting opposition from former ministers, deputies and officials. Newspapers claimed that only low- and medium-ranking civil servants had been charged, while those who had actually been responsible were going free. His former colleagues accused him of ruining their reputations, and attacked him in the press. Maronites complained that members of their community had been singled out, while Muslims alleged that the inquiries had been focused primarily on departments headed by Muslim ministers and officials. Following an inquiry into the Ministry of Finance, which had been headed by Subhi Haidar, his family initiated a campaign for incorporation of the Beqa valley into Syria. In an incident on 22 December 1932, Alfred Tabet, one of the judges, was threatened by Sami al-Sulh and Riad al-Sulh, and later attacked, after Mumtaz al-Sulh, Sami al-Sulh's brother, who was serving in the Justice Department, had came under investigation. Anxious to prevent an open confrontation with the influential Sulh family, the High Commission and Dabbas refrained from taking further measures against the Sulh family.[106]

On the eve of Ponsot's return from Paris, tension rose in Beirut as its leaders awaited the end of Dabbas' temporary regime and the high commissioner's plans for reforming the political system. Before proceeding to Damascus, however, Ponsot announced that since he was occupied with the negotiations with Syria, any decision on Lebanon's problems would have to be postponed; Dabbas would continue in his position for the meantime. The Quai d'Orsay, which clearly feared that restoring the constitution and holding elections would be exploited by the National Bloc to intervene on the coast, had chosen to conclude a treaty with Syria before dealing with Lebanon. This decision, however, ignored the mounting impatience of many Lebanese with French policy in their country, and their distaste for Dabbas' administration. The Lebanese politicians' disappointment turned to anger when, at the beginning of December, details of Ponsot's declaration to the Permanent Mandates Commission reached Beirut. His distinction between a 'treaty' and a 'mandate' zone increased suspicion that France indeed intended to continue its direct control over Lebanon after granting independence to Syria. Moreover, his remarks on the failure of Lebanon's political institutions and the shortcomings of its leaders were regarded as an affront to national pride. Thus, upon his return to Beirut at the beginning of January 1933,

Ponsot faced an organized campaign demanding the dismissal of Dabbas and restoration of the constitution. The campaign was led by an unexpected coalition of Riad al-Sulh, Beshara al-Khuri and Bishops Khuri and Mubarak. In the six months that followed, Lebanon underwent a serious political crisis that undermined French policy both in Lebanon and Syria, and marked a new phase in the cooperation between Sulh and Khuri.[107]

In June 1932, Ibrahim Haidar had proposed to Riad al-Sulh that they exploit the anger of many Lebanese politicians at suspension of the constitution to promote Lebanon's union with Syria. Sulh declined, stressing that although the ministers and deputies resented Ponsot's decision, it had public support. The time to act, he said, would be in another few months, when the Lebanese public was disappointed with the promised reforms and tax reductions. Indeed, the growing opposition to Ponsot's measures and to Dabbas' provisional regime gave Sulh and the National Bloc a unique opportunity to lure Lebanese Christian politicians into cooperating with the Arab nationalists against the French mandate. Sulh's arguments—that the Christians should hasten to reach agreement with the National Bloc and the Arab Muslims in Lebanon before Syria received independence—now fell on more sympathetic ears. Some political figures were even ready to consider his request to participate in the pan-Arab congress, scheduled to convene in Geneva in September to mark Iraq's admission to the League of Nations. By the end of December, Sulh had succeeded in establishing close ties with Yusuf al-Khazin, Bishop Khuri's ally, and Beshara al-Khuri, as well as—through the mediation of Aziz al-Hashem—with Bishop Mubarak.[108]

Despite his opposition to suspension of the constitution and the appointment of Dabbas, Khuri was careful not to confront Ponsot openly, preferring to wait for the restoration of political life. But he grew angry and disillusioned when he was not only held responsible for the failure of the former regime, but publicly accused of corruption. He blamed Dabbas for collaborating with the High Commission to undermine the constitution and for allowing Eddé to ruin his reputation. As Ponsot's intention to maintain Dabbas' provisional administration became apparent, and details of the proposed constitutional revision emerged, Khuri decided to take action. Together with his close allies, he exploited the rising opposition to Dabbas to conduct a campaign to depose him. He believed that Ponsot, anxious to prevent a new crisis in Lebanon that might jeopardize his negotiations with the Syrian government, would be forced to abandon Dabbas, as he had abandoned Eddé. As in 1930, Khuri coordinated his efforts with Riad al-Sulh, aiming to enlist the latter's support in pressuring Ponsot. Sulh, however, had his own agenda—to rally the Christians, especially the Maronites, against the French mandate.[109]

The two politicians, however, could not have won over the Christian public without the involvement of the Maronite church. They found a powerful and willing ally in Bishop Khuri who, throughout 1932, had continued his struggle against Patriarch Arida and Bishops Awad and Aql. He and Gianini had succeeded in convincing the Vatican to withhold from Arida the 'paleum', the formal approval granted by the Pope to every new Maronite patriarch. This delay caused Arida considerable embarrassment and weakened his position in his own community as well as in the church, where he was unable to appoint new bishops. A campaign was conducted against Arida in the press, accusing him of plotting to depose Gianini and of supporting the suspension of the constitution in return for financial benefits for members of his family. Encouraged by Bishop Khuri, at the end of December a Maronite crowd demonstrated against the patriarch in Bkerki. Khuri also exploited Mubarak's increasing resentment of Arida after Mubarak had lost much of his influence to Awad and Aql. Bishops Khuri and Mubarak now coordinated their attacks on Arida, accusing him of failure to defend the political and economic interests of the Maronite community.[110]

Outspoken and naive, a brilliant orator, committed to Lebanon's independence and Maronite rights, Bishop Ignatius Mubarak was especially suited to lead the opposition to Dabbas. His hostility to the latter had become legendary. Twice, in 1926 and again in 1929, he had sought to prevent Dabbas' election as president. On 10 May 1932, he met Ponsot to protest Dabbas' reappointment; only after the high commissioner assured him that it was merely for six months, did he agree to withdraw his objection. In a memorandum to Ponsot after suspension of the constitution, he noted that the inhabitants of Mount Lebanon were satisfied with the dissolution of the previous regime, but warned that the people were impatient for economic and political reform. He appealed for an easing of the tax burden, reorganization of the municipal system and the gendarmerie, and government investment in irrigation projects and road construction. As opposition to Dabbas and the High Commission mounted, Mubarak became an address for complaints from former ministers and deputies, families whose sons had been imprisoned or dismissed from their positions, inhabitants of the Mountain who continued to protest against high taxes, and Beirut merchants who opposed the rise in customs duties. Yet Dabbas rejected his attempts to intervene on their behalf. In October Mubarak travelled to Damascus to inform Ponsot of the deteriorating economic conditions and the growing public unrest, and pressed for Dabbas' immediate removal. Upon Ponsot's return from Geneva, he conferred with him again, reiterating his demand for the High Commission's immediate intervention.[111]

Faced with an organized campaign against Dabbas by politicians and the press, and worried that Dabbas might succumb and resign, Ponsot remained in Beirut for over a month, mediating between the president and his opponents. At the beginning of February 1933, hoping he had convinced the opposition to wait until he had concluded his negotiations with the Syrian government, he left for Damascus. But Ponsot had miscalculated.[112]

On 9 February, at a ceremony in St George's Cathedral to mark St Marun's Day, Bishop Mubarak launched a bitter attack on Dabbas, charging him with responsibility for Lebanon's plight, and called for the French government to dismiss him. Muslim dignitaries, including Riad al-Sulh, were present, and Mubarak thanked the 'Muslim brothers' for participating; 'St Marun was the father not only of the Maronites, but of Lebanon and all its communities,' he told them. But the attempt to stage the ceremony as a demonstration of Christian–Muslim coexistence backfired when Sulh reminded the audience that St Marun had originally come from Hama, testifying to the fact that Syria and Lebanon were one country. He pointed to growing Christian–Muslim cooperation and declared that while he opposed any foreign authority, he was proud of being an Arab Lebanese, and that Syrian unity would be attained through agreement—which the Muslims sought to achieve without violence. His remarks provoked an immediate response from Mubarak, who declared that he was striving for 'Lebanese' and not 'Syrian unity', and proposed 'leaving Lebanon under the shade of its cedars, and Syria with its own treaty'.[113]

Mubarak's declaration signalled the beginning of an organized campaign against Dabbas which soon escalated into attacks on the High Commission. In numerous speeches and interviews Mubarak criticized Dabbas' mishandling of the economy, demanded the formation of a parliamentary committee to examine revision of the constitution, and threatened to follow Hawayik's example and travel to Paris to present his views to the French government. He refused to invite Dabbas to the consular mass, which led to Ponsot's subsequent boycott of the ceremony. This provoked an angry response from Mubarak, who directed his criticism against the High Commission, accusing its officials of incompetence and responsibility for the deteriorating economic situation. He complained that French concessionary companies were exploiting Lebanese resources, charged that increased customs duties were hindering Beirut's ability to compete with Haifa in the transit trade, and demanded that Lebanon's share in the revenue from the Common Interests be increased.[114]

Sulh was quick to exploit Mubarak's attacks on Dabbas and the High Commission. At the beginning of March the drivers' syndicate went on strike to protest taxes on cars and petrol, bringing Beirut to a standstill. The action was tacitly encouraged by Sulh and publicly supported by Mubarak. At the initiative of the Beirut Chamber of Commerce, presided over by Omar Da'uq, all the Chambers of Commerce in the mandated territories convened in protest against the taxes and customs duties. Prominent Sunni leaders called for transforming Beirut into an autonomous town with a free trade zone, while in Tripoli the campaign for union with Syria intensified.[115]

The deteriorating situation in Lebanon was exploited by the National Bloc which tried to pressure Ponsot into either linking Lebanon politically and economically with Syria, or revising its borders. Syrian leaders voiced satisfaction with Mubarak's criticism of the French mandate, and delegations from Damascus and Aleppo travelled to Beirut to express their support. Syrian newspapers commented that events in Lebanon underlined the failure both of France's attempt to divide Syria, and the sectarian concept on which Lebanon was based. One newspaper noted that 'the declaration of Lebanon's independence in extended borders, and its establishment as a republic was merely a clerico-imperialist political plot which, although it had lasted twelve years, could not last much longer.'[116] At a meeting in Aleppo, Faris al-Khuri, a prominent Christian leader, pointed to the Maronites' disillusionment with France, and appealed to the Christians in Syria to support the National Bloc's struggle for independence and unity.[117]

Mubarak's campaign against Dabbas and the High Commission's economic policy caught Ponsot at a sensitive stage in the negotiations with the Syrian government, when French policy was already under attack from militants in the National Bloc and from the Permanent Mandates Commission. Ponsot was certain that Sulh and the Syrian nationalists were exploiting Mubarak's naivete, along with the opposition of some Maronite politicians to Dabbas, to undermine France's status in Lebanon. He was anxious to prevent a public confrontation with Mubarak, but all his efforts to convince the latter, through messengers, including Eddé and Sa'ad, that his attacks were only serving Syria's interests, were to no avail. Encouraged by the High Commission, some Lebanese newspapers criticized Mubarak, claiming that his proposals for improving the economy were impractical. At the same time Ponsot discreetly asked Arida to pressure his bishop to end cooperation with Sulh and cease his attacks on Dabbas and the High Commission.[118]

Arida had failed to provide spiritual and temporal leadership for his divided church and community, and the popular support for Mubarak's campaign underscored this fact. The Patriarch now warned Mubarak that his attacks on Dabbas were undermining relations between the church and the

High Commission, and threatened him with sanctions. At the same time, he assured Dabbas that the Maronite church disapproved of Mubarak's criticism. He also appealed to the drivers to end their strike, since the government had accepted their demands. At this point his position improved to some extent when the Pope—strongly influenced by French claims that the delay in granting the 'paleum' was weakening the position of the Maronites and other Catholic Christian communities in Syria—finally approved Arida's election. Nevertheless, Bishops Khuri and Mubarak continued to denounce his lack of leadership. At a meeting in Diman they requested that he refrain from making any decisions on political issues without prior consultation with all of his bishops. They also demanded that he press Ponsot to oust Dabbas, reduce taxes and ratify the long-awaited Personal Law for the Christian communities. Arida's decision to appoint a clergyman from his home town of Bshari as the new Bishop of Tripoli was exploited by Bishop Khuri to encourage the inhabitants of Zgharta to stage a demonstration in Bkerki.[119] His opponents also conducted a campaign against him in the press: Muslim newspapers condemned him for referring to Lebanon as a 'foyer chrétien'. Meanwhile, a letter he had sent to a Jewish leader, criticizing Nazi Germany's attitude toward the Jews, was leaked to the press, giving rise to charges that he supported the settlement in Lebanon of Jewish refugees from Germany. Bishop Mubarak exploited this incident to denounce him publicly as the 'Patriarch of the Jews'.[120] Bishop Khuri's plans to travel to Paris and Rome added to Arida's concern; he refused to give him letters of recommendation and informed Ponsot that it was merely a private visit.

Efforts by some of his bishops to undermine his authority drove Arida to reassert his leadership and to demonstrate concern for his community's interests. In addition to reduced taxes and ratification of the Personal Law, he demanded that Ponsot restore constitutional life, increase Lebanon's share in the revenue from customs duties and invest in such national projects as irrigation and electricity. His immediate concern, however, was for Ponsot to end Dabbas' provisional regime before departing for Paris, and appoint Habib al-Sa'ad as president. Such a move would undoubtedly have bolstered Arida's prestige and struck at the ambitions of Bishop Khuri and his cousin. But Ponsot, who was shortly to end his term of office, was reluctant to make any decision on Lebanon's future president. He nevertheless raised the possibility of Sa'ad's appointment with Mubarak. The latter was quick to publicize it and thereby effectively undermined the patriarch's initiative. This incident, along with Mubarak's continued public attacks on his leadership, led Arida to impose sanctions on the rebellious bishop and threaten to excommunicate him.[121]

Six months after launching their campaign, Bishop Khuri, Beshara al-Khuri and Riad al-Sulh considered it a success. Bishop Khuri could have felt only satisfaction at Arida's diminishing authority and at seeing Mubarak—who had played a major role in thwarting his election as patriarch—humiliated and losing his influence. He would continue his attacks on Bishops Aql and Awad and his attempts to depose Patriarch Arida. Beshara al-Khuri, on the other hand, had achieved only some of his goals—he had failed to oust Dabbas and restore the constitution. Moreover, faced with the threat of Sa'ad's nomination, he was forced to limit his attacks on Dabbas. He had prevented Ponsot from imposing the revised constitution, but at the same time had undermined efforts to reform the administration. Indeed, on 1 September 1933, the anniversary of Lebanon's independence, Dabbas granted a general amnesty to all those accused of corruption and abuse of their positions. Although Khuri's relations with the Arab Muslim leaders had improved, they continued to distrust him, suspecting that he was only seeking to promote his own political ambitions. His cooperation with Sulh, however, jeopardized his efforts to secure the presidency, for he no longer had the trust of the High Commission.[122]

The success of the campaign strengthened Riad al-Sulh's conviction that severing Maronite ties to France, rather than Lebanon's political union with Syria, should be the immediate Arab nationalist goal. 'When this is achieved', he told Aziz al-Hashem, 'political union will follow.'[123] At the beginning of 1935, he would again successfully manipulate Maronite dissatisfaction with the political and economic situation to provoke a confrontation between Patriarch Arida and de Martel.

During the deliberations that took place in Paris before de Martel assumed office, it was recognized that Lebanon had become more vulnerable to subversion by the National Bloc and the pan-Arab Muslim elements on the coast; it was imperative for France to stabilize the political and economic situation. In the face of continuing division among the Christians, and increasing Muslim unity, officials in the Quai d'Orsay, the High Commission and the military establishment were advising tighter control over the country. A memorandum to the foreign minister noted that France was morally and legally bound to pursue a policy in Lebanon similar to that in Syria, namely of granting independence through a treaty. But Lebanon was 'a conglomerate of minorities' lacking national solidarity: although its population was more advanced than that of Syria or Iraq, it was less ready for self-government. There was, the memorandum argued, a contradiction between the goal for which Lebanon had been established—as a refuge for Christian minorities—and its present demography: half its population was Muslim. It warned, however, that severing predominantly Muslim areas from Lebanon, as advocated by some Christian leaders, would enable Syria to undermine Lebanon's international status and return it to its pre-war borders within a Syrian state. The memorandum particularly opposed the annexation of Tripoli to Syria, pointing to France's strategic interests in the city. It analysed the failure of the political system established in 1926 and queried whether it might not be preferable to control Lebanon directly, rather than through an intermediary. Although such a solution might be welcomed by many Lebanese, it cautioned that France would be exposed to criticism in Geneva and Damascus. It therefore recommended an undefined transitional period during which political life would gradually be restored and the constitution revised in accordance with Ponsot's proposals. The memorandum concluded that France still envisaged a treaty with Lebanon but, in view of personal and sectarian rivalry, it would have to retain authority over the country during that period. In maintaining its presence in Lebanon, France would follow the example of Britain, which had granted independence to Iraq while keeping Palestine under tight control.[124]

Such views, which prevailed in the Quai d'Orsay and the High Commission, were not shared by Joseph Paul-Boncour, the new prime minister and foreign minister, who continued to advocate a more liberal policy. Before his departure for Beirut, de Martel was therefore instructed to implement Ponsot's proposed political reforms and restore constitutional life in Lebanon. But it soon emerged that the new high commissioner's interpretation of these instructions was far more rigid than the prime minister intended.[125]

Fully aware of the complexity of Lebanese society and its sensitivity to symbols of national sovereignty, Ponsot had chosen to govern through an intermediary. The inexperienced de Martel, however, saw no need to conceal the reality of French control, and was determined to pursue a policy he considered in his country's best interests. He was also keen to demonstrate both to his superiors and the population of the mandated territories that he was a man of action who, unlike his predecessor, could take decisions and implement them unhesitatingly. Shortly after his arrival, he informed the French advisers to the local governments that their primary obligation was to carry out his instructions rather than assist the governments that were paying their salaries. He would have pursued an even firmer policy—he remarked to his senior staff—if not for the insistence of Paris and the need to placate the Permanent Mandates Commission. Cynical and tactless, de Martel had no patience for the intrigues of the politicians and clergy, whom he largely despised. He believed that politics in the mandated territories were the realm of a small group motivated by personal ambition, while the general public was indifferent, aspiring primarily to raise its standard of living. His rather frustrating initial encounter with Syrian and Lebanese politicians led him to devote most of the next two years to improving the economy, thus neglecting the deteriorating political situation.[126]

After his attempt to impose a treaty on the Syrian government had been undermined by the National Bloc, de Martel first turned his attention to solving Lebanon's political problems. His Lebanese policy was considerably influenced by his confrontation with the Syrian parliament, and by his fear of Syrian nationalist subversion in Lebanon. On 1 December 1933, he sent Paul-Boncour a plan for revising the constitution, which, although based on Ponsot's recommendations, reflected de Martel's authoritarian character and his determination to exercise direct control. He proposed that the president be nominated by the high commissioner for a period of three years; that the government be replaced with a secretary of state appointed by and responsible to the president, and assisted by a council comprising general directors; that the number of deputies be reduced to 25, of whom 18 would be elected and 7 nominated; and that the power of parliament be limited in legislative and financial matters. He saw no need to follow de Jouvenel's example of submitting the revised constitution for parliament's approval, arguing that holding parliamentary elections and then seeking legislative assent to the revisions, would give the National Bloc an opportunity to stir up trouble in Lebanon. He therefore suggested promulgating the revised constitution himself, declaring that in any case the mandatory power held the ultimate authority. De Martel went so far as to claim that it might be more useful, in light of the extensive modifications, to issue a new constitution altogether. Demonstrating his lack of sensitivity, he suggested abolishing a number of provisions, including Article 52, granting the president the power to negotiate and ratify treaties; Article 91, providing for Lebanon to request admission to the League of Nations; and Articles 92 and 94, which concerned Lebanon's external relations. Although they may not have been of practical use under the mandate, all these had symbolic value, affirming Lebanon's international status. His most controversial proposal, however, was to replace the vaguely-worded articles of the 1926 constitution pertaining to the authority of the high commissioner with new provisions defining more precisely his power over both the president and the parliament. They included appointment of the president and the right to revise the constitution and dissolve parliament, and obliged the president and the parliament to seek the high commissioner's sanction for revision of the constitution. De Martel argued that these amendments were necessary to enable the high commissioner to confront crises without having to resort to such extreme measures as suspending the constitution, as Ponsot had done in May 1932.[127]

Although de Martel claimed that his proposals had been inspired by his predecessor's recommendations and were in accordance with the instructions he had received in Paris, they in fact constituted a return to the tough policy of the early years of the mandate. While Ponsot had sought to strengthen the authority of the president vis-à-vis parliament, de Martel aimed to turn the president into a powerless puppet of the High Commission, and reduce parliament to a mere rubber stamp. De Martel's plans were clearly not compatible with the policy that Paul-Boncour sought to implement. The latter was willing to allow the high commissioner to proceed with his proposals, but only as a temporary measure and after certain adjustments. Reforms that proved successful would be integrated into the 1926 constitution, with the approval of the Lebanese parliament. The prime minister authorized de Martel to appoint a president and hold elections for parliament in accordance with the revised electoral law he had proposed, and to announce when he intended to proceed with revision of the 1926 constitution. But he opposed abolition of articles that pertained to Lebanon's exercise of its foreign policy, arguing that this would be interpreted, both at home and abroad, as a sign of French intentions to retain control over Lebanon and renounce its treaties policy. He was particularly critical of de Martel's attempt to define the power of the high commissioner within the framework of the constitution, maintaining that it would transform the president into 'nothing but an instrument of the high commissioner'.[128]

While de Martel was engaged in exchanges with the Quai d'Orsay on amending the constitution, tension in Lebanon was rising. The arrival of a new high commissioner was always accompanied by a period of uncertainty, when High Commission staff, politicians and religious leaders alike were wary of his intentions and sought his support. This time the disquiet was especially discernible, since it was generally believed that France was about to make a crucial decision on its Syrian and Lebanese policies. For the Sunnis of Lebanon, who nervously witnessed de Martel's confrontation with the National Bloc over ratification of the treaty, the last two months of 1933 were particularly tense. Their leaders were under pressure both from the Syrian nationalists and their own community to demonstrate their support for Syrian unity. Yet they were hoping to persuade de Martel to adopt a more balanced policy toward the Muslims, rather than follow his predecessor's example of cultivating close ties with the Maronite church. The prominent Sunni families of Beirut—the Bayhums, the Salams and the Daʿuqs—who had lost ground to the Sulhs, the mufti and the nationalist youth groups, were seeking to restore their influence. All these factors played a part in the decision to convene the 'Conference of the Coast' in November 1933, marking a new stage in the attempts of the Sunni leadership to redefine its stand toward Syrian unity and the Lebanese state.[129]

The declared goal of the Conference of the Coast was to demonstrate Lebanese Muslim support for the National Bloc's struggle against de Martel's attempts to impose a treaty on Syria without first ensuring Syrian unity. But prominent Sunni leaders, particularly those in Beirut, had their own agenda. They sought to use the conference to persuade de Martel and the Lebanese Christians to grant them equality in the Lebanese state. This became obvious at a meeting held at Omar Bayhum's home on the eve of the conference and attended by Salim Ali Salam, Omar Da'uq and Abd al-Hamid Karameh, to discuss the demands to be presented to the high commissioner. While Karameh suggested that they press for Syrian unity, particularly the annexation of Tripoli to Syria, Da'uq proposed that they limit their requests to improving economic conditions and granting Muslims an equal share in the political and administrative systems. The participants also debated whom to support as president. Da'uq argued that because it was impossible to ensure the presidency for a Muslim, they should back Najib Abu Suan's candidacy. Bayhum and Salam, on the other hand, preferred Beshara al-Khuri, whom they described as 'less harmful', and whose election would enable the Sunnis to request the premiership.[130]

The Conference of the Coast took place on 16 November in Salam's home, and drew scores of delegates from Beirut, Tripoli, Sidon, Tyre, Marjayun and Jabal Amil. Participants repeatedly raised the issue of the political, economic, cultural and religious inequality of the Muslims of Lebanon, and called for annexation to Syria. At the close of the conference, Salam sent a memorandum to de Martel on behalf of the 'people of the coast annexed to Mount Lebanon', reiterating demands for Syrian unity. A large portion of the memorandum, however, was dedicated to a detailed description of the inequality between the Muslims on the coast and the Christians of Mount Lebanon. The signatories pointed out that according to the recent census, Muslims comprised half of Lebanon's population, and argued that although the annexed territories contributed 80 per cent of the revenue in the budget, most of the country's resources were invested in the Mountain. They accused the Lebanese government of neglecting the economy and raising taxes and customs duties to finance an inefficient administration, thereby undermining trade and giving Palestine an advantage. They complained that the Muslims had no control over their wakf, and that unlike the Christians, their religious leaders were appointed by the state. The memorandum ended with a call for Syrian unity. Faced with pressure from the National Bloc, the bourgeois Sunni leaders of Beirut clearly had no choice but to join in supporting union with Syria. Moreover, they assumed that such a demand would help them force the high commissioner and the Christians to grant them their fair share. Thus a different conclusion could have been drawn from the memorandum: inequality was driving the Muslims to demand annexation to Syria; equality could have persuaded them to recognize the Lebanese state.[131]

The Franco–Syrian negotiations, the renewal of Syrian demands for Tripoli and the Beqa valley, and the organized campaign of the Muslims on the coast for union with Syria caused much apprehension among the Christians, particularly in the Maronite church. Arida and his bishops were anxious to ensure the new high commissioner's support for the Christians, as well as his recognition of the church's unique role in Lebanon. Shortly after his arrival, Arida met de Martel and requested not only that Lebanon's territorial integrity be maintained, but that its border with the Alawite region be revised to include villages which, he insisted, had originally been Lebanese. He reiterated the demands he had raised with Ponsot in the summer: nomination of a Maronite president, namely Sa'ad; reforms in the administration; reduction of taxes and customs duties; an increase of Lebanon's share in the revenue from those duties; and formation of a small Lebanese army based on compulsory military service. Although de Martel accorded Arida a cordial reception and repeated his government's support for the Maronites and for Lebanese independence and territorial integrity, he refrained from making any commitments.[132]

Throughout November, the Lebanese politicians waited impatiently for de Martel to conclude his negotiations with the Syrian government and turn to their country's political and economic problems. They paid close attention to his conflict with the National Bloc over ratification of the Franco–Syrian Treaty, knowing well that it would have immediate repercussions on Lebanon. There was much press speculation on the end of Dabbas' provisional regime, the election of a president and reforms in the political system. At the beginning of December, newspapers in Beirut published details—leaked by Dabbas—of de Martel's proposals for revising the constitution. Their publication caused much anxiety among the Lebanese politicians. Some criticized the proposed amendments, but the majority remained silent; with elections looming, few were willing to risk a confrontation with the high commissioner, who had just demonstrated to the Syrians his impatience with opposition. Candidates for the presidency and the parliament hastened to the High Commission to reaffirm their loyalty and impress French officials with their qualifications or denounce their opponents. They were joined by Maronite bishops promoting their own candidates. Although no official decisions had yet been made on the date, the number of deputies, or their distribution among the various communities and regions, Lebanon found itself in the midst of an intense election campaign.[133]

With the news that the next president was to be appointed by the high commissioner, the candidates immediately sought de Martel's support. Some French officials attempted to promote Najib Abu Suan as a compromise candidate, but the main struggle took place between Sa'ad and Khuri, while Eddé remained somewhat on the sidelines.[134] The Maronite church once again became an arena for contention between the two candidates. On publication of de Martel's plans, Arida sent him an urgent message requesting that no decisions be made before consulting him. In other messages, the patriarch and Bishop Aql asked for Sa'ad to be appointed as president before the parliamentary elections. Arida also objected to basing the distribution of deputies on the 1932 census, alleging that the results had been rigged by the Muslims.[135]

The prospect of their sworn enemy being nominated as president and supervising the parliamentary elections drove Bishop Khuri and Beshara al-Khuri to act immediately. The former proposed that the president be selected from another Christian community, thus enabling a Maronite to hold the more influential position of secretary of state. If the community insisted on a Maronite president, Khuri was willing to support Khalil Abu Lama or even Emile Eddé. Following veiled threats, the Sûreté Générale warned that if Sa'ad was appointed, Bishop Khuri's 'religious-political clan' would seek to undermine his administration by cooperating with Riad al-Sulh and Omar Bayhum. Beshara al-Khuri and his close circle of friends and relatives stepped up their efforts to promote his candidacy against Sa'ad. Attempts were also made to gain the backing of the Sunni leaders in Beirut and, indeed, a Muslim delegation met with Privat-Aubouard to express its support for Khuri.[136]

Toward the middle of December, rumours that Khuri had made certain commitments to the Muslims roused concern in the High Commission. At a meeting with a French official on 13 December, Khuri denied having made such pledges. He described himself as a 'good Christian', stressing that unlike other Christian politicians (alluding to Eddé), he had fought to the end against Jisr's candidacy. He spoke of the 'true nature' of his relationship with the Muslims, emphasizing that they appreciated his lack of fanaticism. Although the Muslims supported Syrian unity, he believed that as 'real life was stronger than principles' they would eventually realize that their best interests lay in cooperating with a Christian president, namely himself. He claimed he was a friend of France, noted the various positions he had held, and expressed confidence that he would not be excluded from the presidency. Maintaining that his candidacy was supported by the Maronite clergy, particularly Bishop Mubarak, Khuri described Sa'ad as the representative of a past era, too old to control a Muslim secretary of state effectively.[137]

De Martel's initial exposure to the complexities of Lebanese politics reinforced his belief that Lebanon was not yet ready for independence. He was soon to discover that all his actions were being closely monitored in Paris and that Lebanese politicians could out-manoeuvre him through their access to French politicians. In private correspondence with his associates in the Quai d'Orsay de Martel repeatedly complained that while he had received no clear instructions on his negotiations with the Syrian government, in Lebanon his every move was being scrutinized. Indeed, he was placed in a most embarrassing situation as Dabbas and other Lebanese politicians appealed directly to Paris in an attempt to thwart his initiative to revise the constitution. Details of his plans and Paul-Boncour's reaction to them were being leaked from the Quai d'Orsay and widely publicized in Beirut. He continually warned his superiors that the delay in approving his proposals was undermining his position, with the National Bloc exploiting tension in Lebanon to enlist the support of both Christians and Muslims. De Martel also provided details of the Conference of the Coast and of nationalist activities among the Shiites and the Druze, as well as of Riad al-Sulh's renewed efforts to win the support of Christian religious leaders, particularly that of Mubarak. Yet despite all his warnings, Paul-Boncour refused to approve his recommendations before subjecting them to a thorough examination.[138]

When Paul-Boncour continued to delay his approval, de Martel suggested that he immediately travel to Paris to present his views to the government. On 29 December, almost a month after de Martel's proposals had been forwarded to the Quai d'Orsay, Paul-Boncour finally authorized the high commissioner to partially restore constitutional life in Lebanon. On 2 January 1934, de Martel published two decrees in which he accepted Dabbas' resignation, announced parliamentary elections based on the revised electoral law, and appointed Habib al-Sa'ad as president for a one-year term, to begin after the elections. In the interim period, Privat-Aubouard, the delegate to Lebanon, was to head the administration and supervise the elections.[139]

While Lebanon's unique political problems undoubtedly posed an exceptionally forbidding task, France was morally and legally obliged to help Lebanon overcome the shortcomings of its political system and guide it toward independence. Yet 21 months after Ponsot had dissolved the parliament and government and undertaken to revise the constitution, the temporary administration he had established was replaced by yet another provisional regime. With a new and inexperienced high commissioner and conservative officials in Paris and Beirut who continued to insist on direct control, Paul-Boncour authorized temporary measures to be taken once again—assuming that de Martel would introduce the necessary reforms later with the cooperation of an elected parliament. De Martel, however, preferred the convenience of direct administration. Lebanon thus lost the opportunity to revise its flawed constitution. In addition, de Martel's decrees created complex political and legal difficulties: Lebanon now had two constitutions—one provisional and one permanent. Furthermore, the politicians, led by Khuri and his supporters, would succeed in presenting the 1926 constitution as an answer to Lebanon's political and economic ills, almost erasing its shortcomings from public memory. Finally, the struggle that developed between the politicians and the high commissioner over restoration of the constitution further destabilized Lebanon's political life and precluded an open debate on practical solutions to the country's problems.

By nominating Habib al-Sa'ad, de Martel had sought to defuse the political tension fuelled by the rivalry between Eddé and Khuri, to placate Arida, and to use the 75-year-old president as a tool to control the administration. In fact, Sa'ad's appointment added to political instability, as Bishop Khuri and Beshara al-Khuri embarked upon a campaign to discredit him and his supporters in the Maronite church. He was portrayed in the press as an old, corrupt politician whose views and methods had been shaped during the Ottoman period and who was therefore unable to address the issues of a modern state and the needs of its younger generation. He was also depicted as a weak president, unable to defend either Maronite interests against a Muslim secretary of state, or Lebanon's national interests against the High Commission. Indeed, his appointment deepened resentment of the French mandate and exposed de Martel to criticism from the opposition, which held him responsible for the country's plight. It also left open the question of the presidency; the confrontation between Eddé and Khuri would continue to dominate Lebanese politics for the next two years.[140]

The parliament elected in January 1934 marked a watershed in Lebanese politics. For the first three years, with its limited power and short sessions, it made only a minor contribution to solving Lebanon's pressing social and economic problems. Yet in this parliament, Khuri's Constitutional Bloc emerged as an organized political force that would lead the campaign for restoration of the 1926 constitution. The new political generation that had just been elected would, together with the established leaders, shape Lebanon's politics after independence.

The elections were held according to the revised electoral law, with proportional sectarian representation, the division into five electoral districts and the 'list' system maintained. The electoral colleges, which had given rise to widespread corruption in the 1929 elections were supplanted by direct universal suffrage, which was considered more democratic. To limit the number of deputies, a ratio of 50,000 voters to one deputy was adopted, instead of the previous 20,000 to one. The new parliament therefore comprised 18 elected deputies of whom ten were Christian and eight Muslim, and seven appointed deputies—four Christians and three Muslims. This move was criticized by the politicians, who now had to compete for a smaller number of seats. Opposition was also voiced by the Muslims, who claimed they were under-represented, as well as by the Maronites of the Beqa valley and south Lebanon, who were no longer represented in parliament. Although division of the deputies among the various sects was officially based on the 1932 census, the High Commission increased the number of Christian deputies by readjusting the results in favour of the Christians, and by allocating a seat to the Armenian community in Beirut.[141]

After his failure with the Syrian parliament, de Martel was determined to secure election of a Lebanese parliament amenable to his policies, especially regarding his intended constitutional revisions. He was also anxious to prevent the National Bloc and its supporters on the coast from boycotting the elections or transforming them into a demonstration of anti-French sentiment. Unlike Ponsot, de Martel lacked close links with the established politicians and sought to use the elections to promote young, educated candidates who could assist him in modernizing the country. Yet after Paul-Boncour had expressed his desire for the democratic process to be respected, de Martel had to be cautious in his intervention in the vote. The High Commission, however, was able to considerably influence the results: in addition to nominating seven deputies it decided in which district legislatures would be appointed, and in which elected. Arab nationalist politicians like Riad al-Sulh received messages discouraging them from presenting their candidacies, while French officials actually took part in preparing the electoral lists in the various districts. The High Commission also exploited the rivalry among Sunni politicians over parliamentary seats in order to sow discord among them. In Tripoli, competition was encouraged between the Bisars and the Muqadams, and in Beirut, between the Sulhs and the Bayhums.[142]

The election period was limited to three weeks in order to reduce tension and instability, and politicians were given only five days to register their candidacies. By 11 January, 141 candidates had registered, of whom 123 eventually participated in the elections. The campaign was short but intense. The difficulties of the candidates, who had rapidly to adjust to the revised electoral law, were compounded by the fact that voting took place during a severe snowstorm and shortly after the end of Ramadan. Nevertheless, 55 per cent of the voters went to the polls, compared with 37 per cent in the previous elections. As in 1929, the main struggle was not between communities, but between clans within the same community who were competing for access to the state institutions. Politicians invested large sums of money in buying votes and paying newspapers and journalists to promote their candidacies. Wealthy Lebanese and foreign concessionaires were far more involved than in previous elections in financing the candidates' campaigns. Religious leaders, especially from the Maronite church, again intervened in the elections. Although Khuri was told that he would be appointed in any case, he and his allies ran a very well organized campaign. Under the slogan 'Youth for Lebanon', he promoted various young politicians, and offered political and financial backing to those who undertook to support him.[143]

On Mount Lebanon, there was fierce competition between Habib al-Sa'ad and Bishops Awad and Aql on one side, and Beshara al-Khuri and Bishops Khuri, Mubarak and Bustani on the other. Sa'ad promoted the candidacy of his nephew, Rashid, in the Shuf, against Auguste Adib's nephew, Camille Nimr Chamoun, whose brother Josef served as director of Public Works. Chamoun was also supported by Khuri. In the Kisrawan, Farid al-Khazin competed with his cousin, Yusuf al-Khazin. The phenomenon of sons inheriting their father's seats in parliament thus became an established practice: Hamid Faranjieh succeeded his father in Zghorta, while in Akkar, following French intervention, Muhammad Abd al-Razak replaced his father, Abud Abd al-Razak. In Tripoli, the High Commission thwarted Jisr's attempt to promote his brother's candidacy and tacitly cooperated with Karameh in backing Amin Muqadam. A bitter struggle took place in the Beqa between the Haidars, who had been losing their influence among the Shiites, and their rivals from the north, the Hamadehs. Ibrahim Haidar had little chance against the list comprising Sabri Hamadeh and Elias Toma Sakaf, a wealthy Greek Catholic from Zahleh. In an attempt to sway the French, the Haidars intensified their contacts with the National Bloc, and some of them openly expressed support for annexation of the Beqa valley to Syria. In south Lebanon, a conflict arose among prominent Shiite families when the High Commission chose to support Najib Usayran and Fadel al-Fadel against Yusuf al-Zein and Latif al-As'ad.[144]

In Beirut, an intense campaign was conducted for the Sunni and minority seats. The Sunni community became sharply divided as the well-established families—the Bayhums, Da'uqs and Salams—were challenged on the one hand by the Sulhs, and on the other by the Mufti Tawfik Khalid. The latter, with support from the Fakhuri and Tiarah families, was attempting to follow the example of Hajj Amin al-Husaini in Palestine by building up a political power base of his own. At the same time, the older generation of politicians—including Omar Da'uq, Omar Bayhum, Husain al-Ahdab and Salim Ali Salam—had to allow younger newcomers like Ahmad Da'uq, Muhammad Ali Bayhum, Khair al-Din al-Ahdab and Abdallah al-Yafi to play a more prominent role. A particularly bitter conflict arose between Ahdab—who was supported by his uncle, Husain al-Ahdab, Omar Bayhum and Henri Pharaon—and Yafi, backed by Riad al-Sulh and the Mufti. Sulh had initially sought to incite a Muslim boycott of the elections, but as French officials hinted they might consider the appointment of his cousin Sami to the position of secretary of state, he changed his tactics and decided to cooperate with the High Commission. At a meeting with de Martel, Sulh stressed the need for France to adopt a more balanced policy toward Maronites and Muslims and asked the High Commission not to oppose Yafi's candidacy. De Martel, who received Sulh cordially, chose him to inform the Sunni community of his resolve to appoint a Sunni as secretary of state. The meeting consequently fuelled rumours that the High Commission had decided to nominate Sami al-Sulh to that position and intended to back the Sulhs against their rivals, the Bayhums.[145] Yet neither Yafi nor Ahdab secured the necessary absolute majority in the first round. Under pressure from the latter's camp, and with the High Commission tacitly supporting his rival, Yafi withdrew his candidacy. Another fierce competition took place between Ayub Tabet and Abdallah Ishaq, an Armenian Catholic, for the minority seat. Ishaq was endorsed by a French concessionaire which he served as legal counsel. With the support of the High Commission, Emile Eddé and Christian communities in Beirut that objected to two Armenians representing the city in parliament, Ayub Tabet was eventually elected.[146]

On 28 January, Privat-Aubouard nominated seven deputies, including Eddé, Khuri, Sa'ad and Dabbas. De Martel's decision to appoint Dabbas, who had declared his intention to withdraw from political life and move to Paris, was taken primarily to ensure that he remained in Beirut under de Martel's close supervision. The veteran Khalid Chihab was chosen to represent the Sunnis. There was disagreement in the High Commission over the Greek Catholic seat in Beirut. Some French officials, with whom Henri Pharaon had cultivated close ties, favoured him. With his wealth and standing, they argued, it was preferable to have him in parliament, where he could be better controlled; moreover, in light of his bitter rivalry with Eddé, he could be used, if the need arose, to undermine the latter. His appointment, however, was opposed by Privat-Aubouard, Eddé's close friend, who succeeded in nominating Gabriel Khabaz, the owner of *L'Orient*. As before, the Haidars' threat to support Syrian unity was effective; de Martel not only appointed Ibrahim Haidar as a deputy, but retained his cousin, Subhi Haidar, as a director in the Lebanese administration.[147]

Only nine of the deputies had served in the previous parliament, while prominent figures such as Jisr, Namur, Dammus and Georges Tabet lost their seats. The new legislature was filled with younger politicians who, for the most part, were better educated than their predecessors. Deputies such as Camille Chamoun (aged 34) Hamid Faranjieh (26) Majid Arslan (28) Farid al-Khazin (41) and Khair al-Din al-Ahdab (45) would play an important role in Lebanese politics. The elections had been a major success for Khuri, and nearly half of the deputies allied themselves with him. Eddé, on the other hand, had the backing of only three. On 29 January, Abdallah Bayhum, president of the Chamber of Commerce in Beirut, was appointed secretary of state. The following day, parliament convened an extraordinary session at which it elected Dabbas as speaker and passed a resolution declaring Lebanon's loyalty to France and willingness to cooperate with de Martel. But the high commissioner, who had conveyed his satisfaction to Paris at the election of a pro-French parliament, was soon to discover that the Lebanese parliament was no easier to control than its counterpart in Syria.[148]

Shortly after the Lebanese elections, de Martel left for Paris to re-evaluate French policy in the mandated territories with officials in the Quai d'Orsay. His experiences since arriving in Beirut in October must have been disappointing. He had been unable to impose a treaty on the Syrian parliament, and his attempts to revise the Lebanese constitution had been overruled by Paul-Boncour. On the eve of his departure, he sent the Quai d'Orsay a memorandum analysing the causes of the failure of France's treaties policy, and proposed revising it in light of the events in Syria in November. He argued that French efforts after 1926 to emulate Britain's Iraqi policy in Syria had been unsuccessful because, in contrast to Britain, France had no qualified 'interlocutors' with whom it could reach a concrete agreement. Attempts to conclude a treaty with the Syrian nationalists in 1926, 1928 and 1933 had failed because of the very nature of Arab nationalism, which precluded any compromise. The nationalists in Syria were demanding complete French withdrawal, total independence and Syrian and Arab unity. But France could not give in to such demands without undermining its own interests in the Levant or its international obligation to defend the minorities there—which had, after all, been the *raison d'être* for its mandate. Indeed, the point of departure for the mandate had been the protection of a Christian Lebanon, represented by the Maronite community. De Martel described the leaders of the National Bloc as excitable, unruly agitators, consumed with ambition, greedy for power and money and interested only in personal rivalry. They owed their strength only to incitement; inaction, he claimed, was destroying them and rendering them susceptible to the influence of extremists. The pursuit of a treaty in such circumstances was thus impractical and had to be modified to enable France to ensure its vital interests during the 'transitional period'. He therefore suggested reversing the previous policy by delaying negotiations and observing a transitional period, in which the High Commission would have a free hand to prepare the military and strategic infrastructure and secure protection for the minorities before concluding a treaty. During this interval, the duration of which was not defined, he proposed suspending parliamentary sessions in Syria and forming a government that would cooperate closely with the High Commission to solve the pressing economic, financial and administrative problems. Thus, he argued, France should emulate Britain's policy in Egypt rather than Iraq.[149]

Despite his claims to the contrary, de Martel's proposals constituted, if not a departure from his predecessor's policy, at the least a recommendation to freeze it. Moreover, they strengthened the position of those in Paris and Beirut who in any case disapproved of rapid conclusion of a treaty with Syria. After France's draft treaty had been rejected by the National Bloc, and with France no longer under pressure from the Permanent Mandates Commission, the Quai d'Orsay willingly adopted de Martel's proposals; they became the basis of a policy which he implemented throughout the following year. The French governmental crises in January and February, and the replacement of Paul-Boncour by Louis Barthou, undoubtedly facilitated these changes. De Martel's scheme was also supported by the military establishment, since it offered greater freedom of action in preparing the military infrastructure in the mandated territories.[150]

De Martel returned to Beirut in February with renewed confidence, determined to implement the decisions made in Paris. He reorganized the High Commission, appointing new officials and sending some of the staff back to Paris. A 'committee for the study of the defence of the mandated territories' was established, comprising representatives of the High Commission, the army and navy. One of its first decisions was to initiate studies of the utilization of the Beirut port in the event of war, and creation of a surveillance and communications network along the coast. The moderate nationalist Syrian prime minister, Ayubi, was replaced by al-Hasani, and sessions of the Syrian parliament were suspended until November. In May and July, the High Commission published comprehensive plans for rejuvenating the economy of the mandated territories, which included enlarging the port of Beirut and establishing a free-trade zone there, extending the Tripoli–Aleppo railway through Turkey and the Jazira to Mosul, laying a wide-gauge electrified railway track between Beirut and Damascus, improving the road linking Damascus and Palmyra to Baghdad, and enlarging and modernizing the aerodromes in Damascus and Aleppo. Although one major declared goal of these plans was to revive the transit trade and enable Beirut to compete with Haifa, they were undoubtedly intended to serve France's strategic interests by utilizing the budget of the Common Interests. They also sought to boost agriculture: a major project was construction of a dam near Homs to drain the marshes in the Orontes valley and use the reclaimed land for growing crops, mainly cotton.[151]

De Martel's policy in Syria influenced his stand on Lebanon. In December 1933 he had underlined the need for complete synchronization of French policy in Syria and Lebanon. With the Syrian parliament suspended, he was reluctant to give in to the Lebanese deputies' demands to extend their power and restore the constitution. Moreover, Lebanon had become a major arena of confrontation between the High Commission and the National Bloc. The Syrian nationalists were determined to undermine de Martel's economic policy, force him to restore constitutional life and renew treaty negotiations on their own terms. The emphasis on projects with strategic advantages for France intensified their suspicions that France intended unilateral implementation of the military section of the 1933 treaty. The massive French investment in the construction of the Mosul-Tripoli pipeline, enlargement of the port of Beirut, and formation of a special committee to study the defence of the mandated territories, reinforced their fears that France was planning to transform Lebanon into a major base for its military and naval activities in the region. The nationalists therefore increasingly concentrated their efforts in Lebanon on thwarting French policy. Moreover, they had learned from past experience that opposition in Lebanon was particularly effective in pressuring the High Commission. While the French government, the National Assembly and the press tended to ignore their activities in the interior, they reacted immediately when French interests in Lebanon or their traditional ties with the Christians were under threat.[152]

Throughout 1934 and 1935, the National Bloc pursued its efforts to stir up opposition to the mandate in Lebanon, particularly among the Maronites. Well aware of the unbridgeable national and political gap between themselves and the Lebanese Christians, their leaders emphasized economic issues, in particular the need for a joint stand against the exploitation of Syria and Lebanon by French concessionaires. Such views had been voiced in January 1934 by Fakhri al-Barudi, one of the more sophisticated figures in the National Bloc, during a visit to Beirut, when he encouraged local Muslim leaders to allay Christian fears. He himself visited Bkerki in an attempt to gain Arida's support for a common struggle against the foreign colonial companies', particularly the tobacco monopoly. The National Bloc also stepped up its efforts to rally the Sunnis and Shiites of Lebanon, and at a meeting in Homs at the beginning of February, decided to establish branches in Tripoli, Beirut and Jabal Amil.[153]

Barudi's views and National Bloc attempts to gain Maronite support resulted, to a large extent, from the continued efforts of Riad al-Sulh. The elections had left Sulh convinced that he had been deliberately misled by de Martel. He had been led to believe that his cousin, Sami al-Sulh, would be appointed secretary of state and that the High Commission would not oppose his candidate, Abdallah al-Yafi, in the elections. De Martel, however, had nominated Abdallah Bayhum, while Yafi had been defeated by Ahdab, who was backed by Omar Bayhum. Sulh revealed his anger at the National Bloc meeting in Homs, at which—contrary to his long-held views—he supported a resolution by the radicals, headed by Hananu and Atasi, calling for the return of Tripoli and the Beqa valley to Syria. Bitter and vengeful, he was determined to cause as much trouble as possible for the French in Lebanon. In February, with the help of Adel al-Sulh and Aziz al-Hashem, he attempted to persuade Christian politicians to join in establishing a 'Lebanese National Bloc'. He later exploited the grievances of Lebanese politicians and businessmen against the High Commission, and used *al-Nida* to attack de Martel's policy. After agitating against the mandate throughout the year, in June he initiated a petition for Syrian unity. He also stepped up efforts to incite the Shiites of Jabal Amil against the French, declaring that it was time to end the High Commission's effective control of their lives. His efforts culminated in the tobacco monopoly crisis of February-March 1935, one of the major triumphs of his struggle against the French mandate.[154]

By 1934, growing Lebanese disillusionment with the political and economic situation had afforded the opposition ample opportunity to cause trouble for the mandate authorities. The fears of the Beirut merchants and financiers of competition from Haifa came to a head when the British inaugurated the modern port there. Despite competition from Palestine for transit trade, the merchants complained, the High Commission insisted on maintaining high customs duties, which were financing projects that mainly benefitted French strategic and economic interests. Turkey's decision to raise its own customs duties further undermined the export of agricultural and industrial products from Lebanon. And an economic crisis in Egypt following the collapse of cotton prices affected many Lebanese who had made investments and owned property there. An expanding number of young graduates from the universities in Beirut and Damascus joined the thousands of unemployed. With the United States closing its doors to immigrants, and with countries in the region (particularly Iraq and Sudan) giving priority to their own citizens for public sector jobs, large numbers of educated, unemployed young people remained in Lebanon, where they became a source of political agitation. Sunnis and Shiites continued to protest their under-representation in the administration, and the Greek Orthodox now added voices of displeasure at their community's share. The High Commission's grant of a ten-year concession to a company owned by Emile Eddé's brother Farid, to transfer pilgrims to Mecca and Medina, roused hostility among the Muslims, who complained that Christians were now even taking over areas concerning Muslim religious duties. This issue figured prominently in a petition presented by Sunni leaders to de Martel in November. The signatories, including Salam, Omar Bayhum, Ahmad Da'uq and Karameh, maintained that if the Muslims could not practice their religion and safeguard their culture, they would prefer a population exchange, with Muslims emigrating from Lebanon to Syria, while the Christians of Syria would settle in Lebanon. Although the Sunni notables did not seriously intend to carry out their proposal, the fact that they broached the idea testified to the depth of their resentment.[155]

The Shiites of the south, who until then had refrained from actively opposing the mandate, began to complain of neglect by the Lebanese government and the High Commission, despite their loyalty to Lebanon and the French mandate. During the deliberations prior to the elections, Commandant Pechkof, head of special services in south Lebanon, had cautioned the High Commission not to be misled by the apparent tranquillity of the Shiites in Jabal Amil, who harboured a deep discontent that might be exploited by the pan-Arabist and pan-Islamic opposition. If an uprising broke out among them, he warned, there could be serious repercussions: the region bordered Palestine, and the army would face extreme difficulty suppressing it, due to the harsh mountainous terrain and lack of roads.[156] Pechkof suggested raising the number of southern Shiite deputies in parliament and increasing investment in road construction. But his ideas were ignored by de Martel who, because of France's strategic interests and the need to counter Syrian nationalist influence, continued to give priority to the Shiites in the Beqa valley. Developing rivalries among the leading feudal families added to the dissatisfaction. The High Commission's decision to back the Usayrans and the Fadels in the elections had antagonized the two most prominent clans—the Zeins and the As'ads. Throughout the year, Yusuf al-Zein issued calls for Shiite equality, intending to enhance his own prestige in the community and undermine that of the deputies Najib Usayran and Fadel al-Fadel, who were now forced to take a more radical stand in defending community rights in order to maintain their own popularity.[157]

Two new Shiite sectors—clerics and students—joined in criticizing the neglect of the south by the High Commission and the Lebanese government. Shiite clerics had seldom been politically active, but they now began to take part in internal community politics and voice their concern for Shiite rights. This phenomenon resulted partly from family rivalries and partly from the political role played by religious leaders of other communities. Moreover, the clerics sought to counter the attempts of the Sunni mufti, Tawfik Khalid, to establish himself as the higher spiritual and religious authority of all the Muslims of Lebanon. They insisted on maintaining their own religious autonomy and repeatedly requested that the High Commission and the Lebanese government recognize a supreme Shiite religious authority, similar to that of the other communities in Lebanon. At the same time, young Shiite students, exposed to pan-Arabist ideas at the American University of Beirut and the University of Damascus, were becoming a source of political agitation. Many of them were unemployed and no longer willing to accept Christian claims that there were not enough Shiites qualified to serve in public positions. During the year, Shiites held numerous meetings and demonstrations demanding a greater share in the administration, appointment of a Shiite imam to a position similar to that of the Sunni Mufti of the Republic, additional government schools in the south, more investment in road construction and irrigation projects, and protection of the tobacco industry. In September, Shiite notables signed a petition calling for the south to be severed from the Lebanese state and converted into an autonomous region under a French governor, giving the Shiites a status similar to that of the Alawites. Their initiative was supported by the National Bloc and pan-Arabists in Lebanon, who were hoping to dismantle the Lebanese state and allow Syria access to the sea through Sidon.[158]

The Sa'ad administration, however, was ill-equipped to solve the economic and social problems or satisfy the demands of the Sunnis and Shiites. The power of President Sa'ad and Secretary of State Bayhum was in any case limited, with real authority being held by the French delegate, Privat-Aubouard. His chief concerns continued to be reduction of administrative costs, balancing the budget and suppression of any criticism of, or opposition to, the High Commission. Sa'ad himself reverted to the familiar ways of nepotism and patronage. The municipal elections in May afforded him ample opportunity to promote his supporters and undermine his opponents. He continually clashed with the deputies, especially Khuri and his associates, who were attacking him in the press. His primary goal was to ensure that de Martel reappointed him as president; he therefore cooperated closely with the High Commission and made efforts to retain Arida's backing.[159]

Sa'ad's appointment as president for one year left open the question of the presidency. The struggle between Eddé and Khuri continued to dominate the political scene, with the parliament and press becoming their main battle ground. The collapse of a building in Beirut, in which 14 people were killed and 20 injured, was exploited by Eddé and Khabbaz to call for the dismissal of Salim Taqla, the administrator of Beirut, who was using his influential position to promote Khuri's interests. Khuri's relentless defence of his friend in parliament was therefore understandable. Both contenders sought to ensure their own election when Sa'ad's term of office ended in January 1935. Khuri, who enjoyed the backing of ten deputies, pressed for the restoration of the 1926 constitution, in order to return to parliament the power to elect the next president. Eddé, supported by only six deputies, hoped that he could gain the High Commission's endorsement of his candidacy with the help of Privat-Aubouard. Indeed, in the summer, the High Commission began promoting Eddé, who now attempted to better his chances by dispelling his anti-Muslim image. He allied himself with Abdallah Bayhum and Khair al-Din al-Ahdab, who helped him improve his relations with the Sunni leadership. His visit to Tripoli on 1 July and his meeting with Karameh, which was arranged by Bayhum, was a significant political manoeuvre, considering the role Karameh had played in forcing Eddé out of office at the beginning of 1930. It drove Sa'ad to pay a similar visit to the north in August which was intended both to placate Arida and to gain Muslim support for his candidacy.[160]

Rumours of de Martel's intention to back his rival led Khuri and his followers to initiate an unprecedented campaign against Eddé in the press. Conscious of the support Eddé enjoyed in the High Commission and in Paris, Khuri aimed to discredit his opponent publicly. A French-language newspaper, *Le Jour*, was founded to counter *L'Orient* and expound Khuri's views to the French-speaking public, particularly officials in the High Commission. First published at the beginning of August, it was edited by Michel Chiha, who had invested a large sum of money in its establishment. One of the first editorials set the tone of the campaign against Eddé by stating:

> Everything demoniacal and foul that this person is hiding will one day be revealed. We write this coolly and with pleasure. But everything will come to an end, including the patience of the Lebanese. As for the French, they will decide if their patience can outlast ours. For years Emile Eddé ... did all he could to demolish his country, to build up his personal fortune on lies, strife and hatred and to antagonize the minorities [namely the Muslims] in order to satisfy a raging and unhealthy ambition. For years he has been behaving like someone possessed. We will exorcise him. But for the moment we will take this arrogant censor by the ears, this hypocrite, rotten with arrogance, and we will rub his nose in his depravities.[161]

In the following months, both *Le Jour* and Arabic newspapers affiliated with Khuri published details of alleged corruption during Eddé's term as prime minister four years previously. In response, *L'Orient* exposed cases of nepotism, corruption and embezzlement of public funds involving Khuri and his colleagues. Bishop Mubarak, who was constantly appealing to de Martel to induce the two rivals to cease their violent attacks in the press, expressed the fears of many Lebanese when he warned that the repeated scandals and accusations of corruption were not only discrediting the politicians and the political system, but were eating away 'like gangrene' at the very fabric of Lebanese society. Nevertheless, the tactics of Khuri and Chiha were effective; in the face of such vociferous opposition, details of which reached Paris, de Martel was no longer willing to support Eddé.[162]

The parliamentary elections and the establishment of *Le Jour* marked an important stage in the transformation of Khuri's clan from a loose coalition of politicians, financed mainly by individual bankers and businessmen who were close Khuri associates, into a well-organized bloc backed by the powerful commercial and financial sectors in Beirut. This group, later known as the Constitutional Bloc, was to play a key role in shaping Lebanon's political and economic character after independence. In the fractured, volatile Lebanese political system, politicians tended to shift from one side to another according to their immediate interests; thus the emerging Bloc, a closely-knit political group with long-range goals, substantial financial resources and easy access to the press, enjoyed a considerable advantage. A growing number of Beirut businessmen and financiers now allied themselves with Khuri in order to ensure access to the political and administrative systems if he were elected. Resenting the privileges of the French concessionary companies, they also backed his call for greater political and economic independence. Many of them believed their business opportunities were being jeopardized by de Martel's economic policy and the weakening of the French franc. These close links with the business sector of Beirut considerably influenced the political and economic ideology of the Constitutional Bloc.[163]

In October 1934, shortly after de Martel's return from Paris, three deputies allied with Khuri—Michel Zakur, Farid al-Khazin and Camille Chamoun—sent the high commissioner a memorandum that can be seen as marking the birth of the Constitutional Bloc. They argued that Lebanon was suffering from a severe 'malaise' caused by the frequent changes in its political system, and that it was in desperate need of the stable regime to which its people aspired. For nine months Lebanon had been undergoing a period of stagnation and its government, headed by men 'chosen at random according to the requirements of the moment', was detached from the nation, ignoring the parliament, and pursuing a policy detrimental to the whole country. The solution to this unhealthy situation, they claimed, was to restore the 1926 constitution, which had been unanimously endorsed by the Lebanese people. If the High Commission deemed it necessary to amend certain articles of the constitution, parliament would be willing, as in the past, to cooperate.[164]

Despite these claims, the Lebanese public was far from unanimous in supporting the restoration of full power to parliament and the government. The bitter confrontation between Eddé and Khuri had increased skepticism of the politicians' ability to govern the country. Although Khuri attempted to portray himself as a defender of the constitution and of Lebanon's national dignity, many distrusted him, believing that he was merely seeking election as president. His close ties with financiers and businessmen in Beirut fuelled this suspicion. Mistrust of politicians and the parliamentary system as a whole was reinforced by events in France following the Stavisky affair. Accounts in the French daily press criticizing deputies and senators, accusing them of corruption and inefficiency and describing them as 'chatterboxes', could hardly have reassured the Lebanese on the integrity of their politicians or political system.[165]

The High Commission, which continued to receive appeals from various sectors to solve Lebanon's pressing economic and administrative problems, was fully aware of the national mood, and therefore unwilling to acquiesce in Khuri's calls for restoration of the constitution. French officials believed that his demands reflected the views of only a small group of politicians, intellectuals and journalists, and were not shared by the general public, which was mainly concerned with improving economic conditions. Moreover, the intense hostility between Khuri and Eddé had added to their fears that restoration of the constitution and allowing the deputies to elect the next president might create an unstable political situation which, coupled with the economic crisis, could be exploited by the National Bloc to stir up trouble in Lebanon. Such views were voiced by de Martel during deliberations in the Quai d'Orsay in September 1934; he continued to maintain that Lebanon's political problems were not urgent, and that conditions were not yet ripe for revision and restoration of the constitution. Arguing that the two main contenders, Eddé and Khuri, were effectively neutralizing each other, he proposed that Sa'ad be appointed president for another year.[166]

De Martel's recommendation was also intended to placate Patriarch Arida. After the high commissioner's return from Paris in February, relations between the two deteriorated to such an extent that they ceased to meet. Ponsot had recognized the importance of the church and had regularly consulted Arida, giving him the feeling that his views and advice were being taken into consideration. But de Martel was impatient with Arida's attempts to interfere in the High Commission's policies. In his dispatches to the Quai d'Orsay, he claimed that Arida was isolated from the outside world, and that his bishops had little respect for him. He expressed contempt for the patriarch and downplayed his influence, describing him as old, stubborn, vain, naive, and surrounded by an entourage of family and friends who were taking advantage of him. He particularly resented Arida's attempts to intervene in his economic policy and accused him of seeking to promote his family's financial interests. De Martel increasingly ignored the patriarch and chose instead to use the services of Cardinal Tapuni and Bishop Mubarak to advance the goals of the High Commission, thereby further antagonizing Arida.[167]

De Martel's portrayal of Arida's isolation, the intrigues in Bkerki, and the attempts by politicians and interest groups to use the patriarch to further their own agendas, was well founded. The bishops continued to be deeply divided, with Khuri and Aql unceasingly trying to undermine each other. Arida's relations with Gianini and the Holy See remained tense, and he repeatedly postponed his visit to the Vatican, which was incumbent upon him as the new patriarch. In August, in an attempt to improve matters, he appointed Bishop Khuri to represent him in the negotiations in Rome on the future of the Maronite church's ties with the Vatican, only to learn afterwards that Khuri had used the visit to plot against him. The puritanical Arida deplored what he termed the decline of moral standards in Beirut, with its new casinos, cinemas and prostitution, and repeatedly asked the High Commission to censor films he deemed harmful to public morals. Clearly, de Martel's private life—his affair with the wife of the Belgian consul had become common knowledge—did not add to Arida's respect for him. In his meetings with French officials, the patriarch continually complained that his advice was being ignored. He requested a revision of the 1932 census results, which, he claimed, had been rigged by the Muslim director of the interior at the time. He also protested that Sunnis, Shiites and Druze were taking over the administration, insisted that a Maronite be appointed as director of the department of public works, and asked for additional funds to sustain church schools. Arida's major concern, however, was the deteriorating economic situation. He alleged that the population of Mount Lebanon had enjoyed a better standard of living under the Mutassarifiyya, and objected to the high taxes and customs duties, the granting of subsidies to foreign concessionaires, and the investment of resources in Syria, particularly in the Jazira, which, he argued, was at Lebanon's expense. Although he was pleased with de Martel's decision to reappoint Sa'ad, he claimed that the latter had no real power and that he 'could not even appoint an orderly without the High Commission's approval'.[168]

At the end of 1934, there was a growing realization among National Bloc leaders that public opinion should be mobilized without delay to press the High Commission to change its policies. De Martel's decree in November dissolving the Syrian parliament and the failure of Mardam's visit to Paris convinced even the moderates that France had no intention of agreeing to restoration of constitutional life, resuming treaty negotiations, or revising its stand on Syrian unity. With France pouring resources into improving the strategic infrastructure of the mandated territories, they feared that by the time a new treaty was concluded, it would be too late to change the situation. The dissolution of the Syrian parliament sparked rumours that the High Commission would take similar steps in Lebanon, leading Khuri and his supporters to initiate a new press campaign in support of the Lebanese parliament. When de Martel reiterated his intention not to restore the constitution and reinstate it only after substantial modification, they criticized him openly. His refusal to allow the deputies to elect the president, along with his rumoured plan to reappoint Sa'ad, strengthened antagonism to him among members of Khuri's clan. They were joined by Dabbas who, in October, had lost his position as speaker of the parliament to Petro Trad, after the latter was backed by the High Commission.[169]

In mid-January, Bastide, president of the French parliament's Committee for Foreign Affairs, arrived for the inauguration of the Mosul-Tripoli oil pipeline. His visit afforded de Martel's critics the opportunity to denounce the high commissioner's policies publicly. In Damascus, National Bloc leaders attacked his authoritarian methods and economic measures. In Bkerki, Bastide heard complaints of his failure to solve Lebanon's problems. At a reception held by de Martel in honour of Bastide, Dabbas and Khuri joined Omar Da'uq in attacking French policy and in voicing their hopes that as a member of the French parliament, Bastide would support their request for restoration of the constitution. De Martel, who regarded these attacks as a personal affront, responded at a reception held the following day in parliament, by publicly chastising the deputies. His disappointment and anger were expressed in a dispatch to the Quai d'Orsay: 'After several months in Syria and Lebanon', he wrote, 'the best-intentioned Frenchman, weighed down by responsibilities, has to acknowledge how difficult it is to satisfy everyone in this atmosphere of subtle intrigues. I believe that a few hours would have been sufficient for him [Bastide] to reach the same conclusions.'[170]

The conflict during Bastide's visit, between the National Bloc and the Khuri camp on the one hand, and de Martel on the other, laid the groundwork for the open confrontation that was to be triggered by de Martel's decision to reinstate the tobacco monopoly. Well aware of Syrian and Lebanese concern with the economic situation, the two groups, each for its own reasons, exploited opposition to this measure to provoke a crisis. As in the case of the Mubarak affair two years earlier, Khuri tacitly coordinated his moves with Riad al-Sulh and other Muslim pan-Arabists, and again succeeded in manoeuvering a prominent Maronite religious leader—this time Patriarch Arida—into leading the campaign against French policy in the mandated territories.

In post-independence Lebanese historiography, opposition to the tobacco monopoly was presented as the culmination of the national struggle in the inter-war years against French domination of Lebanon and exploitation of its economy by colonial concessionary companies. There was a direct link, it was claimed, between the events of 1935 and the uprising against the Free French in 1943. According to this interpretation, the tobacco monopoly crisis marked a turning point in the cooperation between Lebanese Christians and Muslims and between Lebanon and Syria against the foreign power. And Arida was portrayed as the champion of Lebanon's quest for political and economic independence from France. Indeed, there were national, political, economic and social aspects to the crisis and to Arida's opposition to the French concessionary companies; it undoubtedly marked unprecedented collaboration between Lebanese Christian leaders and the Syrian National Bloc. But it was hardly a spontaneous uprising by peasants, manufacturers and workers against a colonial company and an allegedly corrupt high commissioner. The crisis was a well-orchestrated event instigated by the National Bloc, Khuri's camp and certain businessmen who had vested interests in the existing system. National Bloc leaders in Damascus and Sulh in Beirut openly exploited opposition to the monopoly by Arida and the Christians of Mount Lebanon to force de Martel to revise his policy; Khuri worked behind the scenes as before, and took advantage of the patriarch's weak character, strong feeling of responsibility for his community's interests, and resentment of de Martel, to incite Arida against the high commissioner. For his part, Bishop Khuri used the crisis to discredit Arida and undermine his relations with France and the Vatican.[171]

The tobacco industry had traditionally been a major source of income for thousands of peasants, workers and manufacturers, as well as for the local governments. Since 1883 all aspects of cultivation, manufacture, taxation, import and export in the Ottoman Empire had been controlled by the 'Régie co-intéressée des tabacs de l'empire', a privately-owned French company; this was one of the financial arrangements with European creditors that followed the Ottoman Empire's bankruptcy in the mid-1870s. Mount Lebanon, however, had been exempt from the monopoly under the privileges it received in the organic law of 1864. After 1920, the company had retained its monopoly in the mandated territories, again excluding Mount Lebanon. The lower taxation on tobacco and the lack of a cultivation quota on the Mountain had led to concentration of the industry there and to widespread smuggling into the surrounding regions. The company's attempts to extend its monopoly to the Mountain, arguing that it was impossible to maintain two different taxation systems in one country, were rejected by the farmers and manufacturers of Mount Lebanon. When the monopoly expired in 1929 Prime Minister Eddé had opposed granting the company a new one that would have included Mount Lebanon. The Lebanese government's stand was a major factor in the High Commission's decision in June 1930 to adopt the banderole system in all the mandated territories, according to which the industry was taxed by the use of labels affixed to the cigarette packages. Under this system too, Mount Lebanon enjoyed lower taxes: 25 per cent compared with 45 per cent in the rest of the mandated territories. This solution, which liberalized the growth, manufacture and trade of tobacco, rapidly led to overproduction and the establishment of thousands of small factories. Large-scale smuggling from Lebanon to Syria continued, giving rise to repeated complaints from successive Syrian and Alawite governments. For their part, Lebanese cultivators and manufacturers resented the rapid growth of the tobacco industry in the Alawite region, which was encouraged by the Régie des Tabacs.[172]

The collapse of tobacco prices in the 1930s severely affected the income of growers and manufacturers, and at the same time caused considerable loss of revenue for the Common Interests budget and consequently for the local governments. In 1932, induced by Jamil Mardam, then Syrian finance minister, Ponsot modified the banderole system by limiting production. The High Commission was also subjected to constant lobbying from the Régie des Tabacs, which argued that restoration of the monopoly would ensure regulation of the industry, help the growers and manufacturers and augment income from taxation on tobacco. Throughout 1934, various committees studied the issue and at the end of the year recommended reinstating the monopoly and extending it to all the mandated territories. It was proposed that the monopoly be granted to a new enterprise, the 'Société anonyme de régie co-intéressée libano–syrienne des tabacs', jointly owned by French, Lebanese and Syrian companies. De Martel believed that restoring the monopoly system would improve the industry, allow the introduction of new species of tobacco for export, limit imports and substantially increase income from taxes, thereby enabling him to reduce customs duties.[173]

In November 1934, details emerged of the High Commission's intention to restore the tobacco monopoly. The National Bloc immediately protested and in early December held a rally in Damascus at which Barudi strongly criticized the decision. The Lebanese parliament—which had received petitions from tobacco growers and manufacturers in Mount Lebanon and Jabal Amil, complaining that representatives of the Régie des Tabacs were preventing them from openly discussing the monopoly—voiced its concern. When parliament convened, Farid al-Khazin and Michel Zakur questioned the government and asked that the matter be examined by parliament. The High Commission, however, turned down their request, arguing that it was not just a Lebanese issue, but involved all the mandated territories. Nevertheless, de Martel agreed that a special committee of three deputies—Zakur, Khabaz and Chihab—elected by parliament, would be consulted. As preparations to renew the monopoly progressed, opposition on Mount Lebanon mounted. Delegations of tobacco-growers and manufacturers sent petitions and telegrams to Bkerki demanding that Arida protect the traditional privileges of inhabitants of the Mountain. Politicians who opposed the monopoly or had other grievances against the High Commission, and prominent businessmen in the industry, descended upon Bkerki, seeking the patriarch's intervention. Among the most vociferous were Yusuf Gemayel, Musa Namur, Michel Zakur, Farid al-Khazin, Yusuf al-Khazin, Yusuf al-Sawda and Khalil Ma'atuk. They were joined by Fakhri al-Barudi and other National Bloc leaders, who urged Arida to also protect the interests of the tobacco-growers in Syria.[174]

Although Arida was to express reservations on extending the tobacco monopoly to Mount Lebanon, he initially took a moderate stand. At a meeting on 12 January with Lafond, the French delegate to Lebanon, he proposed maintaining the banderole system with some revisions and bringing in the army if smuggling posed a problem. In light of his later cooperation with the National Bloc, it is worth pointing out that his distrust of the Syrians was as strong as ever. He presented the Maronites as 'a small island of Christians lost in a sea of Muslims', in need of continued French protection. He repeated his opposition to investment of resources in Syria and Damascus, which, he argued, came at the expense of Lebanon and Beirut, and referred to the Syrian capital as a 'city inhabited only by peasants'. He again complained of Maronite under-representation in certain sectors of the administration and in the allocation of resources for education. As protests multiplied, however, he began to take a firmer stand, believing it was his duty as head of the Maronite church to protect the interests of Mount Lebanon. His feeling of obligation, together with a certain gullibility and distrust of de Martel, was used by Lebanese politicians and businessmen to manoeuvre him into leading the campaign against the monopoly. They knew that without his support it would be impossible to mobilize Christian public opinion.[175]

On 28 January 1935, the French Foreign Minister was surprised to receive a telegram protesting de Martel's intention to reinstate the tobacco monopoly. The telegram had been sent from Haifa and was signed by Patriarch

Arida 'on behalf of the Lebanese and Syrians'. At the same time, telegrams were dispatched to Lebanese and Syrian immigrant communities in North and South America urging them to protest to Paris against the monopoly. Arida's telegram signalled the beginning of an organized campaign, that soon developed into a full-blown movement against the High Commission and the French concessionary companies, continuing well into 1936. The monopoly crisis eventually forced the French government to revise its Lebanese policy and had serious repercussions on the presidential elections in January 1936.[176]

With Arida heading the campaign against the tobacco monopoly, Bkerki became a centre of well-orchestrated opposition to de Martel's political and economic policies, and this quickly turned into a popular protest movement against the French mandate. Strikes and demonstrations were held against the monopoly and the exploitation of the local economy by French and other foreign concessionary companies. Daily life was disrupted as more sectors joined in the struggle—including milkmen, lawyers, the drivers' syndicate and car importers. Property owners demanded a 30 per cent reduction in the *temetu* tax, arguing that the value of their property had fallen as a result of the economic crisis. In May, the traders' association in Beirut, headed by Afred Nasser, joined the campaign, protesting that the high taxes and customs duties were undermining commerce and preventing Lebanese merchants from competing with those in Haifa. Leading Christian and Muslim traders and financiers, including Michel Chiha, Henri Pharaon, Jean Tuaini, Habib Trad, Alfred Nasser, Omar Bayhum, Omar Da'uq, Salim Tyara and Salim Ali Salam formed an economic bloc aimed at protecting the national economy against foreign exploitation.[177]

Throughout the crisis, Beshara al-Khuri and Riad al-Sulh tacitly coordinated their moves against the High Commission. Khuri saw the campaign against the tobacco monopoly as an opportunity to coerce de Martel into restoring the constitution and granting parliament the power to elect the next president. He and his colleagues pressed Arida to insist on restoration of constitutional life in Lebanon in his appeals to the Quai d'Orsay. At meetings with French officials, he constantly stressed that the crisis could have been avoided if the monopoly law had been brought before the parliament for approval. As in the Mubarak crisis two years before, Khuri operated behind the scenes, although some of his close friends, such as Yusuf al-Sawda, Michel Zakur, Henri Pharaon and Farid al-Khazin were directly involved in organizing and encouraging opposition to de Martel.[178]

Riad al-Sulh played an important part in transforming the crisis into a popular national protest against the French, involving Christians and Muslims, Lebanese and Syrians. He considered Arida's willingness to act against the High Commission an important achievement of nationalist efforts to undermine France's position in Lebanon. Moreover, it demonstrated to the French public and to members of the Permanent Mandates Commission in Geneva the baselessness of France's claim that its mandate was essential for the protection of Christian minorities against the Muslim Arab majority. Sulh appealed to Muslim politicians, businessmen and journalists in Lebanon to publicly support the Maronite patriarch. He also urged the National Bloc leadership to back Arida. He was in constant touch with Khalil Ma'atuk, Aziz al-Hashem, Michel Zakur, Farid al-Khazin, Jubran Tuaini and Georges Aql to coordinate the campaign against de Martel and helped instigate strikes by merchants and the drivers' syndicate in Beirut. Yet despite his declarations of support for Muslim–Christian solidarity, he harboured no illusions as to the real motives of the Christian politicians who joined the struggle. His young relative and close associate, Khazim al-Sulh, expressed the same view when, in response to a question from an official of the Régie des Tabacs on whether the nationalists feared that Arida would turn his back on them, he declared: 'We have no illusions on the matter. We compromised him and that is sufficient; we will let him go his own way after he has served our purpose and will continue toward our goal. We did the same to Bishop Mubarak when he opposed the High Commission.'[179]

The National Bloc leaders made use of Arida's naivete and vanity, the Christian politicians' political ambitions and the grievances of Beirut businessmen, to turn distate for the monopoly and other French concessionaires into a national campaign against the mandate. Having failed to force de Martel to revise the policy he had pursued since November 1933, they seized the opportunity to demonstrate its shortcomings to the French government and public. Their timing was significant, for they were well aware of de Martel's plans to travel to Paris at the end of February for discussions in the Quai d'Orsay; they hoped that the large-scale popular protests in Syria and Lebanon would convince the government to change its Syrian policy. The Bloc continued to uphold its territorial demands and opposition to Lebanon's separate existence. Indeed, while expressing satisfaction with the quarrel between de Martel and Arida, Mardam told his colleagues that he had 'no trust in the perseverance of the Lebanese and that a political agreement with them was impossible'.[180] Mardam, Barudi, Afif al-Sulh and other National Bloc leaders stressed the need to take advantage of Lebanese Christian grievances and rally their opposition to the French mandate. They were more than willing to allow Arida, whom they depicted as the 'Patriarch of the Arabs', to lead the national campaign as long as it served their interests. In February and March they went to Bkerki to thank Arida for his patriotic stand and asked him to lead the united Syro–Lebanese struggle against the tobacco monopoly. Muslim politicians in Lebanon were urged to back Arida's campaign against de Martel. In Damascus and other Syrian cities imams publicly acclaimed Arida, students and pupils demonstrated in the streets in his support, and Syrian newspapers praised the new-found solidarity of Muslims and Christians against the mandate. At the end of March, the National Bloc organized an economic conference in Damascus to promote the 'national economy' in which Christian and Muslim businessmen from Lebanon, including Alfred Nasser, took part. After declaring support for Arida, they elected an executive committee to coordinate the campaign. Significantly, in their concluding decision, the Lebanese businessmen were defined as 'representatives of the coast'.[181]

Arida's telegram to the Quai d'Orsay at the end of January and the demonstrations and strikes against the tobacco monopoly caught de Martel by surprise. He had been confident that his assistants and the officials of the Régie des tabacs had prepared the ground in Lebanon to ensure that the monopoly would be accepted with little opposition. The National Bloc's success in exploiting the grievances of the Maronite patriarch provoked criticism in the Quai d'Orsay and the National Assembly of de Martel's mishandling of the whole affair. His position was further weakened by the streams of letters and telegrams of protest to the Quai d'Orsay from Arida and politicians, businessmen and organizations in the mandated territories, as well as from Lebanese and Syrian immigrant groups in North and South America. Rumours spread that de Martel had been bribed by the concessionary companies, and there were calls—by Arida among others—to replace him with a new high commissioner. Although in his dispatches to Paris de Martel claimed that he was making a clear distinction between Arida the man and his position, he was hard put to conceal his anger toward the patriarch and his deep resentment of the Lebanese politicians and businessmen who had exploited Arida's credulity to provoke the attacks against him. He initially attempted to persuade Arida to cease his criticism by warning him that he was being used by enemies of France and Lebanon and that his acts and declarations were endangering France's special relationship with the Maronites. However, as Arida continued to insist on abolition of the monopoly and intensified his attacks on de Martel in Paris, the high commissioner severed all contact with him. He then sought to isolate and weaken the patriarch by discreetly encouraging Maronite bishops and the Jesuits to take action against him. Indeed, as the crisis continued, it gradually took on the form of a personal feud between Arida and de Martel.[182]

Throughout the crisis, Foreign Minister Laval publicly supported de Martel and resisted pressure to replace him. In reply to Arida's letters, he and Léger, his deputy, stressed that they had approved the high commissioner's decision to restore the tobacco monopoly, that he enjoyed their complete confidence, and that he was merely implementing the policy of the French government. They repeatedly warned the patriarch that his collaboration with the National Bloc was undermining not only French interests in the Levant but also those of the Christians in Lebanon, and asked him to cooperate fully with de Martel. While in Paris, de Martel appeared before the Haut-Comité Méditerranéen and later met with the prime minister, who subsequently issued a public statement supporting him and his policies. The High Commission immediately published details of de Martel's meeting with the prime minister in the Lebanese and Syrian newspapers, together with interviews he had given to the French press.[183]

De Martel's concern was to prevent the National Bloc from using opposition to the tobacco monopoly and the grievances of Lebanese politicians and businessmen to instigate a popular protest movement against the mandate. In mid-February, on the advice of the Sûreté Générale, he expelled Barudi from Beirut and later banished Sulh to Kamishli for his role in the drivers' strike. Muslim leaders in Beirut were urged to refrain from joining the anti-French campaign. A message was conveyed to Christian politicians, including Khuri and Chiha, that no political reform could be attained by provoking public disorder, and that Lebanon's future would be decided only within the framework of France's general policy, which was dominated by the threat of a new war in Europe. They were asked to cease their collaboration with the National Bloc and their attacks on French policy and the concessionary companies. The High Commission pressed Christian businessmen and financiers in Beirut not to participate in the economic congress in Damascus. To defuse some of the tension, it announced willingness to acquiesce in some of the demands of the economic sector. Indeed, the tobacco monopoly law included new provisions protecting the rights of growers and manufacturers, as well as an undertaking to maintain local governments' income from the tobacco industry at the same level as under the banderole system. By the end of April, the combination of pressure and concessions had ended most of the strikes. The High Commission's decision to lower the customs duties and *temetu* tax was greeted with much satisfaction by business circles in Beirut. A serious incident that month in Tripoli, in which Abd al-Hamid Karameh shot and killed Abd al-Majid Muqadam, a member of a rival family, led to a strong reaction in the Syrian and Lebanese press and helped the High Commission to divert public attention from the monopoly issue. In early July, on the eve of his third trip to Paris since the beginning of the year, de Martel was able to report to the Quai d'Orsay that the High Commission had succeeded in weakening opposition to his policies and that only a small number of Christian politicians and businessmen in Lebanon still supported the National Bloc's campaign against the mandate. [184]

While de Martel and the Quai d'Orsay were determined not to leave the impression that they had been coerced, they realized that the policy defined in early 1934, particularly toward Lebanon, had to be revised. In a memorandum to the Foreign Minister in mid-March, de Martel admitted that the crisis had convinced him that appointment of the president by the high commissioner was undesirable, since it exposed the latter to direct attack. He therefore recommended that the Lebanese parliament elect the next president in January 1936, when Sa'ad was due to end his term. In the meantime, he proposed that the deputies be granted more freedom to elaborate laws, although their power in fiscal matters would continue to be restricted. He saw only a slim chance of a Muslim being elected president, but stressed that even if this did occur, it would be preferable not to prevent it by force, as Ponsot had done in 1932. His recommendations were approved by the Foreign Minister, who pointed out that although political and economic unrest in Lebanon had been encouraged by Damascus, it did attest to a genuine malaise. He therefore instructed de Martel to do his utmost to forestall a further deterioration in the High Commission's relations with the Christians. Yet neither the Foreign Minister nor de Martel was willing to modify their Syrian policy, especially their boycott of the National Bloc. De Martel reiterated that the Syrian nationalists had not changed their militant, hostile stand and suggested that France continue to strengthen its military interests and its position among the minorities. He proposed that an administrative system based on decentralization be implemented to ensure the autonomous status of Jabal Druze, the Alawite region, Alexandretta and the Jazira before they were linked to Syria.[185]

The National Bloc leaders, especially Riad al-Sulh and Fakhri al-Barudi, were pleased with the crisis in Lebanon. They had succeeded in undermining one of the basic tenets of French policy in the mandated territories—the special relationship with the Lebanese Christians, in particular the Maronites. They had embarrassed de Martel and weakened his position in Paris and Beirut, and exposed the limitations of his political and economic policies to the French government and the National Assembly. They were particularly pleased with the demands of some Lebanese Christians to replace the mandate with a treaty and limit the French military presence in Lebanon. Thus Riad al-Sulh's long-held view that Syria should recognize Lebanon within its 1920 borders, if the Lebanese Christians joined the Muslims in demanding complete independence from France, gained much ground within the National Bloc.[186]

The willingness of Arida and certain Christian politicians to collaborate with the National Bloc made a strong impression on the Muslims of Lebanon. Indeed, the tobacco monopoly crisis helped forge a feeling of patriotism shared by Christians and Muslims alike. The Sunnis were obliged to reconsider their stand on the Lebanese state, and the Maronites to re-evaluate their position on France and Syria. The crisis demonstrated that the two communities had a common goal—Lebanon's political and economic independence from the mandate. The Muslims discovered that even the patriarch, who symbolized the Maronites' historical ties with France, was ready to oppose the mandate and fight for independence. As for the Christians, the intercommunal solidarity manifested during the crisis convinced many of them that by giving up the French mandate, they could not only free their economy from French control, but also win the support of the Lebanese Muslims and Syrian nationalists for Lebanon's separate existence within its 1920 borders. Such views became increasingly common both in the Khuri camp and other Christian sectors.[187]

Beshara al-Khuri and his Constitutional Bloc were also satisfied with the outcome of the crisis. De Martel had been forced to give more power to parliament, and reports from Paris indicated that the deputies might even be allowed to elect the next Lebanese president. Merchants and financiers in Beirut welcomed the High Commission's willingness to relax its hold over the Lebanese economy and its efforts to revive trade. Khuri had enhanced his public image as a patriot fighting for Lebanon's national dignity and political and economic independence from the mandatory power. He also hoped he had improved his position among the Muslims and that Sunni and Shiite deputies would now be more inclined to give him their vote. His decision to defend Abd al-Hamid Karameh in court was also intended to improve his popularity among the Muslim and Arab nationalists. All this satisfaction, however, proved premature. De Martel, holding Khuri and his associates responsible for the attacks against him, was determined to prevent Khuri's election as president; he would take his revenge during the presidential elections in January 1936.[188]

Arida's role in the campaign against the French mandate sparked a serious crisis within the Maronite church. His feud with de Martel, and especially his collaboration with the National Bloc, provoked strong opposition from most of the bishops, who feared that he was undermining the church and the Maronite community's special relations with France. His opponents, particularly Bishops Khuri and Mubarak, tried to take advantage of his deteriorating relations with de Martel to depose Arida. They were joined by Gianini—who frequently warned the Holy See of the danger Arida's stand posed for the Christians in Lebanon and Syria—and by the Jesuits, who had opposed his election from the start. The conflict burst into the open at the synod in Diman convened by Arida in May in order to ensure the bishops' approval for his stand against the high commissioner. But the bishops vehemently crticized him and refused to support his policy. On 17 June five bishops, led by Khuri and Mubarak, secretly sent a letter to the Pope denouncing Arida's behaviour, including his collaboration with the National Bloc, and requesting either that Arida be removed or a committee of bishops be appointed to supervise his activities. This was an extremely unusual step, in view of the traditional autonomy enjoyed by the Maronite church and Maronite opposition to any direct intervention in their affairs by the Holy See. Fearing a strong reaction from his community, Bishop Khuri, who had initiated the move together with Gianini, was anxious to conceal his involvement.[189]

The plot of the five Maronite bishops to depose their patriarch placed de Martel in a sensitive position. He had been informed by Khuri and Mubarak of their letter to the Pope a few days earlier; he had tacitly encouraged the bishops to attack Arida, but had not instigated their attempt to depose him. Realizing the far-reaching consequences of the bishops' initiative, he immediately informed the Foreign Minister, stressing that the High Commission had been careful not to be involved. De Martel's report sparked urgent discussions in Paris. Although the Quai d'Orsay had criticized Arida for his stand during the tobacco monopoly crisis and his collaboration with the National Bloc, it opposed the move to oust him, fearing that this would strengthen the influence of Italy and the Holy See over the Catholic churches in the Levant, and in particular the Maronite community. Indeed, Bishop Khuri, one of the main candidates to replace Arida, was known to have close ties with Italian officials in Beirut and Rome. The foreign minister therefore instructed Charles-Roux, the French ambassador to the Vatican, to oppose attempts to depose Arida, although he indicated that the French government would not object to disciplinary measures being taken against him.[190]

Unaware of his bishops' plot, Arida was taken by surprise when, at the beginning of August, he received a letter from the Pope reprimanding him for his stand. Angry and resentful, he suspected that de Martel and the Quai d'Orsay had been behind the Pope's move. He sent Pharès, one of his trusted bishops, to Paris to learn of the Quai d'Orsay's intentions. But officials there had refrained from informing Arida of his bishops' initiative, fearing it might provoke a crisis within the Maronite church. Bishop Pharès was therefore told that France had no part in Arida's strained relations with the Holy See. In October and November news of growing tension between Arida and the Holy See circulated in Beirut, and France was again held responsible. The Pope continued to receive secret letters from the five bishops, Gianini and the head of the Jesuits in Beirut, claiming that Arida was incompetent and unable to carry out his duties as patriarch. The sudden arrival in Beirut of two top Vatican officials, and the urgent summons of Cardinal Tapuni to Rome, sparked rumours that Arida might even be replaced. After intensive deliberations, the Pope turned down the bishops' request, but he did instruct Bishop Aql, Khuri's main rival, to resign as patriarchal vicar.[191]

As the Quai d'Orsay continued to receive reports blaming France for the Pope's action against Arida, the prime minister rebuked de Martel for his failure to obtain a copy of the bishops' letter, remarking that 'although Arida holds us responsible, we are apparently the only ones who know nothing about it.' He directed de Martel to make it clear to the Maronite patriarch that the French government had nothing to do with the Vatican's move; on the contrary, it had defended Arida. Yet despite the French assurances, the patriarch still suspected that de Martel had been involved.[192]

The crisis in the Maronite church had a direct impact on the forthcoming presidential elections. Arida's position was considerably weakened and his ability to promote a candidate limited. This was precisely one of Bishop Khuri's goals. Unaware of the decision made by the Quai d'Orsay in March to grant the Lebanese parliament the power to elect the next president, Khuri's camp feared that in order to placate Arida, de Martel might reappoint Sa'ad at the last minute, as he had in January 1935. Bishop Khuri once more intervened on behalf of his cousin. In his correspondence with de Martel and the Quai d'Orsay, he repeatedly promoted Khuri's candidacy, hoping that, having demonstrated his willingness to cooperate with the High Commission against Arida, his advice would be heeded. But his involvement in the elections had the opposite effect. As in 1932, warnings were sounded that Bishop Khuri and Beshara al-Khuri would take over the church and the highest political position in Lebanon. De Martel accused Bishop Khuri, whom he deeply distrusted, of maintaining close ties with Italian representatives and complained that the Quai d'Orsay was giving too much weight to his views. In fact, Bishop Khuri's and Gianini's initiative to depose Arida reinforced de Martel's determination to block Beshara al-Khuri's election.[193]

At the beginning of July, before departing for Paris, de Martel instructed his staff to refrain from taking any initiative or revealing any details of the High Commission's intentions with regard to the presidential elections. During the next three months, tension in Lebanon rose, rumours abounded and numerous articles appeared in the press speculating on the plans of de Martel and the Quai d'Orsay. Politicians, clergy and journalists travelled to Paris to promote one candidate or another. Among them was Beshara al-Khuri, who met with French politicians and officials in an attempt to persuade them not to veto his candidacy and to allow the Lebanese deputies to elect the next president. As the time approached for de Martel's return to Beirut, Eddé and Khuri stepped up their efforts to win the deputies' support. Upon his arrival in mid-October, de Martel was greeted by a stream of politicians, clergy and businessmen wishing to learn of his intentions or endorse their candidate. Bishop Mubarak probably expressed the views of most when he told a French official that, if de Martel maintained his neutrality, Khuri would be elected. Yet, despite the pressure, de Martel remained silent.[194]

The election of the speaker of the parliament for the winter session served as the first indication of the power balance between the two camps. While Eddé and the deputies allied to him backed Khair al-Din al-Ahdab, Khuri and his followers presented Khalid Chihab as their candidate. Both sides sought a Sunni's election as speaker, in order to open the way for replacing Abdallah Bayhum, the secretary of state, with a Christian. Eddé undertook to appoint Ayub Tabet to that position in return for his support, while Khuri intended to give it to Salim Taqla, a trusted friend. The Constitutional Bloc's backing assured Chihab's election, but his candidacy was opposed by both the Sunni and Greek Orthodox communities. Prominent Sunni politicians and religious leaders, including the mufti, appealed to de Martel to prevent the Christians from taking a top executive position away from their community, while the Greek Orthodox opposed the initiative to replace Petro Trad as speaker. De Martel, however, refused to intervene and restated his intention to remain completely neutral. Consequently, Chihab was elected by a majority of 17 votes to 6. Najib Usayran was elected as his deputy, and two of Khuri's followers, Hamid Faranjieh and Hikmat Jumblatt, were chosen as secretaries. Chihab's election and de Martel's neutrality strengthened Khuri's confidence. Yet his decision to endorse Chihab had been a political error, since it antagonised both the Sunni and Greek Orthodox deputies. With his opponent enjoying a clear majority in parliament, Eddé openly appealed to de Martel to intervene in the presidential elections. An editorial in *L'Orient* argued that a group of 25 deputies, not necessarily motivated by the general good, should not be allowed to elect the next president; he should be appointed by the high commissioner. The newspaper also maintained that in view of the bitter rivalry between Eddé and Khuri, an 'outside' candidate should not be ruled out.[195]

On 12 November, with the election campaign in full swing, de Martel finally declared that the next Lebanese president would not be appointed but elected by parliament. He refrained, however, from specifying the exact date of the elections, the length of the president's term, or his powers. He also refused to clarify whether he intended to fully restore the constitution. On 3

January 1936, he issued a long-awaited decree announcing that the president would be elected for a three-year term by parliament in an extraodinary session on 20 January, either by a two-thirds majority in the first ballot or a simple majority in the second. The decree also stipulated that the president would continue to be assisted by a secretary of state who would be responsible to him and not to parliament, and who need not necessarily be a member of parliament. The decision to reduce the president's term of office from six years, as defined in the revised 1929 constitution, to only three years, was intended to give the High Commission more freedom in deciding Lebanon's future. However, it created a legal problem—whether the constitutional provision barring the president from serving a second consecutive term was still valid.[196]

De Martel's November declaration threw the Lebanese political system into turmoil. For the next two months, attention was focused on the elections, with political figures and the public disregarding the dramatic international and regional events then taking place—Italy's invasion of Ethiopia and national uprisings in Egypt and Syria. After seven years of bitter rivalry—which had deeply divided the Lebanese politicians, led to suspension of the constitution and jeopardized all efforts to settle political, economic and social problems—Eddé and Khuri found themselves face to face. The elections, however, were not merely to determine the next president: the deputies were to choose between two ideologies regarding the nature of Lebanon's future relations with France and the Arab world.[197]

Since the 1934 parliamentary elections, Khuri and his supporters had been working diligently to ensure his election. They carefully studied each deputy's political, social and financial position and endeavoured to win the support of the Maronite clergy and other religious leaders, as well as of prominent businessmen and financiers in Beirut. Substantial sums were paid to journalists and newspaper owners to publish articles endorsing his candidacy and attacking Eddé. Special efforts were made to secure the votes of undecided Sunni and Shiite deputies. Khuri hoped that his anti-French stand and the close ties he had maintained with the Arab nationalist politicians in Lebanon and the National Bloc leadership would help him obtain the support of the Muslim deputies. His task seemed simple, since he already enjoyed the backing of ten deputies, whose election he had helped. Well aware that his efforts would be in vain if de Martel intervened against him, he attempted to improve relations with the high commissioner. He also sent emissaries to Paris with a message of his loyalty to France and the mandate, reiterating his appeal that the Lebanese parliament be allowed to freely choose the president. His tactics were effective to a certain extent; de Martel and officials in the Quai d'Orsay were extremely careful to forestall accusations of involvement in the elections.[198]

In contrast to Khuri, Eddé began to organize his campaign just a short time before the elections. His chances appeared slim, with only four deputies endorsing his candidacy. His immediate goal was to prevent Khuri from securing the backing of 13 deputies, which would have ensured his victory. With most of the deputies from Mount Lebanon already committed to Khuri, Eddé sought the support of representatives from the coast, the Beqa valley and south Lebanon, the majority of whom were Sunnis or Shiites. The Muslim public, however, still regarded him as a loyal ally of France and an opponent of the Muslim and Arab cause. With the help of Khair al-Din al-Ahdab, he strove to dispel this image and pledged to grant the Sunni and Shiite communities a fair share in the political and administrative systems, in return for their deputies' votes. He even sought Riad al-Sulh's assistance to pressure the Sunni legislators. He also attempted to persuade Habib al-Sa'ad, who was backed by two deputies, to withdraw his candidacy. Sa'ad refused, however, hoping to emerge as a last-minute compromise candidate with the High Commission's support. Eddé repeatedly appealed to de Martel to intervene on his behalf to sway the undecided deputies. He also sent messages to the Quai d'Orsay and prominent French politcians stressing his loyalty to France and the mandate and claiming that Khuri's election would endanger French interests in Lebanon. Newspapers allied to Eddé—*L'Orient* and *Sawt al-Ahrar*—vehemently attacked Khuri, warning that his election would lead to domination of Lebanon's political and economic systems by the 'consortium'.[199]

Never before in any Lebanese election had money been used so extensively to buy votes. Businessmen and foreign concessionaires in both camps contributed large sums to the campaign. Khuri's main financial backers were Pharaon and Chiha, and the latter exploited his position in the Syro–Lebanese Bank to influence deputies. Farid al-Khazin was allocated substantial funds, with which he financed a press campaign. Eddé also bribed deputies, and was aided by Khalil Ma'atuk and the Compagnie Algérienne, a Frenck Bank, to which he served as legal adviser.[200]

Despite Eddé's efforts in November and early December, only two deputies joined his camp. With Khuri's victory almost certain, officials in the High Commission carefully examined whether a compromise candidate could be promoted; but Khuri opposed the initiative, stressing that he was determined to maintain his candidacy. Resolved to prevent Khuri's election, de Martel decided to intervene, thereby drastically shifting the balance of power. Anxious not to expose himself to criticism, he took indirect action. On 15 December, the High Commission announced its decision to remove

Salim Taqla from his position as administrator of Beirut, accusing him of purchasing from Henri Pharaon a large plot of land at a price 30 per cent higher than its market value for the construction of a municipal stadium. A French official who had approved the deal was also transferred from his position. The timing of this revelation was clearly intended to undermine Khuri's candidacy. The affair reinforced accusations that Khuri and his colleagues exploited their public positions for personal profit. Indeed, *L'Orient* seized the opportunity to mount a strong attack on Khuri, while *Sawt al-Ahrar* warned against the election of a 'weak and inconsistent man whose access to power would lead to a republic of friends, brothers and cousins.'[201]

The Taqla affair considerably improved Eddé's public standing and increased the number of deputies willing to endorse him. Nevertheless, neither candidate was able to ensure a majority until the last minute. The main battle was for the votes of four undecided deputies who shifted their support from one candidate to another, either because they were urged to do so, or in order to raise their price. Eddé's position improved even more after Khalil Ma'atuk convinced Sa'ad to withdraw his candidacy and back Eddé. On 15 January, 12 deputies met at Eddé's home and pledged to support him. Finally, with Ma'atuk's help, Eddé succeeded in winning over Elias Toma Sakaf, thus ensuring himself a majority.[202]

On 20 January, parliament met amidst tight security. Before the vote, de Martel told the deputies that they had a national responsibility and stressed the neutrality maintained by the High Commission throughout the election campaign. In the first ballot, 14 deputies voted for Eddé and 11 for Khuri. In the second ballot Eddé was elected by 15 votes to 10. Paradoxically, Eddé was supported mainly by Muslim deputies representing the annexed regions, while Khuri was backed by the deputies from Mount Lebanon, most of whom were Maronites. Thus, despite Khuri's efforts to portray Eddé as anti-Muslim and himself as an advocate of Christian–Muslim cooperation, the majority of the Sunni and Shiite deputies continued to distrust him, regarding him as a representative of the narrow Maronite ideology of the Mountain.[203]

Eddé's election crowned his ten-year campaign for the presidency. In his acceptance speech, he declared that he would loyally serve his country and cooperate closely with the high commissioner. One of his first moves was to appoint Ayub Tabet as secretary of state as a reward for his support. Confident and vengeful, Eddé was determined to weaken Khuri's hold. Yet he came to power at a time when his rival's views were gaining ground. The uprising in Syria, which coincided with his election, intensified the opposition of Muslims and Arab nationalists to the French mandate, which Eddé still regarded as vital for protection of the Christians. The elections had also demonstrated the growing influence of the Muslims in Lebanese politics, and for the next three years Eddé would attempt to maintain his alliance with their leaders.[204]

In his memoirs, written more than 20 years later, Khuri described his emotions during the journey from parliament to his home in Aley after Eddé's victory. His anger, disappointment and humiliation were still apparent, despite the passage of time. The defeat had finally convinced him that as long as France controlled Lebanon, he had no chance of becoming president. During the following months, Khuri reorganized his camp and renewed his demands for ending the mandate and fully restoring the constitution. He then turned the parliament into a centre of opposition to President Eddé.[205]

CHAPTER FOUR

Mirage and Reality

With the election of Emile Eddé in January 1936, the question of the presidency, which had dominated political life in Lebanon for the previous six years, seemed to have been settled. The Lebanese people now hoped that the new president and parliament would apply themselves to the task of solving the country's pressing political, social and economic problems. The Sunni and Shiite deputies who had voted for Eddé expected him to fulfil his pledges and accord them a greater share in running the state. These expectations were short-lived, however: rivalry between Eddé and Khuri continued unabated, while negotiations on treaties to grant Syria and Lebanon their independence widened the rift between Christians and Muslims.

In September 1936, a decade after de Jouvenel had resigned in the wake of Poincaré's refusal to implement his liberal policy, and three years after de Martel had failed to impose a treaty on the Syrian parliament, France finally concluded a treaty with Syria. A pact with Lebanon followed in November. The terms stipulated that Syria and Lebanon were to gain independence and join the League of Nations at the end of a three-year transitional period. But the considerable efforts expended in negotiating the two treaties were in vain. With the growing threat of war in Europe, successive French governments—pressed by right-wing forces in the National Assembly and the army, which insisted on retaining control of Syria and Lebanon—were unable or unwilling to ratify the treaties. When the Second World War broke out in September 1939, the mandate over Syria and Lebanon was still in force, with the two countries under the administration of the French high commissioner.[1]

The failure of the treaties would become apparent, however, only two years after their conclusion; in 1936 the negotiations dominated political life in Syria and Lebanon. With the two states scheduled to gain independence, fundamental issues, hitherto unresolved, resurfaced: relations with France; the incorporation of Jabal Druze, the Alawite region and Alexandretta into Syria; political and economic ties between Syria and Lebanon; and Syria's claims to Tripoli and the Beqa valley. Lebanon, divided between its Christian and Muslim populations, was again torn between conflicting pressures from Paris and Damascus.

Italy's invasion of Ethiopia in October 1935 marked the beginning of a particularly turbulent year in the Middle East. In Egypt, the Wafd resumed its struggle against Britain, and in December strikes and demonstrations throughout the country forced Britain to renew negotiations on a treaty. Events in Ethiopia and Egypt triggered a national uprising in Syria in January and February 1936, impelling France to end its boycott of the National Bloc and negotiate directly with its leaders. In turn, the Syrian crisis precipitated a revolt in Palestine in April, which soon escalated into a national struggle against Britain and the Zionist movement. Throughout the Middle East, the Arabs were rising up against Western colonial powers, demanding independence and unity. Arab solidarity had not been so pronounced since the Syrian–Druze revolt a decade earlier.[2]

The aggressive policies of Hitler and Mussolini and their massive military investments sparked fears in France of an imminent war—not long after after a million and a quarter French soldiers had perished defending the nation against Germany. Moreover, French politicians, generals and diplomats were acutely aware that their country remained demographically and economically inferior to Germany. The collapse of the elaborate European and international order, in which France had invested so heavily to ensure its security in the face of the German threat, forced the leadership back to the drawing board. Military considerations subsequently took on a significant role in France's foreign policy, especially in its mandated territories.[3]

French strategists made a clear distinction between North Africa and the Levant when evaluating their potential contribution in the event of a war in Europe. Based on the experience of the First World War, North Africa was considered vital to France's defense plans. With its proximity, natural resources and the large French population in Algeria, North Africa was an essential strategic hinterland. Indeed, one quarter of the French army and a large part of its navy were stationed there. Italy's reinforcement of its navy and air force in the western Mediterranean, and the outbreak of the Spanish Civil War endangered France's naval routes between North Africa and Toulon. As a countermeasure, the French navy began building a new base in Mars al-Kabir in Algeria to supplement those in Bezerta, Tunisia and Casablanca. At the same time, the railway from Algeria to Morocco was extended to the Atlantic Ocean to provide an alternative route to Bordeaux and La Rochelle.[4]

Until the end of the 1920s, most of the French generals had considered the mandated territories a military and financial burden of little strategic value. Indeed, each time the Ministry of War was urged to cut its budget, it opted to withdraw troops from the Levant. The military establishment in Paris saw its army in the mandated territories as a colonial force whose main task was to ensure law and order. It was wary of retaining large forces in the region, fearing they could not rapidly be recalled to France in the event of war. The views of Generals Weygand and Gamelin, who had served in the Levant, regarding the region's strategic importance, had fallen on deaf ears. The last time the question of France's military interests in Syria and Lebanon had been examined by the government was in 1931, during discussions on replacing the mandate in Syria with a treaty. A recommendation made then to build a naval base in Tripoli was not implemented.[5]

As the threat of war in Europe mounted and Italy emerged as a major naval and air power in the Mediterranean, the French generals changed their stand on the mandated territories. They feared that the Italian naval bases on the mainland, Rhodes and the Dodecanese Islands might endanger French naval routes to its allies in the Balkans, as well as to the Dardenelles Straits and the Suez Canal. They warned that France could not rely solely on the British navy, with its bases in Alexandria, Cyprus and Haifa, to protect its interests in the eastern Mediterranean; France required its own bases in the region. The building of a British naval base in Haifa prompted the French Naval Ministry to press for modernizing the port in Beirut and constructing a new port in Tripoli. With the completion of the pipeline from Mosul in 1935 and the decision to build a large refinery in Tripoli, control of Syria and Lebanon and the securing of naval routes to France became even more vital. Noting Britain's strategy of retaining control over Iraq through its air bases there, the French Air Ministry called for its government to pursue a similar policy in Syria and Lebanon. It also pointed to the importance of airfields in the Levant for France's aerial links with its colonies in Indo-China. Thus, from the mid-1930s, French policy in Syria and Lebanon was influenced by immediate military and strategic concerns.[6]

In March 1935, during the deliberations in Paris that followed the tobacco monopoly crisis, de Martel proposed that the Quai d'Orsay and the Ministries of War, Navy and Air hold joint discussions on the strategic and imperial interests to be secured in the treaties with Syria and Lebanon. He stressed in particular the importance of ensuring French interests in Lebanon, now that the Mosul–Tripoli oil pipeline had been completed. On 21 March, he was instructed by the prime minister to confer with General Huntziger, commander of the French Army in the Levant, and 'to prepare a new study of the military organization in anticipation of the evolution of the mandate system into a treaty system'. It was decided that during Huntziger's forthcoming visit to Paris in May, a meeting would be convened, to be attended by representatives of all the ministries concerned. But in the following months little progress was made, as de Martel became preoccupied with the crisis in Lebanon.[7]

In early May, General Huntziger and Rear-Admiral Rivet, commander of the naval division in the Levant, prepared two memoranda defining France's military interests in the mandated territories. The memoranda were sent to the Ministries of War and Navy, and their recommendations subsequently served as a basis for the army's demands in the treaty negotiations with Syria and Lebanon. Huntziger argued that France should retain its command over seaports and airports in the mandated territories to ensure freedom of operation in the eastern Mediterranean. This would allow it both to guarantee the internal security of the mandated territories, and to reap the benefits of their resources, especially the oil from the IPC pipeline, in time of war. He divided the region into three zones: Syria, where France would maintain a limited military presence; Jabal Druze, the Alawite region and Alexandretta, in which France would station a larger force for a transitional period; and Lebanon, where it was vital to have complete freedom of action. He recommended that the French army maintain control over the strategically important triangle between Tripoli, Homs and Tartus, and station troops in Latakiya and Jabal Druze. He argued that France should also oversee the roads linking its bases in Lebanon to Suwayda, in Jabal Druze, by way of Kuneitra and the Houran, as well as the oil pipeline up to the Iraqi border. He also proposed constructing two air bases in the vicinity of Damascus to oversee the Syrian capital, and three more near Alexandretta, Aleppo and Deir al-Zor to serve as stopovers on the air routes to Indo-China. Both Huntziger and Rivet stressed Lebanon's strategic importance: Beirut was a major eastern Mediterranean port needed by the French navy for reinforcements in times of crisis; Tripoli was essential for oil supplies; the base in Rayak was indispensable for the air force.[8]

In October 1935 the minister of war sent a letter to the prime minister enclosing Huntziger's memorandum and reiterating the need to ensure French military interests in the treaty with Syria. He also proposed that France retain its mandate in Lebanon, the Alawite region and Jabal Druze. The prime minister had heard nothing on the matter from either the Quai d'Orsay or the high commissioner since issuing instructions to de Martel in March and was surprised to receive a copy of the memorandum. In reply to the minister of war he stressed that the issue of retaining the mandate had first to be studied by de Martel and Huntziger in Beirut, and by the Quai d'Orsay and the Ministry of War in Paris. He nevertheless emphasized the advantages of treaties, pointing to the limitations imposed on France by the mandate. France could emulate Britain's example in Iraq, maintaining control of Syria with a small number of bases. Rejecting the proposal to retain the mandate in Jabal Druze and the Alawite region, he stressed it would be impossible to come to any agreement with Syria without returning those areas. Although he shared the minister of war's views on the importance of a military presence in Lebanon, especially in the Tripoli area, he advocated ending the mandate there as well. The letter prompted the prime minister to renew his instructions to the Quai d'Orsay and de Martel. They were to begin consultations with the Ministries of War, Navy and Air on defining the means to secure France's strategic interests in Syria and Lebanon, taking into consideration both military and political constraints.[9]

With the army adamant on safeguarding French military interests in Lebanon, the Quai d'Orsay and the High Commission sought to establish a stable and friendly government in Beirut. The support of the Christians, particularly the Maronites, had to be maintained, and steps taken to prevent the Syrian nationalists and their Arab Muslim allies in Lebanon from undermining the Lebanese state and French interests there. Fully committed to Lebanon's territorial integrity, France would oppose Syrian claims over Tripoli and the Beqa valley. After 1935 it substantially increased investment in strategic installations in Lebanon: the port of Beirut was enlarged; an airport and communications centre were built in Khaldeh; and in Tripoli the port was improved and construction begun on an airport and oil refinery.

This emphasis on military considerations reinforced Syrian nationalist fears that France intended to retain Lebanon as a major Middle East base from which to control Syria even after granting it independence. Thus, while in 1935 and early 1936 the Syrian nationalists had sought the cooperation of the Lebanese Christians, in particular Patriarch Arida, they resumed their territorial claims in Lebanon during the treaty negotiations and encouraged the Muslims on the coast to step up their campaign for union with Syria. Indeed, in the summer of 1936, the Lebanese question became a major point of contention in the Franco–Syrian negotiations.

In October 1935, on the eve of de Martel's return from Paris, tension in Syria was running high. Rumours abounded that the Quai d'Orsay had instructed de Martel to end the two years of political stagnation, restore constitutional life and renew treaty negotiations. With its leaders divided and its influence eroded, the National Bloc was under pressure to take action against the mandate. Resentment mounted after de Martel allowed the Lebanese parliament to elect a president, while in Syria the constitution remained suspended. De Martel planned to decentralize the administrative system in order to grant a larger measure of autonomy to the minority regions before their integration into Syria, and limit the control of the nationalist-dominated towns over the surrounding countryside—strengthening the nationalists' conviction that

France was still seeking to undermine their position and prevent Syria from attaining political unity. The Italian invasion of Ethiopia, the reports of an imminent war in Europe and the uprising in Egypt added to the tension and anxiety in Syria. Growing numbers of Arab leaders now believed that such a war would weaken British and French control in the Middle East and enable them to undo the War Agreements and thus secure independence and unity.[10]

The death in November of Ibrahim Hananu, one of Syria's most admired leaders, served as an opportunity for the nationalists to settle their differences, close ranks and muster public support for their struggle against France. Throughout December the National Bloc organized demonstrations, strikes and a boycott of the electric and tramway companies, which were foreign concessionaires. It also renewed efforts to win the approval of Arida and other Maronite politicians. Preparations were made for a large-scale demonstration in Damascus on 10 January, which marked the 40th day after Hananu's death. For its part, the High Commission took elaborate measures to foil the nationalists' plans. It cautioned their leaders, put the army and police on the alert, and attempted to prevent demonstrators from entering Damascus. Nevertheless, large demonstrations were held in Damascus and other towns in Syria and Lebanon, and the situation rapidly deteriorated into a general uprising. The expulsion of Barudi to Kamishli and the imprisonment of Mardam, Bakri and Sa'dallah al-Jabiri merely added fuel to the fire, forcing General Huntziger to declare a state of emergency on 10 February. In violent clashes with the French army, 13 demonstrators were killed and more than 3000 detained.[11]

The crisis in Syria placed de Martel in a quandary—there had been yet another change in government in early February, and he had not received any clear instructions from Paris. His handling of the crisis was sharply criticized in the National Assembly and by the press, while the Foreign Affairs Committee proposed sending a special commission of inquiry to Syria. Fearing that the strikes and demonstrations might escalate into a wider revolt, de Martel began informal talks with the National Bloc leaders in an attempt to defuse the tension. Flandin, the new foreign minister, approved his initiative, but cautioned him against making any explicit promises and summoned him to Paris to report to the Haut-Comité Méditerranéen.[12]

After boycotting the National Bloc for two years, de Martel reached the same conclusion as had his two predecessors—only an agreement with the nationalists could ensure law and order in Syria. On 23 February he dissolved al-Hasani's government and entrusted Ata al-Ayubi, a moderate nationalist, with forming a new government. In a conciliatory letter to Ayubi two days later, he affirmed France's intention to replace the mandate with a treaty and 'realize the legitimate aspirations of the Syrian nation'. The letter, immediately made public by the High Commission, along with the release of detainees, opened the way for negotiations with the National Bloc. Toward the end of the month, the High Commission held talks in Beirut with a National Bloc delegation, led by Hashem al-Atasi, on the terms for resumption of negotiations. The status of Jabal Druze, the Alawite region and Alexandretta was again a stumbling block. In informal discussions with French officials, Riad al-Sulh suggested that Jabal Druze and the Alawite region be fully integrated into Syria, with France retaining forces there for a transitional period in order to safeguard the rights of the minorities. This initiative, no doubt made with the approval of the National Bloc, broke the deadlock and opened the way for an agreement. De Martel's positive reaction to Sulh's proposal, which he defined as 'elegant', is understandable; it was consistent with General Huntziger's recommendations. On 1 March, on instructions from Flandin, de Martel reached agreement with the Syrian delegation: France would grant Syria a treaty similar to the Anglo–Iraqi treaty; a Syrian delegation would leave immediately for Paris to negotiate terms; and all detainees would be released. In the following months, attention in the mandated territories turned to Paris and the progress of the Franco–Syrian negotiations.[13]

De Martel left for Paris on 17 March and was followed four days later by a six-member Syrian delegation headed by Hashem al-Atasi. One of its advisers was Riad al-Sulh, who had close ties with the socialists and was considered an expert on French politics. De Martel had expected negotiations to last a month, with unsolved issues to be settled later in Beirut and Damascus. But they continued for over five months, and were beset by a series of crises. The gap between the French and the Syrians, particularly on military issues, proved too wide to be bridged. The French elections in April–May, and Syria's political, territorial and economic claims over Lebanon caused further setbacks.[14]

At the meeting of the Haut-Comité Méditerranéen on 25 March, de Martel reviewed the causes of the uprising in Syria and recommended that France negotiate a treaty with the Syrian government and the National Bloc. He was later received by the prime minister, who approved his recommendations. Yet, as in the past, moves to emancipate the mandated territories met with strong opposition from the right wing groups and the army, as well as from officials in the Quai d'Orsay and the High Commission. Military circles doubted that France's strategic interests could be fully guaranteed in a Syrian state controlled by the National Bloc, while politicians and officials warned that an independent, united Syria might jeopardize France's position in Lebanon and even undermine the latter's very existence as a Christian state.[15]

Shortly after arriving in Paris, the Syrian delegation made a courtesy call on the foreign minister. The Quai d'Orsay entrusted de Martel with the negotiations, but veteran conservative officials in the Quai d'Orsay, including de Caix, Saint-Quentin and Chauvel, were also involved. The Syrian delegates, who had arrived with high expectations, were enraged by the attitude of the Quai d'Orsay. Disagreement soon surfaced in the preliminary discussions, which were devoted to ascertaining whether the 1933 treaty could serve as the basis for a new agreement. At the end of April, de Martel presented the delegation with a draft treaty which included appendices pertaining to French military interests in Syria, terms for the union of the Alawite region and Jabal Druze with Syria, and the nature of economic ties between Syria and Lebanon. The French stand was unacceptable to the Syrian delegates, but they chose to delay their formal reply until after the general elections in France, due to be held on 26 April and 3 May.[16]

The victory of Léon Blum's Popular Front, a coalition of socialists, radicals and communists, was welcomed enthusiastically by the Syrian delegation. Its nationalist members expected the French left, which had for years criticized the government's Syrian policy, to support their demands for independence and unity. Informal discussions held in May with socialist and communist deputies, and the delegation's meeting with Blum, the prime minister-designate, reinforced this conviction. The Syrians expected that the new government, after studying the situation in the mandated territories and taking regional and international constraints into consideration, would grant them a treaty far more liberal than that proposed by the previous administration. They therefore continued to stall the negotiations until Blum's regime came to power. After repeated requests from de Martel, Hashem al-Atasi sent him a short letter on 30 May rejecting the French proposals.[17]

Pierre Viénot, the new under-secretary of state for foreign affairs, was appointed to head the negotiations in de Martel's place. A liberal neo-socialist, Viénot believed in the need to emancipate Syria and Lebanon by concluding treaties to replace the mandate. For the next three months, he had to mediate between an uncompromising Syrian delegation, intransigent officials in the Quai d'Orsay, and army generals reluctant to relinquish control of the mandated territories.

The Popular Front's rise to power widened the rift between right and left that had dominated French politics since the war. The right strongly opposed the new government's social and economic reforms, as well as its foreign policy—which sought to maintain peace and stability in Europe through disarmament and a collective security agreement under the aegis of the League of Nations. The generals rejected what they saw as a pacifist policy; they doubted that the leftist government was either willing or able to mobilize the nation against Germany. The government thus faced strong opposition both in domestic and foreign affairs, including the emancipation of Syria and Lebanon, although the latter policy had been initiated by the previous administration.[18]

The right wing used the negotiations with the Syrian delegation, resumed at the beginning of June, as part of its campaign to press the Blum government to guarantee French imperial interests in its colonies. If anything, the army was now more adamantly opposed to terminating the mandate in Syria and Lebanon. In light of Italy's emergence as a major military force in the Mediterranean and its close ties with Germany, the new Ministers of War, Navy and Air immediately came under pressure from their headquarters to secure France's strategic interests in the Levant. Several of the ideas put forward, such as the annexation of the Alawite region and Jabal Druze to Lebanon, were somewhat extreme. De Martel and officials in the Quai d'Orsay inundated Yvon Delbos, the new foreign minister, with memoranda arguing that the French proposals of April and May had integrated French interests with Syrian aspirations for independence and unity. To deter the government from granting further concessions to the Syrians, they exploited public support for France's moral obligation to protect the Christians in the Levant. The High Commission reported that Christians and other minorities feared their interests could not be guaranteed in a Arab Sunni-dominated Syrian state. Robert de Caix cautioned that, following the massacre of the Assyrians in Iraq, the Permanent Mandates Commission would not approve a treaty which failed to safeguard the rights of the minorities in Syria. The Catholic church and missionary orders voiced concern that their educational and cultural activities in Syria and Lebanon might be jeopardized. De Martel warned of a possible conflict over Alexandretta between Syria and Turkey, which could undermine Fernch relations with the latter. Companies with economic interests in Syria and Lebanon also joined the campaign. In an attempt to delay or even foil the negotiations altogether, opponents of the treaty proposed sending a commission of inquiry to the mandated territories before resuming talks.[19]

After years of negotiating with the French, the Syrian nationalist delegates were well aware of the right's capacity to prevent a change in the government's traditional policy on minorities. They were also cognizant of the Maronites' ability to mobilize French political and public support in the face of a threat to Lebanon's independent existence and territorial integrity. At the end of February, Hashem al-Atasi had met in Beirut with Lebanese Sunni notables, who were anxious to learn of their community's fate in the coming negotiations. He informed them that the issue of the territories annexed to Mount Lebanon would be raised in Paris, but not pressed if the conclusion of a Syrian treaty was at risk. Prior to his departure for Paris, de Martel had in fact made clear to the National Bloc that the questions of Lebanese independence and borders would not be up for discussion: the only issue for debate would be its economic ties with Syria. Nonetheless, during negotiations in Paris in April, the Syrian delegation did raise certain political demands in Lebanon. For example, they asked for the words 'les états' in the term 'les états de la Syrie et du Liban' to be replaced by 'les territoires', thus implying that Lebanon should not be regarded as a state. When the French requested air bases in Syria, the Syrian delegates responded that France might retain only those in Rayak and Tripoli—disregarding the fact that both were on Lebanese territory.[20]

The Syrian delegation's new-found confidence was expressed in a letter sent by Hashem al-Atasi to de Martel on 11 June, rejecting the French proposals and demanding resumption of negotiations on all standing issues. Atasi also formally requested the return of 'the Syrian territories which had been annexed to Lebanon', singling out the cities of Rayak and Tripoli, 'which are on Syrian soil'. With the left in power, the nationalists believed they stood a better chance of revising Lebanon's borders or linking it politically to Syria. They also had another goal: to undermine French designs to transform Lebanon into a major base for its army, navy and air force by limiting both the size of the French forces and the duration of their stay.[21]

The French military establishment and officials in the Quai d'Orsay reacted angrily to the Syrian delegation's territorial claims in Lebanon, regarding them as yet another indication of Syrian intentions to remove France from its strategic positions in all its mandated territories. The intimate ties between leftist deputies and Syrian delegates fueled the army's fears that the new socialist government might acquiesce in Arab nationalist demands for access to the sea through Tripoli, thereby weakening French control over this strategically important city. These concerns were not unfounded; some government advisers had expressed willingness to consider such a solution. De Martel hastened to point out that in accordance with the March agreement, Lebanon would not be on the agenda in the Paris negotiations. He reiterated that Lebanon, like Syria, enjoyed an international status recognized by the League of Nations, with borders guaranteed by France. As for Syria's demand for access to the sea, he argued that it would have control over the port of Alexandretta and was merely seeking a pretext to dismember Lebanon. With a certain element of truth, he commented that while the Syrian delegates were claiming Jabal Druze and the Alawite region under the slogan of national unity, they were striving at the same time to divide Lebanon along religious and sectarian lines.[22]

The decision of the Syrian delegates to formally raise political and territorial claims in Lebanon sparked an immediate crisis in the negotiations in Paris as well as Beirut. The French government had to contain the situation in Lebanon before concluding any treaty with the Syrian delegation. Thus, while the French and Syrian representatives were negotiating a treaty in Paris, in Lebanon the High Commission and the National Bloc were at loggerheads. The National Bloc incited the Muslims, especially in Tripoli, to step up their campaign for union with Syria, and strove to split the Christian camp by urging some of its leaders to sever their historical ties with France. The High Commission, for its part, sought to retain the support of the Maronites, while trying to convince both Sunnis and Shiites that their interests would best be served by integration into an independent Lebanese state, in which France would protect the rights of all communities.[23]

The crisis in Syria at the start of the year and the ensuing negotiations in Paris had an immediate impact on Lebanon's internal affairs. Indeed, 1936 was for Lebanon one of the most turbulent years in the inter-war period. The country had not yet recovered from the presidential elections when it was engulfed by the Syrian uprising. Demonstrations and strikes supporting the Syrian national struggle against the French mandate soon spread to Tripoli, Beirut, Sidon and Ba'albeck. The agreement between de Martel and Atasi heightened anxiety among Christians and Muslims alike, and prompted their leaders to take action. Within less than two weeks, two major developments took place that marked a turning point in inter-sectarian relations in Lebanon: the Conference of the Coast, and the letter from seven Constitutional Bloc deputies to the High Commission. The first signalled the beginning of intense public debate among the Sunnis over their relations with Syria; the second was an attempt by the Khuri camp to redefine Lebanese Christian relations with France.

With Syria about to gain independence and secure the return of Jabal Druze and the Alawite region, the Muslims in Lebanon, especially the Sunnis, feared that the National Bloc would abandon them to their fate as a minority in a Christian state dominated by the Maronites and closely linked to France. The ambivalent message conveyed by the National Bloc leaders before their departure for Paris reinforced Muslim anxiety. No longer were they willing to wait passively while their brethren in Syria, Palestine and Egypt rose up against the colonial powers. The Sunni leadership, however, was deeply divided over its goals and course of action. Proponents of Syrian unity, particularly in Tripoli, continued to insist on immediate annexation to Syria. Politicians, ministers, deputies and officials in the Lebanese institutions argued that as the Syrians were focused solely on their own interests, the Muslims needed to secure their rights in Lebanon. Between these two extremes stood the pan-Arabists, who claimed that the most pressing issue was neither Lebanon's borders nor Muslim political rights, but ensuring complete independence from France. When this goal was achieved, they maintained, Lebanon would become an Arab state in which Muslims would enjoy full equality with their Christian compatriots.[24]

Disagreement among the Sunni leaders emerged during the Conference of the Coast and in the ensuing public debate. The Conference was convened on 10 March at the initiative of Salim Ali Salam, Abd al-Hamid Karameh and Salah Bayhum, who sought to press the high commissioner and the Syrian delegation to discuss the future status of the areas annexed to Mount Lebanon in the Paris negotiations. Despite the organizers' efforts to portray the conference as non-sectarian and nationalist in nature, it was primarily a Sunni-Muslim event. It took place at Salam's home, and was attended by 30 delegates and 70 observers from Tripoli, Beirut, Sidon, Tyre, Ba'albeck and Jabal Amil; the Muslim ministers were conspicuously absent. Although the participants failed to agree on a plan of action, Salam, Karameh and Bayhum passed a resolution demanding the immediate return to Syria of the territories formerly annexed to Mount Lebanon. The resolution was sent to the High Commission, the Quai d'Orsay and the Permanent Mandates Commission, as well as to the National Bloc in Damascus.[25]

During the following weeks, Tripoli became the centre of a campaign against the Lebanese state. Immediately after the Conference, Karameh and Bisar went to Damascus to urge the National Bloc leaders to raise the issue of Tripoli's annexation to Syria in the negotiations. They also requested an audience with de Martel in order to expound their views before his departure for Paris. At a meeting with Pati de Clam, the French administrative adviser in north Lebanon, they accused the Lebanese government of treating the inhabitants of Tripoli as second-class citizens and of having neglected the city for years. Indeed, the adviser himself had repeatedly made similar charges and recommended that the Lebanese government invest more in Tripoli.[26]

The opening of the negotiations in Paris, which coincided with the general strike in Palestine declared by the mufti, Hajj Amin al-Husaini, exacerbated tension among the Muslims in Lebanon. In April, demonstrations were held in Tripoli, Beirut and Sidon in support of the Palestinian struggle and Syrian unity. Anti-French sentiment among the Shiites in the south intensified after Fakhri al-Barudi toured the region. Feelings escalated into violent clashes with the Lebanese gendarmerie during the Ashura celebrations in Nabatiya, in which two people were killed and scores injured. In turn, the violence sparked strikes and demonstrations throughout the south against the mandate and the Lebanese government.[27]

The National Bloc leaders took different stands on the campaign conducted in Lebanon by the proponents of Syrian unity. Atasi and Quwatly were determined to encourage their activities, while Jamil Mardam and Riad al-Sulh were concerned that these might jeopardize the treaty negotiations with France. Arguing that the most urgent goal of the Syrian Arab nationalists was to end French control over Lebanon, Sulh opposed any move that might antagonize the Christians and enable France to reinforce its position as their protector. On 5 March, accompanied by Khalil Ma'atuk and Amin Arslan, he went to Bkerki to inform Arida that the National Bloc had refrained from making any territorial claims in Lebanon during the talks with de Martel. He criticized the decision taken by Salam and Bayhum to convene a conference and, reluctant to participate himself, instructed his young cousin, Khazim al-Sulh, to try to foil any decision that might antagonize the Christians. Khazim al-Sulh, however, was prevented from expressing his views and therefore refused to sign the resolution. In the aftermath of the Conference of the Coast, Riad al-Sulh considered organizing another conference, but gave up his plans as he was about to leave for Paris with the Syrian delegation. He nevertheless advised his cousin to convey a message to Arida reiterating Muslim willingness to recognize Lebanon's borders— provided it became an independent, sovereign Arab state and a member of the League of Nations, and that its relations with France were based on a treaty resembling the Franco–Syrian pact about to be concluded. A similar stand was taken by Fakhri al-Barudi and Mazhar Raslan, who arrived in Bkerki on 13 March to inform Arida of their disapproval of the Beirut conference's decision.[28]

The day after the Conference of the Coast, Khazim al-Sulh published an article in *al-Nahar*, testifying to the extent to which the pan-Arabists had modified their stand toward the Lebanese state. The article, which provoked intense public debate, was a response to Sulh's critics and an attempt to calm the Christians, who had been angered by the resolution passed at the conference. He praised Patriarch Arida for his patriotic stand and attacked those who insisted on revision of Lebanon's borders, warning that such a move would transform the country into a irredentist Christian entity closely linked to France—a Malta or Gibraltar in the heart of the Arab world. Sulh also pointed to growing Christian disillusionment with the French mandate, claiming that this development, together with the distancing of Arab nationalism from Islam, would create common ground for a joint Muslim–Christian struggle for Lebanese independence. When this goal was achieved, he argued, the question of Lebanon's relations with Syria and the rest of the Arab world would be resolved naturally, through democratic means. All efforts now had to be directed toward ensuring Lebanon's complete independence from France.[29]

Despite such views, it is doubtful that common ground for genuine cooperation existed at that stage at a national level, either between Christians and Muslims or between Lebanon and Syria. Syrian claims over Lebanon in the Paris negotiations, the resolutions adopted by the Conference of the Coast in March and October that year, and the large-scale Muslim campaign against the Lebanese state in July and November, attested to the fact that neither Syria nor the majority of the Muslims in Lebanon were prepared to recognize a Lebanese state. For their part, even the Christian politicians most critical of the mandate, who strove to replace it with a treaty, were not yet ready to give up French protection altogether.

Since 1920, the Christians, especially the Maronites, had dreaded the rise of a united, independent Muslim Syrian state to the east. With the French decision in early March 1936 to enter negotiations with the National Bloc on ending the mandate, they feared such a state was close to realization. They anxiously observed France's reluctance to take harsh measures to suppress the Syrian uprising, aware that, despite its repeated declarations and pledges, France seemed ready to abandon the minorities in Syria to their fate. They witnessed the minorities' appeals to the High Commission to ensure their rights before Syria was granted independence, and their leaders' desperate attempts to improve relations with the National Bloc. Reflecting the mounting fear of Sunni domination, even among the non-Christian communities, Alawite notables proposed to Eddé and Arida that their region be annexed to Lebanon.[30]

During the spring and summer of 1936, the Maronites faced a dilemma: whether to continue to trust their traditional ally, France, notwithstanding its hesitant policy, or align themselves with Syria, despite the fact that some National Bloc leaders continued to refer to Lebanon as 'coastal Syria'. Should they join Syria in seeking a treaty with France, or retain the mandate with its international guarantee for Lebanon's separate existence? The tide of pan-Arabism engulfing the region, and the separatist declarations of the Muslims in Lebanon led some Maronites to make radical proposals—substitution of the mandate with a French condominium, for example, or the return of Lebanon to its pre-war borders and its transformation into a French canton. Such ideas reflected the deep confusion and divisions within the Maronite community, and its indecisiveness in the face of the most serious challenge since 1926 to Lebanon's territorial integrity and independent existence. The

Maronite political and religious leaders failed, however, to rise above their immediate political interests. The rivalry between Eddé and Khuri continued unabated, while Arida pursued his personal feud with de Martel. For their part, Bishops Khuri and Mubarak renewed their efforts to depose Arida, and in May, Mubarak travelled to Rome and Paris to seek Vatican and French government support for this move.[31]

The Syrian uprising strengthened the belief of the Khuri camp that the Christians should relinquish their historic ties with France and forge an alliance with the pan-Arabist movement both to affirm Lebanon's existence and guarantee their access to power. In talks held in February 1936, Riad al-Sulh advised Constitutional Bloc members of the National Bloc's willingness to recognize Lebanon's independence and territorial integrity, provided the Christians joined the struggle against France to achieve these goals. Two days after the de Martel-Atasi agreement became public, seven deputies from the Constitutional Bloc (excluding Khuri), presented Meyrier, the French delegate-general, with a memorandum requesting France to grant Lebanon the same rights it had given their 'Syrian brethren'. They demanded restoration of the constitution, replacement of the mandate with a treaty and Lebanon's admission into the League of Nations. They also asked permission for a Lebanese delegation to go to Paris to negotiate a treaty with the French government. The memorandum marked another stage in the transformation of the Constitutional Bloc into a national movement against the French mandate. It was a skilful political move, a demonstration that Khuri could undermine French policy if de Martel continued to ignore his political interests. It also enhanced Khuri's public stature among both Muslims and Christians. To the Syrians and the Muslims in Lebanon, he was an anti-French Maronite leader, willing to join the national struggle for independence; to the Christians, he was a patriotic Lebanese statesman, demanding that France treat Lebanon on equal terms with Syria.[32]

De Martel, who was initiating very sensitive negotiations with the National Bloc, angrily rejected the Constitutional Bloc's demands. In his despatches to Paris, he claimed that Khuri's initiative was motivated by his defeat in the presidential elections, and warned that the Syrian nationalists were exploiting rivalry within the Maronite community to undermine French interests in Lebanon. He rejected Khuri's request that a Lebanese delegation be allowed to leave for Paris, stressing that it would hamper efforts to reach an agreement with Syria. And he assured Eddé, who was under opposition pressure to insist on a treaty similar to that being negotiated with Syria, that the French government would not permit the Syrian delegation to make any claims that could endanger Lebanon's independence or territorial integrity. For his part, Eddé believed that Khuri's main objective had been to force de

Martel to restore full power to parliament in order to restrict presidential authority. Thus, after ensuring the election of his candidate, Petro Trad, as speaker of the parliament in April, Eddé declared suspension of further parliamentary sessions, under the pretext that no serious debate could take place whilst the high commissioner was in Paris.[33]

The victory of the Popular Front increased fears among the Lebanese Christians that the new leftist government would be less committed to their protection and might grant Syria concessions at Lebanon's expense, in order to hasten an agreement with the Syrian delegation. Reports from Paris of the latter's intentions to claim Tripoli and the Beqa valley exacerbated tension in Lebanon. The Constitutional Bloc, which only a few months earlier had cooperated with the National Bloc, now denounced Eddé for failing to protect Lebanon's territorial integrity against Syrian ambitions. It renewed its request that a Lebanese delegation, including members of the parliament, be allowed to leave immediately for Paris. Under increasing public pressure, Eddé met Meyrier on 8 June, but his demand that Lebanon be permitted to send its own delegation was again rejected. In a telegram to de Martel, Eddé insisted that 'no decision concerning Lebanon's interests be made during the negotiations with the Syrian delegation'.[34]

Reports of the territorial claims made by Hashem al-Atasi on 11 June reached Beirut the following day and provoked a strong reaction from the Christians. The High Commission and the Quai d'Orsay were inundated by protests: Eddé requested that a Lebanese delegation go to Paris to defend the country's national interests; Arida attacked Syria's attempt to undermine Lebanon's territorial integrity; the Constitutional Bloc demanded that the parliament be urgently convened. Lebanese immigrant organizations in France, Egypt and North and South America protested to their French ambassadors and consuls and sent telegrams to the Quai d'Orsay, reminding France of its moral obligation to protect the Christians in Lebanon. In Paris, Bishop Mubarak and Riad al-Sulh traded insults in the press, while in Beirut, Christian and Muslim newspapers accused each other's communities of lacking patriotism and harming national interests. As tension mounted, Meyrier sent telegrams to the Quai d'Orsay warning of inter-sectarian strife and urging that steps be taken to calm the Christians.[35]

The sharp reaction to Atasi's letter in the army and pro-Lebanese circles in Paris, and among the Christians in Lebanon, in addition to Meyrier's warning, compelled Blum's government to take immediate action. On 18 June the Haut-Comité Mediterranéen convened to review the negotiations with the Syrian delegation and their repercussions in Lebanon. The participants acknowledged the importance of Christian support, particularly that of the Maronites, if France was to safeguard its strategic, economic and cultural interests in Lebanon, and agreed that Lebanon and Syria should be treated on equal terms. It was therefore decided that the mandate in Lebanon be replaced with a treaty, in order to reinforce Lebanon's international status and link it directly to France—thereby ending the intervention of the Permanent Mandates Commission. Two days later Viénot sent a letter to Eddé officially reiterating France's commitment to maintaining Lebanon's independence and territorial integrity and assuring him that Lebanon would be accorded a treaty similar to that of Syria. Thus 17 years after Gouraud had formed Greater Lebanon, and a decade after de Jouvenel's establishment of the Lebanese Republic, France was again obliged to issue an official statement guaranteeing continued existence of the Lebanese state within its 1920 borders.[36]

Viénot's letter, hastily published by the Quai d'Orsay and the High Commission, was received with great satisfaction by the Lebanese Christians and their emigrant organizations, who sent numerous telegrams of support and thanks to Paris. Muslim and pan-Arabist leaders in Lebanon and Syria, however, angrily accused France and the Lebanese Christians of attempting to create a fait accompli. The letter sparked a series of crises in Lebanon which culminated during the negotiations on the Franco–Lebanese treaty in October and November.[37]

The letter, which de Martel had formally sent to Hashem al-Atasi, deepened disagreement over Lebanon among the members of the Syrian delegation. Mardam warned his colleagues that their insistence on revision of Lebanon's borders would jeopardize efforts to secure a treaty and the return of Jabal Druze and the Alawite region to Syria. Atasi and Sa'dallah al-Jabiri, however, believed that only continued pressure on the French government would guarantee Syrian interests in Lebanon and the rights of the Muslims there. A similar stand was taken by the National Bloc leaders in Damascus and, indeed, Shukri al-Quwatly constantly urged Atasi not to give in to French coercion. For his part, Sulh argued that for tactical reasons, the Syrian delegation should maintain its territorial claims over Lebanon as a means of forcing France to limit its military presence in Syria and Lebanon, as well as improving Syria's position in negotiations on the Common Interests. He pointed to the support for the Syrian stand among socialist and communist deputies and regarded Viénot's statement as merely a temporary measure to placate the right. Reports of a conflict between Eddé and Khuri over the constitution, which Sulh received from Beirut in July and August, reinforced his belief that it was possible to use the rivalry between the two Maronite leaders, and the tension between Khuri's camp and the High Commission, to lure part of the Christian leadership into collaboration with the National Bloc.[38]

In a letter to de Martel in early July, Atasi wrote that the Syrian delegation had been 'painfully surprised' by Viénot's statement. He warned that the policy outlined by Viénot could 'create centres of irredentism in Lebanon, which would make it difficult for the Syrian people to remain on friendly terms with Lebanon'. He argued that Lebanon's borders had been unilaterally declared by France in a decree on 31 August 1920, against the wishes of the Syrians in the annexed regions. This decree had been merely an administrative act, to which the French government was now granting international status. He reiterated Syria's right to 'its natural sea ports', and reminded de Martel that both de Jouvenel and Ponsot had recognized that principle, with Eddé also supporting the idea at the time. Atasi concluded by demanding that 'the territories torn away should be allowed to express their wishes in a free plebiscite'. His letter drew an immediate response from Viénot, who warned that if the Syrian delegation continued to make territorial claims in Lebanon, it would 'risk compromising the satisfactory and rapid conclusion of the ongoing negotiations'.[39]

Notwithstanding Viénot's warning, the nationalist members of the Syrian delegation were determined to press their country's claims in Lebanon. They urged the National Bloc leaders in Damascus to instigate a campaign among the Muslims in Lebanon, particularly in Sidon and south Lebanon, in support of union with Syria. Interest in the Sidon region evolved from Sulh's attempt to turn his native city into a Syrian port, both providing Syria with a foothold in Lebanon, and inserting a wedge between Christian Lebanon and a future Jewish state—whose establishment in Palestine was then being considered. Throughout July Quwatly appealed to Muslim notables in Sidon and pro-Syrian Shiites in the south to demonstrate and send petitions requesting their annexation to Syria. Sulh sent similar instructions from Paris to his relatives and friends in Sidon and Jabal Amil.[40]

On 5 July, delegates from Tripoli, Beirut, Nabatiya, Marjayoun, Tyre and Bint Jbeyl met in Sidon and passed a resolution supporting Syrian unity. They also called for a plebiscite to be held among the inhabitants of the regions annexed to Mount Lebanon, and authorized the Syrian delegation in Paris to present their national aspirations. The resolution was forwarded to the French government, the National Assembly and the Permanent Mandates Commission, as well as to the Syrian delegation in Paris and the National Bloc in Damascus. In the days that followed, tension mounted in Sidon. Despite precautionary measures by the High Commission, large-scale demonstrations took place on 12 July, ending in violent clashes with the French army and the Lebanese gendarmerie, in which a number of demonstrators were killed. A three-day general strike was staged in protest, and the demonstrations soon spread from Sidon to other cities in Lebanon and Syria.

In Beirut, Omar Bayhum and Salim Ali Salam convened a meeting of prominent Muslim leaders, at the conclusion of which they wrote to Foreign Minister Delbos that the Muslims 'categorically refused to be governed by a minority'. In another letter to Meyrier, Salam warned that any solution to the Lebanese question which failed to fulfil Muslim aspirations would only exacerbate the situation.[41]

The turmoil in Sidon and the Muslim campaign in support of Syria's territorial claims provoked harsh criticism from the Christians, whose newspapers now intensified their attacks on Syria and its allies in Lebanon. In *L'Orient*, Georges Naqash told the Syrians, 'We don't have anything to offer you—leave us alone,' and warned that 'all the disorder and violence here and in the towns in the interior merely distract from the cause for Syria's independence and delay the conclusion of the negotiations still under way in Paris.' Writing in *Le Journaliste Errant*, Iskandar Riashi cynically proposed that the Christians respond to the campaign for Syrian unity in Sidon and Tripoli by referring the separatists to General Huntziger.[42]

Pressed by the Quai d'Orsay, Meyrier moved quickly to contain pro-Syrian activity among the Muslims in Lebanon. He was joined by Eddé, now being harshly attacked by the Constitutional Bloc for failing to defend Lebanon's independence and territorial integrity. In the south, Aref al-Zein was imprisoned, while Kamil al-As'ad and other moderate Shiite leaders were urged to stage rallies and sign petitions supporting the Lebanese state. Syrian unionists in Sidon, Beirut and Tripoli were warned to cease their activities, and Muslim politicians and officials in the Lebanese administration were asked to declare publicly their allegiance to the Lebanese state. On 7 July, five Sunni deputies (Khalid Shihab, Khair al-Din al-Ahdab, Amin Muqadam, Muhammad Amin Qaz'oun, and Muhammad Abd al-Razak) sent a letter to Eddé announcing their recognition of Lebanon and requesting complete equality for the Muslims. Their letter was criticized by pro-Syrian leaders, who accused the deputies of treason and insisted that they did not represent the Muslims in Lebanon. In response to threats on his life, Muqadam reneged on his decision and signed a petition endorsing Tripoli's annexation to Syria. The deputies' letter deepened divisions within the Sunni community and enabled Meyrier and Eddé to claim that the supporters of Syrian unity were in the minority. By the end of the month, their combined efforts had succeeded in limiting the campaign for Syrian unity in Lebanon.[43]

After failing to organize a large-scale campaign for union with Syria among the Muslims in Lebanon, the Syrian delegation changed tactics. They proposed to the French negotiators that the issues of the Syro–Lebanese borders and economic relations between the two countries be settled in direct negotiations by their governments. Viénot, however, reaffirmed that France would not grant Syria and Lebanon independence or sponsor their admission to the League of Nations until those issues were settled. The Syrian delegation also tried to use the question of the Common Interests to link Lebanon to Syria politically through a confederal system. They proposed that the Common Interests organization, which was under the control of the high commissioner, be replaced by a new agency with considerable political and economic power. Syria and Lebanon would be represented in it in accordance with the size of their populations. This proposal was also rejected by the French negotiators, one of whom remarked wryly that 'after failing to absorb Lebanon piece by piece, the Syrians were now trying to take it over in its entirety.'[44]

At the end of four months of negotiations, the French and the Syrians were still far from agreement on major issues, including the size and duration of France's military presence in Jabal Druze and the Alawite region, the length of the transitional period between approval of the treaty and its coming into force, protection of the minorities, and Syro–Lebanese relations. The French Finance Ministry's demand that Syria reimburse France with part of the FF 4 billion which, it claimed, had been invested in Syria since the beginning of the mandate, became another source of contention. Dissension within the French government continued to hinder progress in the negotiations. Viénot, backed by Foreign Minister Delbos, upheld his view that France had urgently to conclude a treaty with Syria. Pointing to the revolt in Palestine against Britain, he warned that failure of the negotiations in Paris would provoke a general uprising in Syria, which might also endanger French interests in North Africa. The Minister of War and the army command, however, claimed that events in Palestine demonstrated the region's inherent political instability and highlighted France's need to guarantee its strategic imperial interests in Syria. Critics of the treaty pointed to opposition by the Turkish, Druze, Alawite and Christian minorities to integration into an independent Syrian state dominated by an Arab Sunni majority, and argued that France could not morally renounce its minorities policy. In July and August, Alawite notables renewed their appeal to Eddé and Arida to annex their region to Lebanon, prompting Viénot to warn the two Maronite leaders that such a move would reinforce Syrian hostility toward Lebanon and transform the Christians into a minority in their own state.[45]

The Anglo–Egyptian treaty, signed at the end of August, increased pressure on the French government vis-à-vis Syria. Prime Minister Blum now backed Viénot's initiative to speed up the negotiations, even if it entailed compromising some of France's initial terms. After two weeks of intense talks, the two sides finally reached agreement. On 9 September, Viénot and

Hashem al-Atasi signed a 25-year 'treaty of friendship and alliance' between the states, which included protocols and exchanges of letters. This treaty, based on the Anglo–Iraqi treaty, stipulated that Syria would gain independence and become a member of the League of Nations at the end of a three-year transitional period. Jabal Druze and the Alawite region would be integrated into Syria, but would continue to enjoy a certain degree of administrative and financial autonomy, similar to that of Alexandretta. A military protocol specified that France would assist Syria in equipping and training its army and protecting its sovereignty. France would be allowed to retain two military airports, at least 25 miles from any one of the four interior towns, and the transport and port facilities necessary to maintain them. It was also permitted to station forces in Jabal Druze and the Alawite region, but for a five-year period only. The issue of the Common Interests was to be decided in direct negotiations between the Syrian and Lebanese governments. Yet despite French pressure, the Syrian delegation refused to recognize Lebanon's independence and borders. Indeed, during the ceremony at which the treaties were signed, Atasi declared Syria's desire to form a federation with Lebanon.[46]

The Syrian negotiators were justifiably satisfied with the treaty, which they saw as a major step toward ensuring their country's independence and unity; they were therefore anxious to implement it without delay. The treaty restored the National Bloc's prestige among the Syrian public, and the delegation was accorded a hero's welcome on its return to Damascus. In France, on the other hand, the treaty was criticized by the Ministry of War, the army, senators and deputies on the right, and officials in the Quai d'Orsay and the High Commission, as well as by groups with economic or religious-cultural interests in Syria. Viénot and de Martel were accused of having failed to protect French interests and of surrendering the minorities loyal to France to the Arab Muslim nationalists. The army command argued that Lebanon—now more vulnerable to Syrian subversion—could no longer be a viable military base for France. There were, in fact, considerable discrepancies between the proposals originally outlined by Huntziger and de Martel, and the terms of the treaty. Its opponents thus intensified their efforts in the following months to prevent its ratification by the National Assembly.[47]

After signing the pact with Syria, Viénot and de Martel were eager to conclude a treaty with Lebanon. They assumed that guarantees of French strategic, economic and religious-cultural interests in Lebanon would reduce opposition to the Syrian treaty from the army and the right wing. They also sought to reassure pro-Lebanese Christian circles in France, which feared that an independent Syria would endanger Lebanon's existence. Well aware of Syrian ambitions, Viénot and de Martel were likewise concerned that any delay in the negotiations would enable the National Bloc to step up its subversive activities among the Muslims and Christians in Lebanon. It was therefore decided to speed up negotiations with Lebanon and obtain ratification of the treaty in November, when the Syrian politicians would be preoccupied with parliamentary elections. Moreover, the High Commission would still be able to press the National Bloc to avoid intervening in the Franco–Lebanese negotiations, since the Bloc would need French assistance to gain Alawite and Druze support for their union with Syria. Delbos and Viénot chose to hold the talks in Beirut rather than Paris, to prevent their becoming a focus of political controversy in France, as had negotiations on the Syrian treaty. De Martel was consequently entrusted with the task.[48]

In September, Viénot, de Martel and representatives of the army held deliberations in the Quai d'Orsay to define French policy in Syria and Lebanon in the aftermath of the Syrian treaty. The Ministries of War, Navy and Air drafted a military protocol to be incorporated into the agreement. To limit opposition and avoid delay, the Quai d'Orsay decided to base the Lebanese treaty on that of Syria and to leave the issue of economic ties between Lebanon and Syria to be negotiated directly by their governments. De Martel recommended that steps be taken to prevent the National Bloc and its allies in Lebanon, particularly Riad al-Sulh, from intervening in the negotiations; to persuade the Maronite leaders to grant the Muslims a greater share in running the state; and to convince Eddé and Khuri to settle their differences and create a joint front against Syria and its supporters in Lebanon. His recommendations were approved by Delbos and Viénot, who also stressed the need to win support for the treaty among moderate Muslims in Lebanon. From his return to Beirut at the end of September, until the conclusion of the treaty in mid-November, de Martel successfully implemented the policy defined in Paris. Significantly, much of his time was spent on mediating between Eddé and Khuri and between the Christians and Muslims, rather than negotiating with the Lebanese government.[49]

Upon his arrival in Beirut, de Martel had first to solve a constitutional crisis which was impeding agreement on formation of a Lebanese delegation to the negotiations. The crisis had arisen in early July following a request by Khuri and his supporters that the 1926 constitution be restored before the treaty was negotiated and ratified. Their initiative had evolved partly from the conviction that only the Constitutional Bloc could defend Lebanese national interests, and partly from their own political needs. They regarded Viénot's letter as a victory for their cause, assuming that the new French government would be bound to restore the constitution and call for parliamentary elections in Lebanon, as it had in Syria, to obtain ratification of the treaty. Convinced that the treaty would determine Lebanon's relations with France and shape its political system for the next 25 years, they were anxious to prevent Eddé from conducting talks with France by himself. They pointed to the Syrian nationalists' success in negotiating a pact after forcing de Martel to remove Taj al-Din al-Hasani from his position, and maintained that the Constitutional Bloc should adopt similar tactics in Lebanon. Khuri and his followers believed that a well-organized public campaign in Beirut and Paris, coupled with a veiled threat to collaborate with the Arab nationalists, would drive the French government to sacrifice Eddé and acquiesce in their demands for restoration of the constitution and participation in the negotiations. Moreover, with pressure mounting from the army to secure its military interests in Lebanon, they were sure that to prevent opposition to the treaty, the Quai d'Orsay would involve them in the negotiations. Thus, despite Meyrier's efforts to persuade Khuri to delay his initiative, the 12 deputies of the Constitutional Bloc tabled a resolution on 7 July formally requesting restoration of the constitution. The result was a confrontation with Eddé and the High Commission that lasted for the next four months.[50]

Eddé bitterly resented Khuri's efforts to curtail his authority to represent Lebanon in the negotiations. He pointed out that the constitution, whose restoration Khuri was demanding, gave the president the power to negotiate international agreements before presenting them to parliament for approval. Eddé did not believe that Lebanon had reached political maturity, and continued to view the 1926 constitution as a source of political instability and uncontrolled expenditure. With demonstrations against the state by the pro-Syrian Muslims in Lebanon, and attempts by the National Bloc to link Lebanon politically to Syria, he felt that the mandate should continue or be replaced by a French protectorate, remarking to Meyrier that 'it would be better to be guided by France than fall prey to the wolves'. Yet, after the new French government had undertaken to grant Lebanon independence, Eddé could not publicly oppose Khuri's initiative. He therefore instructed his deputies to endorse the resolution of the Constitutional Bloc, initiating at the same time a revision of the constitution. He proposed following the American example and expanding the power of the president, while replacing a government responsible to parliament with a secretary of state responsible to the president. Realizing, however, that Khuri and his deputies would thwart his attempt, Eddé decided to act outside parliament.[51]

On 10 July, Eddé wrote to religious leaders, deputies, heads of professional organizations and prominent businessmen, requesting their views on an appropriate constitution for Lebanon. His initiative provoked a strong reaction from proponents of Syrian unity, as well as from the Constitutional Bloc. The former pressed the Mufti, Tawfik Khalid, and other Muslim religious leaders and politicians, to refrain from replying to Eddé, while the Constitutional Bloc exerted similar pressure on Arida. Khuri's camp sent urgent telegrams to Premier Blum, Delbos, Viénot and senators and deputies in the National Assembly, protesting Eddé's move and demanding immediate restoration of the constitution. If revision was necessary, they argued, it should be made by the parliament after its restoration. Michel Zakur and other members of the Bloc met openly with Syrian leaders in Beirut, and went so far as to warn French officials that if forced to do so, they would cooperate with pan-Arabists in Lebanon and the National Bloc to foil Eddé's scheme. The Constitutional Bloc also launched a press campaign accusing Eddé of unlawfully attempting to revise the constitution and establish a dictatorial regime in Lebanon. Paradoxically, while Maronite deputies from Mount Lebanon threatened to collaborate with their country's enemies if their political demands were not met, five Sunni deputies complied with Eddé's appeal and on 10 July declared their support for the Lebanese state.[52]

On receiving reports from Beirut on the rift within the Christian camp and the growing tension between Christians and Muslims, Viénot instructed Meyrier to act immediately. On 28 July the latter informed Khuri that the High Commission would not allow any revision of the constitution, and asked him to delay his initiative until de Martel's return. Meyrier also warned Khuri that he was weakening the Christian community and undermining French efforts to defend Lebanon's independence and territorial integrity in the negotiations with the Syrians in Paris. But Khuri again rejected his appeal and continued to insist that he be treated as Eddé's equal in the negotiations; that the constitution be restored immediately; and that any modification be made by the parliament. A few days later he sent a letter to Meyrier warning that:

> It is extremely dangerous to place Lebanon today in the tragic situation of having to choose between safeguarding its borders and its freedom, when the two could be reconciled. To put it in such a position at this moment, when the separatist movement is on the rise, is to put the country, with its two elements—one not yet completely assimilated, and the other dissatisfied and disappointed—at risk of throwing itself into the arms of its neighbours, who are all too happy to make the most of the benefits which they will soon reap, adding to Lebanon's misfortune and political disarray.[53]

Khuri's intransigence, along with reports on talks between Constitutional Bloc members and Syrian leaders, prompted Viénot to take firmer action. At the end of the month an official from the High Commission met Arida in Bkerki, told him that Khuri's initiative was having a detrimental effect on the Christians in Lebanon, and informed him of renewed attempts by Bishops

Khuri and Mubarak to depose him. Following the meeting, Arida wrote to Eddé, backing his stand on the constitution. The letter, which Eddé was quick to make public, and a meeting between Meyrier and Arida, helped win Christian public support for the government's position. Newspapers allied with Eddé accused Khuri of selfishly undermining Lebanon's ability to withstand the combined assault of Syria and its allies in Lebanon. In response, Khuri and his deputies now went beyond attacks on Eddé and Arida, openly criticizing French policy and declaring their intention to insist on Lebanon's 'complete national sovereignty'. Constitutional Bloc members, including Michel Zakur, also met with Fakhri al-Barudi and Lutfi al-Haffer, who had arrived in Beirut. When these actions failed to move Meyrier, Khuri proposed that he and his colleagues resign en masse from parliament to demonstrate their resentment of French policy. This idea backfired, however; most of his deputies refused to comply after the High Commission made clear its intention to appoint new deputies in their place.[54]

By the end of August it was clear that Khuri had failed in his attempts to force the Quai d'Orsay to include him in the negotiations and restore the constitution. With his rival discredited, Eddé stepped up pressure on the High Commission to adopt the revised constitution he had prepared. Lebanon's Independence Day was celebrated with much fanfare: for the first time, a parade of the Lebanese gendarmerie and police force was held in Beirut, reviewed by Eddé. His followers now acclaimed him as a Lebanese patriot, successfully defending the country's independence and borders and its unique historical ties with France. Significantly, while Muslim deputies and officials took part in the celebrations, Khuri was conspicuously absent. Nevertheless, he tried to mend relations with the High Commission by reiterating his friendship for France. On Independence Day *Le Jour* published an editorial endorsing a French military presence to guarantee Lebanon's distinct existence and protect it against aggression.[55]

Although he disliked and distrusted Khuri, de Martel recommended during the Paris talks in September that he participate in the negotiations to ensure speedy conclusion of a treaty. But he rejected Khuri's demand for restoration of the constitution, warning that it would deepen divisions within the Christian camp and sharpen tensions between Christians and Muslims, thereby exposing Lebanon to Syrian subversion. On his return to Beirut at the end of September de Martel urged Eddé and Khuri to reach an understanding on the composition of the Lebanese delegation to the negotiations. He made it clear to both leaders that he would not discuss restoration or revision of the constitution until a treaty was negotiated and ratified. Eddé at length was persuaded that Ayub Tabet, the secretary of state, and Khalid Shihab, the Speaker of the parliament, might join him in the negotiations, and later agreed to the participation of a parliamentary advisory committee as well. Khuri, however, continued to insist that the deputies have equal status in the delegation. On 10 October, Eddé and Khuri finally met and reached an agreement. Five days later, the parliament convened and elected a committee of seven deputies, representing the major communities, to take part in the negotiations; Khuri was elected chairman and Gabriel Khabaz his deputy. With his participation in the negotiations guaranteed, and his rival's initiative to revise the constitution thwarted, Khuri was to play an important role in ensuring that negotiations with de Martel would progress smoothly. Talks between de Martel and a ten-member Lebanese delegation headed by Emile Eddé officially began on 20 October.[56]

While mediating between Eddé and Khuri, de Martel also strove to allay Muslim fears for their rights in an independent Lebanon. In discussions with Eddé and other Christian leaders, as well as in his messages to Arida, he repeatedly stressed the importance of avoiding the impression that Lebanon was 'a Maronite dictatorship' imposed by France. He proposed offering the premiership to the Sunnis, guaranteeing equality in taxation and allocation of state funds, and granting Tripoli an autonomous municipal status to weaken its inhabitants' support for union with Syria. Such measures, he emphasized, had to be taken by the Lebanese government rather than the High Commission. He frequently met with Muslim notables, including some of the declared opponents of the mandate, as well as with religious leaders and businessmen, assuring them that France was not concluding a treaty with the Christians alone, but with all the communities in Lebanon. By retaining its influence, he stressed, France would be in a better position to protect the rights of all citizens in an independent Lebanese state.[57]

Acting on instructions from Delbos and Viénot at the beginning of October, de Martel directed Pati de Clam to examine the issue of changing the status of Tripoli. De Clam's report confirmed the inhabitants' claims that since 1920 their city had been systematically neglected by the central government in comparison with the northern district of Mount Lebanon, to which it had been annexed. Most administrative positions in the district, they alleged, were held by Christian functionaries from the Mountain, who were either hostile to the city or innatentive to its needs. They pointed out that Lebanese presidents had visited Tripoli only twice in the last decade and, despite repeated appeals, the government in Beirut had refused to allocate funds for modernizing the port. Moreover, the report argued that support in Tripoli for union with Syria sprang more from economic neglect than from nationalistic sentiment. In this regard it quoted Karameh's declaration: 'We would rather become Syria's main port than continue as a colony of the old Lebanon, which only demonstrates its concern for us by sending tax papers.'[58] As expected, the report opposed Tripoli's annexation to Syria, but warned that if the current situation persisted, the city would remain a source of irredentism and tension between Syria and Lebanon. It recommended that Tripoli be separated from the district of north Lebanon, granted an independent municipal status and its own kaimakam, and that the municipal council be given greater authority in local administrative affairs. With Viénot's approval, French officials presented the proposals to the city leaders, taking the opportunity to emphasize the High Commission's role in ensuring that Tripoli be chosen as the outlet for the oil pipeline from Mosul, as well as French plans for major development projects, including the construction of a refinery and an airport, and modernization of the port.[59]

The High Commission also strove to win the support of the Shiites, especially in the south, for the Franco–Lebanese treaty. Pechkof and officers of the Service de Renseignements reminded Shiite notables and religious leaders of the inferior status of their brethren in Iraq and the fears of the minorities in Syria, and claimed that the Shiite community would be better off in Lebanon than in a Sunni Arab Syrian state controlled by Damascus. They undertook to press the Lebanese government to increase the number of Shiite officials in the administration and allocate more state funds to developing the south. They repeated their argument that by maintaining its influence in Lebanon, France would be in a better position to protect Shiite rights vis-à-vis the Maronites. They urged the Shiite leaders to reject appeals by Sulh and other Syrian unionists to join the campaign against the treaty, and declare their allegiance to Lebanon. At the beginning of November, thousands of Shiites held a rally in Nabatiya in support of the Lebanese state; petitions and telegrams were sent to the High Commission, and delegations went to Beirut, affirming to de Martel and President Eddé their community's commitment to the treaty.[60]

Eddé worked closely with de Martel to allay Muslim fears of the treaty and to weaken and isolate Syria's supporters on the coast. He had, however, his own motives for pursuing an 'Islamic policy'. Since January, with the assistance of Khair al-Din al-Ahdab, he had been cultivating ties with the Muslim community; July's public endorsement of an independent Lebanon by the five Muslim deputies testified to his success. Muslim support was vital for strengthening Eddé's position against Khuri, and for dispelling the Constitutional Bloc's accusations that he was an enemy of Islam and of Arabism. His meetings with Sunni and Shiite leaders in September and October reinforced Eddé's conviction that if their rights were guaranteed, the Muslims would choose to remain part of Lebanon rather than be united with Syria. He shared de Martel's views that the Sunnis should have the second most important executive position after the presidency, and proposed that the new post of vice-president be reserved for a Sunni if his plan to revise the constitution and abolish the government was approved.[61] While he still harboured doubts on the retention of Tripoli, Eddé realized that in view of its increasing strategic importance for France, it could not be severed from Lebanon. In mid-September he visited Tripoli after extensive preparations by Ahdab, once city leaders, including Karameh, had agreed to accord him a courteous reception. But his visit sparked demonstrations by hundreds of youths—many of them members of the League for National Action and the Parti Populaire Syrien—in which scores were wounded. Nevertheless Eddé endorsed de Martel's plan to grant Tripoli independent municipal status, and at the end of October dispatched Ahdab to inform city leaders of his intention to implement it and increase government investment there.[62]

Despite efforts by de Martel and Eddé to allay their fears during treaty negotiations in October and November, the Sunnis upheld their opposition to an independent Lebanese state. Just as in 1920, when Greater Lebanon was established, and 1926, when the Lebanese Republic was declared, now that Lebanon was negotiating its independence, they once again refused to be part of the process. They were concerned that the Maronites would dominate the state after the mandate ended. As a community, however, the Sunnis were divided on the treaty. Some, like those in Tripoli, saw the negotiations as a last chance for union with Syria, while others sought to link Lebanon in a confederation with Syria, or impose a decentralized administrative system that would guarantee autonomy for the annexed areas. Yet, increasing numbers of Muslims viewed the treaty negotiations as an opportunity to press France and the Maronites to safeguard their rights.[63]

The Sunni campaign against the treaty, however, was not merely the popular expression of a minority community anxious to protect its rights and national identity in a Maronite-dominated state closely linked to France. Their apprehension had been fuelled and exploited by the National Bloc and its supporters on the coast, who feared that the Lebanese treaty would harm Syrian interests. The Franco–Lebanese negotiations had indeed presented the Syrian leaders with a dilemma. Before leaving Paris, the Syrian delegation had agreed to refrain from undermining Lebanon's independence and territorial integrity. Moreover, the support of the French government and the High Commission was essential for implementation of their own treaty with France, particularly the immediate incorporation of Jabal Druze and the Alawite region. Well aware of strong resistance to the treaty among rightwing officials and officers in the High Commission, and the minorities in Syria itself, they understood that moves against Lebanon and French interests there might jeopardize implementation of the Franco–Syrian pact. The violent clashes between Christians and Muslims in Aleppo on 11 October, in which eight people were killed and over a hundred wounded, reinforced French opposition to the treaty. Nevertheless, the National Bloc could ignore neither the negotiations in Beirut—in which the extent of French influence in Lebanon was to be determined for the next quarter-century—nor Syria's moral obligation to defend the interests of the Arab Muslims on the coast. As during the Paris negotiations, the Syrian leadership was divided: while Mardam advocated caution, others, including Barudi, Shishakli, Sa'adallah al-Jabiri and Afif al-Sulh, backed Riad al-Sulh, who was spearheading the campaign against the Lebanese treaty.[64]

His prestige considerably enhanced by his role in the Franco–Syrian negotiations in Paris, the confident Sulh was determined to foil a treaty that would transform Lebanon into a French military, economic and cultural centre in the heart of Syria and the Arab world. In talks with his colleagues in the National Bloc in October, he defined three goals for Syria and the Muslims on the coast: to limit France's military presence in Lebanon, to persuade the Christians to agree on a confederal link with Syria or, failing that, to demand decentralization, which would enable the Muslims in Tripoli, the Beqa valley and south Lebanon to enjoy considerable administrative autonomy. He believed those goals could be attained if the Muslims on the coast united in demanding full participation in the treaty negotiations.[65]

Despite the High Commission's elaborate precautions, Sulh's arrival in Beirut at the end of September turned into a major political demonstration as thousands converged on the port to greet him. However, Salam and Omar Bayhum, the two prominent Sunni leaders of Beirut, declined an invitation to attend. Sulh immediately proceeded to Damascus, where a public reception was held for the members of the Syrian delegation. He was welcomed enthusiastically by the National Bloc leadership and Muslim deputations from the coast, which had come to demonstrate their support for Syrian unity. To the delegates, who had voiced their concern for the future, Mardam declared: 'our love for Tripoli, Tyre, Sidon, Beirut, Shuf, Batrun and Bkerki is deep and genuine'. For his part, Sulh warned the French and Christians alike that the Muslims would not allow a continuation of the present situation in Lebanon, or permit the treaty to become a 'consecration of the past'. He called for Muslim-Christian solidarity and invited the Christians 'to return to the fold'. Back in Beirut, he appealed to Khuri, Zakur, Tuaini, Aziz al-Hashem and other Christian leaders to cooperate with the Muslims to ensure Lebanese national sovereignty. Sulh also urged Salam and Omar Bayhum to support his request to represent the Muslims in the negotiations.

But his attempts to mobilize the Shiites in the south were frustrated by the High Commission.[66]

Concerned lest Sulh's activities undermine efforts to form a delegation for the negotiations, de Martel summoned him to the High Commission and accused him of endangering the Franco–Syrian treaty. Sulh was unmoved and declined de Martel's proposal that he meet with Eddé to discuss the Muslims' grievances. He criticized de Martel's attempt to form a delegation comprising only deputies, and charged that the Muslim deputies chosen did not represent their communities. He insisted that Lebanon refrain from undertaking military and economic commitments that would jeopardize its ties with Syria, and demanded that Tripoli, the Beqa valley and south Lebanon be granted administrative autonomy identical to that given to Jabal Druze and the Alawite region in the Franco–Syrian treaty. Although de Martel rejected Sulh's attempt to 'subordinate' an independent Lebanon to Syria, he did express willingness to consider a decentralized administrative system.[67]

De Martel's success in inducing Eddé and Khuri to reach agreement on the formation of a joint delegation prompted the National Bloc, Sulh and other Sunni leaders on the coast to intensify their opposition to the Lebanese treaty. At a meeting in Sofar on 16 October, Sa'adallah Jabiri, Afif al-Sulh, Riad al-Sulh, Bayhum, Salam, Karameh and Bisar decided to urge the Muslim masses to stage demonstrations, send petitions to the French government and the Permanent Mandates Commission, and organize a national congress in Beirut. This marked the start of a well-orchestrated campaign against the treaty and the Lebanese state, which lasted more than a month. The campaign soon escalated into large-scale riots in Tripoli and Beirut in which scores were killed, hundreds wounded, and many arrested. Tension between the Christians and Muslims in Beirut had mounted to the point of inter-sectarian strife.[68]

The day after the Sofar meeting, Karameh and Bisar declared a general strike in Tripoli which continued well into November. In Beirut, a delegation of Sunni notables, including Salam, Bayhum and Sulh, informed de Martel of their community's refusal to recognize the appointed negotiators, and insisted that Lebanon be linked in a confederation with Syria. De Martel responded shortly that France was determined to grant Lebanon its independence, and proposed that they make their request after conclusion of the Franco–Lebanese treaty—increasing the Sunni leaders' resentment. Barred from taking part in negotiations that were to determine Lebanon's future, they organized yet another conference to voice their grievances. On 23 October, hundreds of delegates convened in the home of Omar Bayhum; but despite the organizers' efforts, Shiite participation was limited, while the Christians boycotted the meeting altogether. In a frank and lengthy speech,

Sulh reviewed the Paris negotiations and his exchanges with Maronite leaders, including Khuri and Sawda. He warned the Christians not to rely on French protection, stressing that neither they nor France could impose a solution unacceptable to Lebanese Muslims, to Syria or to the Arab Muslim world. The delegates adopted a resolution that included a refusal to recognize the Lebanese negotiators, along with calls for decentralization and confederation with Syria. Salim Ali Salam, president of the 'Conference of the Coast', sent copies of the document to de Martel, the Quai d'Orsay and the League of Nations.[69]

Sulh revealed his anger and disappointment with the conduct of the Christian leadership to Aziz al-Hashem:

> From now on I will think and act only as a Muslim. If anyone fears or respects me it is because I am a Muslim leader. The title of a nationalist leader bears no weight with the French. Only the Islamic movements disturb them. As a Muslim I cannot have any faith or hope in the Christians. The other Christians, except for you, Aziz al-Hashem, and a handful of your friends, are all in the pay of France. You have only one goal in the East—to fetter Islamic or national politics. This is an indisputable fact of which I have become certain since my stay in Paris. I have been informed by the Quai d'Orsay of letters of certain of your Christian leaders against the National Bloc. I have also read the letters of your Maronite patriarch, Emile Eddé, Beshara al-Khuri and even of Michel Zakur—letters which reveal their anti-Islamic sentiment. I now bear no illusions as to the feelings of the Christians toward the Muslims. That is why I have decided to pursue a distinctly Islamic policy, disregarding your existence as Christians in the East. We will impose unity despite yourselves, within five years. You have the example of the Alawites and Jabal Druze. You saw how the French abandoned them at the last minute. Take heed of that example. You will have no peace in Lebanon—neither the Christians nor the French. Know that henceforth we will be financially supported by the Islamic world and that independent Syria will be a refuge if any problems arise.[70]

Toward the end of October, tension mounted between Christians and Muslims and between Lebanon and Syria. The Syrian press stepped up its attacks on Eddé and the Maronite community, charging that the Lebanese treaty posed a serious threat to Syria, including rights to its own port, and warning that neither France nor Britain, nor the Lebanese Christians could prevent Syrian unity and the eventual union of the entire Arab world. Lebanese newspapers responded by accusing Syria of attempts to undermine Lebanon's independence and territorial unity. They pointed to the inter-sectarian clashes in Aleppo as proof of the need for Christians in the Levant to secure a homeland of their own. Riots broke out in Tripoli on 1 November, and scores were wounded in clashes with the French army. Shots were fired at the French administrative adviser and the commander of the French forces in the region. On 15 November, the first day of Ramadan, only two days after the signing of the Franco–Lebanese treaty, riots erupted in the Muslim quarters of west Beirut following the Friday prayers, during which Sulh and Nasuli had attacked the treaty and the Lebanese state. Thousands of demonstrators marched to the city centre, where they set fire to cars and trams, looted shops, stormed into government offices and French concessionaire companies, and threatened to lay siege to the seat of the Lebanese government. In running battles with the French security forces, over a hundred were injured and many arrested. In the Christian quarters, members of the White Shirts and the Phalanges, as well as Armenians, rushed to defend their homes and properties against the Muslim onslaught, while on the Mountain, Maronites threatened to descend to Beirut to protect their brethren. Only the large-scale intervention of the French security services prevented an escalation into inter-sectarian strife. Five days later, violence again erupted in Tripoli, resulting in numerous casualties. In response, the French arrested several of the city's prominent leaders, including Karameh, Bisar and Mustafa Muqadam.[71]

De Martel accused Sulh and the National Bloc of inciting the demonstrations in Beirut and Tripoli. He immediately summoned Salam and Bayhum, warned them of the dangers of a religious conflict, and pressed them to issue a public statement to defuse the tension. The following day, 12 prominent Muslim and Christian leaders published a declaration urging their communities to maintain law and order. Viénot sent an urgent letter from Paris to the National Bloc leaders threatening that France would not implement its treaty with Syria unless they ceased their subversive activities in Lebanon. For his part, de Martel warned Mardam that further deterioration in Christian–Muslim relations in Lebanon would increase tension among the minorities in Jabal Druze, the Alawite region and the sanjak of Alexandretta. Unless the National Bloc could demonstrate its political maturity in Lebanon, France would be unable to continue its efforts to win the minorities' support for integration into Syria. And French officials cautioned the Syrians that the events in Aleppo, Beirut and Tripoli were jeopardizing the French endeavour to ratify the Syrian treaty in the National Assembly.[72]

The French threats prompted Mardam and Sa'adallah al-Jabiri to leave immediately for Beirut, where they pressed Sulh, Salam and Bayhum to end their campaign. From there they proceeded to Tripoli, and when the imprisoned leaders of that city had undertaken to stop the violent demonstrations, the High Commission released them. Thus it was only when events in Lebanon—which they themselves had instigated—threatened to endanger their own treaty with France, that the Syrian leaders called on the Muslims of the coast to cease their opposition to the treaty and the Lebanese state.[73]

The conclusion of the Franco–Lebanese treaty and the events in Beirut and Tripoli precipitated a shift in the Sunni leadership's stand on Syria and the Lebanese state. Many, including declared supporters of Syrian unity, were bitterly disappointed with the National Bloc. Abandoned by Syria, and with Lebanon on the threshold of independence, they believed that the Muslims' most urgent goal was to ensure their own rights. Sulh had lost much of his prestige and influence: he was blamed in Damascus for endangering Syrian interests with his hasty and irresponsible behavior, while in Beirut he was accused by the French and the Christians of almost provoking inter-sectarian conflict. The violence in Beirut served as a bitter lesson for Sulh, who would henceforth be wary of inciting his community against the Christians to achieve political goals. The clashes reinforced his belief that Lebanon's Muslims should give up their struggle for immediate political union with Syria, and strive instead to strengthen Lebanon's Arab character; only when this goal was achieved should they seek Arab unity.[74]

Sunni and Syrian opposition prompted de Martel and the Lebanese delegation to conclude the negotiations rapidly. Fearing further unrest, de Martel pressed for an agreement while the National Bloc was still preoccupied with parliamentary elections in Syria. The delegation's three prominent Christian members—Eddé, Khuri and Ayub Tabet—hoped agreement would be reached before the election of a Syrian government and reincorporation of Jabal Druze and the Alawite region was complete. In fact, the talks lasted for only three weeks, compared to six months of negotiations on the Franco–Syrian treaty. The Christians no longer viewed the treaty as an act of independence from the mandatory power, but as a direct French guarantee for a Christian Lebanon, against the Syrian threat from without and Muslim opposition from within. Indeed, Eddé proposed a treaty of unlimited duration; it was the French who insisted it remain in force for 25 years, as would the Syrian treaty. De Martel maintained a cloak of secrecy throughout the negotiations, fearing that information might be exploited by the Muslim opposition and the National Bloc to influence the Lebanese negotiators. He presented the military protocol to the Lebanese only two days before ending the negotiations, and insisted on its approval without any modifications.[75]

Disagreement on the treaty was more pronounced between the Christian and Muslim negotiators than between the Lebanese delegation and de Martel. Under pressure from their community, Khalid Shihab and Abud Abd al-Razak demanded that the treaty guarantee Muslim rights, including equality in taxation and allocation of resources, as well as official status for the Arabic language. They also requested immediate implementation of the proposed municipal autonomy for Tripoli. The Shiite delegate, Najib Usayran, accused the central government of failing to grant his community its rights, and insisted that south Lebanon too be accorded local autonomy. Khuri and Tabet, however, opposed raising such issues, arguing that they were internal Lebanese concerns and should not be included in a treaty regulating Lebanon's future relations with a foreign power. Khuri also objected to according greater administrative autonomy to Tripoli and other annexed regions, lest this be exploited by Lebanon's opponents to undermine its territorial integrity. Only after de Martel agreed to limit such autonomy to municipal affairs, and ensure that no distinction would be made between Mount Lebanon and the annexed areas, did Khuri acquiesce.[76]

On 13 November 1936, the treaty was signed by de Martel and Eddé at a ceremony in the High Commission, despite the fact that some of the protocols and letters annexed to it had not yet been finalized. Four days later, in the aftermath of the Beirut riots, an extraordinary session of the Lebanese parliament was convened to debate and ratify the treaty. Khuri presented a report to the deputies setting out in detail the treaty's various articles, including the military protocols. He repeatedly pointed to the similarity between the Lebanese treaty and those of Syria, Iraq and Egypt, and stressed that France's position in Lebanon did not negate Lebanon's independence and national sovereignty. He rejected accusations that the treaty accorded France a unique military status in Lebanon, and argued that the military protocol was identical to that of the Franco–Syrian treaty. Khuri acknowledged that Lebanon aspired to good neighbourly relations with Syria, but insisted that those relations be based on equality between two separate independent states. After a short debate, the treaty was approved by 24 deputies, excluding Amin Muqadam, the deputy from Tripoli, who boycotted the session. Najib Usayran voiced the mixed feelings of many of the deputies, when he declared:

> We have just concluded a treaty similar to that between Syria and France. But the welcome accorded to the two treaties was not the same. While the Syrians received their delegation with joy and enthusiasm, certain persons sought to undermine the signing of our treaty. They purposely distorted the truth and the interpretation of a text which clearly guaranteed the rights of all the communities in the country, without granting any of them the slightest preference or privilege.[77]

The two agreements were almost identical: like Syria, Lebanon was to gain independence and become a member of the League of Nations after an interim three year period. Their military protocols, however, differed considerably. While France's military presence in Syria was limited—both geographically and temporally—in Lebanon, the French airforce, army and navy were to enjoy complete freedom of action for the entire duration of the treaty. The Muslim concern for their rights resulted in an exchange of letters—nos 6 and 6 *bis*—between the high commissioner and the Lebanese president, in which the latter undertook to guarantee representation of all communities in the state institutions, unification of the fiscal system, and implement administrative reforms. Thus, ten years after the Lebanese constitution had guaranteed equal sectarian representation (article 11), the Muslims were still concerned with protecting their rights. Following the signing of the treaty, de Martel sent a letter to Salim Ali Salam, head of the Muslim higher council, assuring him of the High Commission's intention to implement letters 6 and 6 bis. For the next three years, Muslim leaders would use these letters to demand that the High Commission and the Lebanese government honour their pledges.[78]

Pointing to the fact that Lebanon was to become an independent state, soon after ratification, Khuri asked de Martel to restore constitutional life and appoint a government responsible to parliament. This move marked the end of Khuri's cooperation with Eddé and the resumption of their bitter rivalry. Both leaders were uncompromising: Eddé demanded that the constitution first be modified in accordance with his proposals of August and September, while Khuri insisted that it be restored immediately without any revision. Khuri's position raised serious constitutional problems: the 1926 constitution had stipulated a parliament of 45 deputies, while the current parliament, elected in January 1934, comprised only 25. Moreover, Eddé had been elected for a three-year term, not six, as provided by the constitution. A solution proposed by Eddé—to dissolve the parliament and hold new elections, as Syria had done—was rejected by both de Martel and Khuri. Another idea, put forward by officials in the High Commission—to transform the present parliament into a constituent assembly—was turned down by both Eddé and Khuri. De Martel continued to advocate revision of the constitution, in order to prevent a return to the precarious political system that had led to suspension of the constitution in May 1932. The Quai d'Orsay, however, objected to the high commissioner imposing his own solution on the two warring sides in what it regarded as an internal Lebanese affair. Viénot expressed this stance in a letter to de Martel, in which he stressed: 'Now that the treaty has been ratified, the constitutional question interests us less directly than in the past. It is not bad that the Lebanese have to cope with the difficulties involved in the exercise of independence. The mandatory power has, in the meantime, to establish a compromise acceptable to all.'[79]

At the beginning of January 1937, de Martel issued a decree restoring the constitution and affirming that both parliament and president would serve the terms for which they had originally been elected—until January 1938 and January 1939 respectively. He also called for Lebanese politicians to demonstrate maturity, refrain from paralysing the government with their intrigues, and ensure that the political and administrative systems were compatible with the size and needs of their country.[80]

De Martel's appeals fell on deaf ears, however: rivalries between the deputies, the ministers and the president resumed with full intensity. Disagreements immediately surfaced during deliberations on the formation of the government. Eddé proposed that the premiership be allocated to the Sunnis, and chose Ahdab, his close ally since 1934, for that position. It was a clever move, aimed at demonstrating his intention to fulfil the pledges he had made to Muslim leaders in the treaty negotiations, and thus ensure their support for him against Khuri. His initiative, however, provoked strong opposition from Arida and his bishops, who argued that in light of Sunni hostility toward the Lebanese state and Syria's offensive against Lebanon, it would be irresponsible to nominate a Muslim as prime minister. Khuri, who also objected to Eddé's move, noted that a Sunni, Khalid Shihab, already held the prominent position of speaker of the house, and that Ahdab's appointment would upset the delicate balance among the various communities. He therefore proposed that Ayub Tabet, the former secretary of state, continue as prime minister. It was then left to de Martel to mediate between the two political clans. With Lebanon about to begin negotiations on economic ties with Syria, de Martel was anxious to form a strong government in which both rival groups would participate. He nevertheless backed Eddé's proposition to nominate Ahdab, believing it would facilitate integration of the Sunnis in Lebanon and weaken Syria's supporters there. Moreover, he hoped that Ahdab, who was a native of Tripoli, would help in suppressing opposition in the city to the idea of a Lebanese state. After Khuri refused to take part in a government headed by Ahdab, the latter formed a four-member cabinet in which he also retained the influential Ministry of the Interior. The other members were Khalil Abu Lama, Ibrahim Haidar and Habib Abu Shahla. Shahla's appointment was intended to placate the Greek Orthodox community, which had lost the position of speaker of the parliament.[81]

The restoration of the constitution and the formation of a government responsible to parliament marked Lebanon's return to an unstable political system: by September 1939 the country was to have eight governments. Instead of running the country, the prime ministers were constantly engaged in ensuring that their governments were not voted out of power. With 13 deputies supporting Eddé and Ahdab, and 12 allied with the Constitutional Bloc, the opposition had only to convince one deputy to change sides in order to topple the government. Deputies were able to extract favours for themselves, their relatives, or their clients, while money was used freely by both the government and the opposition to purchase political loyalty. Arida and the Maronite bishops again intervened in politics as Eddé and Khuri competed for their support. The rivalry of the Maronite politicians over the presidency was accompanied by a struggle for the premiership among the Sunni leaders. Thus, instead of progressing toward independence, Lebanon became even more dependent on the high commissioner, who was constantly mediating between the various communities and political clans.[82]

The political rivalry between Eddé and Khuri once again turned into a relentless personal feud. Since elections for parliament were due at the end of the year—a parliament which was to elect the next president for a six-year term—Khuri and his supporters were determined to do their utmost to prevent Eddé's re-election. With Lebanon scheduled to gain independence at the end of 1939, they believed that Eddé, once elected and free from French supervision, would use his power as president to suppress them and take revenge. The Khuri camp employed all means to weaken and discredit him and undermine his authority, and exploited their influence in parliament to impose their own government. Their attacks focussed on Ahdab, whom they regarded as a key figure in the coalition behind the president.[83]

Hardly had the government been established, when the Constitutional Bloc began its onslaught on the prime minister. Messages were sent to Arida and Bishop Mubarak, urging them to voice their opposition to Ahdab. The drivers' syndicate was encouraged to strike, while newspapers allied with Khuri attacked both Eddé and Ahdab. Under the barrage of criticism, Ahdab delayed the vote of confidence, hoping to increase his government's majority in parliament. When parliament convened in early February, tempers rose to the point where the session had twice to be adjourned. Khuri spearheaded the attacks on the government, insinuating that Eddé was not legally president, since he had not sworn to defend the constitution; therefore Ahdab's nomination as prime minister was invalid. Further, he accused the government of resting on the vote of one deputy, Amin Muqadam, who in November had declared his opposition to the treaty; indeed to the very existence of the Lebanese state. Chamoun's proposal that each deputy be required to pledge loyalty to the constitution, to Lebanon, and to the defence of its borders before being allowed to vote, angered the Muslim deputies and public. Commenting on the haggling over the formation of the government, the British consul in Beirut predicted: 'If the chamber, as it is at the present constituted, renders the work of the Ministry impossible, he [Eddé] will probably not hesitate to dissolve it.'[84]

The threat to dissolve parliament, in which he had the power to nominate one third of the deputies, and hold new elections was Eddé's main weapon in deterring the Constitutional Bloc from attacking the government. But de Martel firmly opposed such a move, fearing that elections would divide the Maronite community even further, heighten the inter-sectarian tension which had erupted the previous November, and enable Syria to expand its subversive activities in Lebanon. Eddé's request that he be allowed to appoint two more deputies to the present parliament, in accordance with the constitution, was also rejected. (The parliament comprised 18 elected and 7 nominated deputies, while the constitution stipulated that the number of nominated deputies be half of those elected.) Eddé and Ahdab failed in their efforts to lure deputies away from the opposition, and were forced to offer increased favours and handouts just to maintain the loyalty of the coalition deputies. Ahdab, who had emerged during the year as a political force to be reckoned with in Lebanon, became Eddé's main ally against Khuri.[85]

Although he served in the post for only 15 months, Khair al-Din al-Ahdab played an important role in establishing the precedent of a Sunni prime minister. As Muhammad al-Jisr before him, he exploited the rivalry between the two Maronite leaders—as well as the High Commission's desire to cultivate a loyal Sunni Muslim leader who could withstand pressure from Syria and its supporters in Lebanon—to strengthen his position. Despite opposition from the Maronite church and the Constitutional Bloc, and attacks by Syria and Sunni leaders, particularly in Beirut, he succeeded in retaining his influence and was able to form five consecutive governments. Eddé's decision in March 1938 to withdraw his support forced Ahdab to resign, but it also weakened the power of the president himself. Ahdab's political career was characteristic of the radical changes in the Sunni leaders' stand on the Lebanese state. A member of a prominent family that had originated in Tripoli and moved to Beirut, he studied mathematics at the Sorbonne in the mid-1920s. Then, with the help of his uncle, Husain al-Ahdab, administrator of Beirut, he was appointed to an administrative post in the Beqa, where his uncle owned land. While serving there, he married into a distinguished Greek Catholic family from Zahleh. Forced to resign following disciplinary measures against him, he consequently joined the opposition to the French mandate. In 1926 he fled to Palestine after collaborating with Riad al-Sulh in assisting the Syrian rebels. Two years later he was pardoned and returned to Beirut, where, together with Sulh, he established *al-Ahd al-Jadid*, an Arab nationalist newspaper that supported Syrian unity and opposed the mandate and the Lebanese state. His election to the Lebanese parliament in January 1934 marked a turning point in his attitude toward France and Lebanon. During that period, he worked for the Sûreté Générale, which later helped him with his political career. This aspect of his past became public knowledge, and after he was nominated as prime minister, newspapers allied with the Constitutional Bloc used it to discredit him in the Muslim community. Ahdab believed that the Muslims should aspire for integration into Lebanon and work from within state institutions to achieve their rights. Yet he remarked at one time to a French official that although the Muslims comprised half of Lebanon's population, they would attain full equality with the Christians only gradually, since the latter were better educated and dominated the political and economic systems. While in office, Ahdab faced a constant dilemma which was to confront almost all of his successors: how to fulfil his obligation, as the most prominent Muslim politician in the Lebanese political system, to protect and promote the interests of his community, while retaining his position, which depended largely on the goodwill of the Maronite president. He also had to balance the defence of Lebanese independence and national interests against Syrian ambitions, with the need to maintain cordial relations with the government in Damascus. His decision to stand firmly against Damascus led to continued Syrian attempts to undermine him and oust him from his post.[86]

Ahdab's nomination, however, was initially well received by the Sunni community, which expected him to use his power as prime minister to immediately fulfil the pledges made by de Martel and Eddé in the treaty negotiations. In mid-January, Salam held a banquet in honour of Ahdab, attended by hundreds of guests, including many Muslim notables, among them Karameh. The expectant mood was expressed by one of the Muslim guests to a French official:

> This is the first time in 18 years that the Muslims feel they are no longer being treated as poor relations in Lebanon, and you can see that we are flattered that we can welcome the French in our homes. Believe it that we have no interest in being governed by Jamil Mardam. We, the Muslims of Beirut, intend to remain our own masters. But we have commercial interests in the interior, and are seeking sufficiently close contacts in order to avoid differences in legislation.[87]

In January and February, Ahdab took steps to demonstrate to the Muslims his government's intention to fulfil its pledges and improve their status. Efforts were made to place taxation of the annexed areas on a par with that of Mount Lebanon; funds were allocated to development projects in Muslim regions, including Tripoli; an increasing number of Muslims were appointed to the administration, and the Muslim newspaper *Beirut*, previously suspended, was allowed to resume publication. Whilst welcoming these measures, Sunni and Shiite leaders continued to press Ahdab to appoint members of their communities to more prominent administrative positions. Facing mounting opposition from the Maronite church and the Constitutional Bloc, however, Ahdab found it extremely difficult to fulfil their requests.[88]

Ahdab nevertheless succeeded in countering the attacks of the Constitutional Bloc. He put an end to the drivers' strikes, suspended opposition newspapers that were critical of the government, and stepped up pressure on officials allied with Khuri. He also encouraged Muslim newspapers to attack Khuri and portray him as a selfish, ambitious politician who was undermining efforts to achieve Muslim-Christian cooperation. Ahdab shrewdly presented Khuri's attempt to depose him as a ploy by Maronite deputies from the Mountain, seeking to prevent the Muslims on the coast from holding influential political positions in Lebanon. Despite his slim majority, he foiled opposition attempts to topple the government and was able to govern effectively and even increase public support. At the end of February, Khuri sent messages to de Martel expressing willingness to participate in the government, provided the initiative came from the High Commission. Eddé and Ahdab, however, firmly rejected de Martel's proposal to form a government of 'national unity'.[89]

On the eve of the parliament's spring session, the Constitutional Bloc increased its efforts to bring down the government. Tension between the regime and the opposition escalated into violence on 10 March, when a bomb was thrown and shots fired into Khuri's house, where the opposition deputies were meeting. The incident impelled de Martel to act without delay. He sent alarming reports to Paris, warning that the political rivalry might deteriorate into a Christian–Muslim confrontation, and reiterating his proposal to form a national unity government. After obtaining the support of the Quai d'Orsay, de Martel imposed a unity government on Eddé and Ahdab, with Michel Zakur as minister of interior—a key position to hold before any parliamentary election.[90]

While he had averted an immediate crisis, de Martel had deeply antagonized the Sunni community. Sunni notables, who were already critical of the slow implementation of promises made by de Martel and President Eddé, reacted angrily to the new government, regarding it as a French ploy to unite the Maronites against Muslim demands for equality. They no longer believed that Ahdab could promote their interests, seeing him as a collaborator with the French and the Maronites, who was being used to maintain the status quo. Salam expressed the Muslim notables' disappointment with the government in a letter to de Martel: 'One should not attach too much importance to the fact of having given the position of prime minister to a Muslim. Appearances are misleading. The Muslims do not view the ensuing power as a goal, but as a means to safeguard the rights of the community.'[91]

Disillusioned and resentful, Sunni leaders on the coast resumed their attacks on the High Commission, the president and the government. They sent petitions and letters to Paris calling for the French government to fulfil the pledges the Lebanese treaty had made to the Muslim community, while Muslim newspapers criticized Christian predominance in the administration and the Maronite church's meddling in the government. Responding to queries by the Quai d'Orsay, French officials declared that this opposition was the result of both Syrian subversion and the Muslim leaders' personal grievances—Salam's disappointment that his son, Sa'ib, had not been nominated as mayor of Beirut; Bayhum's ambitions to replace Ahdab as prime minister; and Sulh's continued intrigues. Yet it did reflect the genuine concern of many Muslims that the French and the Maronites were reverting to their old tactics.[92]

The High Commission, however, was justified in blaming the National Bloc for fuelling inter-sectarian tension and undermining Lebanon's political stability. With the two countries about to gain independence, Syria pressed the Lebanese government throughout 1937 and 1938 to make concessions on two issues it considered vital: Tripoli and the control of the Common Interests. The question of Tripoli was now linked directly to Turkey's claim to Alexandretta. With Syria about to lose Alexandretta, its only modern port, Damascus intensified its claims in Tripoli. In early February 1937, after the League of Nations had endorsed Turkey's opposition to incorporation of the sanjak of Alexandretta in Syria, Mardam instructed the Syrian newspapers to demand Tripoli as compensation if Alexandretta was lost. The Syrian press subsequently attacked Eddé and Ahdab, threatening that Syria would boycott Beirut and direct its trade through Haifa. Articles advised the Christians to take heed of French readiness to abandon the Armenians in Alexandretta to their Turkish enemies, and called on the Maronites to end their dependence on France and cooperate with Syria and the Arab world, which was proceeding toward independence and unity. The National Bloc urged Karameh and Bisar to initiate a new campaign for their city's annexation to Syria. Indeed, before departing for Paris in June, Mardam received petitions from leaders in Tripoli authorizing him to raise this issue before the French government. A delegation left the city for Paris to plead the same cause.[93]

Although Eddé had endorsed the cession of Tripoli in the mid-1920s and early 1930s, as Lebanon's president, he now firmly opposed Syrian ambitions. In February and again in June, he sent Ahdab to Tripoli to counter the Syrian move with assurances of his government's intention to develop the city.

He also sent a telegram to Blum, appealing to the French government to deter Syria from pressing its claims. Syria's campaign to annex Tripoli also prompted the French Ministers of the Army, Navy and Air to ask their prime minister and foreign minister to prevent a change the city's status. In talks in Paris in June, Delbos and Viénot urged Mardam to cease his government's campaign in Tripoli, but for the next two years, the National Bloc continued to demand the city as compensation for Alexandretta.[94]

The question of Tripoli also became entangled in negotiations between the Syrian and Lebanese governments on the future of economic links between them. As provided by their treaties with France, they were to reach agreement on administration of the Common Interests, and on division of the revenue from customs duties. The negotiations involved issues crucial to the economies of both states: their continuation as one economic bloc, for example, with a common currency and no customs barriers even after independence. A conflict had emerged even before the official negotiations began in April, when the Lebanese government agreed, despite Syrian opposition, to prolong the Banque Syrie–Liban's concession for a further 25 years. Both governments were running budgetary deficits and were anxious to secure a larger portion of the Common Interests budget. Syria demanded 70 per cent of the revenue, based on the size of its population, while Lebanon insisted on parity, arguing that with their higher standard of living, the Lebanese consumed the greater part of the imported goods. The economic negotiations, however, were overshadowed by political considerations. The Syrian government sought close economic links between the states, while Maronite leaders in Lebanon, particularly Eddé and Arida, advocated separation in order to ensure their country's independence. In March 1938 the negotiations broke down, with each side blaming the other.[95]

The resolute stance made by Eddé and Ahdab, both on Tripoli and the future of Lebanon's economic ties with Syria, led the National Bloc to incite Syrian unionists in Lebanon to oust Ahdab and prevent Eddé's re-election. Mardam acknowledged the fact at the end of July 1938, in a closed meeting of the National Bloc held shortly after the Turkish army had entered Alexandretta. Referring to Syria's relations with Lebanon, he told his audience:

> In the future, artificial borders between the peoples of one country will be derided. For the last 18 years an isolationist policy has failed to separate between the coast and the interior. We will never negotiate with a Lebanese government, as it complies with all instructions given from abroad. We have destroyed all the governments, one after another, because they were tools of foreigners. We will negotiate only with a free government which acts for the good of the whole country.[96]

The escalation of the revolt in Palestine following the publication in July 1937 of the Peel Commission's report on its partition heightened inter-sectarian tension in Lebanon. Many of the Muslims with family and business ties in Palestine followed the uprising closely, actively supporting their brethren to the south. They sent money, smuggled out arms and ammunition, held rallies and strikes, boycotted Jewish goods, sent petitions and telegrams of protest to British officials, and denounced Britain and the Zionist movement. The arrival in October of Hajj Amin al-Husaini, Mufti of Jerusalem, drew Lebanon further into the Palestinian imbroglio. The High Commission turned down the mufti's request to reside in Beirut, but permitted him to stay in the Maronite village of Zuq Michael near Junieh after he promised not to intervene in Lebanon's internal affairs. Husaini maintained close ties with the rebels in Palestine. He met frequently with a relative, Dr Samih Fakhuri, who headed the new Muslim Higher Council, Premier Ahdab and other Lebanese Muslim leaders. He remained in Lebanon until the start of the war; whenever there were signs that the High Commission, under British or Zionist pressure, might expel him or curtail his activities, the Muslims rose to his defence.[97]

As France and Britain prepared to withdraw from the region, the revolt in Palestine generated a resurgence of strong pan-Arab sentiment among the Muslims in Lebanon and Syria, deepening the fears of the Lebanese Christians. At meetings with Zionist leaders from 1936-39, Lebanese Christian religious leaders, including Arida and Bishops Mubarak and Khuri; politicians such as President Eddé and Ayub Tabet, and intellectuals like Charles Corm, frequently voiced their concern that a Jewish defeat in Palestine might tempt the Muslims of Lebanon, as well as the Syrians, to use force against the Christians. Plans for an Arab federation, proposed by heads of neighbouring Arab states, such as Amir Abdallah and Nuri al-Said, added to their anxiety. On one occasion, Eddé told Eliyahu Epstein, the Zionist representative in Beirut, that if Amir Abdallah realized his ambition to unite Transjordan with Syria and Palestine, in part of which the Jews would enjoy autonomy, Lebanon might be impelled to join such a federation and thus bring Maronite sovereignty to an end. On the other hand, an independent Jewish state, sharing a border with Lebanon, would strengthen the Christians' ability to withstand an Arab Muslim assault, both from Syria and from within. Thus, Patriarch Arida and Bishop Mubarak publicly expressed their support for Zionist aspirations. At a meeting with Chaim Weizmann in Paris in June 1937, after being informed that the Peel Commission had recommended establishment of a Jewish state in part of Palestine, Eddé told the Zionist leader that he favoured cooperation between Lebanon and a Jewish state. Such views, however, were not shared by Khuri and other members of the Constitutional Bloc, who argued that open Christian endorsement of the Zionist movement could harm relations with the Muslims in Lebanon, as well as with Syria and other Arab states. They doubted whether the various plans for Arab unity would be realized, assuming that at most, these would lead to a closer alliance among independent Arab states, of which an independent Lebanon could also be part.[98]

Relations between de Martel and General Huntziger grew tense after the conclusion of the Syrian treaty in September 1936. Huntziger accused de Martel of having helped the French government impose a treaty that considerably limited the army's freedom of action in Syria, a treaty that would undermine its ability to use the mandated territories to defend French interests in the Middle East and the eastern Mediterranean in the event of a war in Europe. Throughout 1937 and 1938, Huntziger and the commanders of the air force and navy in the Levant pressed their headquarters and ministers in Paris either to oppose ratification of the Syrian treaty, or at least to insist that it be considerably revised. Well aware of the French public's traditional concern with their country's moral obligation to protect Christian minorities in the Levant, they fuelled the fears of local Christian leaders by warning that the treaty would prevent the French army from defending them after Syria gained independence. Similar messages were also conveyed to Patriarch Arida and to Bishops Mubarak and Khuri. Cardinal Tapuni, head of the Syrian Catholic church, became the army's main ally against the Syrian treaty. Tapuni made several trips to Paris, the Vatican and Geneva to mobilize support for better protection of the Christian minorities in Syria. His proposal to grant autonomy to the Jazira, whose population included many minority groups, in the framework of a decentralized Syrian federation, clearly marked a return to the former minorities policy. Despite concessions by Mardam in December 1937, particularly with regard to minority rights, the generals continued to oppose the Syrian treaty. The uprising in Palestine, along with National Bloc support for the rebels there, reinforced their belief that the Syrian nationalists could not be trusted. They criticized de Martel's laxity toward the mufti's activities in Lebanon and Syria and secretly encouraged the Zionists to act against him in Paris.[99]

Although he did not share Viénot's liberal position on the treaties, de Martel believed they were the only way to guarantee France's long-term strategic, economic and cultural interests in Syria and Lebanon; he consequently advocated their rapid ratification. The violence in Palestine reinforced his conviction that France should proceed with its treaty policy, lest it face a similar revolt in Syria. De Martel opposed the Maronite–Zionist dialogue, fearing it could undermine the delicate relations between Christians and

Muslims in Lebanon. By granting refuge to Hajj Amin al-Husaini, he argued, France had improved its standing among the Muslims. He therefore resisted pressure from the British and Zionist representatives in Beirut and Paris to curtail the mufti's freedom of action. De Martel was well aware of Huntziger's efforts against him in Paris, but succeeded in retaining his influence until the rise of Daladier's radical socialist government in April 1938.[100]

Since the conclusion of the Lebanese treaty, de Martel had come to believe that agreements between Maronite politicians on the Mountain and moderate Sunni leaders in Beirut, and between Eddé and Khuri, were essential for Lebanon's political stability. After failing to persuade Eddé, Ahdab and Khuri to work together, he had imposed a unity government in March. His disagreement with the army high command, however, hampered de Martel's efforts to pursue such a policy in Lebanon; as his relations with Eddé deteriorated, the latter began to collaborate with Huntziger.[101]

Eddé's relations with de Martel had been tense since the high commissioner had granted Khuri a major role in the treaty negotiations. They had deteriorated even further after de Martel's refusal to endorse Eddé's plan for revising the constitution. Eddé had expected to exercise power as the elected president following conclusion of the treaty and restoration of the constitution. But he faced a high commissioner who constantly curtailed his authority and exploited internal political rivalries to justify retaining tight control over Lebanon. Eddé was critical of de Martel's declared 'impartiality'; by preventing him from dissolving parliament, de Martel enabled the Constitutional Bloc to sustain its attacks on the government. De Martel's intervention in the March crisis and his readiness to grant the Ministry of the Interior—whose control was vital to the outcome of the elections—to the Constitutional Bloc, weakened him even further. The High Commission's endeavours to cultivate Ahdab as an independent leader further jeopardized Eddé's ability to maintain his coalition with the Muslims. On a national level, Eddé agreed with Huntziger that a long-term French military presence in Syria was essential for the protection of the Lebanese Christians. When opposition to ratification of the Syrian treaty became more pronounced in the National Assembly, he took steps—against de Martel's advice—to ensure that Lebanon's treaty would be approved separately from that of Syria. The army, which objected primarily to the Syrian treaty, backed Eddé's initiative.[102]

Arida's scheduled visit to Paris in June 1937 afforded Eddé the opportunity to travel to France and present his views directly to the French government. At the end of April, he asked to be invited on a official visit to Paris to counter any attempts by Arida to speak on behalf of Lebanon. The

Quai d'Orsay, concerned that views expressed by the outspoken patriarch might undermine its policies in Syria and Lebanon, approved Eddé's request, but invited the Syrian prime minister, Jamil Mardam, as well. The inauguration of the Syro–Lebanese pavilion at an exhibition in Paris offered a pretext for the visits of the two leaders. Eddé arrived in Paris in mid-June, accompanied by Habib Abu Shahla, the minister for national defence. Faced with the right's continued attacks on the Syrian treaty, the Blum government accorded him an especially warm welcome. He was decorated with the title of Grand Officer of the Legion of Honor; breakfasted with the French president in the Elysée Palace; met the prime minister, foreign minister, senators and deputies; talked to groups with economic, cultural and religious interests in Lebanon; and granted interviews to the Parisian press. In meetings with officials at the Quai d'Orsay, Eddé stressed the need to ensure protection for the Christians of Lebanon vis-à-vis the Muslim Syria which was about to gain independence. He pointed to the political instability in Lebanon that had followed restoration of the constitution, which was preventing the government, in the face of a small and evenly divided parliament, from effectively exercising power. Eddé asked for permision to dissolve parliament and elect an expanded legislature, thus enabling the government to enjoy a solid majority. His public statements referred to differences in the military protocols of the Lebanese and Syrian treaties: in contrast to Syria, the French army enjoyed complete freedom of action in Lebanon. The Christians, he noted, surrounded by a sea of Muslims, would constantly require French protection. He appealed to the French government and National Assembly to ratify the Lebanese treaty without waiting for the outcome of deliberations on the Syrian treaty. He also opposed the French navy's plans to build a modern port in Tripoli, arguing that in view of the large expenditure involved, it was preferable to enlarge the existing harbour in Beirut. This stand was in stark contrast to his former declaration that Tripoli was essential for Lebanon.[103]

Eddé's statement in Paris describing Lebanon as a bastion of French influence in the Middle East, and his attempts at unilateral ratification of the Lebanese treaty, added to the tension between the Syrian and Lebanese governments. Viénot disapproved of Eddé's initiative and made it clear that the Quai d'Orsay would insist that both treaties be ratified simultaneously. Taken by surprise, de Martel pointed out the hostile reaction that the Lebanese president's declaration had evoked in Syria and among Muslims in Lebanon. However, General Gamelin, who had replaced General Weygand as French chief of staff, and General Huntziger, both welcomed Eddé's words.[104]

Throughout May, de Martel had urged Ahdab and Khuri to refrain from any intrigues that might endanger the government. The sudden death of interior minister Michel Zakur on 18 June, however, provoked a serious political crisis. Having succeeded in tempting one deputy away from the coalition, the Constitutional Bloc sought to impose its own government on Eddé, or at least retain the Ministry of the Interior in a national unity government. Eddé, however, was determined that the portfolio be allocated to his trusted ally, Habib Abu Shahla, whom he immediately despatched by air to Lebanon. Eddé himself returned to Beirut in early July, and was greeted by thousands of supporters. With his confidence bolstered by the warm welcome accorded him in Paris, he threatened to dissolve parliament and declare new elections unless his conditions were met. After his demands were turned down by the opposition, he empowered Ahdab to form a new government comprising five members, four of whom were Eddists. The Constitutional Bloc responded by tabling a motion, signed by 13 deputies, calling for an extraordinary session of parliament to vote the government out. On 24 July, facing certain defeat, Eddé dissolved parliament and declared new elections. This move marked the beginning of a particularly stormy three-month period during which, as Khuri would recount later, the country had been on the verge of civil war.[105]

Concerned that a confrontation between Eddé and Khuri might destabilize the Lebanese state, de Martel strove to defuse the tension by separating the parliamentary elections from those for the presidency. He proposed that the High Commission extend Eddé's term of office for another three years, at the end of which, however, in accordance with the constitution, he would not be eligible for re-election for another six years. The Quai d'Orsay approved the plan, which Eddé, after some hesitation, had agreed to as well. Khuri, however, rejected the idea, proposing instead that the president's term be limited to three years—which meant that Eddé could not be re-elected at the end of his current term. When this proposal was turned down, Khuri suggested that in the forthcoming vote, the president be elected for three instead of the six years stipulated by the constitution. After the failure of his initiative, de Martel did succeed in convincing both Eddé and Khuri that the next parliament should comprise 60 deputies, 40 of whom would be elected and 20 nominated.[106]

The news that parliamentary elections were to be held within three months sparked frenzied activity throughout Lebanon. Politicians set about organizing their supporters, and candidates engaged in intense negotiations over electoral lists, while religious leaders, businessmen and foreign concessionaire companies promoted their respective candidates. The High Commission, for its part, took precautions to preclude the election of any-

one unfriendly to France. The events of the first week of the campaign reinforced de Martel's worst fears. Determined to win an overwhelming majority
in parliament and assure his election as president, Eddé, assisted by Ahdab,
conducted an aggressive campaign against the opposition. Both took steps to
ensure their control of the administrative system, essential for winning any
election in Lebanon. They installed their clients in key positions, and harassed relatives of Constitutional Bloc members, as well as officials known as
Khuri supporters, forcing them to resign. When opposition newspapers protested these measures, Ahdab suspended them *sine die*. Eddé also let de
Martel know that he intended to use his authority to nominate one third of
the deputies to the new parliament. Khuri desperately pleaded for de Martel
to intervene, but to no avail. Faced with certain defeat, Khuri left for Paris
at the beginning of August, staying there for almost two months and constantly appealing to the Quai d'Orsay to ensure free, fair elections. Once
again the 'Muslim card' was being played to press the Quai d'Orsay and the
High Commission to impose their own electoral solutions.[107]

The elections caused profound discord among the Sunni leaders. Anxious
to broaden his own power base in Beirut's Sunni community, Ahdab cooperated closely with the High Commission to undermine his rivals—Sulh,
Salam and Bayhum. To that end, he also collaborated with members of less
prominent clans, including the Fakhuris. The establishment of a new Muslim higher council by Samih Fakhuri in July was intended to compete with
that headed by Salam. Ahdab also attracted several of the younger Sunni
leaders allied with Riad al-Sulh, among them Abdallah al-Yafi and Muhi al-
Din al-Nasuli, head of the Muslim scouts and editor of the influential
Muslim newspaper, *Beirut*. He enlisted many of the *qabadayat* (strongmen)
in Beirut, Sidon and Tripoli, whose services were always in great demand
during elections. Under the joint attack of Ahdab and the High Commission, Salam, Bayhum and Sulh closed ranks. Although he himself was not a
candidate, Salam contributed large sums of money to ensure the election of
Bayhum and Sulh. The rivalry between Ahdab and Bayhum, who had his
own ambitions for the premiership, was especially intense; it almost erupted
into violence after the government prevented Bayhum from leaving for Paris
to plead his case to the Quai d'Orsay. For his part, Sulh, who was determined
to enter parliament, conducted an aggressive campaign. Mobilizing his followers, he held discussions with Christian candidates in Beirut aimed at
forming a joint electoral list. Mardam took up Sulh's case and pleaded with
de Martel not to veto his candidacy. Sulh even made it known to French officials and Christian politicians that if elected, he would be willing to
recognize Lebanon's territorial integrity. Faced with strong opposition from
the High Commission, however, he again collaborated with Khuri.[108]

With relatives and clients harassed by the government, and the High Commission refusing to intervene, the Constitutional Bloc candidates began to cooperate with Muslim politicians known for their hostility to France. In Beirut, Henri Pharaon and Jubran Tuaini coordinated their moves with Sulh and Bayhum, and Khalid Shihab pressed the mufti, Tawfik Khalid, to oppose Ahdab; in Tripoli, Taqla sought Karameh's support for the opposition candidate. The Constitutional Bloc's initiative in Tripoli prompted Ahdab to visit Karameh and persuade him to maintain neutrality.[109]

The High Commission was highly critical of the Constitutional Bloc's collaboration with the Arab Muslim nationalists. French officials were concerned that Sulh would exploit the rivalry between the two Maronite leaders to gain access to parliament, thence to act against French and Lebanese interests. They also sensed danger in the election of anti-French Christian politicians, such as Aziz al-Hashem and Khalil Ma'atouk. Meyrier and Lafond warned Taqla, Shihab, Tuaini, Pharaon and other members of the Constitutional Bloc that they were compromising Lebanon's national interests, but to no avail. When officials in the Quai d'Orsay sought to persuade Khuri to have his supporters end cooperation with the Muslims, their efforts came to naught.[110]

The Arab Congress convened at Bludan in Syria on 8 September to discuss assistance to the Palestinians following the report of the Peel Commission, added to French fears of an Arab nationalist attack on Lebanon. The congress became a major display of pan-Arabist sentiment. Four hundred delegates from Syria, Palestine, Iraq and Egypt took part; Lebanon was represented by a delegation of 59 members, including Sulh, Da'uq, Karameh, Bisar, Yafi, Hashem and Tuaini. The latter tabled a resolution criticizing the Lebanese government for its refusal to condemn the Peel Report. The Quai d'Orsay, dismayed at Tuaini's cooperation with Sulh and other opponents of France, warned Mardam that an anti-Lebanese resolution would jeopardize Franco–Syrian relations.[111]

Urgent dispatches from the High Commission were warning the Quai d'Orsay of the danger of an alliance between the Constitutional Bloc and the Muslim opposition. The situation prompted François de Tessan, under-secretary for foreign affairs, to summon Khuri and caution him that his supporters' conduct would enable anti-Lebanese politicians to enter parliament, and make it difficult for France to protect Lebanon's independence. Khuri responded that he did not object to the Lebanese government taking steps to prevent the election of 'undesirable elements' in Beirut, Sidon and Tripoli, but on Mount Lebanon, where all the candidates were 'staunch Lebanese', the election campaign had to be free.[112]

Despite its criticism of Khuri's duplicity, the Quai d'Orsay was anxious to curtail the Constitutional Bloc's cooperation with the pro-Syrian Arab Muslim nationalists and adopted de Martel's recommendation. After meeting with Khuri in mid-September, de Tessan instructed his high commissioner, who had arrived in Paris in August for deliberations on the Lebanese crisis, to prolong Eddé's term for another three years. This, he hoped, would ensure political stability by guaranteeing the government a majority in the parliament, and prevent election of pro-Syrian candidates. De Martel left for Beirut on 27 September; with him on the boat was Khuri. For the next three days they had ample opportunity to exchange views on a way out of the crisis.[113]

Upon Khuri's arrival in Beirut, tension between the two rival camps burst into open confrontation. Hundreds of his supporters accorded him an enthusiastic welcome at the port, and one hundred vehicles escorted his car to his summer house in Aley. To avoid congestion in the narrow streets of the village, the gendarmerie directed the procession through a shorter route. Majid Arslan, Camil Chamoun, Henri Pharaon and some of Khuri's relatives, who suspected that the gendarmes were under government orders to prevent them turning the event into a political demonstration, brandished their guns. The government issued warrants for their arrest and Chamoun, Arslan and others involved in the incident fled to the Baruk Mountain, where they threatened to mobilize their supporters and forcibly resist the government. With emotions running high, de Martel, fearing escalation into violence, ordered Ahdab to cease harassing the opposition and cautioned Khuri to refrain from further provocation. He publicly called on both sides to demonstrate political maturity, reminding them that the mandatory power was still responsible for maintaining law and order. The policy formulated in Paris was immediately put into force. Khuri now agreed that Eddé remain in office for another three years, provided he confined himself strictly to his constitutional prerogatives—in particular with regard to relations between the government and parliament. He also insisted that Eddé end his intervention in the forthcoming parliamentary elections, and that the Constitutional Bloc be represented fairly in parliament. These conditions were intended to erode Eddé's political power and forestall his plan to revise the constitution and transform Lebanon into a presidential republic. Barred from taking part in the elections, Eddé would be left without a strong political base of his own in parliament. His ability to intervene in the formation of the government would thereby be limited, since the government depended on a majority in parliament, where the Constitutional Bloc retained considerable influence. In the face of almost certain defeat, Khuri's conditions were somewhat extreme.

Yet de Martel accepted them, despite the fact that they exceeded the instructions given to him in Paris.[114]

De Martel's *volte-face* was so marked that rumours abounded in Beirut that the Constitutional Bloc had bribed high-ranking officials in the High Commission. There was no need, however, to seek such a sinister cause. De Martel genuinely feared the repercussions of a violent confrontation over Lebanon within the Christian community and, subsequently, on French interests there. His relations with Eddé were already tense, since the latter was collaborating with Huntziger and insisting on exercising his power as president. Eddé's aggressive policy toward the opposition, and the ensuing crisis, reinforced de Martel's belief that as high commissioner he had to maintain his position as an impartial mediator between the political factions and communities. He continued to seek an agreement between the Maronites on the Mountain and the Sunnis on the coast, which would entail allocating the premiership to the Sunnis, while allowing the Maronites to retain the presidency. An alliance between Eddé and Ahdab, however, could not achieve this goal, because Eddé, unlike Khuri, lacked a power base among the Maronites on the Mountain. Thus, de Martel pointed out, each time Eddé barred Khuri and his supporters from state institutions, they collaborated with the militant pro-Syrian Muslims on the coast to put pressure on the High Commission. His solution to the crisis was twofold: first, to contain the rivalry between Eddé and Khuri over the presidency by prolonging Eddé's term of office, and then to confine Eddé to the role of an impartial president, standing above the various communities and political factions. The daily business of governing would be carried out by the prime minister and his cabinet. With the question of the presidency settled, the High Commission would urge Khuri and Ahdab to cooperate in the elections and in forming a unity government.[115]

After Ahdab and Khuri had agreed to work together, de Martel on 5 October informed a surprised, then resentful, Eddé that his term in office was being prolonged for an additional three years, at the end of which he would not be eligible for re-election for another six. The deputies would be divided between the government and the opposition, and their nomination determined in deliberations involving the High Commission, Eddé, Ahdab and Khuri. The Lebanese public learned of the extension of their president's term from a decree published by the High Commission in the press on the following day. Throughout the first week of October, Ahdab, Khuri, Kieffer and Lafond met secretly at the high commissioner's residence to choose the deputies. The negotiations were extremely complex, requiring agreement on an acceptable division of the 60 elected and nominated deputies between government and opposition, while ensuring that the various communities and regions were fairly represented in parliament. Only after de Martel issued yet another decree increasing the number of deputies to 63, did they reach consensus. Thirty-seven deputies were allocated to the government (24 elected and 13 nominated), and 26 to the Constitutional Bloc (18 elected and 8 nominated). After the candidates for the combined electoral lists in each of the five electoral districts had been decided upon, de Martel published another decree dividing the 42 elected deputies among the various communities and regions.[116]

The elections, held on 24 and 25 October, were merely a nominal act. Nevertheless, the High Commission, Ahdab and the Constitutional Bloc had invested much time and effort to secure the success of their candidates. The French had been particularly anxious to prevent Sulh's election. As expected, all the candidates of the government and the opposition were elected. Sulh, who had initially insisted on participating, withdrew on the first balloting day after his supporters were prevented from voting. In Beirut both Sunni-backed government candidates, Abdallah al-Yafi and Salim Lababidi, won over 22,000 votes, while Sulh and Bayhum received less than 2,000 votes each. In the other electoral districts, the government and the Constitutional Bloc candidates also won by overwhelming majorities.[117]

After publication of the election results, Ahdab and Khuri began negotiations on forming a national unity government; Eddé did not take part. On 29 October parliament held its first session at which Petro Trad was elected speaker. The Shiite deputies, however, voted for Rashid Baydun, arguing that as their community was the third largest, a Shiite was entitled to the position. The following day, a seven-member government was formed, comprising Habib Abu Shahla, Georges Tabet, Ibrahim Haidar, Musa Namur, Salim Taqla and Majid Arslan, with Ahdab as prime minister. It was approved almost unanimously, with 57 deputies voting in favour.[118]

The October 1937 elections had far-reaching consequences for Lebanese politics. Khuri re-emerged as a major political force and as the main contender for the presidency at the end of Eddé's term. He exploited the elections to increase the number of Constitutional Bloc members in parliament, many of whom owed their election to him. Access to government institutions and state funds enabled him to broaden his circle of followers. His prestige among the Lebanese public, however, did not fare so well. Many young and educated Lebanese voiced their dismay at his conduct and accused him of having 'let them down'. After a five-year struggle for a constitution and a democracy, and against French intervention in Lebanon's internal affairs, he had struck a shady deal with de Martel. Eddé lost much of his power as his coalition with the Muslim deputies disintegrated and Ahdab formed his own power base in parliament. With his ability to inter-

vene in the government and the administration limited, Eddé was unable to
retain the loyalty of his supporters. His prestige declined as well, since he had
consented to serve a second term as president by decree of the high commissioner—despite the fact that Lebanon had its own legislature. Ahdab fared
no better. He was viewed by his community as ambitious, opportunistic and
a collaborator with France. He was soon to discover that without the constant backing of the president, he was unable to withstand the growing public
criticism. Muslim leaders, who had hoped that Lebanon was entering a new
era, realized that the High Commission and the Maronites were continuing
their old tactics of cultivating only the Muslim politicians they could control. On the eve of independence, Lebanese politicians not only discredited
themselves, but undermined the state institutions, and with them the country as a whole. The Lebanese public again questioned the need for such a
large government and parliament and an ever-growing administration, when
most of the state budget was spent on its upkeep. In the next two years the
disappointment of the young and educated generation would turn into unprecedented anti-parliamentary sentiment. The outbreak of the war and the
emergence of Khuri and the Constitutional Bloc as champions of Christian–
Muslim solidarity in the struggle for independence from France, slowed
down this trend. It would revive in the early 1950s with dissent against
Khuri's regime.[119]

At the end of October, de Martel sent a report to the Quai d'Orsay analysing the results of the Lebanese elections. He praised Ahdab for having
effectively isolated the pro-Syrian militants, and for winning the support of
younger Sunni leaders, including Yafi and Nasuli, for the government. He
also pointed out that 67.11 per cent of the registered voters had cast their
ballots, and that even in Tripoli, which had in the past boycotted elections,
12,000 had voted for the government. In these elections, he noted with satisfaction, the intervention of the Maronite church had been successfully
restricted. He congratulated himself on having averted a serious crisis, and
expressed confidence that Lebanon would enjoy a stable government, with
the two camps cooperating under the guidance of the High Commission.
Over the following five months, however, it became obvious that his expectations had been unfounded; Ahdab was forced to resign despite the High
Commission's backing, while de Martel himself came under attack for his
handling of the elections in both Beirut and Paris.[120]

Criticism of de Martel and Ahdab came from all directions. Many of the
unsuccessful candidates, whether Christian or Muslim, protested to the Quai
d'Orsay and to the senators and deputies, that the High Commission had
rigged the elections. Riad al-Sulh was particularly vociferous. In early 1938,

he travelled to Paris where, at meetings with left-wing politicians and journalists, he accused de Martel of continuing the old tactics of direct
administration and of 'divide and rule'—despite the fact that Lebanon and
Syria had concluded treaties granting them independence from France. Eddé,
bitter and resentful, collaborated closely with Huntziger against de Martel.
He sent his son Raymond to Paris to complain to the Quai d'Orsay of his
mistreatment by the high commissioner. Surprisingly, de Martel explained
that his decision to intervene in the elections and impose a solution had been
intended to prevent Eddé's defeat on Mount Lebanon. When Eliyahu
Epstein, a Zionist official, complained of the freedom Hajj Amin al-Husaini
enjoyed in Lebanon, Eddé laid the blame on de Martel and proposed that
the Zionists use their influence in the Quai d'Orsay against him. He accused
Ahdab of betrayal, telling him angrily: 'You are the reflection of de Martel
and Kieffer, and refrained from committing yourself, which was to my det-
riment.' Vengeful, he constantly strove to oust Ahdab, and to this end even
resigned himself to the fact that the next government would be formed by
the Constitutional Bloc. He met with Ahdab's Sunni opponents in Beirut,
including Salam and Bayhum, with whom he coordinated his moves. Eddé
also urged Patriarch Arida and Bishop Mubarak to insist on Ahdab's replacement with a Christian prime minister. A similar demand was made by
Cardinal Tapuni, Mgr Leprêtre, the apostolic delegate, and the Jesuits in Beirut, who criticized what they termed the high commissioner's 'Islamic policy'.
De Martel's attempts to point out the services rendered by Ahdab both to
France and Lebanon, were to no avail. Even Robert de Caix's visit to Beirut
in early 1938 and his meetings with Eddé, Arida and other Christian clergy,
failed to change their stand.[121]

Despite mounting attacks on the government, Ahdab could not be removed as long as Khuri adhered to his agreement with de Martel. But
Khuri's policy now faced strong opposition from his own camp, led by
Michel Chiha, who insisted that the Bloc resign from the government and
resume its attacks on Eddé and Ahdab. Chiha was joined by Henri Pharaon
and younger members of the Bloc, including Charles Amoun, editor of *Le
Jour*, Hamid Karameh and Ibrahim Azar. Khuri pointed out to his colleagues
that he had had no choice but to strike a deal with de Martel in October;
after an exhausting two-year campaign in the opposition, which had necessitated considerable financial resources, the group needed access to the
government and to positions in the administration to ensure the loyalty of
its followers. He also argued that some of the new members, such as Namur,
Sakaf and Zein, would be reluctant to join the Constitutional Bloc in
opposition. Yet Chiha was unconvinced, and began to reduce his contribu-
tions, including support of *Le Jour*. With his two main financial backers

opposing his policy, Khuri desperately appealed to de Martel to replace Ahdab.[122]

Deputies from both camps allied to either Eddé or Chiha began to criticize the government. Ahdab's request for an additional budget to cover government outlays in the elections provoked bitter attacks by Khabaz and Amoun. Despite explanations that the money had been spent on preventing the election of candidates hostile to Lebanon, and that the Constitutional Bloc had been involved in these efforts, he failed to end the campaign against the government. Both *L'Orient* and *Le Jour* chastised Ahdab, alluding to rumours that he had received large sums from deputies in return for his support of their election or nomination to parliament. But it took a government decision to dissolve the paramilitary organizations, and the ensuing clashes with the Phalangists, to unite the Christian public against Ahdab and his government.[123]

In 1936 and 1937, Beirut and other Lebanese cities witnessed the emergence of paramilitary youth organizations with clear fascist tendencies. Their uniformed members marched through the streets carrying flags and placards; they staged rallies, sports competitions and military drills. Their proliferation attested to the deep dissatisfaction of Lebanese youth with the traditional politicians and their corrupt and inefficient institutions, along with a growing political and social awareness and a desire to take part in shaping their country's future. The politicians and the various parties and factions directed this strong patriotic sentiment toward defined national and political goals. In Syria, Fakhri al-Barudi formed the Iron Shirts, the National Bloc's youth movement, and in early 1936 attempted to establish branches in Beirut, Tripoli and Sidon. In the same year, three similar paramilitary youth organizations were formed in Lebanon—the White Shirts, the Lebanese Phalanges and the Najjada. These movements were of a religious bent and became entangled in sectarian and political rivalries. The White Shirts, the youth organization of the L'Unité Libanaise, established by Tawfik Awad in June 1936 with Eddé's backing, advocated the defence of Lebanon's independence and territorial integrity. It attracted many young Maronites who frequently demonstrated against Syrian claims to Lebanon.[124] The Lebanese Phalanges also staunchly supported Lebanon's independence and borders. The group's first political activity took place on 21 November 1936 to counter Muslim demonstrations in Beirut against the treaty and the Lebanese state.[125] Supporters of both Eddé and Khuri were among their founders, but as rivalry between the two camps mounted in early 1937, it was reflected in the movement. In April, Pierre Gemayel, a Phalanges founder, who advocated neutrality, was elected its leader. The Phalanges were better organized than the White Shirts and attracted hundreds of Maronite youths from the Mountain and the Christian quarters of east Beirut. According to their doctrine, independent Lebanon, within its 1920 borders, was a separate and distinct geographical and historical entity. After 1937, they adopted a more pronounced anti-French stance and called for an end to the mandate. In contrast, the Najjada was an Arab Muslim organization which stood for Arab unity, the independence of the Arab world from foreign rule, and an Arab Lebanon.[126] It was formed at the end of 1936 from a Muslim scout organization established by Nasuli, to protect Muslim Beirut and counter Christian paramilitary organizations. Its members marched through the streets of the Muslim quarters hoisting the Syrian flag and banners with slogans calling for Arab unity, and held demonstrations in support of the Muslim struggle in Palestine.

The more veteran Parti Populaire Syrien had been established as a secret organization in 1932 by the Greek Orthodox Antoine Khalil Sa'adeh, who taught at the University of Beirut, and whose students were among its first members. Sa'adeh preached that Syria was one geographical entity extending from the Taurus mountains in the north to the Suez Canal in the south, and from the Mediterranean to the Syrian desert. The population of the region, regardless of religion or sect, comprised one Syrian nation which had existed since historical times. This geographical Syria, distinct from the rest of the Arab Muslim world, had to be united and independent. In a way, his ideology mirrored the Phoenician ideas advocated by the Maronites with regard to Lebanon. The party did not recognize Lebanon's separate existence and called for its annexation to Syria. The Sûreté Générale learned of its existence in November 1935, from the president of the American University of Beirut. The French security services began to suspect that the party was being funded by Italian intelligence, after papers seized in members' homes included plans of Rayak airport and other French military installations. In June 1936, Sa'adeh was arrested for the second time, after party members tried to assassinate the editors of two Lebanese newspapers that had attacked the organization. In May 1937 however, he was released with Ahdab's intervention after undertaking to recognize Lebanon's separate existence and support the government in the elections.[127]

The marked sectarian and paramilitary character of the Lebanese youth movements roused the High Commission's fears of violent confrontations between their members. At the beginning of November the Najjada staged a demonstration in support of the Muslims in Palestine, while the Phalanges planned to hold a rally on 21 November to mark the first anniversary of its establishment. This prompted Colombani, the new director general of the Sûreté Générale, to recommend dissolution of all paramilitary organizations.

De Martel, however, preferred that this unpopular step be taken by the Lebanese government. On 18 November Abu Shahla, the minister of the interior, issued a decree dissolving the organizations and forbidding all paramilitary militias. He charged that they were no longer engaged in sports activities, but were conducting military training, and that their religious and sectarian character contradicted the government's goal of ensuring harmony among the communities. The decree provoked an angry reaction from the Maronite community, led by Bishop Mubarak, who chastised the government for its action against the 'young Lebanese patriots'. On 20 November, Pierre Gemayel published a statement in the press denying that the Phalanges had military tendencies and describing its members as the elite of Lebanese youth, inspired by genuine patriotic sentiments, whose aim was to root anarchy out of the country. He ended with the call 'camarades, à demain'.[128]

On the following day, a Sunday, violent clashes broke out in Beirut between hundreds of Phalangists and the Lebanese police and French security services. In the riots, which lasted throughout the day, two demonstrators and a French soldier were killed, scores were injured on both sides, and many members of the Phalanges were arrested, among them the wounded Pierre Gemayel. To prevent further disturbances, the High Commission imposed press censorship. On 26 November, a general strike was held in Beirut and in Maronite villages on the Mountain to protest the brutal measures of the security forces. A statement issued by de Martel, calling for an end to the demonstrations and stressing the High Commission's determination to maintain law and order, did little to defuse the tension. In parliament, the government was harshly criticized by the deputies. Although it survived a vote of non-confidence, the damage to its standing in the Maronite community proved irreversible.[129]

In mid-January 1938, Salim Taqla and Majid Arslan resigned from the government and were joined by Habib Abu-Shahla, who had been flirting with Khuri since November. Reluctant to dismiss Ahdab, but unable to impose his own solution, de Martel left it to the Lebanese politicians to find a way out of the crisis—for which he had been primarily responsible. He advised Eddé and Khuri, however, to delay Ahdab's replacement until after the parliament passed the annual budget, which included the unpopular measure of higher taxes. He also stressed the need to continue allocating the premiership to the Sunni community. At a meeting in early February, Eddé offered Khuri the premiership and after Khuri declined, proposed the formation of an emergency government comprising three veteran prime ministers—Khuri, Ahdab and Ayub Tabet. Khuri, who saw himself as a potential presidential candidate, refused to take direct responsibility for the government's actions. Despite warnings from his aides that a government headed by the Constitutional Bloc would weaken his position even further, Eddé, anxious to be rid of Ahdab, acquiesced in Khuri's conditions and nominated Khalid Shihab to form the new government. On 20 March, Ahdab finally resigned and Shihab formed a seven-member cabinet in which both parties were represented. Control of the premiership and the important Ministries of Finance and Public Works enabled Khuri to strengthen his camp. Yet, with its members in power, dissension soon arose in the ranks of the Constitutional Bloc, especially between Khuri and Chamoun, as the latter adopted an independent stand. For his part, Eddé, whose authority in the government, parliament and administration had been eroded, renewed his appeals to the Quai d'Orsay to dissolve parliament and adopt his proposal for revising the constitution. In November 1938, Shihab's government was replaced by yet another, headed by Abdallah Yafi, thus continuing the tradition of a Sunni prime minister. It was during Yafi's tenure that the Second World War broke out.[130]

With war against Germany looming on the horizon following Hitler's 'anschluss' with Austria in March 1938, the Quai d'Orsay, the High Commission and the army command had little patience for the intrigues of Lebanese politicians. Faced with the prospect of a war in Europe and the Mediterranean, France was no longer ready to give up direct control over the mandated territories. Additional concessions made by Mardam at the end of the year failed to persuade the French government and the National Assembly to ratify the Syrian treaty. The Quai d'Orsay also turned down Eddé's appeals for ratification of the Lebanese treaty when he came to Paris in July. In Lebanon, the French army, navy and air force accelerated work on military projects. New port facilities built in Beirut especially for the navy were inaugurated in June, and 14 French warships arrived for the ceremony. French destroyers constantly patrolled the Lebanese coast. A month later, a new airport was opened in Khaldeh near Beirut—the largest and most modern in the Middle East at the time. A communications centre was built nearby, and used to relay French radio broadcasts in the Middle East. The airport in Rayak was extended, and new barracks and ammunition dumps were constructed in army camps in Zahleh, Beirut and other towns, to serve the thousands of French troops arriving in Lebanon. Fortifications were built along the coast and heavy guns were installed in the mountains above Beirut. Tripoli was also fortified, and work on the refinery there accelerated. A civil defence system was organized, and in September the High Commission issued a decree, stipulating that all offenses against national security would be brought before French military courts. The Sûreté Générale increased its supervision of the thousands of foreign citizens in Lebanon, who were also forbidden to live near military installations. The French army now considered Lebanon, and especially Beirut, as a vital strategic base in the eastern Mediterranean in the event of a war with Italy. The fortification of Lebanon, along with reports from Europe of an impending war, compounded Lebanese fears that their country would become a major battlefield for the European powers.[131]

Meanwhile, the pressure from Huntziger in Beirut and Gamelin in Paris finally bore fruit. On 22 October 1938, the Quai d'Orsay announced the replacement of de Martel by Gabriel Puaux. Having decided not to ratify the treaty, the French government had sought a high commissioner who would cooperate with the army command in the Levant. The news of de Martel's departure pleased the Maronite church and President Eddé, but in Damascus it was seen as further indication of France's intention to abandon its treaty policy. De Martel left Beirut in mid-November from the airport in Khaldeh, which he had helped construct. The muted ceremony stood in stark contrast to the grand reception accorded him on his arrival in Beirut five years before. Like his predecessors, de Martel had failed to establish a new basis for France's relations with its mandated territories. During the first two years he had tried, unsuccessfully, to impose on Syria a treaty on French terms, and isolate the National Bloc. In March 1936, when he was finally forced to change his stance and seek an agreement with the National Bloc, it was already too late. Political instability in Paris, mounting tension in the international arena and the opposition of the army and the right in the National Assembly had jeopardized such a policy. De Martel had been caught between foreign ministers—who pressed him to proceed with moderation and caution, either for fear of a new uprising in Syria or a belief in the need to emancipate the mandated territories—and the army, which insisted on maintaining firm control. He had failed to provide Lebanon with a stable, efficient political system, and had become increasingly involved in local intrigues, often encouraging them, either to retain his influence or safeguard what he considered French interests. His contribution to the economy of the mandated territories, however, was more positive. Despite the depression and the devaluations of the French franc, de Martel succeeded in modernizing the infrastructure of both Syria and Lebanon. Hundreds of kilometers of roads were laid, the railway in northern Syria was extended to Iraq, large irrigation projects were begun, and the pipeline from Mosul to Tripoli was completed. With its modernized port and new airport and communications centre, Beirut would establish itself in the 1940s and 1950s as a leading regional and international commercial and financial centre.[132]

Like his two predecessors, Puaux was a career diplomat with some experience in Muslim affairs. He held the post of high commissioner until December 1940, when the Vichy government replaced him with General Henri Dentz. Puaux arrived in Beirut in early January 1939 and spent the months before the war tightening French control over Syria and Lebanon. At that time, France's Middle East policy, like that of Britain, was almost exclusively determined by military and strategic considerations. But while Britain pursued a pan-Arab policy—which culminated in the White Paper on Palestine in May 1939—France returned to its traditional minorities policy. With war in Europe inevitable, it was unwilling to allow the National Bloc, which it had never trusted, to exercise its authority, preferring to rely on the more friendly minorities in Mount Lebanon, Jabal Druze and the Alawite region. In May, after returning from talks in Paris, Puaux declared in a radio broadcast that France no longer intended to ratify the 1936 treaties, but was ready to resume negotiations on new agreements, in which its interests and those of the minorities would be better safeguarded. In fact, since the end of 1938, officers of the Service de Renseignements had been inciting the Druze and the Alawites, as well as Christians and Kurds in the Jazira, to demand greater autonomy from Damascus, while in the Quai d'Orsay and the High Commission, officials were again considering the formation of a Syrian federation.[133] With their only tangible achievement—the incorporation of the Alawite region and Jabal Druze into Syria—denied them, Mardam, who had advocated cooperation with France, resigned. Hostility to France became even more pronounced after Alexandretta was formally relinquished to Turkey. In July, Puaux suspended the Syrian constitution, dissolved parliament, granted greater autonomy to Jabal Druze, the Alawite region and the Jazira, and replaced the government with a directorate. These steps were accompanied by the transfer of 10,000 French soldiers from Lebanon to Syria, where they took up positions around Damascus and other major cities.[134]

The High Commission could not suspend the Syrian constitution while elected political institutions in Lebanon were retained. Officials in the High Commission and army officers therefore exploited the contempt and resentment felt by many Lebanese toward their own politicians to instigate a campaign among both Christians and Muslims for the restoration of direct French control. News from Europe on the general mobilization, along with rumours of French plans to introduce compulsory military service in the mandated territories caused much alarm. So did the steady arrival of French troops, including soldiers from the French Foreign Legion, and the sale of gas masks by the government. The fear of war was particularly noticeable among the Christians. It drove Eddé to appeal again to Puaux and the Quai d'Orsay to ratify the Lebanese treaty without delay. Another idea aired by Christian leaders was to establish a 'Shiite state' comprising Jabal Amil and the Beqa valley, and to link it to the Alawite region in the north. Such an entity, they argued, would serve as a buffer between the Christians in Lebanon—whose majority would thereby be increased—and Syria. They also proposed that the High Commission help the Christians from the densely populated Mount Lebanon to settle in Muslim regions near Tyre and Sidon, or in Tripoli itself. Such ideas were clearly impractical, but attested to the Christians' deep concern for the future of their state.[135]

Even as the Lebanese public was gripped by fear at the prospect of a new war, Eddé and Khuri continued their feud to the last minute. Eddé, attempting to exploit the High Commission's intention to tighten its control, tried to persuade Puaux to transform Lebanon into a presidential republic. For his part, Khuri argued that if the High Commission was determined to suspend the constitution, not only should the government and parliament be dissolved, but the president should also end his term. The suspension of the Syrian constitution and Puaux's return to the Quai d'Orsay for deliberations, prompted the two rivals to take their case to Paris. Eddé left for France in the middle of July, and was followed soon after by Khuri, accompanied by Taqla. Although the mood in the French capital was tense, with the threat of war mounting daily, the conflict between Eddé and Khuri persisted throughout August. At the end of the month, the foreign minister instructed Puaux and Eddé to return immediately to their posts in Lebanon. Having missed the last scheduled passenger boat, Khuri had to travel through Naples to Alexandretta, where he took a Romanian ship bound for Beirut.[136]

Upon his arrival in Beirut on 31 August, Puaux met with General Weygand, who had been appointed by the French government as superior commander in the Middle East arena. The following day Germany invaded Poland; the Second World War had begun. The High Commission immediately declared a state of emergency and deployed forces to defend the mandated territories. On 21 September, Puaux issued decrees suspending the Lebanese constitution, dissolving parliament and the government, and appointing Eddé as head of state, with Abdallah Bayhum as his secretary. Eddé's appointment was merely a nominal act, however; it was the High Commission that effectively controlled Lebanon.[137]

With memories of their traumatic experience in the Great War still fresh in their minds, the Lebanese now anxiously awaited the outcome of this second war between the European powers.

CHAPTER FIVE

Conclusion

When the Maronite Christians, assisted by France, established Greater Lebanon in 1920, they achieved a national objective which had thus far eluded other, larger minorities in the Middle East. Six years later, the Lebanese Republic was proclaimed, and the Maronites embarked upon transforming their homeland, within its extended borders, into a politically and economically viable state. They envisioned a modern, Western nation, closely linked to France and Europe, in which Christians would be secure— an island of prosperity and progress in a hostile, Muslim Arab Middle East.

By the eve of the Second World War, despite numerous problems that continued to trouble Lebanon, the Maronites appeared to have taken giant steps toward the realization of their dream. Lebanon enjoyed international recognition and had its own symbols of statehood, along with a Western constitution that provided for a democratic parliamentary system. Its economy had recovered from the recession of the early 1930s and its entrepreneurs had taken full advantage of the economic opportunities available under the mandate, turning Lebanon into a leading commercial and financial centre for the entire Middle East. A modern infrastructure had been laid, thousands of miles of roads paved, bridges constructed, the railway system improved and Beirut's port enlarged and modernized to cope with the sharp rise in trade with Europe. A new airport and communications centre ensured rapid links with Europe and North America. With its elegant new buildings and wide avenues, Beirut was a vibrant, modern city. Young people from all over the region came to study in its universities, where they were exposed to a unique mix of East and West, intellectual openness, and a cosmopolitan atmosphere. Lebanese newspapers, magazines and books, printed by the ever-increasing number of publishing houses, were read throughout the Middle East. Lebanon had indeed become an island of modernity in a region yet to emerge from the Ottoman legacy. But beneath the surface, fundamental problems remained that would continue to plague Lebanon even after independence. It was far easier, the Maronites would discover, to declare statehood, build an infrastructure and economy and formulate a constitution, than to transform their country into a nation-state and mould its communities into a civil society.

A reassessment of Lebanon's political history in the interwar years reveals that this was a formative period for both its political and economic systems. Indeed, the political experience and outlook of the leadership that was to struggle for independence from France in 1943 and steer Lebanon for the next two decades was shaped during the 1920s and 30s. What were the forces that spurred the Lebanese to take their own particular path toward statehood and discard other alternatives? The answer to this question—the concern of this work—can be found in the complex interplay between French policy in its mandated territories, inter- and intra-communal and factional relations within Lebanon, and Syrian involvement in the Lebanese domestic scene.

In contrast to Syria, which France considered a burden, Lebanon was the cornerstone of French policy in the Middle East, a showcase of its 'mission civilisatrice'. France's traditional religious and cultural ties with the Catholic communities of the Levant, especially the Maronites, and its moral obligation to protect them, was the basis of this policy. After establishing Grand Liban as an entity distinct and independent from Syria and extending its borders, France spent the next two decades defending Lebanon's separate existence and territorial integrity from both internal and external threats. The High Commission helped elaborate Lebanon's constitution and build its political and administrative systems and modern infrastructure. Lebanon was treated favourably, at Syria's expense. Indeed, France held Lebanon together until the political, social and economic forces that would help integrate the annexed areas into the state began to take effect. French representatives prevented the Maronites from dominating state institutions completely, while eroding the opposition of the Sunnis and other communities to Lebanese independence. As Muslim Syria and the Arab nationalists continued to express hostility toward France—the Syrian–Druze revolt made this abundantly clear—the French government focused on Lebanon's importance as a stronghold in the Middle East. Completion of the oil pipeline from Mosul to Tripoli in 1935, Italy's emergence as a major power in the Mediterranean, and the growing threat of war in Europe all reinforced Lebanon's strategic value.

While France helped consolidate the Lebanese state, its policies also encouraged negative trends, whose consequences would be felt in Lebanon's political and economic systems and its relations with Syria after independence. Once they had rejected de Jouvenel's initiative, successive French governments pursued policies that lacked initiative, merely reacting to events. France failed to forge a strategy that would secure its own interests in the mandated territories, guarantee Lebanon's independence and territorial integrity, and be acceptable to the Arab Muslim majority in Syria. France's minorities policy, its continued conflict with the Syrian Arab nationalist movement, and its inability to solve the issue of Syrian unity all worked to transform Lebanon into an arena for Franco–Syrian confrontation. In the second half of the 1930s, French efforts to turn the Lebanese state into a major strategic base in the eastern Mediterranean reinforced Syrian hostility toward Lebanon. As a result of the divide-and-rule policy of French officials and the political institutions and culture they allowed to flourish, Lebanon was left with a legacy it has been unable to overcome. Finally, tertiarization of the economy accelerated rapidly under the mandate; for this, Lebanon would pay dearly decades later.

The question of revising Lebanon's 1920 borders provides the clearest demonstration of the French tendency to maintain the status quo and avoid unpopular decisions. This was not merely a territorial or economic issue; it had far-reaching consequences for Lebanon's ability to become a viable nation-state. Both Robert de Caix and Henry de Jouvenel recognized that Lebanon's main problem lay in the weakness of its Christian majority. They failed, however, to persuade their governments to annex predominantly Sunni Tripoli and part of the Shiite Beqa valley to Syria—a step they believed would also have weakened Syrian hostility toward Lebanon. Although Ponsot also understood the need for such a move, he was reluctant to act in the face of opposition from the Maronite church and community, as well as from his own army and staff. Even discreet appeals in 1932 by Christian leaders, particularly Eddé, for territorial reduction failed to convince the Quai d'Orsay and the High Commission. Lebanon thus remained within its 1920 borders, with a large, alien Muslim population, facing a hostile, powerful neighbour that continued to press political and territorial claims.

The Syrian shadow loomed constantly over Lebanon: Syria's refusal to recognize Lebanon's separate existence posed a permanent threat to the country's very survival. Both moderate and nationalist Syrian leaders demanded that the Lebanese Christians give up French protection and agree either to link Lebanon with Syria politically or return to the borders of the Mutasarrifiya—reinforcing the Christians' sense of vulnerability and their fears that the achievements of 1920 might be reversed. Rebel raids in Lebanon during the Syrian–Druze revolt attested to the depth of Syrian nationalist hostility toward the Christians, and demonstrated the formers' willingness to use force against the Lebanese state. As France continued to reject their demands for unity and independence and prevented their access to power, the Syrian Arab nationalists targeted the French presence in Lebanon and strove to destabilize the young state. They exploited national, sectarian, factional and personal divisions to undermine Lebanon's political stability—as illustrated in their involvement in the Eddé government crisis; in the 1930 controversy over replacement of the mandate with a treaty; in the role they played behind the scenes during the presidential crisis of 1932; in instigating the crises of Mubarak and Arida; and in their incitement of violent demonstrations in the summer of 1936. Even after concluding a treaty with France, in which the National Bloc grudgingly agreed to relinquish its territorial claims over Lebanon, the Syrian government tried to exploit negotiations over the Common Interests to force Lebanon to agree to close political and economic ties between the two states. And the French decision to concede Alexandretta, Syria's only modern port, to Turkey, drove the Syrian government to renew its claims on Tripoli. Thus, 20 years after the establishment of Grand Liban in the aftermath of the Maisalun defeat, which had stripped the Muslim Arab majority of its independence and unity, Syrian animosity toward Christian Lebanon remained as strong as ever.

As the cradle of Arab nationalism, Syria challenged Lebanon's national identity as well. Unlike other newly-created Arab states in the Fertile Crescent, Lebanon—the outgrowth of a Lebanese-Maronite national movement—could not capture the loyalty of its Arab Muslim population by professing allegiance to pan-Arabism or Islam. Attracted by the ideals of pan-Arabism, the Muslims viewed Lebanon as an artificial entity, unworthy of their loyalty. Attempts in the 1930s by Christian intellectuals, politicians and businessmen to stress Lebanon's Phoenician heritage was meaningless to them. The controversy over Lebanon's national identity was particularly evident in the educational system and the role of the French and Arabic languages; this was reflected in the 1929 crisis following Eddé's closure of the schools. In the long run, Christian–Muslim disagreement on their country's national identity would jeopardize efforts to create a nation-state commanding the allegiance of all its citizens.

During the 1930s, especially after the conclusion of the Syrian and Lebanese treaties, the Muslims grew more disposed to relinquish their ambitions for union with Syria and recognize the Lebanese state. They demanded, however, that the Christians sever their historical ties with France, that Lebanon secure its independence and national sovereignty, assume an Arab identity and grant its Muslim citizens full equality. At the same time, many Christians came to understand that Lebanon could not remain in permanent conflict with Arab nationalism or with Syria and other Arab countries, which were breaking free from the colonial powers. They were willing to end their reliance on France and become part of the emerging Arab state system, provided that Lebanon retain its unique identity and Christian dominance be assured. Intellectuals, professionals and businessmen from both communities began to promote the idea of Lebanon as a model of Christian-Muslim symbiosis. In the Middle East, where religious and sectarian conflict was rife, they asserted, Lebanon would become a state in which the two religions and the diverse communities would coexist harmoniously within the framework of a liberal, democratic parliamentary system. Such ideas, however, were held by only a small minority. Most Maronites continued to view Lebanon primarily as a homeland for the Christians, while Muslims—especially the Sunnis—adamantly opposed a Maronite dominated-state with its own distinct national identity.

Facing Muslim rejection and continued Syrian attempts to undermine Lebanon, Christian leaders and French representatives alike were concerned with reinforcing the symbols of statehood. The 1926 constitution and the newly-formed political institutions—the presidency, government and parliament—together with defined territories and citizenship, would bear witness to the existence of the Lebanese state. And those institutions would play a key role in the integration of the annexed regions into Lebanon. By 1939, thirteen years after the proclamation of the Lebanese Republic, the character of these institutions had to a large extent been shaped, and the balance between the executive and legislative powers had been defined.

While the constitution provided for Western institutions, Lebanese political culture was, in reality, largely determined by traditional forces. What emerged was a unique mix of the experience accrued from practising a parliamentary democracy, and the successful penetration of the new state institutions by the primordial forces at work within Lebanese society— community, feudalism and kinship. Paradoxically then, while Lebanon appeared to be the most Westernized country in the Arab Middle East, it retained more features of Ottoman society and politics than any other state in the Fertile Crescent.

During the mandate years, critics were already denouncing political sectarianism, blaming it for the chronic instability and incompetence of the Lebanese political and administrative systems. While they admitted that sectarian differences were being channelled into a well-defined framework, thus preventing open conflict, they argued that sectarianism was jeopardizing efforts to create a Lebanese nation. Particularly harmful for Lebanon in the long term was Maronite success in exploiting sectarianism to dominate the new political institutions, thereby further marginalizing the other communities. The balance of power that emerged after 1926 between the president and the government and parliament, was a clear illustration of this process. The 1927 and 1929 constitutional revisions considerably increased presidential authority, and altered the balance between the executive and legislative powers. Parliament's ability to effectively supervise the power of the president was restricted. Representing all of Lebanon's communities, it became a mere forum for debate, rather than a sovereign authoritative body. The inherent instability of the government and the prime minister's dependence on the president also became apparent. After 1937, the pattern of a Maronite president and Sunni prime minister was established. Under the mandate, presidential power was held in check by the high commissioner, but after 1943, Maronite presidents would wield considerable clout, with a detrimental effect on the delicate balance between the communities. The presidency thus became a means for the Maronites to maintain their dominance.

Political sectarianism also gave rise to a trend that can be termed 'political feudalism'. The significance of this process, often confused with the general phenomenon of sectarianism, has invariably been overlooked. In fact, inter-sectarian conflict frequently reflected power struggles between elites for access to state institutions and wealth. The power of the new, predominantly Maronite, political elite that emerged under the mandate derived not from land ownership, but from its members' newly acquired positions in the political or administrative systems. And they used their positions primarily to promote their own and their families' interests. Eddé, Khuri, Dabbas, Sa'ad, Chamoun, Namur, Zakur and Taqla belonged to this class of political and bureaucratic *zu'ama*. Well-established feudal families from the Mountain and the peripheral regions, including the Arslans, the Junblatts, the Khazins, the Franjiehs, the As'ads, the Zeins, the Haidars, the Hamadehs and the Razaks would also be integrated in the state apparatus. Prominent Sunni families in Beirut, Sidon and Tripoli—the Sulhs, the Bayhums, the Salams, the Da'uqs and the Karamehs—who had mostly been denied access to the state institutions under the mandate, would become part of these elites after independence. The success of both old and new elites in strengthening their control over the state evolved partly from French policy and partly from their ability to portray themselves as guardians of their communities' rights. While the land-owning elites of Egypt, Syria and Iraq lost their political and economic power in the wake of the military coup d'états and agrarian reforms of the 1950s, political feudalism became entrenched in Lebanon, reinforcing the country's oligarchic character. This political class would perpetuate sectarianism and perfect the system of political patronage and clientelism to retain its influence. Its close links with the mercantile-financial Christian elites in Beirut would eventually determine the nature of Lebanon's laissez-faire economy. Under the mandate, the Lebanese state became not only a corporation of 'communities' but of 'beys'.

The rise of the political and bureaucratic *za'im* was accompanied by the emergence of political clans, groups of politicians cutting across sectarian lines that promoted the interests of their members, families and clients. This process originated in the electoral law of 1922 and the list system adopted by the Lebanese Republic. In order to secure their seats in the legislature, politicians from different communities would cooperate in the electoral districts and later in the parliament itself. Groups like these formed in the parliament and government around Dabbas–Khuri, Sa'ad, Eddé, Namur and Jisr. During the 1920s, these alliances were mainly of a provisional nature, with deputies constantly regrouping according to changing circumstances. Hence the volatility and instability of Lebanese political life under the mandate. The 1930s, however, saw the emergence of well-organized political blocs, whose members shared long-term goals and a common vision of Lebanon's future. These groupings were supported by companies and businessmen outside parliament, and owned newspapers in which they were able to air their views and attack their opponents. The two major clans were headed by Emile Eddé and Beshara al-Khuri, whose bitter struggle over the presidency dominated Lebanese politics throughout the 1930s.

Lebanon's political history from 1926–39 clearly demonstrates how the contest between Eddé and Khuri developed into a power struggle between two political clans which subsequently assumed an ideological character as well. Eddé for the most part remained a lone leader, who at various stages established alliances either with politicians and factions that shared mutual interests, or with those who supported his ideas. Khuri, however, brought together a closely-knit group whose members were linked by familial and business interests; they were determined to attain power and shape Lebanon politically and economically according to their vision. Maronite political elites from the Mountain and Christian business circles in Beirut developed firm ties within this bloc. While both groups were headed by Maronites, they were supported by politicians from other communities as well. Indeed, the rivalry between Eddé and Khuri facilitated the integration of the Muslim elites in the annexed regions, especially the Sunnis, into Lebanese politics. Eddé, who was identified with Christian Lebanon and supported continued French protection, was elected president in 1936 by mainly Sunni and Shiite deputies. Until 1932, Khuri cooperated openly with Jisr, and tacitly with Riad al-Sulh in 1930, 1933, 1935 and 1937. Eddé supported Jisr in 1932 in order to undermine Khuri's candidacy, and from 1934 onwards worked closely with Khair al-din al-Ahdab. In 1937, this alliance established the precedent of a Maronite president and a Sunni prime minister, which was adopted by Khuri and Sulh in the National Pact.

Eddé played a prominent role in Lebanese politics during the 1920s and 30s, and served as president after 1936. The Constitutional Bloc, however, effectively thwarted his initiatives—including territorial reduction, decentralization, and a presidential republic—either through their control of government and parliament, or by pressuring the High Commission with threats to collaborate with the Arab nationalists. After the French defeat in 1940 and Eddé's downfall in 1943, Khuri and Chiha were free to implement the ideas and policies they had formulated during the previous decade.

Among the states established in the Fertile Crescent after the collapse of the Ottoman Empire, Lebanon was probably the only one that could claim a continuous history as a distinct political entity. But the original ideal of Lebanon as a refuge for persecuted Christian minorities was no longer credible; half of its population was Muslim. Now there was a new and morally valid vision of Lebanon: that of a liberal, democratic state in which diverse communities could coexist and Christian–Muslim symbiosis be attained. It may have been a utopian idea, but it was never really given a chance. While superficially paying homage to the new vision, a small group of political and economic elites, with their own agendas and interests, were virtually to transform the Lebanese state into a 'merchant republic'.

Notes

Chapter One

1. Elie Kedourie, *In the Anglo–Arab Labyrinth: The MacMahon-Husayn Correspondence and its Interpretation, 1914–1939* (Cambridge, 1976) pp. 130–1; George Antonius, *The Arab Awakening* (London, 1938) pp. 152–9; Ernest C. Dawn, *From Arabism to Ottomanism* (Chicago, 1973) pp. 27–30; Daniel Pipes, *Greater Syria: The History of an Ambition* (Oxford, 1990) pp. 3–9.

2. Ministère des Affaires Etrangères, Les Archives diplomatiques de Nantes, Mandat Syrie–Liban, 1918–1948 (henceforth MAE, Nantes, Syrie et Liban), carton 2367, a copy of Faisal's declaration, November 1918; Meir Zamir, 'Faisal and the Lebanese Question, 1918–1920', *Middle Eastern Studies* 27/3 (July 1991), pp. 404–26; Pipes, *Greater Syria*, pp. 22–8.

3. Ministère des Affaires Etrangères, Paris, Série E-Levant 1918–1940 (henceforth MAE, Paris, Syrie et Liban), vol. 31, 'Esquisse de l'Organisation de la Syrie sous le Mandat français', memorandum by Robert de Caix; vol. 203, 'Note pour le Ministre', Paris, 24 January 1928; Philip S. Khoury, *Syria and the French Mandate* (Princeton, 1987), pp. 19–20; Meir Zamir, *The Formation of Modern Lebanon* (London, 1985), pp. 107–8; Stephan H. Longrigg, *Syria and Lebanon under French Mandate* (London, 1958), pp. 116–17; Said Murad, *Al-harakat al-wahdawiyya fi Lubnan* (Beirut, 1986), pp. 147–51.

4. Khoury, *Syria and the French Mandate*, pp. 57–60; Edmond Rabbath, *L'Unité syrienne et devenir arabe* (Paris, 1937), pp. 11–21; Pipes, *Greater Syria*, pp. 52–5; Zamir, *The Formation of Modern Lebanon*, pp. 179–81.

5. MAE, Nantes, Syrie et Liban, carton 2366, Col. Toulat's interview with Faisal, Damascus, 2 July 1919; carton 412, 'L'Unité syrienne', Damascus, June 1928, Captain Olive of the S.R. in Syria to the head of the S.R. in Syria and Jabal Druze; 'L'Union économique Syro–Libanaise', *Correspondance d'Orient* (henceforth CO) (Paris), no. 340, April 1926, pp. 154–5; Rabbath: *L'Unité syrienne*, pp. 162–73, 197–9; Pipes, *Greater Syria*, pp. 55–6; Zamir, *The Formation of Modern Lebanon*, pp. 179–81.

6. Centre de Hautes Etudes sur l'Afrique et l'Asie Modernes, (henceforth CHEAM), no. 197, 'Une Opinion chrétienne libanaise sur le rôle du Liban auprès des pays arabes' (anonymous); Rabbath, *L'Unité syrienne*, pp. 153–60; Zamir, *The Formation of Modern Lebanon*, pp. 59, 80–1, and 'Faisal and the Lebanese Question', pp. 404–26.

7.   Muhammad Kurd 'Ali, *Memoirs of Muhammad Kurd 'Ali* (Washington, D.C., 1954), pp. 199–204; Raghid Solh, *Lebanon and Arab Nationalism 1935–1945* (Ph.D. thesis, Oxford University, 1986), pp. 9–12; Zamir, *The Formation of Modern Lebanon*, p. 180, and 'Faisal and the Lebanese Question', pp. 404–26.

8.   'Les doléances des Damascains', CO, no. 303, March 1923, p. 176; Khoury, *Syria and the French Mandate*, pp. 7–8, 57.

9.   MAE, Paris, Syrie et Liban, vol. 31, 'Esquisse de l'Organisation de la Syrie sous le Mandat français', memorandum by Robert de Caix; Khoury, *Syria and the French Mandate*, pp. 168–9.

10.   MAE, Paris, Syrie et Liban, vol. 31, 'Esquisse de l'Organisation de la Syrie sous le Mandat français', p. 43; Rabbath, *L'Unité syrienne*, pp. 174–7; Zamir, *The Formation of Modern Lebanon*, pp. 93–4, and 'Faisal and the Lebanese Question', pp. 404–26.

11.   MAE, Nantes, Syrie et Liban, carton 363, Letter of six Syrian ministers to their prime minister, Damascus, 22 May 1926; carton 450, no. 147, 'Les revendications syriennes d'après Ata al Ayoubi', Damascus, 9 March 1927; Kurd 'Ali, *Memoirs*, pp. 130–1; Rabbath: *L'Unité syrienne*, pp. 187–8; Zamir, *The Formation of Modern Lebanon*, p. 152.

12.   MAE, Paris, Syrie et Liban, vol. 31, 'Esquisse de l'Organisation de la Syrie sous le Mandat français'; vol. 200, report by de Caix, 'L'organisation donnée à la Syrie et au Liban', October 1926; 'Pour l'Unité syrienne: il faut reviser l'arrêté du général Gouraud', in CO, no. 344, August 1926, pp. 64–7; 'L'Organisation de la Syrie sous le Mandat français', *Revue des deux Mondes* (Paris), December 1921, pp. 633–63; Zamir, *The Formation of Modern Lebanon*, pp. 108–12; Khoury, *Syria and the French Mandate*, pp. 57–60.

13.   MAE, Nantes, Syrie et Liban, carton 412, 'Unité ou Fédération', memorandum by de Caix, Beirut, 9 March 1921; carton 1561, 'Note historique nationale: Les sources de la mentalité syrienne', 29 March 1921; MAE, Paris, Syrie et Liban, vol. 200, report by de Caix, 'L'organisation donnée à la Syrie et au Liban', October 1926, pp. 27–40; vol. 203, 'Note pour le Ministre', Paris, 24 January 1928; 'Les gouvernements autonomes de la Syrie', *l'Asie française* (henceforth AF) (Paris), no. 190, March 1921, pp. 94–8; Raymond O'Zoux, *Les Etats du Levant sous mandat français* (Paris, 1931), p. 72; Zamir, *The Formation of Modern Lebanon*, pp. 90–6.

14.   MAE, Paris, Syrie et Liban, vol. 200, report by de Caix, 'L'organisation donnée à la Syrie et au Liban', October 1926; Zamir, *The Formation of Modern Lebanon*, pp. 108–12, 151–2.

15.   MAE, Paris, Syrie et Liban, vol. 200, report by de Caix, 'L'organisation donnée à la Syrie et au Liban', October 1926; Zamir, *The Formation of Modern Lebanon*, p. 152.

16.   Speech by Abdallah Sfer Pasha, President of the League for the Defence of Greater Lebanon, at the Comité France-Orient, Paris, 6 November 1926, *Bulletin Officiel du Comité France-Orient*, Paris, no. 55, November 1926, pp. 9–18; Zamir, *The Formation of Modern Lebanon*, pp. 93–4.

17.   'L'Unité Syrienne', *CO*, no. 364, April 1928, pp145–7; Zamir, *The Formation of Modern Lebanon*, pp. 113–7.

18.   For the Syrian-Druze revolt, see G. Carbillet, *Au Djébel Druse* (Paris, 1929); C.J.E. Andréa, *La Révolte druze et l'insurrection de Damas 1925–1926* (Paris, 1937); Elizabeth MacCallum, *The Nationalist Crusade in Syria* (New York, 1928); Amin Said, *al-Thawra al-'arabiyya al-kubra* (Cairo, 1934); Muhi al-Din al-Safarjalani, *Tarikh al-thawra al-suriyya* (Damascus, 1961); Khoury, *Syria and the French Mandate*, Chapters 6–8.

19.   Archives Départementales de la Corrèze, Fonds Henry de Jouvenel, Tulle (henceforth FHJ), 'Note pour le Ministre', Paris, 23 October 1925; 'Les affaires de Syrie à la Chambre Française', *CO*, no. 337, January 1926, pp. 1–5; Zamir, *The Formation of Modern Lebanon*, pp. 168, 184–5.

20.   Zamir, *The Formation of Modern Lebanon*, pp. 168–74.

21.   MAE, Paris, Syrie et Liban, vol. 287, 'Service de la presse - Rapport bi-mensuel', Beirut, 17 August 1926. See in particular article in *al-Bashir* (Beirut); Zamir, *The Formation of Modern Lebanon*, pp. 174–9, 195–6.

22.   Zamir, *The Formation of Modern Lebanon*, p. 188.

23.   MAE, Nantes, Syrie et Liban, Letter from the Syrian delegation to Foreign Minister Paul-Boncour, Geneva, 3 November 1926; MAE, Paris, Syrie et Liban, vol. 203, Paris, 16 July 1927, p. 51, Khadour Bin Ghabrit to Briand; vol. 287, 'Service de la presse - Rapport bi-mensuel', Beirut, 12 July and 12 September 1926. See in particular the exchanges between the Syrian and Lebanese Christian press on Lebanon's independence and Syrian unity.

24.   FHJ, 'Note pour le Ministre', Paris, 23 October 1925; 'Le changement du Haut Commissaire en Syrie et au Liban', *AF*, no. 236, December 1925, pp. 336–9; Joyce L. Miller, 'The Syrian Revolt of 1925', *International Journal of Middle East Studies*, 8 (1977), pp. 545–63; Zamir, *The Formation of Modern Lebanon*, pp. 184–5.

25.   FO 371/11516 5013/146, no. 1617, Paris, 27 August 1926, Crewe to Chamberlain; *The Times* (London), 31 August 1926; Khoury, *Syria and the French Mandate*, p. 202.

26.   MAE, Nantes, Syrie et Liban, carton 453, 'Note de M. de Jouvenel pour M. Briand, Ministère des Affaires Etrangères', Paris, 3 August 1926; carton 1359, letter from de Jouvenel to Briand, Paris, August 1926; MAE, Paris, Syrie et Liban, vol. 224, nos 333–6, Beirut, 14 May 1926, de Jouvenel to Briand; 'Un discours de M. Henry de Jouvenel à l'Institut Colonial Français', *CO*, no. 336, December 1925, pp. 257–60.

27.   MAE, Paris, Syrie et Liban, vol. 224, Briand's letter to de Jouvenel, Paris, 18 January 1926, pp. 68–91, and de Caix's memorandum, Paris, 25 January 1926, pp. 92–4; MAE, Nantes, Syrie et Liban, carton 1359, letter from de Jouvenel to Briand, Paris, August 1926.

28.   MAE, Nantes, Syrie et Liban, carton 453, 'Note de M. de Jouvenel pour M. Briand, Ministère des Affaires Etrangères', Paris, 3 August 1926; carton 450, de Caix's memorandum, Paris, 27 March 1926.

29.   MAE, Nantes, Syrie et Liban, carton 363, Letter by six Syrian ministers to their prime minister, Damascus, 22 May 1926; MAE, Paris, Syrie et Liban, vol. 274, pp. 63–4;'Le nouveau chef de l'Etat de Syrie', CO, no. 341, May 1926, pp. 225–7; Khoury, *Syria and the French Mandate*, pp. 197–201; Zamir, *The Formation of Modern Lebanon*, pp. 193–4.

30.   MAE, Paris, Syrie et Liban, vol. 200, report by de Caix, 'L'organisation donnée à la Syrie et au Liban', October 1926, in particular from p. 53 onwards; press cuttings - Weygand's declaration in *Le Temps* (Paris), 25 November 1926, pp. 295–6.

31.   MAE, Paris, Syrie et Liban, vol. 224, no. 305, Beirut, 6 May, and nos 333–6, 14 May 1926, de Jouvenel to Briand; nos 325–6, Paris, 17 May 1926, Bertholot to de Jouvenel; 'Note pour le ministre', Paris, 3 July 1926; vol. 422, p. 71, extract from *Le Temps*, 12 June 1926; Pour l'Unité syrienne: il faut reviser l'arrêté du général Gouraud', CO, no. 344, August 1926, pp. 64–7. The author, Jean Mélia, was de Jouvenel's adviser. Zamir, *The Formation of Modern Lebanon*, pp. 198–9.

32.   MAE, Paris, Syrie et Liban, vol. 199, no. 444, Beirut, 29 June 1926, de Reffye to Briand; vol. 201, 'Evénements de Syrie, du 27 Mai au 12 Octobre 1926', de Reffye's report, Beirut, 24 January 1927, pp. 150–1, 153; MAE, Nantes, Syrie et Liban, carton 450, no. 2307/3, Beirut, 21 August 1926, General Gamelin to the Ministry of War; FHJ, nos 600–4, Beirut, 30 June 1926.

33.   MAE, Paris, Syrie et Liban, vol. 199, nos 514–18, Beirut, 3 August 1926, de Reffye to de Jouvenel.

34.   MAE, Paris, Syrie et Liban, vol. 202, 'Réflexions d'un Français sur la Syrie', extract from *Le Temps*, 31 March 1927, p. 99.

35.   MAE, Nantes, Syrie et Liban, carton 453, 'Note de M. de Jouvenel pour M. Briand, Ministère des Affaires Etrangères', Paris, 3 August 1926.

36.   MAE, Paris, Syrie et Liban, vol. 199, Paris, 13 August 1926, Berthelot to de Reffye; vol. 397, an interview with M. de Jouvenel, pp. 35–7; MAE, Nantes, Syrie et Liban, carton 925, Information no. 54, 30 August 1926; Ministère de la Guerre, Service Historique de l'Armée, Section Outre-Mer (Vincennes), (henceforth SHA), carton 9B3, Revue de la Presse, Beirut, 17 August 1926; FO 371/11516 5013/146, no. 1617, Paris, 27 August 1926, Crewe to Chamberlain.

37.   SHA, carton 32B3, Bulletin d'Information no. 8, Beirut, 16 September 1926; MAE, Nantes, Syrie et Liban, carton 363, copy of decree appointing Ponsot as High Commissioner, Paris, 3 September 1926; MAE, Paris, Syrie et Liban, vol. 199, no. 408, London, 4 September 1926, Chargé d'Affaires to Briand; FO 371/11516 5074/146 no. 1643, Paris, 30 August 1926, Crewe to Chamberlain; FO 371/12303 471/44 no. 11, Beirut, 17 January 1927, Satow to Chamberlain; 'La situation en Syrie et les changements du Haut Commissaire', AF, no. 243, August-September 1926, pp. 267–8.

38.   MAE, Nantes, Syrie et Liban, carton 1359, letter from de Jouvenel to Briand, Paris, August 1926; MAE, Paris, Syrie et Liban, vol. 477, 'Statut Organique: Projet du Département approuvé par le Conseil des Ministres', 26 August 1926; FO 371/12303 471/44 No. 11, Beirut, 17 January 1927, Satow to

Chamberlain; 'Le programme politique du Haut Commissariat en Syrie et au Liban', *AF*, July-October 1927, pp. 283–9; 'La tâche du nouveau Haut-Commissaire de France en Syrie', *CO*, no. 346, October 1926, pp. 145–50.

39.   MAE, Nantes, Syrie et Liban, carton 450, no. 2307/3, Beirut, 21 August 1926, General Gamelin to the Ministry of War. For a different point of view, see General Billotte's memorandum, MAE, Paris, Syrie et Liban, vol. 200, 'Réflexions succintes sur la situation politique et militaire de la Syrie', Beirut, 14 November 1926.

40.   MAE, Nantes, Syrie et Liban, carton 841, no. 93, Direction de la Sûreté Générale, 'Rapport à M. le Directeur du Service des Renseignements' (henceforth S.R.), Beirut, 6 January 1927; carton 840, S.R., Beirut, 1 October 1930; carton 441, 'Circulaire', Beirut, 1 January 1928, Ponsot to his delegates and the directors of the S.R. and the Sûreté Générale; MAE, Paris, Syrie et Liban, vol. 199, nos 605–8, Beirut, 4 September 1926, de Reffye to Ponsot; vol. 200, no. 634, 11 October 1926, de Reffye to the Foreign Minister; Bulletin d'Information no. 1, Beirut, 16 January 1927; vol. 201, Note, 24 January 1927, 'Evénements de Syrie du 27 mai au 12 octobre 1926'; FO 371/12302 2215/21 no. 90, Beirut, 26 April 1927; FO 371/12303 5450/44, no. 184, Beirut, 28 November 1927, Satow to Chamberlain.

41.   MAE, Paris, Syrie et Liban, vol. 203, 'Note pour le Ministre', Paris, 24 January 1928; vol. 199, nos 605–13, 4 September 1926, de Reffye to Ponsot; no. 596, Beirut, 18 September 1926, and vol. 200, no. 634, 11 October 1926, de Reffye to Briand; vol. 201, Note, 24 January 1927, 'Evénements de Syrie du 27 mai au 12 octobre 1926'; MAE, Nantes, Syrie et Liban, carton 841, no. 1740, Beirut, 27 April 1927, Report of the Director of the Sûreté Générale; FO 371/12303 5450/44, no. 184, Beirut, 28 November 1927, Satow to Chamberlain.

42.   MAE, Nantes, Syrie et Liban, carton 925, file of reports on Ponsot's inquiry from December 1926–January 1927; carton 364, Beirut, 25 January 1927, Ahmad Nami to Poincaré; carton 412, no. 8900, Damascus, 22 October 1926, copy of Jamal al-Elchi's proposal sent by Pierre Alype to Ponsot; carton 450, no. 147, 'Les revendications syriennes d'après Ata al Ayoubi', Damascus, 9 March 1927; Letter from the Syrian delegation to Foreign Minister Paul-Boncour, Geneva, 3 November 1926; MAE, Paris, Syrie et Liban, vol. 201, Bulletin d'Information, no. 10, Beirut, 1 December 1926; FO 371/12303 471/44 no. 11, Beirut, 17 January 1927, and FO 371/11516 6219/146 no. 197, Beirut, 14 October 1926, Satow to Chamberlain; speech by Abdallah Sfer Pasha, President of the League for the Defence of Greater Lebanon, at the Comité France-Orient, Paris, 6 November 1926, in *Bulletin Officiel du Comité France-Orient*, no. 55, November 1926, pp. 9–18; 'Sur une politique d'abandon', *AF*, no. 245, December 1926, pp. 354–8; MacCallum, *The Nationalist Crusade*, pp. 195–6.

43.   MAE, Nantes, Syrie et Liban, carton 364, 12 April 1927, 'Suggestions relatives à la politique à suivre au Levant'.

44.   MAE, Paris, Syrie et Liban, vol. 422, 'Questions à exposer à la Commission des Affaires Etrangères', Paris, 31 March 1927; vol. 202, 'Réflexions

d'un Français sur la Syrie', extract from *Le Temps*, 31 March 1927, p. 99; vol. 201, p. 105, extract from *Bulletin Officiel du Comité France-Orient*, 15 January 1927.

45.   MAE, Paris, Syrie et Liban, vol. 422, 'Questions à exposer à la Commission des Affaires Etrangères', 31 March 1927; MAE, Nantes, Syrie et Liban, carton 364, 'Suggestions relatives à la politique à suivre au Levant', 12 April 1927; FO 371/1156 6713/146 no. 2319, Paris, 6 December 1926, Crewe to Chamberlain.

46.   MAE, Nantes, Syrie et Liban, carton 364, 'Suggestions relatives à la politique à suivre au Levant', Paris, 12 April 1927.

47.   MAE, Paris, Syrie et Liban, vol. 203, 'Note pour le Ministre', Paris, 15 November 1927 and 24 January 1928; 'Note de M. de Caix', Paris, 5 August 1927; vol. 225, Ponsot's memorandum, Paris, 3 May 1927.

48.   MAE, Nantes, Syrie et Liban, carton 364, 'Statut organique de la Syrie et du Liban', Paris, 2 March 1927; MAE, Paris, Syrie et Liban, vol. 225, Ponsot's memorandum, Paris, 3 May 1927. See p. 49.

49.   MAE, Nantes, Syrie et Liban, carton 364, Ponsot's plan of action, Paris, 1 June 1927; MAE, Paris, Syrie et Liban, vol. 203, 'Note de M. de Caix', Paris, 5 August 1927.

50.   SHA, carton 32B3, Bulletin d'Information no. 8, Beirut, 16 September 1926; MAE, Paris, Syrie et Liban, vol. 224, Briand's declaration to the League of Nations in Geneva, 12 March 1927, pp. 209–10.

51.   MAE, Nantes, Syrie et Liban, carton 925, file on reactions to the declaration; Information no. 657, Beirut, 21 June 1927; MAE, Paris, Syrie et Liban, vol. 203, 'Note de M. de Caix', Paris, 5 August 1927; vol. 225, no. 532, Beirut, 22 July 1927, Ponsot to Briand; FO 371/12303 3647/44 no. 141, Beirut, 28 July 1927, Satow to Chamberlain; 'Le Programme de M. Ponsot', CO, no. 358, August 1927, pp. 49–53; Khoury, *Syria and the French Mandate*, p. 246.

52.   MAE, Nantes, Syrie et Liban, carton 925, file on reactions to the declaration; carton 409, file on the National Bloc's conference in Beirut; carton 933, Rens. no. 1222, and Information no. 895, Beirut, 12 October 1927; MAE, Paris, Syrie et Liban, vol. 225, no. 611, Beirut, 2 September 1927, Ponsot to Briand; vol. 287, Service de la Presse - Rapport Bi-mensuel, Beirut, 31 August 1927; vol. 433, Bulletin d'Information no. 4, Beirut, 15 August 1927; FO 371/ 12303 3647/44 no. 141, 28 July 1927, Satow to Chamberlain. See p. 49–50.

53.   MAE, Nantes, Syrie et Liban, carton 933, Information no. 895, Beirut, 12 October 1927; MAE, Paris, Syrie et Liban, vol. 225, no. 841, Beirut, 29 October 1927, Ponsot to Briand; Khoury, *Syria and the French Mandate*, p. 247.

54.   MAE, Nantes, Syrie et Liban, carton 441, 'Circulaire', Beirut, 1 January 1928, Ponsot to his delegates and the directors of the S.R. and the Sûreté Générale; carton 367, note no. 119, Beirut, 7 January 1928, Ponsot to his staff; carton 364, no. 611, Beirut, 2 September 1927, Ponsot to Briand; carton 953, Information no. 55, Beirut, 24 January 1928, petition by nationalists in Beirut against Catroux's return; MAE, Paris, Syrie et Liban, vol. 203, 'Note de M. de Caix', Paris, 5 August 1927; nos 602–3, Beirut, 28 September and no. 993, 31

December 1927, Ponsot to Berthelot; no. 51, Paris, 1 February 1928, Quai d'Orsay to Ponsot; vol. 225, no. 922, Paris, 22 December 1927 and nos 21–24, 16 January 1928, Briand to Ponsot; no. 18, Beirut, 7 January and no. 57, 21 January 1928, Ponsot to Briand; MacCallum, *The Nationalist Crusade*, p. 198.

55.   MAE, Paris, Syrie et Liban, vol. 203, 'Note pour le Ministre', Paris, 24 January 1928; MAE, Nantes, Syrie et Liban, carton 364, 'Conférence des Délégués', Beirut, 28 December 1927; FO 371/12303 5484/44 no. 2513, Paris, 20 December 1927, Crewe to Chamberlain; FO 371/13079 486/141 no. 9, Beirut, 11 January 1928, Satow to Chamberlain.

56.   MAE, Paris, Syrie et Liban, vol. 225, de Caix's memorandum to Berthelot, Paris, 10 May 1928. De Caix predicted that the Syrian nationalists would prevent Ponsot from implementing his plan.

57.   MAE, Nantes, Syrie et Liban, carton 364, file on the constitutional crisis; carton 412, Information no. 376, 25 June, and no. 420, 27 July 1928; carton 411, Information nos 443–4, Beirut, 22 August 1928; MAE, Paris, Syrie et Liban, vol. 434, Bulletins d'Information nos 6–9, June-September 1928.

58.   MAE, Nantes, Syrie et Liban, carton 412, 'L'Unité syrienne', Damascus, June 1928, Captain Olive of the S.R. in Syria to the head of the S.R. in Syria and Jabal Druze; carton 953, Information no. 439, 16 August 1928; carton 363, 'Parti Républicain Socialiste et Socialiste Français'; FO 371/13074 3944/141 no. 64, Damascus, 31 July 1928, and 371/13074 4390/141 no. 67, Damascus, 9 August 1928, Hole to Chamberlain; FO 371/13074 5766/141 no. 2016, Paris, 3 December 1928, Tyrrell to Chamberlain.

Chapter Two

1.   On the Muslims' reaction during the Syrian revolt, see Zamir, *The Formation of Modern Lebanon*, pp. 182–4, and Murad, *Al-harakat al-wahdawiyya*, pp. 169–73.

2.   On the elaboration of the May 1926 constitution, see Zamir, *The Formation of Modern Lebanon*, pp. 199–215.

3.   The Lebanese Constitution, Beirut, 1960.

4.   Ibid.

5.   See, for example, Samir Khalaf, *Lebanon's Predicament* (New York, 1987).

6.   Arnold Hottinger, 'Zu'ama' in Historical Perspective', in Leonard Binder (ed.) *Politics in Lebanon* (New York, 1965), pp. 85–105.

7.   Philippe Rondot, 'The Political Institutions of Lebanese Democracy', in Binder, pp. 127–141. On the parliament see Abdo I. Baaklini, *Legislative and Political Development: Lebanon 1842–1972* (Durham, NC, 1976).

8.   For the election law of March 1922, see Zamir, *The Formation of Modern Lebanon*, pp. 142–3.

9.   Claude Dubar and Salim Nasr, *Les Classes Sociales au Liban* (Paris, 1976), pp. 51–61; Caroline L. Gates, *The Formation of the Political Economy of Modern Lebanon: The State and the Economy from Colonialism to Independence, 1939–1952*

(Ph.D. thesis, Oxford University, 1985), pp. 3–4, 12–15, 56–63; Fawaz N. Traboulsi, *Identités et solidarités croisées dans les conflits du Liban contemporain* (Ph.D. thesis, University of Paris, 1993), vol. 1, pp. 278–95; Jacques Couland, *Le mouvement syndical au Liban 1919–1946* (Paris, 1970), p. 75. For the importance of kinship in Lebanese political, social and economic life, see Khalaf, *Lebanon's Predicament*, pp. 102–20, 146–84.

10. Beshara al-Khuri, *Haqa'iq lubnaniyya* (Beirut, 1961), 3 volumes. For a description of Khuri, see Kamal S. Salibi, *The Modern History of Lebanon* (London, 1965), pp. 171–4. For a positive evaluation of Khuri's presidency, see Michael C. Hudson, *The Precarious Republic* (New York, 1968), pp. 264–73.

11. Adil Arslan, *Mudhakkirat Adil Arslan* (Beirut, 1983), vol. 3, p. 1383; Iskandar al-Riyashi, *Qabla wa ba'ada* (Beirut, n.d.); Hudson, *The Precarious Republic*, pp. 264–73.

12. On Hector Klat's literary activities, see Rachid Lahoud, *La littérature libanaise de langue française* (Beirut, 1945), pp. 60–6. See his poem, frontispiece. While in Egypt, he dedicated poems to Chiha, which he signed as 'Tite'. In the early 1930s Klat was active in Charles Corm's 'Young Phoenicians'.

13. Khuri, *Haqa'iq lubnaniyya*, vol. 1, pp. 45–9, 63–6, 70, 76–9, 86–7, 97, 101–3, 129–30. See also MAE, Nantes, Syrie et Liban, carton 1365, biographical note.

14. Traboulsi, *Identités et solidarités*, vol. 1, pp. 283–6; Mas'ud Daher, *Ta'rikh lubnan al ijtima'i 1914–1926* (Beirut, 1974), p. 234.

15. On Sawda's activities in the *Alliance libanaise*, and in the early years of the mandate, see Yusuf al-Sawda, *Fi sabil al-istiqlal* (Beirut, 1967); MAE, Nantes, Syrie et Liban, carton 1365, biographical note. See also Zamir, *The Formation of Modern Lebanon*, pp. 49–50, 192.

16. Khuri, *Haqa'iq lubnaniyya*, vol. 1, pp. 70, 73–4, 80–5. See also Fadia Kiwan, 'La Perception du Grand-Liban chez les maronites dans la période du mandat', in Nadim Shehadi, and Dana Haffar Mills (eds) *Lebanon: A History of Conflict and Consensus* (London, 1988), p. 130.

17. Albert Hourani, *Arabic Thought in the Liberal Age 1798–1939* (Oxford, 1970), pp. 319–23; Kamal S. Salibi, *A House of Many Mansions* (London, 1988), pp. 179–81; Jean Salem, *Introduction à la pensée politique de Michel Chiha* (Beirut, 1970). For a critical view of Chiha's philosophy, see Traboulsi, *Identités et solidarités*, vol. 1, pp. 300–67.

18. On Henri Pharaon, see MAE, Nantes, Syrie et Liban, carton 1365, biographical note; U.S. Department of State, Office of Intelligence Research, Biographies of the Lebanese cabinet of Riad al-Sulh, 13 February, 1947; Traboulsi, *Identités et solidarités*, p. 285; Gates, *Formation of the Political Economy*, p. 62.

19. Salem, *La pensée politique de Michel Chiha*, pp. 13–19; Traboulsi, *Identités et solidarités*, pp. 303–6.

20. On Charles Corm and the Phoenician movement, see Hourani, *Arabic Thought*, pp. 319–23; Salibi, *A House of Many Mansions*, pp. 170–9. On Corm's literary activities, see Lahoud, *La littérature libanaise*, pp. 47–50.

21.   On Chiha's role in the elaboration of the constitution, see Michel Chiha, *Politique intérieure* (Beirut, 1964), Preface, pp. 7–11; Salibi, *A House of Many Mansions*, p. 180; Traboulsi, *Identités et solidarités*, pp. 303, 306; Zamir, *The Formation of Modern Lebanon*, p. 207.

22.   Salem, *La pensée politique de Michel Chiha*; Traboulsi, *Identités et solidarités*, Chapter 7. For his literary activities, see Lahoud, *La littérature libanaise*, pp. 55–9.

23.   Nadim Shehadi, 'The Idea of Lebanon: Economy and State in the Cénacle Libanais 1946–1954', in *Papers on Lebanon*, no. 5, (Centre for Lebanese Studies, Oxford, 1987); Traboulsi, *Identités et solidarités*, pp. 307–10.

24.   Traboulsi, *Identités et solidarités*, Chapter 7; Zamir, *The Formation of Modern Lebanon*, p. 192.

25.   Albert H. Hourani, 'Ideologies of the Mountain and the City', in Roger Owen (ed.) *Essays on the Crisis in Lebanon* (London, 1976), pp. 33–41, and 'Visions of Lebanon', in Halim Barakat (ed.) *Toward a Viable Lebanon* (Washington, 1988), pp. 3–11; Traboulsi, *Identités et solidarités*, pp. 312–17.

26.   Baaklini, *Legislative and Political Development*, p. 261; Traboulsi, *Identités et solidarités*, pp. 315–16.

27.   Gates, *Formation of the Political Economy*, p. 40; Marwan R. Buheiry, 'Beirut's Role in the Political Economy of the French Mandate 1919–1939', in Lawrence I. Conrad (ed.) *The Formation and Perception of the Modern Arab World* (Princeton, 1989), pp. 537–59.

28.   In 1914 there were three motor vehicles in Beirut. By 1932, there were 17,647 in all of Syria, of which 9895 were in Lebanon, mostly in Beirut. On road construction and the rapid increase in the number of motor vehicles, see Said B. Himadeh (ed.) *Economic Organization of Syria* (Beirut, 1936), pp. 180–187; Gates, *Formation of the Political Economy*, pp. 43–4.

29.   Buheiry, 'Beirut's Role in the Political Economy of the French Mandate'.

30.   From 1921–1932 Beirut's population increased as follows:

	1921	1932
Sunnis	32,884	51,906
Shiites	3,274	11,379
Druze	1,522	4,225
Maronites	17,763	28,995
Greek Orthodox	12,672	19,943
Greek Catholic	4,256	8,347
Protestant	544	3,684
Armenian Gregorian	-	18,604
Armenian Catholic	-	4,385
Syrian Orthodox	-	1,745
Syriac Catholic	-	2,169
Jews and others	4,907	6,000
Total	77,820	161,382

Buheiry, p. 548. See also Himadeh, *Economic Organization of Syria*, pp. 408–9.

31.   M. Anis, *La Presse libanaise* (Paris, 1977), p. 2. From 1858–1958 the Lebanese established 198 newspapers in Lebanon and abroad. Among the politicians who founded their own newspapers, or journalists who became politicians, were Gabriel Khabaz, Jubran Tuaini, Khair al-Din al-Ahdab, Michel Chiha and Michel Zakur.

32.   Zamir, 'Faisal and the Lebanese Question', pp. 62–84.

33.   MAE, Nantes, Syrie et Liban, carton 933, Bulletin de Rens. no. 26, Beirut, 3 February 1927. For a study of the Maronite church, see David A. Kerr, *The Temporal Authority of the Maronite Patriarchate, 1920–1958: A Study in the Relationship of Religious and Secular Power* (Ph.D. thesis, Oxford University, 1977).

34.   U.S. Department of State, Office of Strategic Services, 'The Position and Influence of the Catholic Church in Lebanon', 15 November 1944.

35.   FO 371/13074 486/141 no. 9, Beirut, 11 January 1928, Satow, the British Consul General in Beirut, to Chamberlain.

36.   Walid Awad, *Ashab al-fakhama: ru'assa lubnan* (Beirut, 1977), pp. 13–53; Khuri, *Haqa'iq lubnaniyya*, vol. 1, pp. 134–5; Zamir, *The Formation of Modern Lebanon*, pp. 214–15.

37.   MAE, Paris, Syrie et Liban, vol. 202, 'Bulletin Trimestriel d'Information', no. 2, Beirut, 15 April 1927; FO 371/11516 4157/146 no. 138, Beirut, 30 June, and no. 165, 13 August 1926, Satow to the Secretary of State for Foreign Affairs; FO 371/11507 4268/12 no. 26, 30 June 1926, General Staff Headquarters, Palestine Command; Khuri, *Haqa'iq lubnaniyya*, vol. 1, p. 139.

38.   FO 371/11516 3917/146 no. 130, Beirut, 15 June 1926; 4157/146 no. 138, 30 June 1926, Satow to the Secretary of State for Foreign Affairs. See also Yusuf Quzma al-Khuri, *Al-bayyanat al-wizariyya al-lubnaniyya wa-munaqishatuha fi majlis al-nuwwab, 1926–1984* (Beirut, 1986), vol. 1, pp. 1–3.

39.   The Constitution allowed for only three deputies in the government. Adib's government comprised the following: Prime Minister - Auguste Adib Pasha; Minister of the Interior - Beshara al-Khuri; Justice - Najib Qabani; Public Works - Yusuf Aftimas; Education - Najib Amouni; Agriculture - Ali Nasrat al-As'ad; Health - Dr. Salim Talhuk. On Auguste Adib, see MAE, Paris, Syrie et Liban, vol. 263, p. 142.

40.   MAE, Nantes, Syrie et Liban, carton 933, Rens. (n.d.); Information no. 719/A, 25 May 1926; FO 371/12303 471/44 no. 11, Beirut, 17 January 1927, Satow to Chamberlain. Khuri, *Haqa'iq lubnaniyya*, vol. 1, pp. 131, 139–41; Zamir, *The Formation of Modern Lebanon*, pp. 155–7.

41.   MAE, Nantes, Syrie et Liban, carton 933, telegram no. 1607, Beirut, 19 October 1926, Catroux to Ponsot. This move was orchestrated by Colonel Catroux. See last minute attempt to replace Chihab with Torbay in order to defeat Namur, in Information no. 146/85, Beirut, 14 October 1926. See also FO 371/ 12303 471/44 no. 11, Beirut, 17 January 1927, Satow to Chamberlain.

42.   MAE, Nantes, Syrie et Liban, carton 933, no. 126/D, 'Attitude de la Chambre à l'égard du Ministère', Delegate to the Lebanese Republic to the High Commissioner, Beirut, 11 February 1927; MAE, Paris, Syrie et Liban, vol. 202,

nos 93–5, Beirut, 12 February 1927, de Reffye to Ponsot; FO 371/11516 4157/146 no. 138, Beirut, 30 June 1926, and 371/12303 5450/44 no. 184, 28 November 1927, Satow to Chamberlain. Ralph E. Crow, 'Confessionalism, Public Administration and Efficiency in Lebanon', in Binder, *Politics in Lebanon*, pp. 167–86.

43.   SHA, carton 32B3, BIR no. 2, 15 April 1927; MAE, Paris, Syrie et Liban, vol. 263, 'Note pour M. le Ministre', Paris, 24 December 1926; vol. 201, Beirut, 22 January 1927, Dabbas to Poincaré; vol. 203, Bulletin d'Information no. 3, 15 June 1927, pp. 11–12. MAE, Nantes, Syrie et Liban, carton 364, 'Statut Organique de la Syrie et du Liban', 2 March 1927. See also FO 371/12306 1651/426 no. 68, 30 March 1927; 1843/426 no. 73, Beirut, 11 April 1927; the budget for 1927 in *Journal Officiel de la République Libanaise*, in 2253/426, no. 96, Beirut, 6 May 1927; FO 371/12303 3058/426 no. 126, Beirut, 30 June 1927, Satow to FO.

44.   MAE, Nantes, Syrie et Liban, carton 933, no. 125/D, 'L'Attitude de la Chambre à l'égard du Ministère', Delegate to the Lebanese Republic to the High Commissioner, Beirut, 12 February 1927.

45.   MAE, Nantes, Syrie et Liban, carton 933, nos 407–10, Beirut, 27 April 1927, de Reffye to Ponsot; MAE, Paris, Syrie et Liban, vol. 202, no. 251, Paris, 2 May 1927, Ponsot to de Reffye.

46.   SHA, carton 32B3, BIR no. 3, Beirut, 16 June 1927.

47.   MAE, Paris, Syrie et Liban, vol. 202, nos 421–2, Beirut, 5 May 1927, de Reffye to the Quai d'Orsay; vol. 203, Bulletin d'Information no. 3, Beirut, 15 June 1927.

48.   MAE, Paris, Syrie et Liban, vol. 202, nos 421–2, Beirut, 5 May 1927, de Reffye to the Quai d'Orsay; Khuri, *Haqa'iq lubnaniyya*, vol. 1, pp. 146–8.

49.   FO 371/12306 3058/426 no. 126, Beirut, 30 June 1927, Satow to FO.

50.   MAE, Paris, Syrie et Liban, vol. 263, 'Note pour M. le Ministre', Paris, 24 December 1926. MAE, Nantes, Syrie et Liban, carton 933, Rens. no. 1222, Damascus, 12 October 1927; carton 364, 'Note pour le Ministre', Paris, 24 January 1928.

51.   MAE, Paris, Syrie et Liban, vol. 263, nos 563–5, Beirut, 9 July 1927, pp. 153–5, Ponsot to the Quai d'Orsay; vol. 225, Memorandum by Ponsot, 3 May 1927, pp. 8–9.

52.   MAE, Nantes, Syrie et Liban, carton 453, no. 649, Beirut, 10 August 1927, Beshara al-Khuri to Solomiac; MAE, Paris, Syrie et Liban, vol. 225, Ponsot's memorandum, 3 May 1927, pp. 8–9; vol. 263, nos 563–5, Beirut, 9 July 1927, Ponsot to the Quai d'Orsay.

53.   MAE, Nantes, Syrie et Liban, carton 2902, 'Révision de la Constitution Libanaise', Beirut, 24 August 1927, Ponsot to Briand; carton 453, no. 446, Paris, 14 September 1927, Briand to Ponsot; MAE, Paris, Syrie et Liban, vol. 263, 'Révision de la Constitution'; no. 632, Beirut, 7 August 1927, Ponsot to the Quai d'Orsay; 'Réforme de la Constitution Libanaise', Paris, 10 September 1927, pp. 249–53.

54.   MAE, Nantes, Syrie et Liban, carton 925, Information no. 657, Beirut, 21 June 1927; carton 933, Rens. (n.d.); Information no. 694, 5 July 1927; 'La Révision de la Constitution', Information, 5 July 1927; MAE, Paris, Syrie et Liban, vol. 203, 'Note de M. de Caix', Paris, 5 August 1927.

55.   MAE, Nantes, Syrie et Liban, carton 933, Rens., Beirut, 4 October 1927; Rens., 7 October 1927; carton 453, no. 166, Beirut, 26 October 1926, Solomiac to Ponsot.

56.   MAE, Nantes, Syrie et Liban, carton 933, Rens., Beirut, 29 September 1927; Information no. 882, 7 October 1927; MAE, Paris, Syrie et Liban, vol. 203, nos 749–51, Beirut, 1 October 1927; nos 767–9, 8 October 1927, Ponsot to the Quai d'Orsay.

57.   MAE, Nantes, Syrie et Liban, carton 933, Information no. 882, 7 October 1927; Bulletin de Rens. no. 228, Beirut, 15 October 1927; FO 371/12303 4745/44 no. 169, Beirut, 25 October 1927, Satow to Chamberlain.

58.   For details of the modification of the constitution, see reports in MAE, Nantes, Syrie et Liban, cartons 933, 2902; carton 453, no. 166, Beirut, 26 October 1927, Solomiac to Ponsot. See also FO 371/12303 4791/44 no. 172, Beirut, 31 October 1927, Satow to Chamberlain.

59.   MAE, Nantes, Syrie et Liban, carton 933, Rens. no. 582, 4 October 1927; no. 590, 7 October 1927; Information nos 882 and 893, 7 October 1927; no. 895, 12 October 1927; FO 371/12303 4791/44 no. 172, Beirut, 31 October 1927, Satow to Chamberlain.

60.   The Lebanese Constitution.

61.   Ibid. See also FO 371/12303 4791/44 no. 172, Beirut, 31 October 1927, Satow to Chamberlain.

62.   MAE, Nantes, Syrie et Liban, carton 933, Rens., Beirut, 22 August 1927; Information no. 85, and Rens., Beirut, 7 September, 15 October and 18 October 1927; Bulletin de Rens. no. 202, 13 September, no. 204, 15 September 1927; no. 228, 15 October, no. 231, 19 October 1927. For Jisr's speech on 19 October, see carton 933, no. 697, 'Compte rendu succinct de la Séance de la Chambre des Députés en date du 28 décembre 1927'; no. 472, 22 August 1927; no. 513, 7 September 1927; no. 607, 15 October 1927; no. 610, 18 October 1927. At a meeting in Diman, the three bishops, Eddé, other Maronite politicians and Jisr formed an 'alliance' of senators and deputies to ensure Jisr's election. Shortly before the elections, Jisr secured 18 votes and Namur 15, while Ayub Tabet, who had also declared his candidacy, was backed by three deputies. The various camps continued to pressure the undecided senators and deputies. Beshara al-Khuri announced that he would abstain from voting, as he was replacing Namur's deceased brother in the senate, while Michel Chiha told Jisr's supporters that he would back Jisr 'in order to ensure his brother-in-law's interests'. In a last-minute attempt to prevent Jisr's election, Namur withdrew his own candidacy in favour of Ayub Tabet.

63.   MAE, Nantes, Syrie et Liban, carton 933, no. 697, 'Compte rendu succinct de la Séance de la Chambre des Députés en date du 28 décembre 1927', 29

December 1927; Information no. 943, 10 November, no. 1028, 20 December, and no. 1054, 22 December 1927. When Khuri, at a meeting of the parliament, defended his government's record, including its part in the revision of the constitution, Namur replied: 'que le gouvernement ne devrait pas être fier de prendre à son actif la révision de la Constitution. C'est précisément, dit-il, ce que je lui reproche.' Similarly, Omar Da'uq declared that he would vote against the government following its role in the modification of the constitution, which was 'jeopardizing the country's independence'; FO 371/12303 4745/44 no. 169, Beirut, 25 October 1927, Satow to Chamberlain.

64.   FO 371/13074 388/141 no. 4, Beirut, 9 January 1928, Satow to FO.

65.   MAE, Nantes, Syrie et Liban, carton 933, Information no. 37, 16 January 1928; FO 371/13074 388/141 no. 4, Beirut, 9 January 1928, Satow to FO.

66.   MAE, Nantes, Syrie et Liban, carton 933, Rens. no. 6, 9 January 1928.

67.   MAE, Nantes, Syrie et Liban, carton 933, Rens. no. 6, 9 January 1928; no. 7, 10 January 1928; Information no. 37, 16 January 1928; Rens., 7 February 1928; MAE, Paris, Syrie et Liban, vol. 203, Petitions and press comment, 22 February 1928, pp. 252–9. After journalists, led by Gabrial Khabbaz and Alfred Naqash from *l'Orient*, protested in Paris, Ponsot was forced to intervene; Khuri, *Al-bayyanat al-wizariyya al-lubnaniyya*, vol. 1, pp. 7–15.

68.   MAE, Nantes, Syrie et Liban, carton 933, Information no 388, 2 July 1928; no. 44, 'Chambre des Députés, Compte rendu de la 2ᵉ séance', 9 August 1928; no. 93, 'Economies réalisées dans l'Administration du Liban depuis la formation du second Ministère Cheikh Bechara el Khoury', Beirut, March 1928.

69.   MAE, Nantes, Syrie et Liban, carton 933, no. 44, 'Chambre des Députés, Compte rendu de la 2ᵉ séance', 9 August 1928; MAE, Paris, Syrie et Liban, vol. 264, Emile Tabet's letter to Briand, 3 October 1928, pp. 109–16.

70.   MAE, Nantes, Syrie et Liban, carton 933, Information no. 388, Beirut, 2 July 1928; FO 371/13074 3077/141 no. 53, Beirut, 24 May 1928, Satow to FO.

71.   MAE, Nantes, Syrie et Liban, carton 412, Bulletin de Rens. nos 430–1, Damascus, 23 June 1928; carton 933, Rens. no. 70, 7 February 1928; Bulletin de Rens. no. 746, 27 October 1928. For Sa'ad's statement in the parliament, see Khuri, *Al-bayyanat al-wizariyya al-lubnaniyya*, vol. 1, pp. 16–18.; FO 371/13074 4391/141 no. 65, Beirut, 14 August 1928, Acting Consul-General Ellison to Lord Cushendun.

72.   MAE, Nantes, Syrie et Liban, carton 364, no. 881, Beirut, 23 December 1927, Ponsot to the Quai d'Orsay; FO 371/13075 349/349, no. 7, Beirut, 12 January 1928; 371/13074 3077/141. no. 53, Beirut, 24 May 1928, Satow to Chamberlain.

73.   MAE, Paris, Syrie et Liban. For various press reports see vol. 289, in particular pp. 10, 18. For the reaction in the Syrian press see pp. 30–2 and vol. 290, pp. 116, 126, 288.

74.   On April 27, 1929, Prime Minister Sa'ad presented the proposed modifications to the parliament, which approved them the same day with a majority of 37 against three. MAE, Nantes, Syrie et Liban, carton 934,

Information no. 1152, 19 April 1929; MAE, Paris, Syrie et Liban, vol. 264, nos 209–12, Beirut, 18 April 1929, Ponsot to the Quai d'Orsay; no. 239, Paris, 19 April 1929, the Quai d'Orsay to Ponsot; no. 235, Beirut, 27 April 1929, Ponsot to the Quai d'Orsay. FO 371/13803 3741/182, 'Loi Constitutionelle', Beirut, 13 July 1929, Satow to FO. See also Edmond Rabbath, *La Formation Historique du Liban Politique et Constitutionnel* (Beirut, 1973), pp. 384–6.

75.   MAE, Nantes, Syrie et Liban, carton 934, no. 1808, 'Note sur la situation politique au Liban', 29 November 1929; on the economic situation, taxation and budget, see a comprehemsive report prepared by Michel Chiha in vol. 934, 'La matière imposable et les impôts au Liban'. See also press reports in MAE, Paris, Syrie et Liban, vol. 290, for example article in *al-Bashir* in the press report of 27–30 April, 1929.

76.   MAE, Nantes, Syrie et Liban, carton 934, 'Crise Ministérielle Libanaise', Beirut, 12 April 1929. In March 1929 *al-Ahwal* published a series of articles by Ayub Tabet, harshly criticizing the ministers for abusing their power.

77.   MAE, Nantes, Syrie et Liban, carton 396, no. 795, 'Note de Service', 16 May 1929; carton 934, no. 1808, 'Note sur la situation politique au Liban', Beirut, 25 November 1929; FO 371/13803 2823/182, no. 54, Beirut, 14 May 1929, Ellison to FO. Khuri claimed that Dabbas had initially offered the premiership to Eddé, but that the latter had declined. It is unlikely that Dabbas, Solomiac and Khuri would have allowed Eddé to serve as prime minister and supervise elections for a parliament which was to elect the president in 1932. MAE, Paris, Syrie et Liban, vol. 264, no. 279, Beirut, 9 May 1929, Ponsot to the Quai d'Orsay. For Khuri's statement in the parliament, see Khuri, *Al-bayyanat al-wizariyya al-lubnaniyya*, vol. 1, pp. 19–20; Khuri, *Haqa'iq lubnaniyya*, vol. 1, pp. 163–4.

78. ⁄ MAE, Nantes, Syrie et Liban, carton 934, no. 1801. Bayhum delivered the speech on 30 May 1929.

79.   MAE, Nantes, Syrie et Liban, carton 934, no. 607, 'Rapport au sujet de l'établissement du quotient électoral pour les élections législatives de 1929', Beirut, 5 April 1929. For the 1922 election law see Zamir, *The Formation of Modern Lebanon*, pp. 142–3.

80.   MAE, Nantes, Syrie et Liban, carton 933, no. 2464, Compte-Rendu, Beirut, 15 October 1928; Rens. no. 501, 8 September 1928; carton 934, no. 607, 'Rapport au sujet de l'établissement du quotient électoral pour les élections législatives de 1929', Beirut, 5 April 1929. The distribution of the deputies between the sects was as follows:

Rite	Nombre	Quotient	Sièges	Fractions
Maronites	199,181	20,302	9+1	16,463
Sunnis	124,786		6	2,974
Shiites	104,947		5	3,437
Orthodox	81,409		4	802
Druze	43,633		2	3,029
Catholics	42,462		2	1,858
Others	12,651		1	12,651

Source: MAE, Nantes vol. 396, no. 941/SRRL, 'Etudes sur les elections libanaises', 10 June 1929.

81.   For a detailed description of the elections see reports in MAE, Nantes, Syrie et Liban, cartons 396 and 934. See in particular comprehensive study of the elections in carton 396, no. 941/SRRL, 'Rapport sur les élections libanaises', Beirut, 5 July 1929.

82.   Ibid.

83.   Ibid.

84.   Ibid.

85.   Ibid.

86.   MAE, Nantes, Syrie et Liban, carton 934, Information no. 167, Beirut, 3 May 1929; no. 291, 14 June 1929, and no. 1595, 21 June 1929; MAE, Paris, Syrie et Liban, vol. 264, pp. 194–9.

87.   MAE, Nantes, Syrie et Liban, carton 396, no. 941/SRRL, 'Etudes sur les elections libanaises', 10 June 1929.

88.   Ibid.

89.   MAE, Nantes, Syrie et Liban, carton 934, no. 1251, 'Note au sujet des Incidents survenus à Tripoli lors des élections au second degré, 14–15 et 16 Juin 1929.' Khuri, *Haqa'iq lubnaniyya*, vol. 1, pp. 165–7.

90.   MAE, Nantes, Syrie et Liban, carton 934, Information no. 201, Beirut, 14 June 1929. On May 16, the head of the S.R. in Lebanon had issued an order to his officers reminding them that '… the elections must take place in complete freedom, without pressure of any kind on the voters. It is therefore strictly forbidden to intervene in the electoral process. The role of the officers is merely to keep. my intermediary, M. le Délégué, informed of what is going on and, in agreement with the gendarmerie, to maintain public order.' in carton 396, S.R. no. 795/SRRL, 16 May 1929.

91.   MAE, Nantes, Syrie et Liban, carton 934. no. 1808, 25 November 1929. Altogether sixteen deputies were reelected and eight senators reappointed. Nearly one third of the members of the parliament were lawyers. There were also two doctors, one agricultural engineer, two journalists, two merchants, and 13 landowners, carton 396, 'Rapport sur les élections libanaises'.

92.   MAE, Nantes, Syrie et Liban, carton 934, Information no. 211, Beirut, 24 June 1929.

93.   MAE, Nantes, Syrie et Liban, carton 934. no. 1808, 25 November 1929. Twenty-nine out of 36 present. Khuri, *Haqa'iq lubnaniyya*, vol. 1, pp. 167–8.

94.   MAE, Nantes, Syrie et Liban, carton 934, Information no. 213, 26 June 1929; no. 1808, 25 November 1929; FO 371/13803 5828/182 no. 99, 22 October 1929, Satow to Henderson.

95.   Although Ponsot approved Habib Trad's proposal, he was unwilling to implement it. In protest, Trad resigned from the parliament in July. MAE, Nantes, Syrie et Liban, carton 934, no. 1808, 25 November 1929.

96.   Ibid.

97.   FO 371/13803 5828/182, no. 99, Beirut, 22 October 1929, Satow to Henderson.

98.   Khuri, *Haqa'iq lubnaniyya*, vol. 1, pp. 116, 140, 167.

99.   See Chapters 3 and 4.

100.   Awad, *Ashab al-fakhama*, pp. 119–250; P. Hobeika, *Emile Eddé* (Beirut, 1939).

101.   Zamir, *The Formation of Modern Lebanon*, pp. 155–6.

102.   Ibid. pp. 194–6. See also Meir Zamir, 'Emile Eddé and the Territorial Integrity of Lebanon' *Middle Eastern Studies*, 14/2 (May 1978), pp. 232–5.

103.   See Eddé's behaviour during his government's crisis in March 1930. See also Chapter 4.

104.   MAE, Paris, Syrie et Liban, vol. 497, 'Memorandum d'un entretien entre M. Tetreau et M. Emile Eddé au sujet de sa candidature à la Présidence de la République Libanaise', Beirut, 27 April 1932.

105.   MAE, Nantes, Syrie et Liban, carton 933, Bulletin d'Information, Beirut, 30 November 1928.

106.   MAE, Nantes, Syrie et Liban, carton 454, a comprehensive report on Eddé's government's crisis.

107.   Ibid.

108.   FO 371/13803 6580/182, no. 111, Beirut, 26 November 1929; Satow to Henderson; MAE, Nantes, Syrie et Liban, carton 935, Information no. 384, 12 November 1929. Khuri, *Al-bayyanat al-wizariyya al-lubnaniyya*, vol. 1, pp. 21–55.

109.   Ibid. Khuri and his three supporters, Sawda, Khazin and Zakur, voted against the government.

110.   MAE, Paris, Syrie et Liban, vol. 497, nos 89–90, Beirut, 11 February 1930, Ponsot to the Quai d'Orsay. Those dismissed included 550 of the 2000 employees in the judicial system. Seventy per cent of Lebanon's budget went on salaries, compared to 40 per cent in Syria and the other mandated states.

111.   MAE, Paris, Syrie et Liban, vol. 203, 'Note de M. de Caix', Paris, 5 August 1927. De Caix proposed granting Beirut a certain degree of municipal autonomy and implementing a decentralized administrative system in Lebanon. Vol 497, no. 392, Beirut, 23 May 1930, Ponsot to the Quai d'Orsay; MAE, Nantes, Syrie et Liban, carton 454, detailed report on Eddé's government's crisis; carton 933, Information no. 877.

112.   Najla W. Atiyah, *The Attitude of the Lebanese Sunnis towards the State of Lebanon* (Ph.D. thesis, University of London, 1973), p. 89. See also J.A. Babikian, *Civilization and Education in Syria and Lebanon* (Beirut, 1936).

113.   MAE, Nantes, Syrie et Liban, carton 935, Information nos 388 and 411, Beirut, March 1930.

114.   MAE, Nantes, Syrie et Liban, carton 935, Information no. 83, Beirut, 29 January 1930; The attacks were led by *al-Nida* and *al-Ahd al-Jadid*, owned by Khair al-Din al-Ahdab, who refuted *L'Orient's* accusations against his uncle, Husain al-Ahdab, the Minister for Public Works.

115.   MAE, Nantes, Syrie et Liban, carton 935, 'Compte-Rendu de la Presse Libano–Syrienne', no. 46, Beirut, 22 February 1930; Information no. 493, 24 March 1930; MAE, Paris, Syrie et Liban, vol. 497, Jerusalem, 17 February 1930, Hajj Amin al-Husaini's letter to Mustafa al-Ghailani, President of the Muslim Council of Beirut published in *al-Ahd al-Jadid*, p. 21. See also p. 29, and pp. 30–1, no. 70, 7 March 1930, in which the French Consul in Iraq reported that the reforms in Lebanon had provoked resentment among the Iraqi public, which saw them as a Christian offensive.

116.   MAE, Nantes, Syrie et Liban, carton 935, *al-Sha'ab* (Damascus), no. 752, 22 January 1930.

117.   At the meeting Eddé told Karameh that he would not allow the reunion of the Muslim Congress to take place on Lebanese soil. MAE, Nantes, Syrie et Liban, carton 935, Information no. 411. For details of Karameh's activities see vol. 934, 'Rapport Politique', Tripoli, 4 April 1930, sent by the French representative there who was following them closely. Karameh's brother had been arrested three months before.

118.   MAE, Nantes, Syrie et Liban, carton 935, Information no. 64, Beirut, 22 January 1930. For a general report on Eddé's government's crisis see carton 454, particularly Chapter VII — 'L'agitation musulmane'; carton 935, Information, no. 64, 22 January 1930; MAE, Paris, Syrie et Liban, vol. 497, no. 138, 26 February. and no. 200, 25 March 1930. It was alleged that Eddé had not kept his promise not to harm Jisr and his proteges.

119.   Pharaon's house became the centre for opposition to Eddé. Pharaon, then 24 years old, declared that that he was willing to use all his wealth to topple Eddé. MAE, Nantes, Syrie et Liban, carton 935, Information no. 314, 4 March 1930.

120.   Ibid. See also MAE, Paris, Syrie et Liban, vol. 497, no. 138, 26 February 1930, Ponsot to the Quai d'Orsay.

121.   MAE, Nantes, Syrie et Liban, carton 934, 'Rapport Politique', Tripoli, 4 April 1930; carton 935, Information no. 411; vol. 454, general report on Eddé's government's crisis, see in particular Chapter 8; MAE, Paris, Syrie et Liban, vol. 497, no. 200, Beirut, 25 March 1930, Ponsot to the Quai d'Orsay.

122.   MAE, Paris, Syrie et Liban, vol. 497, no. 138, Beirut, 26 February, and no. 200, 25 March 1930, Ponsot to the Quai d'Orsay.

123.   Ponsot claimed that Eddé refused to heed his advice, declaring that he solely was responsible for governing and was therefore willing to bear the

consquences. MAE, Paris, Syrie et Liban, vol. 497, no. 200, Beirut 25 March 1930, Ponsot to the Quai d'Orsay.

124.   MAE, Nantes, Syrie et Liban, carton 935, Information no. 240, 29 March 1930; no. 247, 31 March 1930; Rens. no. 470; no. 493, 24 March 1930, and general report on Eddé's government's crisis in carton 454. For Karameh's activities and Muslim opposition see Information nos 388, 411, 192. For Eddé's and his supporters' criticism of Ponsot, particularly in *L'Orient*, see carton 934, no. 262, 9 April 1930 and no. 612, 9 April 1930. See also MAE, Paris, Syrie et Liban, vol. 497, no. 392, 23 May 1930, Ponsot to the Quai d'Orsay; FO 406/65 2072/23 no. 39, Beirut, 1 April 1930, Satow to Henderson.

125.   MAE, Nantes, Syrie et Liban, carton 934, Information no. 233, 27 March 1930.

Chapter Three

1.   For a comprehensive study of Lebanon's economy, see Gates, *Formation of the Political Economy of Modern Lebanon*. The author published some of her findings in 'The Historical Role of Political Economy in the Development of Modern Lebanon', in *Papers on Lebanon* (Centre for Lebanese Studies, Oxford, 1989), no. 10. See also Zvi Y. Hershlag, *Introduction to the Modern Economic History of the Middle East* (Tel Aviv, 1965), (in Hebrew), Chapter 10, and Khoury, *Syria and the French Mandate*, p. 375.

2.   MAE, Paris, Syrie et Liban, vol. 482, 'Situation des Etats du Levant au cours de l'année 1932', Beirut, 5 November 1932, pp. 124–32; Gates, *Formation of the Political Economy*, pp. 39–45. Exports decreased from FF 265 million to FF 194 million and imports from FF 747 million to FF 550 million. Association des Commerçants de Beyrouth, 'Mémoire présenté en date du 15 mars 1933 à S.E. M. Henry Ponsot', in FHJ.

3.   Gates, *Formation of the Political Economy*, pp. 28–34. It was estimated that the average annual remittances from 1920–1926 amounted to FF 30 million. In comparison, Lebanon's budget in 1921 was FF 46 million and, in 1926, FF 93 million.

4.   Gates, *Formation of the Political Economy*, p. 30.

5.   The total tonnage of goods passing through the port of Haifa increased from 236,000 in 1930 to 473,000 in 1933 (the year the modern port was officially inaugurated), to 689,000 in 1934 to 926,000 in 1935 and to 966,000 in 1939. In comparison, in the port of Beirut the tonnage was as follows: in 1929, 567,00; 1933, 555,000; 1934, 463,000; 1939, 633,000. See Mordechai Na'or and Yossi Ben-Artzi (eds) *The Development of Haifa*, (Yitzhak Ben-Zvi Institute, (Jerusalem) (in Hebrew) p. 76. See also Shimon Stern, 'The Struggle to Establish the Port of Haifa during the British Mandate', in *Cathedra* (Jerusalem, October 1981), no. 21, pp. 171–86, and Himadeh, *Economic Organization of Syria*, pp. 233–4.

6.   For the decline in agriculture see Gates, *Formation of the Political Economy*, pp. 36–9. In 1910–11 Syria exported 400 tonnes of silk, most of it produced in Lebanon, to the value of 2,604,000 Syrian Pounds. In 1929 silk exports recovered and reached 387 tonnes, with a value of 1,879,000 Syrian Pounds. In 1933, exports dropped to 106 tonnes, with a value of 223,000 Syrian Pounds. See Hinadeh, *Economic Organization of Syria*, p. 127.

7.   Gates, *Formation of the Political Economy*, pp. 45–53. For example, the number of industrial enterprises increased from 400 in 1930 to 900 in 1939.

8.   Khoury, *Syria and the French Mandate*, pp. 347–50, 397–400. For the emergence of trade unions see Couland, *Le Mouvement Syndical au Liban 1919–1946*.

9.   MAE, Paris, Syrie et Liban, vol. 487, Translation of article in *The Times*, Service d'Information et de Presse, no. 34, Damascus, 29 December 1933. Many Lebanese compared their own economy with that of Palestine and Iraq, which they considered to be superior. This comparison was misleading, however, as the prosperity in Palestine resulted mainly from the large-scale investments of Jewish immigrants, while Iraq received revenue from oil. See also Khoury, *Syria and the French Mandate*, pp. 348–9.

10.   MAE, Paris, Syrie et Liban, vol. 477, no. 107, Beirut, 18 February 1930; vol. 497, no. 21, Beirut, 11 March 1933, Ponsot to the Quai d'Orsay; vol. 480, memorandum, Beirut, 13 April 1932, pp. 79–85.

11.   MAE, Paris, Syrie et Liban, vol. 486, no. 2265, Paris, 2 October 1933, the Prime Minister and Minister of War to the Foreign Minister; vol. 481, pp. 168–72. A close examination of the Lebanese budget in the 1920s shows that the proportion of income from direct and indirect taxes indeed grew from 55 per cent in 1921 to 70.5 per cent in 1929. This percentage increased further during the recession years. At the same time the High Commission reduced its contribution from the Common Interests to the local governments when these governments were facing difficulties in balancing their own budgets. Until 1928 Lebanon had received a higher proportion of the income from the Common Interests than warranted by the size of its population. For example, in the mid-1920s its income from the Common Interests comprised 40 per cent of its total budget. By 1928 this had fallen to 32.5 per cent, and by 1929 to 19.5 per cent. The proportion of the Lebanese budget in the general budget was as follows: 1921 - 29.5 per cent; 1925 - 21 per cent; 1928 - 16 per cent; 1932 - 20.6 per cent. For 1932 the Lebanese budget was FF 104 million out of FF 503 million. By the end of August 1932 Lebanon had accumulated a deficit of FF 8 million. (In 1932 the budget of the Common Interests comprised FF 165 million out of a total budget of FF 503 million.)

12.   MAE, Paris, Syrie et Liban, vol. 482, Beirut, 5 January 1932, pp. 124–32, 'Situation des Etats du Levant au cours de l'année 1932'. See also Gates, *Formation of the Political Economy* , pp. 32–4.

13.   J. Néré, *The Foreign Policy of France from 1914 to 1945* (London, 1974). See in particular Chapter 6. Paul Kennedy, *The Rise and Fall of the Great Powers*

(Glasgow, 1989), pp. 400–6; Elizabeth Monroe, *The Mediterranean in Politics* (Oxford, 1938), pp. 71–89.

14.   Monroe, *The Mediterranean in Politics*, pp. 139–205; Kennedy, *The Rise and Fall of the Great Powers*, pp. 376–85.

15.   MAE, Paris, Syrie et Liban, vol. 483, no. 19, Beirut, 27 January 1933, Ponsot to the Quai d'Orsay; 'Note pour le Ministre', Paris, 15 February 1933; no. 42, Damascus, 17 February 1933, Ponsot to the Quai d'Orsay. Segré, C.G., 'Liberal and Fascist Italy in the Middle East, 1919–1939' and Erlich, H., 'Mussolini and the Middle East in the 1920s: the Restrained Imperialist', in Uriel Dann (ed.) *The Great Powers in the Middle East 1919–1939* (New York, 1988), pp. 197–212.

16.   C.A. MacDonald, 'Radio Bari: Italian Wireless Propaganda in the Middle East and British Countermeasures 1934–1938', *Middle Eastern Studies*, 13/2, (May 1977), pp. 195–207.

17.   For the emergence of fascist paramilitary organizations, see Chapter 4.

18.   MAE, Paris, Syrie et Liban, vol. 483, 'Note pour le Ministre', Paris, 15 February 1933; no. 42, Damascus, 17 February 1933, Ponsot to the Quai d'Orsay. Andreas Hillgruber, 'The Third Reich and the Near and Middle East, 1933–1939', in Dann, pp. 274–82. See also Lukasz Hirszowicz, *The Third Reich and the Arab East* (Toronto, 1966).

19.   MAE, Nantes, Syrie et Liban, carton 926, Revue de la presse, no. 4, Beirut, 14 February 1933; MAE, Paris, Syrie et Liban, vol. 483, no. 42, Damascus, 17 February 1933; vol. 484, 'Note pour le Ministre', Paris, 30 March 1933; and vol. 498, nos 1005–7, Beirut, 26 March 1933, Ponsot to the Quai d'Orsay.

20.   William L. Shirer, *The Collapse of the Third Republic* (New York, 1969), pp. 188–96, 199–210. See also Richard D. Challener, 'The French Foreign Office: The Era of Philippe Berthelot', in Gordon A. Craig, and Felix Gilbert (eds) *The Diplomats 1919–1939* (New York, 1963), vol. 1, pp. 49–85.

21.   The instability of France's political system increased scepticism among many Lebanese regarding their own, which was based on that of France. On the reaction in Beirut to the Stavsky affair, see MAE, Nantes, Syrie et Liban, carton 833, Information no. 522, Beirut, 9 February 1934.

22.   MAE, Paris, Syrie et Liban, vol. 477, no. 15, Beirut, 26 February 1930, Ponsot to the Quai d'Orsay; MAE, Nantes, Syrie et Liban, carton 496, 'Observations sur la préparation des traités avec la Syrie et le Liban', October 1931.

23.   MAE, Paris, Syrie et Liban, vol. 477, no. 15, Beirut, 26 February 1930, Ponsot to the Quai d'Orsay; MAE, Nantes, Syrie et Liban, carton 496, 'Observations sur la préparation des traités avec la Syrie et le Liban', October 1931; FO 371/15364 2627/294 no. 1, Baghdad, 1 May 1931, Sir F. Humphrys to Lord Passfield.

24.   Haut Commissariat de la République Française en Syrie et au Liban, *Statut Organique des Etats du Levant sous Mandat Français* (Paris, 1930); MAE, Nantes, Syrie et Liban, carton 496, 'Observations sur la préparation des traités avec la Syrie et le Liban', October 1931.

25.   MAE, Nantes, Syrie et Liban, carton 364, 'Politique française en Syrie', 10 November 1930; FO 371/15364 2627/294, no. 1, Baghdad, 1 May 1934, Sir F. Humphrys to Lord Passfield.

26.   MAE, Nantes, Syrie et Liban, carton 364, 'Politique francaise en Syrie', 10 November 1930.

27.   Ibid; MAE, Paris, Syrie et Liban, vol. 480, no. 18, Beirut, 2 April 1931, Ponsot to the Quai d'Orsay. In March 1931 Ponsot sent Briand a plan for a treaty based on the Anglo–Iraqi treaty.

28.   Khoury, *Syria and the French Mandate*, pp. 360–6.

29.   MAE, Nantes, Syrie et Liban, carton 411, no. 39, Tripoli, 22 August 1931, Lafond to Ponsot; Extrait du Bulletin d'Information no. 3, 29 July 1931. For criticism of the army's disregard for political considerations see carton 496, 'Observations sur la préparation des traités avec la Syrie et le Liban', October 1931; MAE, Paris, Syrie et Liban, vol. 480, no. 18, Ponsot to the Quai d'Orsay. On the consequences of the oil supply see Itamar Rabinovich, 'Oil and Local Politics: The French-Iraqi Negotiations of the Early 1930s', in Dann, *The Great Powers*, pp. 172–82; Khoury, *Syria and the French Mandate*, p. 441.

30.   MAE, Nantes, Syrie et Liban, carton 364, 'Politique française en Syrie', 10 November 1930.

31.   MAE, Paris, Syrie et Liban, vol. 482, 'Note pour le Président du Conseil', Paris, 7 October 1932.

32.   The Hashemite crown was used by the French to sow discord among the Syrian leaders. See Khoury, *Syria and the French Mandate*, pp. 351–359; Ahmed M. Gomaa, 'The Syrian Throne: Hashemite Ambition and Anglo–French Rivalry, 1930–1935,' in Dann, *The Great Powers*, pp. 183–95.

33.   Khoury, *Syria and the French Mandate*, pp. 375–80.

34.   MAE, Paris, Syrie et Liban, vol. 482, 'Note pour le Président du Conseil', Paris, 7 October 1932.

35.   Ibid. The government agreed to consider Ponsot's proposal to move the negotiations to Paris if they ran into difficulties.

36.   Ibid.

37.   MAE, Nantes, Syrie et Liban, carton 364, Ponsot's testimony to the Permanent Mandates Commission; MAE, Paris, Syrie et Liban, vol. 483, 'Note pour le Ministre', Paris, 15 February 1933; vol. 509, no. 445, Rome, 28 November 1932, Charles-Roux to the Quai d'Orsay; 'Syria and the Lebanon: Examination of the Annual Report for 1931', The League of Nations, the Permanent Mandates Commission, Thirty-Sixth Meeting, 1 December 1932, pp. 259–98 in FO 371/16973 908/120.

38.   MAE, Paris, Syrie et Liban, vol. 483, no. 19, Beirut, 27 January 1933, Ponsot to the Quai d'Orsay, and memorandum 'La situation politique en Syrie', Beirut, 22 February 1933.

39.   MAE, Nantes, Syrie et Liban, carton 926, Revue de la presse, no. 4, Beirut, 14 February 1933; MAE, Paris, Syrie et Liban, vol. 483, no. 42, Damascus, 17

February 1933; vol. 484, 'Note pour le Ministre', Paris, 30 March 1933; and vol. 498, nos 1005–7, Beirut, 26 March 1933, Ponsot to the Quai d'Orsay.

40.   MAE, Paris, Syrie et Liban, vol. 483, no. 26, 3 February, and no. 30, Beirut, 13 February 1933, Ponsot to the Quai d'Orsay; nos167–9, Paris, 11 March 1933, Minister for Foreign Affairs to Ponsot; vol. 484, 'Note pour le Ministre', Paris, 30 March 1933; nos 105–10, Paris, 29 April 1933, Minister for Foreign Affairs to Ponsot; memorandum, 'Evolution du problème syrien', pp. 64–71; and 'Note pour le Ministre', 15 May 1933.

41.   MAE, Paris, Syrie et Liban, vol. 484, 'Note pour le Ministre', 13 May 1933. Druze and Allawite opposition to their integration into Syria was encouraged by French officials. The negotiations in May were in part intended to gain time in view of the pending meeting of the Mandates Commission.

42.   MAE, Paris, Syrie et Liban, vol. 485, nos 1018–20, Paris, 12 June 1933; 1022–23, 16 June and 1025–6, 23 June 1933, Foreign Minister to Ponsot; 'Note de Robert de Caix', 7 June 1933.

43.   For harsh criticism of Ponsot see Khoury, *Syria and the French Mandate*, pp. 389–91. Ponsot was later appointed as ambassador to Turkey, where he played an important role in the problem of Alexandretta. See Arslan, *Mudhakkirat*, vol. 1, pp. 123–40.

44.   MAE, Nantes, Syrie et Liban, carton 832, Press reports on de Martel's assuming office, Beirut, October 1933.

45.   MAE, Paris, Syrie et Liban, vol. 486, 'Note pour le Ministre', Paris, October 1933.

46.   Ibid.

47.   MAE, Paris, Syrie et Liban, vol. 487, nos 751–60, Paris, 23 November 1933, Foreign Minister to de Martel.

48.   For the National Bloc's reaction to the suspension of the negotiations on a treaty see Khoury, *Syria and the French Mandate*, pp. 441–4.

49.   MAE, Nantes, Syrie et Liban, carton 408, no. 613, Beirut, 29 July 1932, Delegate of the High Commissioner to the Quai d'Orsay; MAE, Paris, Syrie et Liban, vol. 484, nos 1012–17, Paris, 16 May 1933, Minister for Foreign Affairs to Ponsot; vol. 499, 'Le problème libanais', November 1933.

50.   Khoury, *Syria and the French Mandate*, pp. 386–90.

51.   Hasan Ali Hallaq, *Mu'atamar al-sahil wa'l-aqdiyya al-arba'ah* (Beirut, 1982); Murad, *Al-harakat al-wahdawiyya*; Solh, *Lebanon and Arab Nationalism*. The rivalry within the National Bloc was reflected in the efforts of each faction to win the support of the Muslim leaders in Lebanon.

52.   MAE, Nantes, Syrie et Liban, carton 411, Information no. 334, 22 June 1932; no. 340, 23 June 1932; no. 344, Ba'albeck, 25 June 1932; Rens. 17 and 18 September 1931; MAE, Paris, Syrie et Liban, vol. 482, no. 619, Beirut, 29 July 1932, Delegate of the High Commissioner to the Quai d'Orsay.

53.   MAE, Paris, Syrie et Liban, vol. 482, no. 619, Beirut, 29 July 1932, Delegate of the High Commissioner to the Quai d'Orsay; vol. 484, no. 113, Beirut, 21 April 1933, Ponsot to the Quai d'Orsay; vol. 485, Paris, 23 June 1933, Subhi

Barakat, President of the Syrian parliament, to Paul-Boncour, Minister for Foreign Affairs; vol. 486, Note de Subhi Barakat, Paris, 24 August 1933; see Mardam's letter p. 84, Damascus, 18 April 1933; MAE, Nantes, Syrie et Liban, carton 411, Information no. 334, 22 June 1932; no. 340, 23 June 1932; carton 940, Information no. 579, 30 December 1933.

54.　MAE, Nantes, Syrie et Liban, carton 1560; memorandum 'Abdul Hamid Karamé', Tripoli, 10 May 1931, Lafond, French representative in Tripoli, to Ponsot; carton 408, Information no. 4724, Beirut, 22 October 1932. For Sulh's role in the Jerusalem Conference see carton 409, no. 1945, 'Note sur la réunion d'un congrès général arabe', Beirut, 29 July 1930.

55.　MAE, Nantes, Syrie et Liban, carton 935, Information no. 2119, Beirut, 3 June 1931; Information 'Beyrouth, municipe autonome', 24 April 1931; MAE, Paris, Syrie et Liban, vol. 497, no. 38, Beirut, 22 April 1930, Ponsot to the Quai d'Orsay.

56.　MAE, Nantes, Syrie et Liban, carton 1365, Muhammad al-Jisr, biographical note; carton 454, report on a meeting with Muhammad al-Jisr, Beirut, 4 April 1932; Zamir, *The Formation of Modern Lebanon*, pp. 204, 211.

57.　MAE, Nantes, Syrie et Liban, carton 1560, 'Abdul Hamid Karamé', Tripoli, 10 May 1931, Lafond, French representative in Tripoli, to Ponsot; carton 408, Information no. 4724, Beirut, 22 October 1932.

58.　MAE, Nantes, Syrie et Liban, carton 1365, Abdul Hamid Karamé, biographical note; carton 411, Rens. 17 September 1931; carton 1560, 'Fiche de Rens.', May, 1931; Zamir, *The Formation of Modern Lebanon*, pp. 186–7, 196–7, 211. See also John Gulick, *Tripoli: A Modern Arab City* (Oxford, 1967).

59.　Biographical sketch of Riad al-Sulh in report of American Consulate in Beirut, no. R-33–47, 22 January 1947, Centre for Lebanese Studies, Oxford.

60.　MAE, Nantes, Syrie et Liban, carton 926, and carton 1365, Riad al-Sulh, biographical note, Beirut, 25 April 1935; MAE, Paris, Syrie et Liban, vol. 497, no. 38, Beirut, 22 April 1930, Ponsot to the Quai d'Orsay. See also Hilal el-Solh, *Riad el-Solh 1894–1951* (Ph.D. thesis, Lyon University, 1981).

61.　MAE, Nantes, Syrie et Liban, carton 455, 'Rapport adressé à M. le Commandant Pechkof', December 1933; Information no. 3, Beirut, 9 March 1934; Hilal el-Solh, *Riad el-Solh*.

62.　MAE, Paris, Syrie et Liban, vol. 497, Report on a meeting between Ponsot and Eddé, 12 April 1930, pp. 61–3; Report on a reception organized by Riad al-Sulh in honour of M. Besnard of the Radical Party, Beirut, 22 April 1930; MAE, Nantes, Syrie et Liban, carton 411, Rens. 17 and 18 September 1931.

63.　For the tobacco monopoly crisis see the end of this chapter.

64.　MAE, Nantes, Syrie et Liban, carton 934, Information nos 268 and 270, 11 April 1930; no. 614, 10 April 1930; MAE, Paris, Syrie et Liban, vol. 497, no. 29, 9 April 1930; no. 38, Beirut, 22 April 1930, Ponsot to the Quai d'Orsay; report on a meeting between Ponsot and Eddé, 12 April 1930, pp. 61–3.

65.　MAE, Nantes, Syrie et Liban, carton 411, *L'Orient*, 26 August and 10–12 September 1931; on Habib Bustani see CHEAM, no. 687, Pierre Rondot, 'Les organisations professionnelles et les plans de réforme politique au Liban', Paris, 15 July 1939.

66.   MAE, Nantes, Syrie et Liban, carton 411, *L'Orient*, 26 August, 10–12 and 17 September and 20 October 1931; *La Syrie*, 25 September 1931.

67.   Zamir, *The Formation of Modern Lebanon*, pp. 219–22.

68.   Salibi, *The Modern History of Lebanon*, pp. 171–6.

69.   MAE, Nantes, Syrie et Liban, carton 934, 'La situation politique au Liban', Beirut, 3 September 1930; Information no. 883, Beirut, 24 December 1930.

70.   MAE, Nantes, Syrie et Liban, carton 934, Information no. 2772, Beirut, 30 October 1930; MAE, Paris, Syrie et Liban, vol. 497, no. 782, Beirut, 24 July 1931, High Commission to the Quai d'Orsay.

71.   MAE, Nantes, Syrie et Liban, carton 454, 'L'élection présidentielle au Liban', Beirut, 10 August 1931. Article 73 stipulated that the successful candidate was to be elected by the parliament with either a two-thirds majority in the first ballot, or a simple majority in the second.

72.   MAE, Paris, Syrie et Liban, vol. 497, Report on a meeting between Ponsot and Eddé, 12 April 1930, pp. 61–3. Khuri, *Haqa'iq lubnaniyya*, vol. 1, pp. 175–8.

73.   MAE, Nantes, Syrie et Liban, carton 934, Information no. 270, Beirut, 11 April 1930; Information no. 612, 9 April 1930; Information no. 642, 11 April 1930. Eddé's wife mentioned the possibility of his withdrawing from political life altogether. MAE, Paris, Syrie et Liban, vol. 497, Report on a meeting between Ponsot and Eddé, 12 April 1930, pp. 61–3.

74.   MAE, Nantes, Syrie et Liban, carton 411, Rens., Beirut, 11 July 1931, Bishop Khuri's letter to Bishop Feghali attached; 'Revue de la presse' no. 30, 19 September 1931; carton 454, no. 1933, Beirut, 4 August 1931, Adviser to the Acting Delegate of the High Commissioner to the Lebanese Republic, to Ponsot; carton 2990, Rens., Beirut, 10 August 1931; 'Election pour la présidence de la République libanaise', Beirut, 21 August 1931.

75.   MAE, Nantes, Syrie et Liban, carton 2990, Information: 'Le Patriarcat maronite et l'élection présidentielle au Liban', Beirut, 12 September 1931; Information no. 4288, 12 November 1931; Information no. 460, Beirut, 26 January 1932; MAE, Paris, Syrie et Liban, vol. 498, no. 446, Beirut, 3 June 1932, Ponsot to the Quai d'Orsay.

76.   MAE, Nantes, Syrie et Liban, carton 595, 'Intrigues des évêques maronites en vue de la succession de leur Patriarche', Beirut, 22 August 1930.

77.   MAE, Nantes, Syrie et Liban, carton 595, no. 911, Beirut, 31 December 1931, Ponsot to the Quai d'Orsay; MAE, Paris, Syrie et Liban, vol. 509, nos 1004–6, Beirut, 9 January 1932; no. 640, Beirut, 15 January 1932, Ponsot to the Quai d'Orsay. Mubarak received nine votes and Khuri six.

78.   MAE, Nantes, Syrie et Liban, carton 595, no. 116, Beirut, 8 January 1932, Ponsot to the Quai d'Orsay.

79.   Aql was appointed as a patriarchal vicar instead of Khuri in reward for his support of Arida.

80.   MAE, Nantes, Syrie et Liban, carton 2990, Information no. 1016, Beirut, 25 February 1932.

81.   MAE, Nantes, Syrie et Liban, carton 454, 'L'élection présidentielle au Liban', Beirut, 10 August 1931.

82.   MAE, Paris, Syrie et Liban, vol. 497, 'Memorandum d'un entretien entre M. Tetreau et M. Emile Eddé au sujet de sa candidature à la Présidence de la République Libanaise', Beirut, 27 April 1932.

83.   MAE, Paris, Syrie et Liban, vol. 497, no. 64, Beirut, 22 January 1932, Ponsot to the Quai d'Orsay.

84.   For details of the census see MAE, Nantes, Syrie et Liban, carton 1851; for an analysis of the 1932 census see Zamir, *The Formation of Modern Lebanon*, pp. 99–100.

85.   MAE, Paris, Syrie et Liban, vol. 509, no. 190, Beirut, 29 February 1932, Ponsot to the Quai d'Orsay.

86.   MAE, Nantes, Syrie et Liban, carton 2990, Information 'Déclarations du Cadi des Cadis sur la campagne pour l'élection présidentielle au Liban', Beirut, 3 September 1931. Jisr's campaign in the Muslim press was financed in part by Bank Misr.

87.   MAE, Paris, Syrie et Liban, vol. 497, 'L'Election présidentielle libanaise: Rens. fournis par Negib Armanazi', Beirut, 22 April 1932, pp. 162–5.

88.   MAE, Paris, Syrie et Liban, vol. 497, p. 157; MAE, Nantes, Syrie et Liban, carton 938, Information no. 225, Beirut, 4 April 1933.

89.   MAE, Nantes, Syrie et Liban, carton 454, report of a meeting with Muhammad al-Jisr, Beirut, 4 April 1932; MAE, Paris, Syrie et Liban, vol. 497, no. 337, Beirut, 23 April 1932, Ponsot to Tardieu.

90.   Khuri was willing to accept Jisr's proposal that Namur be a compromise candidate provided that he (Khuri) remained the candidate in the first ballot. If he failed in the first ballot, he and Jisr would vote for Namur. Jisr also offered Yusuf al-Khazin the premiership if the latter backed his bid for the presidency.

91.   MAE, Paris, Syrie et Liban, vol. 497, p. 157.

92.   MAE, Paris, Syrie et Liban, vol. 497, 'Memorandum d'un entretien entre M. Tetreau et M. Emile Eddé au sujet de sa candidature à la Présidence de la République libanaise', Beirut, 27 April 1932.

93.   MAE, Paris, Syrie et Liban, vol. 497, nos 1008–9, 22 March nos 1010–11 and 11 April 1932, Ponsot to the Quai d'Orsay; no. 1008, 23 March 1932, and nos 1009–10, Paris, 20 April 1932, Minister for Foreign Affairs to Ponsot; nos 1012–18, Beirut, 13 April 1932, Ponsot to the Quai d'Orsay; 'L'Election presidentielle au Liban', Beirut, 12 April 1932. Jisr claimed that he had been led to believe that Ponsot did not oppose his candidacy. Khuri blamed Yusuf al-Khazin, who translated for them at the meeting, for misleading Jisr.

94.   MAE, Paris, Syrie et Liban, vol. 497, no. 364, Beirut, 5 May 1932, Ponsot to the Quai d'Orsay; no. 782, Beirut, 24 July 1931, the High Commission to the Quai d'Orsay.

95.   MAE, Nantes, Syrie et Liban, carton 454, 'La crise présidentielle libanaise', Beirut, 13 May 1932; MAE, Paris, Syrie et Liban, vol. 497, no. 337, Beirut, 23 April 1932, Ponsot to Tardieu; nos 1019–22, 21 April 1932; nos 1023–8, 25 April 1932; no. 320 and nos1029–32, Beirut, 4 May 1932, Ponsot to the Quai d'Orsay; 'Communiqué à la Presse', 9 May 1932; nos 1011–12, Paris, 23 April 1932, the Minister for Foreign Affairs to Ponsot. Jisr tried to convene the parliament on May 10, probably aware of Ponsot's intentions to dissolve it.

96.   MAE, Nantes, Syrie et Liban, carton 408, no. 613, Beirut, 29 July 1932, Delegate of the High Commissioner to the Quai d'Orsay; MAE, Paris, Syrie et Liban, vol. 482, no. 619, Beirut, 29 July 1932, Delegate of the High Commissioner to the Quai d'Orsay. See Zamir, 'Emile Eddé'.

97.   MAE, Nantes, Syrie et Liban, carton 411, anti-government pamphlets distributed among the Muslims in Beirut, 18 May 1932; Information no. 2394, Beirut, 19 May 1932.

98.   MAE, Nantes, Syrie et Liban, carton 2990, Service de la presse, no. 92, Beirut, 11 May 1932; Rens., Beirut, 11 May 1932; Information no. 2287, 11 May 1932; nos 2295 and 2307, 12 May 1932; MAE, Paris, Syrie et Liban, vol. 498, 'Accueil fait par l'opinion libanaise à la suspension de la constitution', Beirut, 30 May 1932; no. 381, Beirut, 10 May 1932, Ponsot to the Prime Minister; Arida's letter to Ponsot, Bkerki, 10 May 1932.

99.   MAE, Nantes, Syrie et Liban, carton 2990, Service de la presse, no. 92, Beirut, 11 May 1932; Information no. 2306, 12 May 1932.

100.   MAE, Nantes, Syrie et Liban, carton 2990, Information: 'Déclarations de M. Murr et de M. Aziz Hachem', Beirut, 13 May 1932.

101.   MAE, Paris, Syrie et Liban, vol. 498, no. 448, Beirut, 3 June 1932, Ponsot to the Quai d'Orsay.

102.   MAE, Paris, Syrie et Liban, vol. 498, no. 422, Beirut, 27 May 1932; no. 1042, 16 May 1932, Ponsot to the Quai d'Orsay.

103.   MAE, Nantes, Syrie et Liban, carton 1542, 'Aperçu général sur l'activité du gouvernement libanais depuis le 9 mai 1932'; carton 2990, Information: 'Déclarations de M. Aboussouen', 25 May 1932; Information: 'Déclarations de Sami Solh', Beirut, 26 May 1932; carton 411, Information no. 344, Ba'albeck, 25 June 1932. After protests by Lebanese officials, the staff of the High Commission also agreed to a wage reduction.

104.   MAE, Nantes, Syrie et Liban, carton 453, 'Révision de la Constitution libanaise'. In fact it was a departure from the March 1922 election law.

105.   MAE, Nantes, Syrie et Liban, carton 453, 'Révision de la Constitution libanaise' (2nd project). Dabbas proposed 50,000 instead of the 25,000 votes for one deputy, as suggested by Privat-Aubouard. Based on the 1932 census, the distribution between the various sects was as follows:

Sect	1922 (seats)	1932 (seats)
Sunnis	6	4
Shiites	5	3
Druze	2	1
Maronites	10	5
Greek Catholic	2	1
Greek Orthodox	4	2
Minorities	1	1
Total	30	17

106.   MAE, Nantes, Syrie et Liban, carton 938, Information no. 105, Beirut, 23 December 1932; no. 48, Damascus, 30 December 1932, Delegate of the High Commissioner to the Quai d'Orsay; carton 2990, Information no. 18, Beirut, 23 November 1932; MAE, Paris, Syrie et Liban, vol. 498, nos 376–7, Beirut, 27 May 1932, Ponsot to the Quai d'Orsay; no. 28, Damascus, 9 December 1932, Delegate of the High Commissioner to the Quai d'Orsay; no. 10, 18 January 1933, Ponsot to the Quai d'Orsay. Dabbas was frequently forced to suspend newspapers that attacked him. Khuri, *Haqa'iq lubnaniyya*, vol. 1, pp. 180–2.

107.   MAE, Nantes, Syrie et Liban, carton 364, Ponsot's testimony to the Mandates Commission; carton 832, Rapport de M. Pierre Alype, Paris, 17 March 1933; MAE, Paris, Syrie et Liban, vol.498, Beirut, 18 December 1932, pp. 181–4.

108.   MAE, Nantes, Syrie et Liban, carton 411, Information no. 208, Beirut, 30 March 1933; Information no. 2831, Beirut, 16 June 1932; carton 408, no. 613, Beirut, 29 July 1932, Delegate of the High Commissioner to the Quai d'Orsay; carton 2990, Information no. 139, Beirut, 30 December 1932; MAE, Paris, Syrie et Liban, vol. 482, no. 619, Beirut, 29 July 1932, Delegate of the High Commissioner to the Quai d'Orsay; vol. 498, 'Note sur le Parti de l'Indépendance républicaine', pp. 290–8.

109.   MAE, Paris, Syrie et Liban, vol. 498, 30 June 1933, pp. 300–4.

110.   MAE, Nantes, Syrie et Liban, carton 595, Information no. 9, Beirut, 9 January 1933; MAE, Paris, Syrie et Liban, vol. 510, no. 34, Beirut, 20 February 1933; Khuri, *Haqa'iq lubnaniyya*, vol. 1, pp. 182–3.

111.   MAE, Nantes, Syrie et Liban, carton 832, Ponsot to Pierre Alype, 14 January 1933; carton 452, Bishop Mubarak's memorandum 'Réformes demandées par les habitants de la montagne', 19 May 1932.

112.   MAE, Paris, Syrie et Liban, vol. 498, no. 40, Damascus, 17 February 1933, Ponsot to the Foreign Minister.

113.   MAE, Nantes, Syrie et Liban, carton 411, Information no. 214, Beirut, 30 March 1933; carton 938, Revue de la presse, no. 41, 20 February 1933; MAE, Paris, Syrie et Liban, vol. 498, no. 40, Damascus, 17 February 1933; no. 47, Beirut, 24 February 1933; no. 81, Beirut, 24 March 1933, Ponsot to the Quai d'Orsay; vol. 511, no. 212, Beirut, 29 May 1934, de Martel to the Quai d'Orsay.

114.   MAE, Nantes, Syrie et Liban, carton 938, Information no. 1461, 1 April 1933; 'Une interview de Mgr. Moubarak', Beirut, 7 March 1933; Information no. 254, 14 April 1933; MAE, Paris, Syrie et Liban, vol. 498, 'Rapport de Mgr.

Moubarak', Beirut, 15 March 1933; no. 93, Beirut, 31 March 1933, Ponsot to the Quai d'Orsay; Mubarak's letter, Beirut, 18 April 1933, pp. 283–5.

115.   MAE, Nantes, Syrie et Liban, carton 411, no. 28, 'Agitation pro-unitaire', Tripoli, 21 February 1933; Information no. 739, Beirut, 17 February 1933; carton 832, Beirut, 7 April 1933, Ponsot to Pierre Alype; carton 938, Revue de la presse, no. 46, 25 February and no. 51, 8 March 1933; carton 939, no. 103, Tripoli, 21 April 1933, Lafond to Ponsot; MAE, Paris, Syrie et Liban, vol. 498, no. 221, Beirut, 14 March 1933, Ponsot to the Quai d'Orsay.

116.   MAE, Nantes, Syrie et Liban, carton 938, Revue de la presse, no. 40, 22 February 1933; carton 595, no. 164, Beirut, 19 May 1933, Ponsot to the Quai d'Orsay.

117.   MAE, Paris, Syrie et Liban, vol. 483, no. 26, Beirut, 3 February 1933; vol. 484, no. 110, Beirut, 21 April 1933, Ponsot to the Quai d'Orsay; vol. 498, pp. 190, 239; MAE, Nantes, Syrie et Liban, carton 938, Revue de la presse, Damascus, no. 40, 22 February 1933.

118.   MAE, Paris, Syrie et Liban, vol. 498, no. 60, Beirut, 10 March 1933, Ponsot to the Quai d'Orsay.

119.   MAE, Nantes, Syrie et Liban, carton 938, Information no. 317, Beirut, 10 May 1933; carton 832, Beirut, 26 May 1933, Ponsot to Pierre Alype; MAE, Paris, Syrie et Liban, vol. 498, no. 82, Beirut, 24 March 1933, Ponsot to the Quai d'Orsay.

120.   MAE, Paris, Syrie et Liban, vol. 510, no. 210, 'Le patriarche maronite et les Juifs', Beirut, 16 June 1933. A second letter had been sent on 18 March. Mubarak's attack on Aql was published in an interview in *al-Itihad al-Lubnani*.

121.   MAE, Nantes, Syrie et Liban, carton 938, 'Note pour M. Chauvel', Beirut, 19 June 1933; carton 595, Information no. 216, Tripoli, 10 November 1933; MAE, Paris, Syrie et Liban, vol. 510, no. 88, Bkerki, 9 May 1933, Arida to Ponsot; no. 547,18 May 1933, Ponsot to Arida; no. 177, Beirut, 26 May 1933, Ponsot to the Quai d'Orsay; vol. 499, no. 241, 7 July, no. 262, 28 July 1933, Ponsot to the Quai d'Orsay.

122.   Khuri, *Haqa'iq lubnaniyya*, vol. 1, pp. 182–3.

123.   MAE, Nantes, Syrie et Liban, carton 411, Information no. 208, Beirut, 30 March 1933.

124.   MAE, Nantes, Syrie et Liban, carton 455, memorandum 'Au sujet du problème libanais', Paris, September 1933; MAE, Paris, Syrie et Liban, vol. 486, 'Note pour le Ministre', October 1933.

125.   MAE, Paris, Syrie et Liban, vol. 499, nos 810–19, Paris, 19 December 1933, Paul-Boncour to de Martel. On Paul-Boncour's role in the elaboration of the May 1926 constitution, see Zamir, *The Formation of Modern Lebanon*, pp. 203–6.

126.   MAE, Nantes, Syrie et Liban, de Martel's letter to Pierre Alype, Beirut, 8 December 1933; MAE, Paris, Syrie et Liban, vol. 499, no. 979, Beirut, 7 December 1933 and no. 391, 8 December 1933, de Martel to the Quai d'Orsay.

127.   MAE, Paris, Syrie et Liban, vol. 499, no. 380, 1 December 1933; nos 973–4, Beirut, 4 December 1933, de Martel to the Quai d'Orsay; MAE, Nantes, Syrie et Liban, de Martel's letter to Pierre Alype, Beirut, 8 December 1933.

128.   MAE, Paris, Syrie et Liban, vol. 499, no. 380, Beirut, 1 December 1933, de Martel to the French Foreign Minister; nos 810–19, Paris, 19 December 1933, Foreign Minister to de Martel. In 1925 Paul-Boncour had opposed Sarrail's attempts to impose an organic law on Lebanon and supported the Lebanese deputies's requests to elaborate their own constitution. See Zamir, *The Formation of Modern Lebanon*, pp. 205–6.

129.   MAE, Nantes, Syrie et Liban, carton 455, Information no. 567, Beirut, 5 December 1933.

130.   MAE, Nantes, Syrie et Liban, carton 455, Information no. 543, Beirut, 15 November 1933.

131.   MAE, Nantes, Syrie et Liban, carton 940, no. 1250, 'Enquête au sujet de quatre mazbatas en faveur de l'Unité Syrienne', Tripoli, 30 December 1933; carton 455, no. 50, Beirut, 2 February 1934, de Martel to the Quai d'Orsay; memorandum from the participants of the Conference of the Coast to de Martel, Beirut, 16 November 1933.

132.   MAE, Paris, Syrie et Liban, vol. 499, nos 1046–7, Beirut, 30 October 1933, de Martel to the Quai d'Orsay; MAE, Nantes, Syrie et Liban, carton 938, Information no. 516, Beirut, 24 October 1933; carton 962, Information no. 679, Ba'albeck, 7 December 1933.

133.   MAE, Nantes, Syrie et Liban, carton 938, Information no. 7523, Beirut, 4 December 1933; MAE, Paris, Syrie et Liban, vol. 499, no. 979, Beirut, 7 December and no. 391, 8 December 1933, de Martel to the Quai d'Orsay.

134.   Eddé had apparently reached an understanding with Sa'ad that he would back the latter's candidacy, as Sa'ad had a better chance of defeating Khuri.

135.   MAE, Nantes, Syrie et Liban, carton 938, Note: 'Patriarchat maronite et les élections', Beirut, 1 December 1933; Information no. 7523, Beirut, 4 December 1933; carton 455, Information no. 563, Beirut, 4 December 1933; carton 962, Information no. 679, Ba'albeck, 7 December 1933.

136.   MAE, Nantes, Syrie et Liban, carton 941, 'Note sur les prochaines élections', Beirut, 10 October 1933.

137.   MAE, Nantes, Syrie et Liban, carton 938, Note, 13 December 1933; carton 941, 'Note sur les prochaines élections', Beirut, 10 October 1933; carton 455, no. 93, Beirut, 24 December 1933, de Martel to Saint-Quentin.

138.   MAE, Nantes, Syrie et Liban, carton 455, Information no. 569, Beirut, 5 December 1933; carton 1542, Information, Beirut, 21 December 1933; carton 832, de Martel's letter to Pierre Alype, Beirut, 15 December 1933; MAE, Paris, Syrie et Liban, vol. 499, no. 979, Beirut, 7 December 1933; no. 391, Beirut, 8 December 1933, de Martel to the Quai d'Orsay; 'Résumé d'une dépêche du 5 décembre 1933', Beirut, 13 December 1933; no. 397, 15 December 1933; nos 1203–6, 16 December 1933; and nos 1237–41, Beirut, 24 December 1933, de Martel to the Quai

d'Orsay; no. 836, Paris, 25 December 1933, Minister for Foreign Affairs to de Martel.

139.   MAE, Paris, Syrie et Liban, vol. 499, no. 1244, Beirut, 26 December 1933, de Martel to the Quai d'Orsay; no. 841, Paris, 26 December 1933; nos 844–5, Paris, 28 December 1933, Minister for Foreign Affairs to de Martel; nos 1–5, Beirut, 2 January 1934, de Martel to the Quai d'Orsay; Dabbas' letter of resignation to de Martel, Beirut, 2 January 1934; MAE, Nantes, Syrie et Liban, carton 832, de Martel's letter to Pierre Alype, Beirut, 29 December 1933.

140.   MAE, Nantes, Syrie et Liban, carton 832, de Martel's letter to Pierre Alype, Beirut, 4 January 1934.

141.   MAE, Nantes, Syrie et Liban, carton 396, Report with details of elected deputies, 25 January 1934.

142.   MAE, Nantes, Syrie et Liban, carton 1542, minutes of meetings at the High Commission concerning the elections, 8 and 15 January 1934; carton 397, 'Procès-verbal de la réunion tenue le 25 janvier 1934 dans le cabinet du Haut Commissaire au sujet des élections libanaises'; carton 832, de Martel's letter to Pierre Alype, Beirut, 12 January 1934; MAE, Paris, Syrie et Liban, vol. 499, no. 19, Beirut, 12 January 1934, de Martel to the Quai d'Orsay. The large Sunni communities in Beirut and Tripoli were represented by one deputy each, as were the smaller communities in Akkar and the Beqa. The French preferred to allow the peripheral regions to elect their own representatives, as they were better able to influence the results. On the other hand, they nominated the Sunni deputies in the south for fear that the influential Sulh family in the Sidon area might promote its own candidate.

143.   MAE, Nantes, Syrie et Liban, carton 941, 'Note sur les prochaines élections', Beirut, 10 October 1933.

144.   MAE, Nantes, Syrie et Liban, carton 455, 'Note du Commandant Pechkof, chargé de mission au Liban Sud', Beirut, 16 and 30 December 1933; 'Note au sujet de la situation électorale dans la Bekaa au 14 décembre 1933'; carton 938, Information no. 7620, Beirut, 11 December 1933. The High Commission ceased supporting Yusuf a-Zein following his role in the presidential crisis and increasing criticism from his community. Latif al-As'ad was considered weak and the High Commission was suspicious of his ties with Riad al-Sulh. French intervention in Tripoli increased the tension between Karameh and Bisar as the Muqadams were related to latter's family.

145.   MAE, Nantes, Syrie et Liban, carton 397, 'Procès-verbal de la réunion tenue le 25 janvier 1934 dans le cabinet du Haut Commissaire au sujet des élections libanaises'; MAE, Paris, Syrie et Liban, vol. 499, 'Entretien avec Riad Solh', Beirut, 12 January 1934.

146.   MAE, Nantes, Syrie et Liban, carton 938, Information no. 7612, 11 December 1933; Information no. 7626, Beirut, 12 December 1933; carton 940, Information no. 284, 25 January 1934; no. 306, 27 January 1934; no. 317, 29 January 1934. Yafi was reimbursed by Husain al-Ahdab, Omar Bayhum and Henri Pharaon for his expenses in the election campaign.

147.   Dabbas' nomination was opposed by the Greek Orthodox leaders in Beirut, especially by the influential Sursuk family, which supported Petro Trad, and by Jubran Tuaini and Khalil abu-Shahla, who had also competed for this seat.

148.   MAE, Paris, Syrie et Liban, vol. 499, no. 38, 26 January 1934, and nos 79–83, Beirut, 30 January 1934, de Martel to the Quai d'Orsay; MAE, Nantes, Syrie et Liban, carton 396, Report with details of elected deputies, 25 January 1934; carton 832, de Martel's letter to Pierre Alype, Beirut, 26 January 1934. For minutes of the parliamentary session see carton 941.

149.   MAE, Nantes, Syrie et Liban, carton 960, Memorandum by de Martel, 31 January 1934.

150.   Shirer, *The Collapse of the Third Republic*, pp. 205–10.

151.   MAE, Nantes, Syrie et Liban, carton 367, no. 181, 'Commission d'Etudes de la Défense des Territoires sous Mandat: Procès-verbal de la séance du 6 mars 1934'; carton 832, de Martel's letter to Pierre Alype, Beirut, 23 February 1934; MAE, Paris, Syrie et Liban, vol. 488, 'Communiqué à la presse de Damas', Damascus, 5 July 1934; vol. 838, Note de Service no. 83, Beirut, 12 June 1934; vol. 252, no. 153, 'Note pour M. le Conseiller du Haut Commissariat au Relations Extérieures', Beirut, 14 March 1933.

152.   MAE, Nantes, Syrie et Liban, carton 926, Information:'Fakhri al-Barudi', Beirut, 4 February 1934; MAE, Paris, Syrie et Liban, vol. 499, 'Le problème libanais', November 1933.

153.   Khoury, *Syria and the French Mandate*, pp. 441–4.

154.   MAE, Nantes, Syrie et Liban, carton 940, Information no. 367, Beirut, 31 January 1934; carton 409, no. 58, Beirut, 9 February 1934, the delegate of the High Commissioner to the Quai d'Orsay; carton 959, Information, Beirut, 9 February 1934; carton 411, Information no. 2308, 27 June 1934.

155.   MAE, Nantes, Syrie et Liban, carton 606, memorandum to de Martel from the Sunni Mufti concerning inequality of the Muslims in the administration, Beirut, 3 April 1934; petition from Sunni notables to de Martel, Beirut, 23 November 1934; Information no. 210, Beirut, 12 December 1934; carton 833, Information no. 1842, Beirut, 23 May 1934; carton 456, Letter from Elias Saliby, Greek Orthodox Archbishop of Beirut, to de Martel, Beirut, 9 July 1934.

156.   MAE, Nantes, Syrie et Liban, carton 455, 'Note du Commandant Pechkof, chargé de mission au Liban Sud', Beirut, 16 December 1933; carton 1933, Petition by 37 Shiite notables to de Martel, 14 December 1933; carton 940, Information no. 579, Beirut, 30 December 1933.

157.   MAE, Nantes, Syrie et Liban, carton 397, 'Compte rendu des deux réunions tenues à Saida et à Kfar Roummane le 23 et 24 février, 1934.'

158.   MAE, Nantes, Syrie et Liban, carton 2424, Information: 'Mufti chiite', Ba'albeck, 13 April 1933; carton 455, Information no. 3:'Les voeux de la population du Liban Sud', Sidon, 9 March 1934; carton 456, 'Visite des deux députés chiites du Liban Sud. Desiderata des Chiites', Note, Administrative adviser in South Lebanon, Sidon, 15 September 1934; carton 607, Information no. 101, Beirut, 17 May 1934; carton 411, Information no. 66, Damascus, 24 September 1934.

159.   MAE, Nantes, Syrie et Liban, carton 1542, 'Conseil des Directeurs', Beirut, 26 March 1934; carton 402, Bulletin d'Information no. 18, Beirut, 31 May 1934.

160.   MAE, Nantes, Syrie et Liban, carton 941, no. 872, 'Compte rendu succint de la séance de la Chambre des Députés en date du 20 mars, 1934'; carton 832, de Martel's letter to Pierre Alype, Beirut, 23 March 1934; carton 926, Information no. 3558, Beirut, 23 October 1934. Eddé succeeded in increasing the number of deputies allied to him in the parliament from three to six, including Ahdab.

161.   MAE, Nantes, Syrie et Liban, carton 1542, *Le Jour* (Beirut), 2, 6 and 7 August 1934.

162.   MAE, Nantes, Syrie et Liban, carton 943, 'Visite de Mgr. Mobarak', Beirut, 17 August 1934; 'Extrait de la lettre avion addressée au Département sous le no. 594, du 17 août 1934'; carton 455, Letter from Bishop Mubarak to de Martel, Beirut, 23 September 1934; carton 940, Information no. 203, Beirut, 22 November 1934.

163.   On the close cooperation between Khuri and the commercial and financial sectors in Beirut see Traboulsi, *Identités et solidarités*, vol. 1, pp. 253–6, 283. See Khuri, *Haqa'iq lubnaniyya*, vol. 1, pp. 189–90. In his memoirs Khuri avoided mentioning Chamoun's role in the establishment of the Constitutional Bloc.

164.   MAE, Nantes, Syrie et Liban, carton 455, Memorandum from Michel Zakur, Farid al-Khazin and Camille Chamoun to de Martel, 28 October 1934. In an attempt to conceal the role played by Chamoun, Khuri claimed in his memoirs that the events marking the establishment of the Constitutional Bloc took place in March 1934, when the issue of the restoration of the constitution was raised in the new parliament by Khazin. In fact, the first to raise this issue had been Ibrahim Munzer. See *Haqa'iq lubnaniyya*, vol. I, pp. 189–90. See also carton 941, no. 872, 'Compte rendu succint de la séance de la Chambre des Députés en date du 20 mars 1934'; carton 497, no. 1249, 'Compte rendu succint de la séance de la Chambre des Députés en date du 23 avril 1934'.

165.   MAE, Nantes, Syrie et Liban, carton 833, Information no. 522, Beirut, 9 February 1934.

166.   MAE, Nantes, Syrie et Liban, carton 455, de Martel's note to the Quai d'Orsay, Beirut, 30 September 1934.

167.   MAE, Nantes, Syrie et Liban, carton 940, Information: 'Conversation entre le patriarche maronite et M. Alphonse Ayoub', Beirut, 2 May 1934; MAE, Paris, Syrie et Liban, vol. 511, no. 393, Beirut, 22 June 1934, de Martel to the Quai d'Orsay.

168.   MAE, Nantes, Syrie et Liban, carton 596, 'Visite au patriarche maronite le 2 mai', Beirut, 4 May 1934; MAE, Paris, Syrie et Liban, vol. 511, no.191, Beirut, 18 May 1934, de Martel to Saint-Quentin (Ministre Plénipotentiaire, Sous-Directeur d'Afrique-Levant, in the Quai d'Orsay); vol. 595, 'Visite à Mgr. Arida', Beirut, 28 July 1934.

169.   MAE, Nantes, Syrie et Liban, carton 455, note no. 424, Sidon, 6 November 1934; carton 942, Information no. 272, 26 January 1935; MAE, Paris, Syrie et Liban, vol. 489, no. 89, Beirut, 25 January 1935, and vol. 490, no. 139, Beirut, 8 February 1935, de Martel to the Quai d'Orsay; Khuri, *Haqa'iq lubnaniyya*, vol. 1, pp. 443–4.

170.   MAE, Paris, Syrie et Liban, vol. 489, no. 89, Beirut, 25 January 1935, and vol. 490, no. 139, Beirut, 8 February 1935, de Martel to the Quai d'Orsay; Arslan, *Mudhakkirat*, vol. 1, p. 76.

171.   Al-Batriyark Antun Arida, *Lubnan wa Faransa* (Beirut, 1987). See introduction by Mas'ud Dahir.

172.   Elias Gannage, *L'Imposition des Tabacs au Liban*, (Beirut, 1956).

173.   MAE, Paris, Syrie et Liban, vol. 498, no. 446, Beirut, 3 June 1932, Ponsot to the Quai d'Orsay. For a extensive study of the tobacco industry in Lebanon see Gannage, *L'Imposition des Tabacs*, p. 104. Under the Régie, total annual production in the mandated territories was 3,250,000 kg. distributed as follows: Lebanon - 1.5 million; Syria and Latakia - 1.5 million; Alexandretta - 250,000. In 1932 production was doubled to 6 m kg: Lebanon - 2 m; Latakia 2.5 million; Syria - 1 million; Alexandretta - 500,000. In September 1932 a quota was fixed: Lebanon - 880,000; Syria and Alexandretta - 300,000; the Allawite region - 1 million.

174.   MAE, Nantes, Syrie et Liban, carton 941, no. 3893, 'Compte rendu succint de la séance de la Chambre des Députés en date du 4 décembre 1934'. A delegation met Bastide and asked him to help prevent the restoration of the monopoly. Tension increased following a particularly violent strike by butchers in Zahleh in protest against the high municipal taxes; carton 942, Information, 25 March, 1935; MAE, Paris, Syrie et Liban, vol. 489, no. 89, Beirut, 25 January 1935, and vol. 490, no. 139, Beirut, 8 February 1935, de Martel to the Quai d'Orsay.

175.   MAE, Nantes, Syrie et Liban, carton 457, Memorandum on a conversation with Patriarch Arida in Bkerki on January 12 1935, Beirut, 13 January 1935; carton 596, Information, Beirut, 24 January 1935.

176.   MAE, Nantes, Syrie et Liban, carton 595, no. 1213, Beirut, 7 February 1935, de Martel to Arida.

177.   MAE, Nantes, Syrie et Liban, carton 1066, Detailed file on tobacco monopoly, 1934/35; carton 457, no. 383, Beirut, 12 April 1935, de Martel to the Quai d'Orsay; no. 540, 17 May 1935, Lagarde to the Quai d'Orsay; carton 595, no. 865, Beirut, 16 August 1935, Lagarde to the Foreign Minister; carton 942, no. 1057, minutes of the parliamentary meeting of 17 April 1935. Particularly active were Khalil Ma'atuk and Yusuf al-Sawda. The former helped finance and organize the campaign against the monopoly, while the latter exploited his position as Arida's adviser to steer him into pursuing a nationalist and anti-French stand. See for example a detailed report compiled by Sawda and sent by Arida to de Martel in MAE, Paris, Syrie et Liban, vol. 513, Beirut, 1 March 1935, pp. 58–72.

178.   MAE, Nantes, Syrie et Liban, carton 943, Information no. 181, 29 September 1934; carton 942, Information no. 113, 1 March 1935.

179.   MAE, Nantes, Syrie et Liban, carton 1542, Information, 4 February 1935; carton 961, Information no. 827, 12 March 1935; carton 456, Note no. 197, Saida, 2 April 1935; carton 457, nos 107–8, Beirut, 15 February and nos 115–17, 17 February 1935, de Martel to the Quai d'Orsay; MAE, Paris, Syrie et Liban, vol. 500, no. 370, Beirut, 5 April 1935, de Martel to the Quai d'Orsay.

180.   MAE, Nantes, Syrie et Liban, carton 961, intelligence reports for February/March; Information no. 104, Damascus, 25 February 1935; Information no. 111, Damascus, 28 February 1935; Information no. 707, 1 March 1935; MAE, Paris, Syrie et Liban, vol. 490, no. 392, Beirut, 12 April 1935, de Martel to the Foreign Minister.

181.   MAE, Paris, Syrie et Liban, vol. 490, no. 392, Beirut, 12 April 1935, de Martel to the Quai d'Orsay; vol. 500, no. 482, Beirut, 3 May 1935, the High Commission to the Quai d'Orsay. Mardam cynically proposed to French officials that he mediate between Arida and de Martel. See also Barudi's letter to the High Commission after being forced to leave Beirut. MAE, Nantes, Syrie et Liban, carton 596, Information, 11 March 1935; carton 942, Information no. 72, 9 January 1935.

182.   MAE, Nantes, Syrie et Liban, carton 457, no. 58, Beirut, 18 January 1935, de Martel to the Quai d'Orsay; carton 595, no. 1213, Beirut, 7 February 1935, de Martel to Arida; no. 200, Bkerki, 1 March 1935, Arida to Laval; no. 591, Beirut, 24 May 1935, Lagarde to Laval; no. 713, 28 June 1935, de Martel to the Quai d'Orsay; carton 596, report on a meeting with Arida, Beirut, 9 March 1935; MAE, Paris, Syrie et Liban, vol. 500, 'Situation politique du Liban', Paris, 20 April 1935; vol. 513, no. 208, Bkerki, 15 April 1935, Arida to Laval.

183.   MAE, Nantes, Syrie et Liban, carton 834, de Martel's declaration, Paris, 30 March 1935; Paris, 28 May, 1935, de Martel to Kieffer; carton 595, Paris, 9 May 1935, Léger to Arida.

184.   MAE, Paris, Syrie et Liban, vol. 500, no. 370, Beirut, 5 April 1935, and no. 383, 12 April 1935, de Martel to the Quai d'Orsay; vol. 490, no. 648, Beirut, 14 June 1935, de Martel to Laval; MAE, Nantes, Syrie et Liban, carton 607, file on Muqadam's killing by Karameh; Information no. 1873, 17 June 1935; carton 596, Barudi's letter to de Martel, Damascus, 10 February 1935; Khairiya Qasimiya, *Al-ra'il al-arabi al-awal*, (London 1991), p. 268, Riad al-Sulh's letter to Nabih al-Azma, Beirut, 27 July 1935.

185.   MAE, Paris, Syrie et Liban, vol. 500, no. 276, Paris, 21 March 1935, the Quai d'Orsay to de Martel.

186.   MAE, Paris, Syrie et Liban, vol. 491, 'Fakri Baroudi et les manoeuvres des nationalistes de Damas', pp. 19–20; vol. 513, no. 24, Beirut, 10 January 1936, de Martel to the Foreign Minister; MAE, Nantes, Syrie et Liban, carton 596, Barudi's letter to de Martel, Damascus, 10 February 1935; Information no. 76, Damascus, 11 February 1935.

187.   Murad, *Al-harakat al-wahdawiyya*, pp. 228–33; Solh, *Lebanon and Arab Nationalism*, pp. 20–21.

188.   MAE, Nantes, Syrie et Liban, carton 607, Information no. 2032, 3 July 1935; Khuri, *Haqa'iq lubnaniyya*, vol. 1, p. 193.

189.   MAE, Paris, Syrie et Liban, vol. 513, no. 270, Beirut, 8 March; no. 310, 23 March, and no. 343,18 June 1935, de Martel to Laval; MAE, Nantes, Syrie et Liban, carton 595, Information no. 544, 18 February 1935; carton 457, Beirut, 10 April 1935, report by Lafond, the French delegate to Lebanon, on his meeting with Arida, and 'Note Pour L'Ambassadeur', Beirut, 8 May 1935.

190.   MAE, Paris, Syrie et Liban, vol. 513, no. 391, Beirut, 12 April 1935, de Martel to Laval; MAE, Nantes, Syrie et Liban, carton 595, nos 315–17, Beirut, 11 June 1935, de Martel to the Quai d'Orsay; nos 284–8, Paris, 13 June, and nos 341–4, 14 July 1935, the Quai d'Orsay to de Martel; Paris, 24 June 1935, the Prime Minister to the French Ambassador to the Vatican; Rome, 26 July 1935, Charles-Roux to the Quai d'Orsay; report by Lt. Colonel Baron on his meeting with Arida, 17 June 1935.

191.   MAE, Nantes, Syrie et Liban, carton 595, Report on Bishop Pharès' visit to the Quai d'Orsay, Paris, 28 August 1935; no. 749, Paris, 9 September 1935, the Prime Minister and Foreign Minister to Lagarde; MAE, Paris, Syrie et Liban, vol. 514, no. 1086, Beirut, 1 November 1935, nos 646–7, 20 November 1935, no. 1289, 27 December 1935, and no. 122, 31 January 1936, de Martel to the Foreign Minister; vol. 1542, no. 1110, Beirut, 8 November 1935, de Martel to the Foreign Minister.

192.   MAE, Nantes, Syrie et Liban, carton 595, no. 866, Paris, 17 October 1935, the Prime Minister and Foreign Minister to Lagarde; no. 900, Paris, 24 October 1935, the Prime Minister to de Martel; vol. 943, Rens., Beirut, 3 September 1935; MAE, Paris, Syrie et Liban, vol. 514, no. 1030, Beirut, 18 October 1935, no. 622, 7 November 1935, and no. 76, 23 January 1936, de Martel to the Quai d'Orsay; nos 554–5, Paris, 8 November 1935, the Foreign Minister to de Martel.

193.   MAE, Nantes, Syrie et Liban, carton 595, 'Note pour l'Ambassadeur', Beirut, 18 October 1935; no. 3895, Beirut, 31 October 1935, Lafond to de Martel; MAE, Paris, Syrie et Liban, vol. 514, no. 6, Beirut, 3 January 1936, de Martel to the Foreign Minister.

194.   MAE, Nantes, Syrie et Liban, carton 943, for details on the elections see file:'La question présidentielle au Liban'; carton 364, no. 2889, Beirut, 2 April 1935, de Martel's note to the French delegate in Lebanon; 'Note pour les délégués et les délégués-adjoints', Beirut, 13 July 1935; carton 457, Bishop Feghali's visit, 22 July, 1935; Bishop Khuri's visit, 23 October 1935; Bishop Mubarak's visit, 24 October 1935.

195.   MAE, Nantes, Syrie et Liban, carton 942, no. 3785, minutes of the parliamentary meeting of 22 October 1935; carton 943, Information no. 2861, 15 October and no. 2898, 18 October 1935; carton 606, Note, October 1935; carton 457, no. 1156, Beirut, 22 November 1935, de Martel to the Quai d'Orsay; Khuri, *Haqa'iq lubnaniyya*, vol. 1, pp. 193–4.

196.   MAE, Paris, Syrie et Liban, vol. 501, no. 7, Beirut, 3 January and no. 25, 10 January 1936, de Martel to the Foreign Minister. The election was to coincide

with the introduction of administrative reforms for decentralization, presuming the Syrian politicians would be busy with the reforms and would not have the time to intervene.

197.   MAE, Nantes, Syrie et Liban, carton 457, no. 1248, Beirut, 14 December 1935, de Martel to the Quai d'Orsay.

198.   MAE, Nantes, Syrie et Liban, carton 943, file: 'La question présidentielle au Liban', Information no. 993, 28 February 1935; no. 2257, 3 August 1935; no. 2739, 30 September 1935; no. 2959, 24 October 1935; no. 3016, 30 October 1935; no. 3482, 18 December 1935.

199.   MAE, Nantes, Syrie et Liban, carton 943, Information no. 2861, 15 October 1935; report on Eddé's and Ma'atuk's meeting with Sa'ad on 13 December; Information no. 3328, 2 December, no. 3357, 5 December, and no. 3432, 12 December 1935. In an attempt to persuade the deputies from the Beqa to withdraw their support of Khuri, Eddé proposed that if he failed, he would back Musa Namur in the second ballot. His intiative however, was blocked by Khuri who made Namur a similar proposal.

200.   MAE, Nantes, Syrie et Liban, carton 943, Information no. 3482, 18 December 1935. A particularly popular tactic was to bribe deputies with cars.

201.   MAE, Nantes, Syrie et Liban, carton 944, no. 1260, 19 December 1935; no. 1272, Beirut, 20 December 1935, de Martel to the Quai d'Orsay; carton 943, Information no. 3560, 16 December 1935; carton 457 no. 370, Beirut, 12 December 1935, Khalid Shihab to de Martel; no. 1282, Beirut, 27 December 1935, de Martel to the Quai d'Orsay; carton 1542, no. 3136, 12 November 1935; MAE, Paris, Syrie et Liban, vol. 491, no. 604, Paris, 21 November and no. 661, 11 December 1935, Leger to de Martel; nos 705–6, Beirut, 7 December 1935, de Martel to the Quai d'Orsay; Khuri, *Haqa'iq lubnaniyya*, vol. 1, pp. 194–5.

202.   MAE, Nantes, Syrie et Liban, carton 943, details on the political maneouvres and intrigues can be found in the file on the elections; Information, 3 January, no. 33, 4 January, Information, 13 January, no. 155, 16 January and no. 157, 17 January 1936; Khuri, *Haqa'iq lubnaniyya*, vol. 1, pp. 195–6.

203.   MAE, Nantes, Syrie et Liban, carton 943, no. 169, Minutes of the parliamentary session of 20 January 1936; MAE, Paris, Syrie et Liban, vol. 501, no. 41, 20 January 1936, and no. 84, 24 January 1936, de Martel to the Quai d'Orsay. See de Martel's denial of any intervention in the elections. In his memoirs Khuri gives different results: in the first ballot 13 voted for Eddé and 12 for him, and in the second ballot, 14 for Eddé and 11 for him. Khuri, *Haqa'iq lubnaniyya*, vol. 1, pp. 196–7.

204.   MAE, Paris, Syrie et Liban, vol. 501, no. 84, Beirut, 24 January 1936, and no. 120, 31 January 1936, de Martel to the Quai d'Orsay.

205.   MAE, Paris, Syrie et Liban, vol. 501, no. 120, Beirut, 31 January and no. 215, 28 February 1936, de Martel to the Quai d'Orsay; MAE, Nantes, Syrie et Liban, carton 943, Information no. 208, 23 January 1936; Khuri, *Haqa'iq lubnaniyya*, vol. 1, pp. 197–8.

Chapter Four

1.   MAE, Guerre, 1939–1945, London, CNF, vol. 43, 'Projects des Traités Franco–syriens et Franco–Libanais de 1936', January 1943; 'Les relations de la France et de la Syrie', conference held at the Centre d'Etudes de Politique Etrangère in February and March 1939 attended by Pierre Viénot and the senators Henry-Haye and Bergeon, members of the Senate Foreign Affairs Commission, in document no. 212.092 CHEAM; Pierre Viénot 'Le traité franco–syrien', pamphlet containing four articles published in the French newspaper *Le Populaire*, 11–14 January, 1939.

2.   Claudio G. Segré,'Liberal and Facist Italy in the Middle East, 1919–1939: The Elusive White Stallion' in Dann, *The Great Powers*, pp. 199–212. On the emergence of pan-Arabism see reports by Sir Miles Lampson, the British High Commissioner in Egypt, Cairo, 24 February 1936 and Gilbert MacKereth, the British Consul in Damascus, 4 March 1936, in Michael G. Fry and Itamar Rabinovich, *Despatches from Damascus: Gilbert MacKereth and British Policy in the Levant, 1933–1939* (Tel Aviv, 1985), pp. 122–40. See also M. Cohen and M. Kolinsky (eds) *Britain and the Middle East in the 1930s: Security Problems* (London, 1992), pp. 21–40.

3.   Shirer, *The Collapse of the Third Republic*, pp. 247–50, 281–4; Kennedy, *The Rise and Fall of the Great Powers*, pp. 401–7, 434–7.

4.   Monroe, *The Mediterranean in Politics*, pp. 71–6.

5.   Monroe, *The Mediterranean in Politics*, pp. 77–89; Arnold J. Toynbee, *Survey of International Affairs 1936* (London, 1937), pp. 753–4.

6.   *ibid*; Rabinovich, I.,'Oil and Local Politics: The French-Iraqi Negotiations of the Early 1930s', in Dann, *The Great Powers*, pp. 172–82.

7.   MAE, Paris, Syrie et Liban, vol. 490, de Martel's memorandum, Paris, 12 March 1935; no. 276, Paris, 19 March 1935, Foreign Minister to de Martel.

8.   MAE, Paris, Syrie et Liban, vol. 491, no. 589/3, Huntziger's memorandum, 6 May, and Rivet's memorandum, Beirut, 9 May 1935.

9.   MAE, Paris, Syrie et Liban, vol. 491, no. 2953, Paris, 31 October 1935, the Prime Minister and Foreign Minister to the Minister of War.

10.   MAE, Paris, Syrie et Liban, vol. 491, no. 1058, Beirut, 25 October 1935, de Martel to the Foreign Minister. See also report by Gilbert MacKereth, the British Consul in Damascus, to Eden, Damascus, 31 January 1936, in Fry and Rabinovich, *Despatches from Damascus*, pp. 115–18.

11.   MAE, Nantes, Syrie et Liban, carton 927, no. 169, Beirut, 16 February 1936, de Martel to the Foreign Minister; MAE, Paris, Syrie et Liban, vol. 493, report on the Franco–Syrian negotiations, Paris, 7 July 1936.

12.   *ibid.*; Marcel Homet, *Syrie terre irrédente: l'histoire secrète du traité franco–syrien* (Paris, 1938), p. 102; MaKereth's report to the Foreign Office, Damsacus, 24 February 1936, in Fry and Rabinovich, *Despatches from Damascus*, pp. 121–2.

13.   MAE, Paris, Syrie et Liban, vol. 492,'Note pour le cabinet du Ministère, Paris, 19 May 1936;'Note de M. de Martel', 3 June 1936; vol. 493, report on the Franco–Syrian negotiations, Paris, 7 July 1936.

14.   MAE, Guerre, 1939–1945, London, CNF, vol. 43, 'Projects des Traités Franco–syriens et Franco–Libanais de 1936', January 1943; FO 371/20065 2656/195 no. 46, Beirut, 5 May 1936, Havard to Eden; Qasimiya, *Al-ra'il al-arabi al-awal*, pp. 282–3, Riad al-Sulh's letter to Nabih al-Azma on the negotiations in Paris, 7 April 1936.

15.   MAE, Paris, Syrie et Liban, vol. 502, 'Note verbale: Organisation future des Etats du Levant - Maintien d'un établissement naval sur les côtes de Syrie' by Fernet, commander of the naval division in the Levant, Beirut, 2 October 1936, and the Quai d'Orsay's reply. The Haut-Comité Méditerranéen was an interministerial body formed to coordinate French policy in North Africa and the Levant.

16.   MAE, Paris, Syrie et Liban, vol. 492, no. 585, Beirut, 28 May 1936, Meyrier to the Foreign Minister; vol. 493, report on the Franco–Syrian negotiations, Paris, 7 July 1936; Qasimiya, *Al-ra'il al-arabi al-awal*, p. 67.

17.   MAE, Paris, Syrie et Liban, vol. 492, Hashem al-Atasi to de Martel, Paris, 30 May 1936; Qasimiya, *Al-ra'il al-arabi al-awal*, pp. 284–5, Kuwatli's letter to Nabih al-Azma, Damascus, 4 June 1936.

18.   MAE, Paris, Syrie et Liban, vol. 493, no. 993, Paris, 29 June 1936, Minister of the Navy to the Foreign Minister. On the Blum government's colonial polcy see William B. Cohen, 'The Colonial Policy of the Popular Front', *French Historical Studies*, vol. 7, 1972, pp. 368–93.

19.   MAE, Paris, Syrie et Liban, vol. 492, de Caix's memorandum 'La commission des mandats et le futur traité franco–syrien', Paris, June 1936; vol. 493, 'Aide mémoire des représentants officiels au pays alaouites', August 1936; no. 993, Paris, 29 June 1936, Minister of the Navy to the Foreign Minister; FO 371/20066 3794/195 no. 802, Paris, 22 June 1936, Sir G. Clerk to Eden.

20.   MAE, Paris, Syrie et Liban, vol. 493, Report on the Franco–Syrian negotiations, Paris, 7 July 1936; vol. 590, no. 566, Beirut, 3 July, Meyrier to the Quai d'Orsay.

21.   MAE, Paris, Syrie et Liban, vol. 478, 'Délégation de la République syrienne: études critiques des projets français', Paris, 11 June 1936. For Sulh's initiative to raise the issue of Syria's access to a port, see vol. 492, note 10 June, and vol. 493, note 25 June 1936; MAE, Nantes, Syrie et Liban, carton 364, 'Notes sur les négociations franco–syriens', Paris, 13 June 1936.

22.   MAE, Paris, Syrie et Liban, vol. 502, 'Note verbale: Organisation future des Etats du Levant - Maintien d'un établissement naval sur les côtes de Syrie' by Fernet, commander of the naval division in the Levant, Beirut, 2 October 1936, and the Quai d'Orsay's reply; vol. 492, Massignon's memorandum in which he proposed granting Tripoli a special status, 10 June 1936.

23.   MAE, Nantes, Syrie et Liban, carton 457, Information no. 2510, Beirut, 15 June 1936.

24.   MAE, Nantes, Syrie et Liban, carton 411, Information no. 772, Beirut, 5 March 1936; MAE, Paris, Syrie et Liban, vol. 492, nos 508–13, Beirut, 17 June, and vol. 590, no. 566, Beirut, 3 July, Meyrier to the Quai d'Orsay.

25.   MAE, Nantes, Syrie et Liban, carton 411, Information no. 861, Beirut, 11 March 1936; Hallaq, *Mu'atamar al-sahil*, pp. 43–64.

26.   MAE, Nantes, Syrie et Liban, carton 411, no. 467, Beirut, 30 April 1936, Meyrier to the Foreign Minister; Information no. 852, Beirut, 10 March 1936; no. 59, 'Agitation pro-unitaire', Tripoli, 17 March 1936, the Administrative Adviser in North Lebanon to the Delegate in Lebanon.

27.   MAE, Nantes, Syrie et Liban, carton 411, no. 973, Beirut, 2 April 1936, Lafond to Meyrier; no. 176, 'Evénements de Beint Jbail', Sidon, 4 April 1936; no. 191, Sidon, 11 April, no. 194, 15 April, no. 199, 17 April, and no. 204, 20 April 1936; FO 371/20069 3128/2746 no. 51, Beirut, 21 May 1936, Havard to Eden.

28.   MAE, Nantes, Syrie et Liban, carton 411, Information no. 769, Beirut, 5 March; no. 859, 10 March; no. 891, 12 March, and no. 951, 17 March 1936; carton 457, 'Situation au Liban', Beirut, 6 March 1936, de Martel to the Foreign Minister; Homet, *Syrie terre irrédente*, pp. 105–6; Hallaq, *Mu'atamar al-sahil*, pp. 66–7, Salam's letter to Hashem al-Atasi, 14 March 1936, and Atasi's reply.

29.   Khazim al-Sulh, 'Mushkilat al-infisal wa'l ittisal', Hallaq, *Mu'atamar al-sahil*, pp. 63–4, 73–89.

30.   MAE, Nantes, Syrie et Liban, carton 490, letter from Bishop Mubarak to de Martel, Beirut, 4 March 1936; carton 457, 'Situation au Liban', Beirut, 6 March 1936, de Martel to the Foreign Minister; FO 371/20065 1716/195 no. 11, 10 March, and 1516/195 no. 13, Aleppo, 14 March 1936, Consul-General Parr to Eden.

31.   MAE, Nantes, Syrie et Liban, carton 596, 'Livre vert du Patriarche', Beirut, 24 February 1936; carton 961, Information no. 327, Beirut, 3 February 1936; carton 595, no. 124, Paris, 30 April 1936, Foreign Minister to Charles Roux; report on Bishop Mubarak's visit to the Quai d'Orsay, Paris, 26 May 1936; J. Tabet, 'Pour sauver l'entente Franco–Libanaise', Paris, 1937 (pamphlet). Ben-Gurion Archives, Sede Boker (henceforth BGA), Correspondence, Dov Yosef's memorandum on a visit to Paris, including a conversation with Bishop Mubarak, London, 14 June 1936.

32.   MAE, Paris, Syrie et Liban, vol. 501, no. 215, Beirut, 28 February 1936, de Martel to the Foreign Minister; MAE, Nantes, Syrie et Liban, carton 457, no. 237, Beirut, 6 March 1936, de Martel to the Quai d'Orsay; no. 2003/D, 'Opinion publique et traité libanais', Beirut, 27 June 1936, the Delegate to Lebanon to Meyrier; FO 371/20065 2656/195 no. 46, Beirut, 5 May 1936, Havard to Eden.

33.   MAE, Nantes, Syrie et Liban, carton 457, no. 536, Beirut, 15 May 1936, Meyrier to the Foreign Minister.

34.   MAE, Nantes, Syrie et Liban, carton 595, no. 468, Paris, 9 June 1936, the Foreign Minister to Meyrier; carton 457, nos 487–8, 6 June 1936, Eddé to de Martel, and nos 481–6, 8 June 1936, Meyrier to the Quai d'Orsay; no. 2003/D, 'Opinion publique et traité libanais', Beirut, 27 June 1936, the Delegate to Lebanon to Meyrier; letter from Michel Zakur to Meyrier, Beirut, 10 July 1936; MAE, Paris, Syrie et Liban, vol. 501, no. 704, Beirut, 10 July 1936, Meyrier to the Foreign Minister.

35.   MAE, Nantes, Syrie et Liban, carton 457, no. 1869, Beirut, 17 June 1936, Meyrier to de Martel; letter from Tawfik Awad to Meyrier, Beirut, 12 June 1936; carton 595, no. 476, Paris, 9 June 1936, the Foreign Minister to Meyrier, including Arida's letter to Delbos of 12 June 1936.

36.   MAE, Nantes, Syrie et Liban, carton 478, letter from Viénot to Eddé, Paris, 20 June 1936; carton 460, nos 399–403, Paris, 20 June 1936, the Foreign Minister to Meyrier; FO 371/20066 3794/195 no. 802, Paris, 22 June 1936, Clerk to Eden.

37.   MAE, Nantes, Syrie et Liban, carton 457, nos 540–1, Beirut, 25 June 1936, Eddé to de Martel; nos 548–9, 26 June 1936, Meyrier to the Quai d'Orsay; no. 246, Diman, 29 June 1936, Arida to de Martel, and no. 248, 1 July 1936, Arida to Viénot; carton 595, no. 671, Beirut, 3 July 1936, Meyrier to the Foreign Minister.

38.   MAE, Paris, Syrie et Liban, vol. 493, letter from Atasi to de Martel, Paris, 25 July 1936; MAE, Nantes, Syrie et Liban, carton 457, Information no. 2510, Beirut, 15 June 1936; no. 302, Sidon, 2 July 1936, Pechkof to Lafond. On the constitutional crisis see pages 29–33.

39.   MAE, Paris, Syrie et Liban, vol. 493, Paris, 6 and 25 July 1936, Atasi to de Martel; MAE, Nantes, Syrie et Liban, carton 478, 7 July 1936, Viénot to Atasi.

40.   MAE, Nantes, Syrie et Liban, carton 457, Information no. 2370, Beirut, 6 July; no. 2510, 15 July; nos 2602 and 2604, 21 July, and no. 2635, 23 July 1936; no. 747, Beirut, 24 July 1936, Meyrier to the Foreign Minister; MAE, Paris, Syrie et Liban, vol. 501, on the activities of the Sulh family in Sidon, pp. 240–1; no. 823, Beirut, 21 August 1936, Meyrier to the Foreign Minister; Arslan, *Mudhakkirat*, vol. 1, p. 481.

41.   MAE, Nantes, Syrie et Liban, carton 457, Beirut, 15 July 1936, letter from Salam to Meyrier; no. 316, 'Manifestations à Saida', Sidon, 12 July 1936; no. 722, Beirut, 18 July, and no. 748, 24 July 1936, Meyrier to the Foreign Minister. One of the young demonstrators was Ma'aruf al-Sa'ad, whose assassination half a century later conributed to the outbreak of the civil war.

42.   MAE, Nantes, Syrie et Liban, carton 457, no. 747, 24 July 1936, Meyrier to the Quai d'Orsay; BGA, Correspondence, Epstein's report on the reaction in Syria and Lebanon to the Franco–Syrian treaty in Paris, Beirut, 1 October 1936.

43.   MAE, Nantes, Syrie et Liban, carton 457, letters from Amin Muqadam to the Foreign Minister, 17 July, and to the French Administrative Adviser in North Lebanon, Tripoli, 18 July 1936; letter from Abud Abd al-Razak to Viénot, Beirut, 6 July 1936; letter from Salim Ali Salam and Omar Bayhum to the Quai d'Orsay, Beirut, 10 July, and to Meyrier, 15 July 1936; no. 718, Beirut, Meyrier to the Foreign Minister; nos 578–80, Beirut, 8 July, 1936, Eddé to the Foreign Minister; carton 606, Information no. 2880, 12 August, and no. 2891, 14 August 1936.

44.   MAE, Nantes, Syrie et Liban, carton 478, 'Réunion tenue le 15 juillet 1936 par la Sous-Commission chargée de la question de la Conférence des Intérêts Communs'.

45.   MAE, Paris, Syrie et Liban, vol. 493, 'Le traité franco–syrienne', Paris, 1 August 1936, the Minister of War to the Foreign Minister; no. 2495, Paris, 4 August 1936, Foreign Minister to the Minister of War; no. 2559, Paris, 8 August 1936, Minister of War to the Foreign Minister; nos 531–2, Paris, 13 August 1936, the Foreign Minister to Meyrier; 'Note: envoi d'une commission d'enquête dans les Etats du Levant sous mandat français', Paris, 4 August 1936; 'Note: Créance civile et militaire', pp. 168–9; vol. 494, no. 2891, Paris, 7 September 1936, the Minister of War to the Minister of Foreign Affairs; no. 909, Beirut, 11 September 1936, Meyrier to the Foreign Minister; no. 580, London, 16 September 1936, the French Ambassador to London to the Foreign Minister.

46.   For the Franco–Syrian Treaty negotiations, see MAE, Nantes, Syrie et Liban, carton 478: "Cabinet Politique, Syrie: Traité Franco–syrien, 1936–1941"; FO 371/20066 6599/195, memorandum by J. G. Ward, Eastern Department, Foreign Office, London, 6 November 1936.

47.   MAE, Paris, Syrie et Liban, vol. 494, nos 587–8, Paris, 8 September 1936, Viénot to de Martel; no. 3047, Paris, 13 September 1936, the Foreign Minister to the Minister of War; 'Retour de la délégation en Syrie', Beirut, 3 October, and vol. 495, no. 1052, Beirut, 27 October 1936, de Martel to the Foreign Minister; 'Le traité franco–syrien et la protection des minorités', Paris, 25 October 1936; vol. 502, 'Note verbale: Organisation future des Etats du Levant - Maintien d'un etablissement naval sur les cotes de Syrie' by Fernet, commander of the naval division in the Levant, Beirut, 2 October 1936, and the Quai d'Orsay's reply; 'Les relations de la France et de la Syrie', conference held at the Centre d'Etudes de Politique Etrangère in February and March 1939 attended by Pierre Viénot and the senators Henry-Haye and Bergeon, members of the Senate Foreign Affairs Commission, in document no. 212.092 CHEAM; FO 371/20066 6968/195 no. 79, Damascus, 27 October 1936, Consul-General Mackereth to Eden.

48.   MAE, Paris, Syrie et Liban, vol. 494, note, 'La situation en Syrie et au Liban', Paris, 10 September 1936; vol. 495, no. 713, 23 October and no 739, Paris, 26 October 1936, Viénot to de Martel; MAE, Nantes, Syrie et Liban, carton 2990, nos 615–18, Paris, 24 September 1936, the Quai d'Orsay to de Martel.

49.   MAE, Paris, Syrie et Liban, vol. 494, note, 'La situation en Syrie et au Liban', Paris, 10 September 1936; vol. 501, nos 733–44, 'Situation au Liban', Beirut, 21 September 1926, Meyrier to the Quai d'Orsay; nos 752–3, Beirut, 25 September 1936, de Martel to Viénot; no. 599, 16 September, and no. 625, 'Programme d'action politique', Paris, 28 September 1936, Viénot to de Martel; MAE, Nantes, Syrie et Liban, carton 457, nos 607–9, Paris, 19 September 1936, the Quai d'Orsay to Meyrier.

50.   MAE, Nantes, Syrie et Liban, carton 457, resolution adopted by the Lebanese parliament and sent to Eddé, requesting the restoration of the constitution, Beirut, 7 July 1936. In the margin, Gabriel Khabbaz and Petro Trad added in writing the condition that the constitution be revised; 'Opinion publique et traité libanais', no. 2003/D, Beirut, 27 June 1936, the Delegate to Lebanon to Meyrier; carton 478, Beirut, letter from Khuri to Meyrier, Beirut, 31 July 1936;

MAE, Paris, Syrie et Liban, vol. 501, no. 700, Beirut, 10 July 1936, Meyrier to the Quai d'Orsay.

51. MAE, Nantes, Syrie et Liban, carton 457, 'Opinion publique et traité libanais', no. 2003/D, Beirut, 27 June 1936, the Delegate to Lebanon to Meyrier; carton 453, Memorandum summarizing articles in the press on the Lebanese constitution, Beirut, 20 July 1936; MAE, Paris, Syrie et Liban, vol. 501, no. 700, Beirut, 10 July 1936, Meyrier to the Quai d'Orsay.

52. MAE, Nantes, Syrie et Liban, carton 453, letter from the Mufti, Tawfik Khalid, to Eddé, Beirut, 8 August, 1936, Chamoun's memorandum to Eddé, 9 July, 1936, and Tuéni's letter to Eddé (nd); carton 457, letter from Michel Zakur to Meyrier, Beirut, 10 July 1936; carton 606, Information no. 2891, Beirut, 14 August 1936; MAE, Paris, Syrie et Liban, vol. 501, no. 938, Beirut, 18 September 1936, Meyrier to the Quai d'Orsay.

53. MAE, Nantes, Syrie et Liban, carton 478, Beirut, letter from Khuri to Meyrier, Beirut, 31 July 1936; carton 457, 'Aide-mémoire', Beirut, 3 August 1936; no. 796, Beirut, 7 August 1936, Meyrier to the Foreign Minister.

54. MAE, Nantes, Syrie et Liban, carton 457, 'Visite à Mgr. Arida à Diman', Beirut, 27 July 1936; 'Note: démission des députés d'opposition', Beirut, 22 August 1936; letter from Arida to Eddé, Beirut, 7 August 1936; carton 411, Information no. 2781, Beirut, 4 August 1936; carton 2967, no. 775, Beirut, 31 July 1936, Meyrier to the Foreign Minister; MAE, Paris, Syrie et Liban, vol. 501, no. 807, 14 August and no. 826, Beirut, 21 August 1936, Meyrier to the Foreign Minister.

55. MAE, Nantes, Syrie et Liban, carton 595, no. 885, Beirut, 5 September 1936, Meyrier to the Foreign Minister; MAE, Paris, Syrie et Liban, vol. 501, no. 878, Beirut, 4 September 1936, Meyrier to the Foreign Minister; no. 599, Paris, 16 September 1936, the Foreign Minister to Meyrier.

56. MAE, Paris, Syrie et Liban, vol. 501, nos 733–44, 'Situation au Liban', Beirut, 21 September 1926, Meyrier to the Quai d'Orsay. Other members were Najib Usayran Hikmat Jumblatt, Petro Trad, Muhammad Abd al-Razak, and Warham Lilikian; MAE, Nantes, Syrie et Liban, carton 2990, no. 3213, Beirut, 15 October 1936 'Proceedings of a session of the Lebanese parliament on 15 October'; FO 371 20066 6753/195, no. 98, Beirut, 23 October 1936, Furlonge to Eden.

57. MAE, Nantes, Syrie et Liban, carton 2990, nos 607–9, Paris, 19 September 1936, the Quai d'Orsay to Meyrier; no. 1104, Beirut, 6 November 1936, de Martel to the Quai d'Orsay; carton 460, 'Information no. 3902, Beirut, 20 October, 1936.

58. MAE, Paris, Syrie et Liban, vol. 501, 'Situation politique en Syrie et en Liban', Paris, 19 September 1936; no. 625, Paris, 28 September 1936, Viénot to de Martel; MAE, Nantes, Syrie et Liban, carton 457, no. 226, 'Note au sujet de Tripoli', Tripoli, 6 October 1936.

59. MAE, Nantes, Syrie et Liban, carton 457, no. 226, 'Note au sujet de Tripoli', Tripoli, 6 October 1936; carton 2990, nos 806–808, Beirut, 11 October 1936, de Martel to the Quai d'Orsay.

60.   MAE, Nantes, Syrie et Liban, carton 459, no. 8618 'Visit de Riad bey Solh', Beirut, 14 October 1936, de Martel to the French administrative adviser in Sidon; no. 8817, Report by the adminstrative adviser in south Lebanon, Sidon, 2 Novermber 1936; carton 456, Information: letter from Ahmad al-As'ad, Beirut, 27 October 1936.

61.   MAE, Paris, Syrie et Liban, vol. 501, nos 733–44, Beirut, 21 September 1936, Meyrier to the Quai d'Orsay.

62.   MAE, Paris, Syrie et Liban, vol. 501, no. 938, Beirut, 18 September 1936, Meyrier to the Quai d'Orsay; no. 599, Paris, 16 September 1936, Léger to Meyrier. The fact that Salim Taqla, Khuri's close ally, served as administrator of the north Lebanon district, only reinforced Eddé's determination to grant it an independent administrator.

63.   MAE, Nantes, Syrie et Liban, carton 2990, nos 798–800, Beirut, 9 October 1936, de Martel to the Quai d'Orsay; carton 459, Information no. 3529, Beirut, 28 September, and no. 3564, 30 September 1936.

64.   MAE, Nantes, Syrie et Liban, carton 2990, nos 615–18, Paris, 24 September 1936, the Quai d'Orsay to de Martel; nos 821–7, Beirut, 13 October, and carton 458, no. 998, 9 October 1936, de Martel to the Quai d'Orsay; carton 459, Information no. 3262, Beirut, 6 October, and no. 3966, 22 October 1936; MAE, Paris, Syrie et Liban, vol. 495, nos 881–882, Beirut, 23 October 1936, de Martel to the Quai d'Orsay.

65.   MAE, Nantes, Syrie et Liban, carton 459, Information no. 3595 'Attitude de la délégation syrienne à l'égard du Traité Franco–Libanais', Beirut, 3 October; no. 3620, 6 October, and no. 3677, 8 October 1936.

66.   MAE, Paris, Syrie et Liban, vol. 501, nos 733–44, Beirut, 21 September 1936, and nos 749–50, 25 September, Meyrier to the Quai d'Orsay; MAE, Nantes, Syrie et Liban, carton 459, Information no. 552, Damascus, 2 October 1936, and no. 446, Report on Sulh's visit to Jabal Amil, Sidon, 13 October 1936; carton 2990, nos 798–800, Beirut, 9 October 1936, de Martel to the Quai d'Orsay.

67.   MAE, Nantes, Syrie et Liban, carton 2990, nos 821–7, Beirut, 13 October 1936, de Martel to the Quai d'Orsay.

68.   MAE, Nantes, Syrie et Liban, carton 460, Information no. 3840, Beirut, 16 October 1936.

69.   MAE, Nantes, Syrie et Liban, carton 460, Sulh's speech at the Conference of the Coast, published in the newspaper *Beirut*, 25 October 1936; Salam's letters to de Martel, Beirut, 28 October, and 28 November 1936; Information no. 3868, Beirut, 19 October; no. 3902, 20 October, and no. 4037, 24 October 1936; no. 3351, Report on the Conference of the Coast, Beirut, 24 October 1936, Lafond to de Martel.

70.   MAE, Nantes, Syrie et Liban, carton 595, no. 1077, Beirut, 29 October 1936, Aziz al-Hashem to Arida.

71.   MAE, Nantes, Syrie et Liban, carton 459, Information, 30 October 1936; 'Rapport Spécial: Réunion à la Mosquée & discours des leaders musulmans', Beirut, 15 November 1936; carton 460, no. 275, Tripoli, 20 November 1936, the

administrative adviser in north Lebanon to de Martel; Information no. 4038, 24 October 1936.

72.   MAE, Nantes, Syrie et Liban, carton 460, nos 937–9, Beirut, 2 November 1936, and carton 2990, no. 1148, Beirut, 20 November 1936, de Martel to the Quai d'Orsay; Hasan Ali Hallaq, *Mudhakkirat Salim Ali Salam* (Beirut, 1981), pp. 313–14.

73.   MAE, Nantes, Syrie et Liban, carton 2990, no. 1104, Beirut, 6 November 1936, de Martel to the Quai d'Orsay; carton 459, no. 1648, Report by the French delegate to Syria on a telephone conversation with Hashem al-Atasi, Damascus, 16 November 1936; Report on a conversation with Faris al-Khuri and Shukri al-Kuwatli, Damascus, 19 November 1936; no. 9841, Report by the Sûreté Générale on the events in Beirut on 15 November, Beirut, 24 November 1936; FO 371/20066 6610/195 no. 56, Aleppo, 20 October 1936, Parr to Eden, and 7488/195 no. 108, Beirut, 24 November 1936, Havard to the Foreign Office.

74.   MAE, Nantes, Syrie et Liban, carton 2990, no. 1179, Beirut, 27 November 1936, de Martel to the Quai d'Orsay; carton 606, Information no. 5007, Beirut, 16 December 1936.

75.   MAE, Paris, Syrie et Liban, vol. 502, Report by Beshara al-Khuri to the parliament on the Franco–Lebanese treaty, Beirut, 17 November 1936; MAE, Nantes, Syrie et Liban, on the treaty negotiations see carton 459, 'Cabinet Politique: Traité Franco–Libanaise, 1936–1941'; see also carton 2990, no. 1147, Beirut, 20 November 1936, de Martel to the Quai d'Orsay.

76.   MAE, Nantes, Syrie et Liban, carton 457, nos 918–21, Beirut, 29 October 1936, de Martel to the Quai d'Orsay; MAE, Paris, Syrie et Liban, vol. 502, no. 1029, Beirut, 21 November 1936, de Martel to the Quai d'Orsay.

77.   MAE, Nantes, Syrie et Liban, carton 944, no. 3575, 'Compte rendue succinct de la séance de la chambre des députés en date du 20 novembre 1936', Beirut, 21 November 1936; carton 2990, Khuri's speech in the parliament, 17 November 1936; carton 458, no. 1139, Beirut, 20 November 1936, de Martel to the Quai d'Orsay; MAE, Paris, Syrie et Liban, vol. 502, Report by Beshara al Khuri to the parliament on the Franco–Lebanese treaty, Beirut, 17 November 1936; Khuri, *Haqa'iq lubnaniyya*, vol. 1, pp. 203–5.

78.   MAE, Nantes, Syrie et Liban, carton 461, no. 36, Paris, 20 January 1937, de St-Quentin to de Martel; no. 46, Beirut, 19 February 1937, de Martel to the Quai d'Orsay; for the original Franco–Lebanese treaty see carton 457; FO 371/20066 7315/195 no. 103, Beirut, 17 November 1936, Furlonge to Eden; Hallaq, *Mudhakkirat Salim Ali Salam*, pp. 310–11, de Martel's letter to Salam, 13 November 1936.

79.   MAE, Paris, Syrie et Liban, vol. 502, nos 992–4, Paris, 28 December, 1936, Viénot to de Martel; nos 1149–51, Beirut, 26 December, and no. 1156, 29 December 1936, de Martel to the Quai d'Orsay; MAE, Nantes, Syrie et Liban, carton 2990, no. 1233, Beirut, 11 December 1936, de Martel to the Quai d'Orsay.

80.   MAE, Paris, Syrie et Liban, vol. 502, nos 1149–51, Beirut, 26 December, and no. 1156, 29 December 1936, de Martel to the Quai d'Orsay.

81.   MAE, Nantes, Syrie et Liban, carton 461, no. 88, Beirut, 22 January, and carton 2990, no. 989, 27 October 1937, de Martel to the Quai d'Orsay; FO 371 20848 252/252, no. 1, Beirut, 6 January 1937, Havard to the Foreign Office.

82.   MAE, Nantes, Syrie et Liban, carton 461, Information, 'Opposition Parlementaire', Beirut, 21 January 1937.

83.   MAE, Nantes, Syrie et Liban, carton 461, no. 88, Beirut, 22 January, and carton 2990, no. 989, Beirut, 27 October 1937, de Martel to the Quai d'Orsay.

84.   MAE, Nantes, Syrie et Liban, carton 944, no. 393, Report on the proceedings of the Lebanese parliament on 2 February 1937; MAE, Paris, Syrie et Liban, vol. 502, no. 115, Beirut, 29 January, nos 166–9, Beirut, 3 February, and no. 158, 5 February 1937, de Martel to the Quai d'Orsay; FO 371/20848 252/252 no. 1, Beirut, 5 January 1937, Havard to the Foreign Office; Khuri, *Haqa'iq lubnaniyya*, vol. 1, pp. 209–13.

85.   MAE, Paris, Syrie et Liban, vol. 502, no. 1156, Beirut, 29 December 1936, and no. 283, 12 March 1937, de Martel to the Quai d'Orsay.

86.   MAE, Nantes, Syrie et Liban, carton 461, no. 62, Beirut, 15 January, and carton 2990, no. 989, Beirut, 27 October 1937, de Martel to the Quai d'Orsay.

87.   MAE, Paris, Syrie et Liban, vol. 502, no. 21, Beirut, 8 January 1937, de Martel to the Quai d'Orsay; MAE, Nantes, Syrie et Liban, carton 461, no. 62, Beirut, 15 January 1937, de Martel to the Quai d'Orsay; carton 460, Salam's letter to de Martel, Beirut, 20 January 1937.

88.   MAE, Nantes, Syrie et Liban, carton 460, no. 39, Report on Ahdab's visit to Tripoli, Tripoli, 8 February 1937; Report submitted to Viénot on the question of Tripoli, 24 May 1937; carton 461, no. 258, Beirut, 5 March 1937, de Martel to the Quai d'Orsay; Hallaq, *Mudhakkirat Salim Ali Salam*, pp. 315–19, Salam's letter to de Martel, 8 February 1937.

89.   MAE, Nantes, Syrie et Liban, carton 461, no. 258, Beirut, 5 March 1937, de Martel to the Quai d'Orsay; FO 371/20848 937/252 no. 20, Beirut, 6 February 1937, Havard to the Foreign Office.

90.   FO 371/20848 1655/252 no. 54, Beirut, 18 March 1937, Havard to the Foreign Office; MAE, Paris, Syrie et Liban, vol. 502, nos 284–5, Beirut, 10 March, nos 292–3, 11 March, no. 283, 12 March, nos 298–9, 12 March, and nos 301–3, 14 March, 1937, de Martel to the Quai d'Orsay; nos 273–5, Paris, 11 March 1937, Viénot to de Martel; MAE, Nantes, Syrie et Liban, carton 944, Proceedings of the Lebanese parliament on 17 March 1937; Khuri, *Haqa'iq lubnaniyya*, vol. 1, pp. 214–16.

91.   MAE, Nantes, Syrie et Liban, carton 460, Beirut, 23 April 1937, Salam to de Martel; carton 606, Information no. 2183, Beirut, 27 April, and no. 2473, 13 May 1937; MAE, Paris, Syrie et Liban, vol. 503, Beirut, 2 June 1937, Salam to the Quai d'Orsay.

92.   MAE, Nantes, Syrie et Liban, carton 606, Information: 'Politique musulmane', Beirut, 19 and 26 April 1937; Information no. 2949, 10 June 1937; MAE, Paris, Syrie et Liban, vol. 502, nos 486–7, Beirut, 25 April 1937, de Martel to the Quai d'Orsay.

93.   MAE, Nantes, Syrie et Liban, carton 2990, no. 174, Beirut, 12 February 1937, de Martel to the Quai d'Orsay; carton 460, no. 137, Paris, 6 March 1937, Viénot to de Martel; Information no. 56, Damascus, 12 February 1937; MAE, Paris, Syrie et Liban, vol. 502, no. 199, Paris, 17 February 1937, Léger to de Martel; no. 276, Beirut, 8 March 1937, de Martel to the Quai d'Orsay.

94.   MAE, Nantes, Syrie et Liban, carton 460, no. 39, Report on Ahdab's visit to Tripoli, Tripoli, 8 February 1937; no. 442, Paris, 24 February 1937, the Air Minister to the Foreign Minister; SHA, carton 9B2, no. 764, Beirut, 9 March 1937, the Foreign Minister to the Minister of War; MAE, Paris, Syrie et Liban, vol. 502, nos 180–1, Beirut, 10 February 1037, de Martel to the Quai d'Orsay.

95.   MAE, Nantes, Syrie et Liban, carton 944, Proceedings of the Lebanese parliament on 2 June 1937; Information: 'Clergé maronite', Beirut, 15 November 1937; MAE, Paris, Syrie et Liban, vol. 495, no. 383, Beirut, 10 April 1937, de Martel to the Quai d'Orsay; FO 371/20850 3794/910 no. 51, Beirut, 8 June, and 371/20849, 4876/252 no. 65, Beirut, 13 August 1937, Havard to the Foreign Office; BGA, Correspondence, Boneh's report on Syro–Lebanese economic relations following a visit to Damascus, 19 April 1937; Nabil Frangié and Zeina Frangié, *Hamid Frangié, l'autre Liban* (Beirut, 1993), vol. 1, pp. 109–18, a report presented by Hamid Franjieh, 2 June 1937.

96.   BGA, Correspondence, report on Franco–Syrian relations sumitted to the French Senate Foreign Affairs Committee, Paris, September 1938; MAE, Nantes, Syrie et Liban, carton 460, no. 56, Damsacus, 11 June 1937, the French delegate in Damascus to Meyrier.

97.   MAE, Nantes, Syrie et Liban, carton 606, Information: an anti-Christian tract posted on the street in Beirut, 28 April 1937. In fact, France's agreement to allow the mufti to remain in Lebanon was coordinated with Britain, which sought to supervise his activities.

98.   MAE, Nantes, Syrie et Liban, carton 2990, no. 458, Beirut, 23 April 1937, de Martel to the Quai d'Orsay; carton 606, Information no. 2247, Beirut, 29 April 1937; BGA, Correspondence, Epstein's diary - reports on conversations with Patriarch Arida and French officials in the Quai d'Orsay, Paris, 5–14 June 1937. On Maronite-Zionist relations, see Laura Z. Eisenberg, *My Enemy's Enemy: Lebanon in the Early Zionist Imagination, 1900–1948* (Detroit, 1994); Qasimiya, *Al-ra'il al-arabi al-awal*, pp. 328–9, Asad Dagher's letter to Nabih al-Azma, Cairo, 8 July 1937.

99.   MAE, Paris, Syrie et Liban, vol. 495, nos 881–2, Beirut, 23 October 1936, de Martel to the Quai d'Orsay; no. 733, Paris, 27 October 1936, Viénot to de Martel; Note: 'Situation en Syrie', Beirut, 27 October 1936; BGA, Correspondence, Epstein's letters to Moshe Shertouk on his conversations with Captain Bertrand, Jerusalem, 29 March, and Beirut, 25 October 1938; Eliyahu Sasson's letter to Shertouk, Damascus, 24 April 1938.

100.   MAE, Nantes, Syrie et Liban, carton 2967, no. 325, Beirut, 24 March, and carton 2990, no. 989, Beirut, 27 October 1937, de Martel to the Quai d'Orsay;

BGA, Correspondence, Sasson's report on his conversation with Khair al-Din al-Ahdab, Jerusalem, 28 June 1938.

101.   MAE, Nantes, Syrie et Liban, carton 461, no. 310, Beirut, 19 March, and carton 2990, no. 989, Beirut, 27 October 1937, de Martel to the Quai d'Orsay; MAE, Paris, Syrie et Liban, vol. 503, nos 593–4, Beirut, 21 May 1937, Meyrier to de Martel.

102.   MAE, Nantes, Syrie et Liban, carton 461, no. 310, Beirut, 19 March 1937, de Martel to the Quai d'Orsay; SHA, carton 9B2, no. 764, Beirut, 9 March 1937, the Foreign Minister to the Minister of War.

103.   MAE, Paris, Syrie et Liban, vol. 502, nos 502–4, Beirut, 20 April, and vol. 503, no. 670, 14 July 1937, de Martel to the Quai d'Orsay; Note: 'Séjour à Paris du Président de la République libanaise', Paris, 9 June 1937; FO 371/20848 3985/252 no. 849, Paris, 10 July, and 3735/252 no. 826, 5 July 1937, Phipps to Eden.

104.   MAE, Paris, Syrie et Liban, vol. 503, no. 670, Beirut, 14 July 1937, de Martel to the Quai d'Orsay; Amin Muqadam's letter to de Tessan, Paris, 8 July 1937; no. 685, Paris, 18 June 1937, Eddé to Ahdab; MAE, Nantes, Syrie et Liban, carton 459, no. 417, Beirut, 8 July 1937, Lafond to de Martel; carton 460, nos 675–6, Beirut, 11 June 1937, Meyrier to the Quai d'Orsay.

105.   MAE, Paris, Syrie et Liban, vol. 503, nos 593–4, Beirut, 21 May 1937, Meyrier to de Martel; no. 609, Beirut, 23 June 1937, Meyrier to the Quai d'Orsay; nos 754–5, 19 July, and no. 801, 24 July 1937, de Martel to the Quai d'Orsay; no. 607, Paris, 22 May 1937, Viénot to Meyrier; FO 371/20849 4185/252 no. 58, Beirut, 13 July 1937, Havard to the Foreign Office.

106.   MAE, Nantes, Syrie et Liban, carton 2990, no. 742, Beirut, 4 August 1937, Meyrier to the Quai d'Orsay; FO 371/20849 4653/252 no. 63, Beirut, 3 August 1937, Havard to the Foreign Office.

107.   MAE, Nantes, Syrie et Liban, carton 2990, Khalid Shihab's memorandum to de Martel, Beirut, 24 July 1937; no. 3305, Note, Ahdab's visit to Tripoli and north Lebanon, Beirut, 29 August 1937; MAE, Paris, Syrie et Liban, vol. 503, no. 689, Beirut, 21 July 1937, de Martel to the Quai d'Orsay; no. 805, Beirut, 25 August 1937, Meyrier to the Quai d'Orsay.

108.   MAE, Nantes, Syrie et Liban, carton 606, Information no. 3048, Beirut, 16 June, no. 3109, 18 June, and no. 3290, 28 June 1937; carton 397, Information no. 1067, Beirut, 4 October 1937; Note for de Martel on the financing of the opposition's campaign, Beirut, 26 October 1937; MAE, Paris, Syrie et Liban, vol. 503, no. 682, Paris, 18 June 1937, the Quai d'Orsay to Meyrier.

109.   MAE, Nantes, Syrie et Liban, carton 397, Information no. 5266, Beirut, 4 October 1937. Angered by the cooperation of his colleagues with Sulh, Salam and Karameh, Ayub Tabet, resigned from Khuri's camp.

110.   MAE, Nantes, Syrie et Liban, carton 2990, telegram from the Quai d'Orsay to Meyrier on the anti-Lebanese activities in the Bludan congress, Paris, 8 September 1937; carton 457, no. 878, Beirut, 15 September 1937, Meyrier to the Quai d'Orsay; MAE, Paris, Syrie et Liban, vol. 503, nos 957–8, Beirut, 14 September 1937, Meyrier to the Quai d'Orsay; Elie Kedourie, 'The Bludan

Congress on Palestine, September 1937', *Middle Eastern Studies*, vol. 17, (1981) pp. 108–25.

111.   MAE, Paris, Syrie et Liban, vol. 503, a memorandum criticizing Khuri, 20 August 1937, pp. 133–6.

112.   MAE, Nantes, Syrie et Liban, carton 2990, no. 567, Paris, 20 September 1937, de Tessan to de Martel.

113.   MAE, Nantes, Syrie et Liban, carton 2990, no. 989, Beirut, 27 October 1937, de Martel to the Quai d'Orsay; no. 567, Paris, 20 September 1937, de Tessan to de Martel.

114.   MAE, Nantes, Syrie et Liban, carton 2990, no. 989, Beirut, 27 October 1937, de Martel to the Quai d'Orsay; MAE, Paris, Syrie et Liban, vol. 503, no. 905, Beirut, 29 September, nos 995–7, 30 September, nos 1013–15, 5 October, and no. 1025, 8 October 1937, de Martel to the Quai d'Orsay; FO 371/20849 5877/252 no. 73, Beirut, 30 September 1937, Havard to the Foreign Office.

115.   MAE, Nantes, Syrie et Liban, carton 2990, no. 989, Beirut, 27 October 1937, de Martel to the Quai d'Orsay; BGA, Correspondence, Epstein, 'A letter from Beirut', 4 November 1937.

116.   MAE, Nantes, Syrie et Liban, carton 2990, no. 989, Beirut, 27 October 1937, de Martel to the Quai d'Orsay; FO 371/20849 6150/252 no. 76, Beirut, 11 October 1937, Havard to the Foreign Office; CHEAM, no. 183, Pierre Rondot, 'Les griefs de l'opposition libanaise au lendemain des élections législatives', 17 January 1938.

117.   On the elections see MAE, Nantes, Syrie et Liban, carton 396, 'Rapport sur les élections législatives libanaises de 24 et 25 octobre 1937'; carton 2990, no. 989, Beirut, 27 October 1937, de Martel to the Quai d'Orsay; FO 371/20849 6150/252 no. 76, Beirut, 11 October 1937, Havard to the Foreign Office; CHEAM, no. 183, Pierre Rondot, 'Les griefs de l'opposition libanaise au lendemain des élections législatives', 17 January 1938.

118.   MAE, Nantes, Syrie et Liban, carton 944, Proceedings of the Lebanese parliament on 30 October and 9 November 1937; MAE, Paris, Syrie et Liban, vol. 503, nos 1154–6, 29 October 1937, de Martel to the Quai d'Orsay; FO 371/ 20849 6563/252 no. 85, Beirut, 2 November 1937, Havard to the Foreign Office.

119.   MAE, Nantes, Syrie et Liban, carton 2990, Lafond's report: 'Information: Séance parlementaire du 9 novembre', Beirut, 8 November 1937; no. 61, Beirut, 19 January 1938, de Martel to the Quai d'Orsay.

120.   MAE, Nantes, Syrie et Liban, carton 2990, no. 989, Beirut, 27 October 1937, de Martel to the Quai d'Orsay.

121.   MAE, Nantes, Syrie et Liban, carton 595, no. 298, Tripoli, 30 November 1937, the French administrative adviser in north Lebanon to Meyrier; Arida's letter to de Martel, Bkerki, 7 February 1938; carton 596, Information: 'Clergé Maronite', 1 March 1938; carton 2990, no. 1006, Beirut, 27 October 1937, and no. 61, Beirut, 19 January 1938, de Martel to the Quai d'Orsay; carton 461, Information no. 2520, Beirut, 18 March 1938; MAE, Paris, Syrie et Liban, vol. 503, no. 1128, Beirut, 1 December 1937, de Martel to the Quai d'Orsay; BGA,

Correspondence, Epstein's letter to Shertouk on his conversation with Eddé, Jerusalem, 29 March 1938; 'A letter from Beirut', 26 January, and 9 March 1938; CHEAM, no. 183, Pierre Rondot, 'Les griefs de l'opposition libanaise au lendemain des élections législatives', 17 January 1938. See also 'Rapport et Motion du Congrès National Démocrate du Liban', Beirut, 27 November 1938, sent by Gabriel Menassa and Georges Aql to the French Prime Minister, Daladier and the Quai d'Orsay, in the pamphlet collection, Middle East Centre, St. Antony's College, Oxford.

122.   MAE, Nantes, Syrie et Liban, carton 2990, Lafond's report: 'Information: Séance parlementaire du 9 novembre', Beirut, 8 November 1937; carton 461, Information: 'Parti Constitutionnel', Beirut, 11 December 1937; carton 944, Proceedings of the meeting of the Lebanese parliament on 30 December 1937.

123.   MAE, Nantes, Syrie et Liban, carton 2990, no. 61, Beirut, 19 January 1938, de Martel to the Quai d'Orsay; MAE, Paris, Syrie et Liban, vol. 503, no. 1041, Beirut, 10 November 1937, de Martel to the Quai d'Orsay; FO 371/21913 501/47 no. 9, Beirut, 18 January 1938, Havard to the Foreign Office; BGA, Corrrespondence, Epstein, 'A letter from Beirut', 8 January 1938.

124.   MAE, Nantes, Syrie et Liban, carton 460, no. 675, Beirut, 12 June 1937, Meyrier to the Quai d'Orsay; carton 457, Information no. 2285, Beirut, 27 June 1936; carton 459, Information no. 3565, 1 October 1936; carton 397, Information no. 4093, Beirut, 13 August 1937.

125.   MAE, Nantes, Syrie et Liban, carton 459, 'Rapport Spécial: Réunion à la Mosquée & discours des leaders musulmans', Beirut, 15 November 1936; carton 460, no. 675, Beirut, 12 June 1937, Meyrier to the Quai d'Orsay; MAE, Paris, Syrie et Liban, vol. 503, no. 4304, Paris, 29 November 1937, the Minister for National Defence to the Foreign Minister; BGA, Correspondence, Epstein, 'A letter from Beirut', 17 December 1937. After President Eddé failed to persuade Colombani, head of the Sûreté Générale to transfer his wounded nephew, Pierre Gemayel, to the hospital, Yusuf Gemayel angrily told Eddé: 'I express my deep sympathies for the dead President Eddé'. See 'A letter from Beirut', 25 November 1937; John P. Entelis, *Pluralism and Party Transformation in Lebanon—Al Kata'ib, 1936–1970* (Leiden, 1974).

126.   MAE, Nantes, Syrie et Liban, carton 2990, no. 1103, Beirut, 24 November 1937, de Martel to the Quai d'Orsay; carton 606, Information no. 2419, Beirut, 11 May 1937; BGA, Correspondence, Sasson, 'News from Syria', 18 November 1937.

127.   MAE, Nantes, Syrie et Liban, carton 629, no. 703, Beirut, 10 July 1936, Meyrier to the Quai d'Orsay; carton 397, Information no. 3734, Beirut, 30 July 1937; MAE, Paris, Syrie et Liban, vol. 495, 'Le Parti Populaire Syrien', pp. 120–8; vol. 503, no. 537, Beirut, 25 May 1937, including Sa'adeh's letter; FO 371/19022 7198/571 no. 92, Beirut, 2 December 1935, Havard to the Foreign Office; BGA, Correspondence, Epstein, 'A letter from Beirut', 10 December 1937.

128.   MAE, Nantes, Syrie et Liban, carton 2990, no. 1103, Beirut, 24 November 1937, de Martel to the Quai d'Orsay; MAE, Paris, Syrie et Liban, vol.

503, nos 1275–8, Beirut, 21 November, and no. 1104, 24 November 1937, de Martel to the Quai d'Orsay; FO 371/20849 7038/252 no. 90, Beirut, 22 November 1937, Havard to the Foreign Office.

129.   MAE, Paris, Syrie et Liban, vol. 503, Proceedings of the Lebanese parliament on 29 November 1937, pp. 277–85; FO 371/20849 7178/252 no. 93, Beirut, 30 November 1937, Havard to the Foreign Office; CHEAM, no. 183, Pierre Rondot, 'Les griefs de l'opposition libanaise au lendemain des élections législatives', 17 January 1938.

130.   MAE, Nantes, Syrie et Liban, carton 2990, Lafond's report on the meeting between Eddé and Khuri, Information, 8 February 1938; no. 284, Beirut, 23 March, and no. 1045, 2 November 1938, de Martel to the Quai d'Orsay; carton 461, Information: 'Cabinet Ahdab', Beirut, 1 March 1938; Information no. 2435, Beirut, 16 March, no. 2520, 18 March, and no. 821, 30 August 1938; carton 945, Proceedings of the Lebanese parliament on 25 March 1938; FO 371/21913 501/47 no. 9, Beirut, 18 January 1938, Havard to the Foreign Office; BGA, Correspondence, Epstein, 'A letter from Beirut', 2 and 25 December 1937, and 17 March 1938.

131.   MAE, Nantes, Syrie et Liban, carton 844, Report on the activities of the Sûreté Générale for 1938; SHA, carton 13B2, de Martel's decree on the establishment of a 'Commission de Défense passive du Liban', 12 May 1938; FO 371/21914 6654/47 no. 71, Beirut, 2 November 1938, Havard to the Foreign Office; BGA, Corrrespondence, Epstein, 'A letter from Beirut', 31 May, 10 June, 28 July and 22 September 1938.

132.   FO 371/21914 7143/47 no. 81, Beirut, 19 November 1938, Havard to the Foreign Office; BGA, Correspondence, Sasson's letter to Shertouk, Damascus, 24 April 1938; Sasson's report on his conversation with Khair al-Din al-Ahdab, Jerusalem, 22 May 1938; Epstein's report on his conversations with Captain Bertrand and Charles Corm in Beirut, 9 November 1938.

133.   BGA, Correspondence, Sasson's report on Puaux's enquiry in Syria and Lebanon, Jerusalem, 8 March 1939; Sasson's report on his conversation with Jamil Mardam, Jerusalem, 16 April 1939. On Puaux, see his memoirs, Gabriel Puaux, *Deux Années au Levant: Souvenirs de Syrie et du Liban 1939–1940*, (Paris, 1952).

134.   MAE, Nantes, Syrie et Liban, carton 460, Information no. 1868, Beirut, 16 March, and no. 3209, 4 May 1939; FO 406/77 473/5 no. 4, Beirut, 11 January 1939, Havard to Halifax; BGA, Correspondence, Epstein, 'A letter from Beirut', 13 March and 11 July 1939; Epstein's report on his conversation with Captain Bertrand in Jerusalem, 19 May 1939.

135.   MAE, Nantes, Syrie et Liban, carton 460, Information: 'Révendications des notabilités musulmanes du Liban', Beirut, 23 January 1939; Eddé's visit to Tripoli, no. 48, Tripoli, 13 February 1939, the French administrative adviser in north Lebanon to Meyrier; BGA, Correspondence, Epstein's report on his conversation with Ayub Tabet, Jerusalem, 5 April, and with Captain Bertrand and Gabriel Khabaz, Jerusalem, 2 August 1939.

136.   MAE, Nantes, Syrie et Liban, carton 463, Information: 'Voyage en France du Président Eddé', Beirut, 21 July 1936; 'Note sur la réforme éventuelle de la constitution du Liban et sur les principes de collaboration Franco–Libanaise après la mise en vigueur du traité'; carton 462, Khuri's memorandum, 'Note sur la situation politique au Liban et sur l'évolution de la politique libanaise', Beirut, 24 January 1939; see also detailed report presented by Khuri to Puaux on the constitutional reforms, including resolutions adopted by the Constitutional Bloc on 21 June 1939, Beirut, 26 June 1939; BGA, Correspondence, Epstein, 'A letter from Beirut', 28 July 1939.

137.   FO 406/77 7014/5 no. 98, Beirut, 2 October 1939, Havard to Halifax; BGA, Correspondence, Epstein, 'A letter from Beirut', 1 September 1939.

Bibliography

I Archival Sources

A France

Ministère des Affaires Etrangères, Les Archives diplomatiques de Nantes, Mandat Syrie-Liban, 1918-1948.
Ministère des Affaires Etrangères, Paris, Série E-Levant 1918-1940.
Ministère des Affaires Etrangères, Guerre 1939-1945. Londres: Comité National Français.
Ministère de la Guerre, Service Historique de l'Armée, Section Outre-Mer (Vincennes).
Archives Départementales de la Corrèze, Fonds Henry de Jouvenel, Tulle.
Centre de Hautes Etudes sur l'Afrique et l'Asie Modernes (CHEAM), Paris.

B Great Britain

Public Record Office (PRO), London.
Foreign Office:
    FO 371 General correspondence (Syria and Lebanon).
    FO 406 Confidential print, Eastern affairs.
    FO 424 Confidential print, Turkey.

C Israel

Ben-Gurion Archives, Sede Boker, Correspondence and general chronological documentation.

II Works cited

Andréa, C. J. E., *La Révolte druze et l'insurrection de Damas 1925-1926* (Paris, 1937).
Anis, M., *La Presse libanaise* (Paris, 1977).
Antonius, George, *The Arab Awakening* (London,1938).
Arida, Antun P., *Lubnan wa Faransa* (Beirut, 1987).
Arslan, Adil, *Mudhakkirat Adil Arslan* (Beirut, 1983) 3 vols.

Atiyah, Najla W., *The Attitude of the Lebanese Sunnis towards the State of Lebanon* (Ph.D. thesis, University of London, 1973).

Awad, Walid, *Ashab al-fakhama: ru'assa lubnan* (Beirut, 1977).

Baaklini, Abdo, I., *Legislative and Political Development: Lebanon 1842-1972* (Durham, NC, 1976).

Babikian, J. A., *Civilization and Education in Syria and Lebanon* (Beirut,1936).

Barakat, Halim (ed.), *Toward a Viable Lebanon* (Washington, 1988).

Binder, Leonard (ed.), *Politics in Lebanon* (New York, 1965).

Carbillet, G., *Au Djébel Druse* (Paris, 1929).

Chiha, Michel, *Politique intérieure* (Beirut, 1964).

Cohen, M. and M. Kolinsky (eds), *Britain and the Middle East in the 1930s: Security Problems* (London, 1992).

Cohen, William B., 'The Colonial Policy of the Popular Front', *French Historical Studies*, vol 7, 1972, pp 368-93.

Conrad, Lawrence I. (ed.),*The Formation and Perception of the Modern Arab World* (Princeton, 1989).

Couland, Jacques, *Le mouvement syndical au Liban 1919-1946* (Paris, 1970).

Craig, Gordon A. and Gilbert, Felix (eds), *The Diplomats 1919-1939* (New York, 1963), 2 vols.

Daher, Mas'ud, *Ta'rikh lubnan al-ijtima'i 1914-1926* (Beirut, 1974).

Dann, Uriel (ed.),*The Great Powers in the Middle East 1919-1939* (New York, 1988).

Dawn, Ernest C., *From Arabism to Ottomanism* (Chicago, 1973).

Dubar, Claude and Nasr, Salim, *Les Classes Sociales au Liban* (Paris, 1976).

Eisenberg, Laura Z., *My Enemy's Enemy: Lebanon in the Early Zionist Imagination, 1900-1948* (Detroit, 1994).

Entelis, John P., *Pluralism and Party Transformation in Lebanon—Al Kata'ib, 1936-1970* (Leiden, 1974).

Frangié, Nabil and Zeina Frangié, *Hamid Frangié, l'autre Liban* (Beirut, 1993), 2 vols.

Fry, Michael G. and Itamar Rabinovich, *Despatches from Damascus: Gilbert MacKereth and British Policy in the Levant, 1933-1939* (Tel Aviv, 1985).

Gannage, Elias, *L'Imposition des Tabacs au Liban* (Beirut, 1956).

Gates, Caroline L., *The Formation of the Political Economy of Modern Lebanon: The State and the Economy from Colonialism to Independence, 1939-1952* (Ph.D. thesis, Oxford University, 1985.

—'The Historical Role of Political Economy in the Development of Modern Lebanon', *Papers on Lebanon* (Centre for Lebanese Studies, Oxford, 1989), no. 10.

Gulick, John, *Tripoli: A Modern Arab City* (Oxford, 1967).

Hallaq, Hasan Ali, *Mudhakkirat Salim Ali Salam* (Beirut, 1981).

—*Mu'atamar al-sahil wa'l-aqdiyya al-arba'ah* (Beirut, 1982).

Haut Commissariat de la République Française en Syrie et au Liban, *Statut Organique des Etats du Levant sous Mandat Français* (Paris, 1930).

Hershlag, Zvi Y., *Introduction to the Modern Economic History of the Middle East* (Tel Aviv, 1965) (in Hebrew).

Himadeh, Said B. (ed.),*Economic Organization of Syria* (Beirut, 1936).

Hirszowicz, Lukasz, *The Third Reich and the Arab East* (Toronto, 1966).

Hobeika, P., *Emile Eddé* (Beirut, 1939).

Homet, Marcel, *Syrie terre irrédente: l'histoire secrète du traité franco-syrien* (Paris, 1938).

Hourani, Albert, *Arabic Thought in the Liberal Age 1798-1939* (Oxford, 1970).

Hudson, Michael C., *The Precarious Republic* (New York, 1968).

Kedourie, Elie, *In the Anglo–Arab Labyrinth: The MacMahon–Husayn . Correspondence and its Interpretation, 1914–1939* (Cambridge, 1976).

—'The Bludan Congress on Palestine, September 1937', *Middle Eastern Studies*, vol. 17 (1981), pp. 108–25.

Kennedy, Paul, *The Rise and Fall of the Great Powers* (Glasgow, 1989).

Kerr, David A., *The Temporal Authority of the Maronite Patriarchate, 1920–1958: A Study in the Relationship of Religious and Secular Power* (Ph.D. thesis, Oxford University, 1977).

Khalaf, Samir, *Lebanon's Predicament* (New York, 1987).

Khoury, Philip S., *Syria and the French Mandate* (Princeton,1987).

al-Khuri, Beshara, *Haqa'iq lubnaniyya* (Beirut,1961) 3 vols.

al-Khuri, Yusuf Quzma, *Al-bayanat al-wizariyah al-lubnaniyya wa-munaqishatuha fi majlis al-nuwwab, 1926–1984* (Beirut, 1986) 3 vols.

Kurd 'Ali, Muhammad, *Memoirs of Muhammad Kurd 'Ali* (Washington, D.C., 1954).

Lahoud, Rachid, *La littérature libanaise de langue française* (Beirut, 1945).

Longrigg, S. H., *Syria and Lebanon under French Mandate* (London, 1958).

MacCallum, Elizabeth, *The Nationalist Crusade in Syria* (New York, 1928).

MacDonald, C. A.,'Radio Bari: Italian Wireless Propaganda in the Middle East and British Countermeasures 1934-1938', *Middle Eastern Studies*, 13/2 (May 1977), pp. 195–207.

Miller, Joyce L.,'The Syrian Revolt of 1925', *International Journal of Middle East Studies*, 8 (1977), pp. 545–63.

Monroe, Elizabeth, *The Mediterranean in Politics* (Oxford, 1938).

Murad, Sa'id, *Al-harakat al-wahdawiyya fi lubnan* (Beirut, 1986).

Na'or, Mordechai and Yossi Ben-Artzi (eds), *The Development of Haifa* (Yitzhak Ben-Zvi Institute (Jerusalem) (in Hebrew).

Néré, J., *The Foreign Policy of France from 1914 to 1945* (London, 1974).

Owen, Roger (ed.), *Essays on the Crisis in Lebanon* (London, 1976).

O'Zoux, Raymond, *Les Etats du Levant sous mandat français* (Paris, 1931).

Pipes, Daniel, *Greater Syria: The History of an Ambition* (Oxford, 1990).

Puaux, Gabriel, *Deux Années au Levant: Souvenirs de Syrie et du Liban 1939-1940* (Paris, 1952).

Qasimiya, Khairiya, *Al-ra'il al-arabi al-awal* (London, 1991).

Rabbath, Edmond, *L'Unité syrienne et devenir arabe* (Paris, 1937).

—*La Formation Historique du Liban Politique et Constitutionnel* (Beirut, 1973).

al-Riyashi, Iskandar, *Qabla wa ba'ada* (Beirut, n.d.).

al-Safarjalani, Muhi al-Din, *Tarikh al-thawra al-suriyya* (Damascus, 1961).

Said, Amin, *al-Thawra al-'arabiyya al-kubra* (Cairo, 1934).

Salem, Jean, *Introduction à la pensée politique de Michel Chiha* (Beirut, 1970).

Salibi, Kamal S., *The Modern History of Lebanon* (London, 1965).

—*A House of Many Mansions* (London, 1988).

al-Sawda, Yusuf, *Fi sabil al-istiqlal* (Beirut, 1967).

Shehadi, Nadim, 'The Idea of Lebanon: Economy and State in the Cénacle Libanais 1946-1954', in *Papers on Lebanon*, no. 5 (Centre for Lebanese Studies, Oxford, 1987).

—and Dana Haffar Mills (eds), *Lebanon: A History of Conflict and Consensus* (London, 1988).

Shirer, William L., *The Collapse of the Third Republic* (New York, 1969).

el-Solh, Hilal, *Riad el-Solh 1894-1951* (Ph.D. thesis, Lyon University, 1981).

Solh, Raghid, *Lebanon and Arab Nationalism 1935-1945* (Ph.D. thesis, Oxford University, 1986).

Stern, Shimon, 'The Struggle to Establish the Port of Haifa during the British Mandate', in *Cathedra* (Jerusalem, October 1981), no. 21, pp. 171–86.

Toynbee, Arnold J., *Survey of International Affairs 1936* (London, 1937).

Traboulsi, Fawaz N., *Identités et solidarités croisées dans les conflits du Liban contemporain* (Ph.D. thesis, University of Paris, 1993).

Zamir, Meir, 'Emile Eddé and the Territorial Integrity of Lebanon', *Middle Eastern Studies*, 14/2 (May 1978), pp. 232–5.

—*The Formation of Modern Lebanon* (London, 1985).

—'Faisal and the Lebanese Question, 1918–1920', *Middle Eastern Studies* 27/3 (July 1991), pp. 404–26.

III Periodicals.

L'Asie française, Paris.

Bulletin Officiel du Comité France-Orient, Paris .

Correspondance d'Orient, Paris.

Journal Officiel de la République Libanaise, Beirut.

Revue des deux Mondes, Paris.

Index

Abd al-Razak, Abud 32, 65, 150, 211
Abd al-Razak, Muhammad 150, 197
Abdallah, Amir of Jordan 78, 221
Abid, Ali 98, 99, 104
Abu Lama, Khalil 146, 214
Abu–Nader, Rukhus 66
Abu Shahla, Habib 214, 224, 225,
   235
Abu Suan, Najib 74, 144, 146
Adib Pasha, Auguste 32, 35, 46-9
   passim, 65, 66, 70, 83, 113, 117,118,
   124, 150 background and outlook
   45
Afiuni, Ahmad Zaki 78
al-Ahd al-Jadid 78, 216
al-Ahdab, Husain 216
al-Ahdab, Khair al-Din 56, 74, 118,
   151, 152, 155, 158, 174, 176, 177,
   205, 206, 246; appointment as
   prime minister 214; background
   and outlook 216–8; and
   Constitutional bloc 215, 218, 225,
   229–30
al-Ahrar 58, 65, 68, 80, 118, 130
Aix–en–Provence, University of 71
Akkar 64, 65, 123, 150
Alawite region 2, 6, 8, 12. 15, 17, 23,
   26, 93-101 *passim*, 106, 107, 123,
   145, 164, 170, 179, 182–9 *passim*,
   195, 198, 207, 208, 210, 211, 238,
   233; ceded to Syria 199
Aleppo 2, 5, 6, 7, 18, 19, 100, 104,
   106, 111, 138, 153, 182, 207, 209,
   210
Alexandretta, autonomous province

of 2-8 *passim*, 12, 20, 23, 26, 96
   106, 120, 170, 179, 182, 185, 187,
   188, 199, 210, 220, 239, 243;
   ceded to Turkey 238
Alexandria 34, 71
Aley 178
'Alliance libanaise' 35
American University of Beirut 234
Amoun, Charles 35, 232, 233
Anatolia 4, 5
Anglo–Iraqi treaty (1930), impact of
   on French mandatory policy 93–
   5, 97, 98–9, 100, 103, 113, 135,
   141, 152, 153, 180, 181, 183, 185,
   198, 199
Anti–Lebanon Mountains 1, 10
Aql, Bishop Paul 66, 67, 121, 122,
   136, 140, 146, 150, 161, 167, 173
Aql, Georges 167
Arab nationalism 1, 2, 3, 4, 6, 9, 10,
   11, 12, 16, 26, 37, 39, 43, 81, 91,
   115, 243; Syrian 1, 72, 91, 95,
   102, 106, 241; French attitude to
   7, 94–5, 152; and Lebanese
   Christians 4, 37, 39, 71, 243; and
   Lebanese nationalism 37, 39, 71,
   114; and Lebanese Sunnis 110–
   11, 112, 191*see also* Pan-Arabism
Arab Revolt 2
Arida, Bishop Antoine Pierre 42,
   121–2, 124, 131, 136–40 *passim*
   148, 154, 157, 158, 183, 184,
   191–204, *passim*, 243; attempts to
   depose 116, 139, 140, 161, 172–
   3, 202; and campaign against